Educational Communications and Technology: Issues and Innovations

Series Editors
J. Michael Spector
M.J. Bishop
Dirk Ifenthaler

For further volumes:
http://www.springer.com/series/11824

Brad Hokanson • Andrew Gibbons
Editors

Design in Educational Technology

Design Thinking, Design Process,
and the Design Studio

 Springer

Editors
Brad Hokanson
College of Design
University of Minnesota
St. Paul, MN, USA

Andrew Gibbons
Brigham Young University
Provo, UT, USA

ISBN 978-3-319-00926-1   ISBN 978-3-319-00927-8 (eBook)
DOI 10.1007/978-3-319-00927-8
Springer Cham Heidelberg New York Dordrecht London

Library of Congress Control Number: 2013946217

Printed on acid-free paper

Springer is part of Springer Science+Business Media (www.springer.com)

Introduction

Design—from the Latin *designare*, to "mark out, point out, describe, design, contrive"—is a focus for many of the ideas and theories of contemporary educational technology.

As a field of study, design usually includes such disciplines as architecture, industrial design, graphic design, fashion, landscape architecture, and interior design. Each has a strong history of research and theory, as well as an established integration with application and practice, and therefore each parallels in many ways the work of instructional design and educational technology.

As an architect and graphic designer, I came to the field of educational technology quite recently. I found that the processes of instructional design mirrored that of architecture, and I found that the values of graphic design were critical to the design and development of educational projects. Many of the ideas, concepts, and methods of these and other design fields are directly useful and supportive of innovation and planning in educational design.

Three components of the broader concept of design formed the framework of the 2012 AECT Summer Research Symposium and this subsequent volume: *design thinking*, *design process*, and the *design studio*. The conscious adoption of aspects of design thinking, evident in a range of divergent professions (including business, government, and medicine), is widespread in the field of education. Design thinking is future-oriented, concerned with "the conception and realization of new things," and at its core is focused on "planning, inventing, making, and doing" (Cross, 1997, p. 1), all of which are of value to the field of educational technology. For an instructional designer, understanding the design process is critical, and this understanding often draws from other traditional design fields such as architecture or industrial design. Much of the curriculum in educational technology deals with application of conceptual models of design through an examination of the design process as practiced, of new models for designing, and of ways to connect theory to the development of educational products. Expanding the focus on design process, a number of leading schools of instructional design have adopted the studio form of education for their professional programs. Studio-based education is intrinsic to design education in many fields and is increasingly important within educational technology. Research and praxis-based observations are critical to effective use of this educational method and were examined as part of the symposium.

For this symposium, proposals focused on design thinking, design process, and the design studio were solicited from the general membership of the Association of Educational Communications and Technology and then evaluated by a panel of experts and the two symposium cochairs. Selected contributors developed their proposal ideas into full chapters, and each chapter draft was distributed to the other participants for review. All authors gathered for the in-person symposium in July 2012 in Louisville, KY, where discussions and presentations provided a rich and engaging synergy. Examples and experiences from outside the traditional boundaries of instructional design and educational technology also enriched and balanced the discussion. This structure formed the basis and the inspiration for the chapters of this book. From their own viewpoints, from their own academic venues, 15 authors have expressed their experience and views of design in a process fashioned to elicit and develop their best ideas and explanations. This design has been critical to this rich project.

The symposium was structured using conversational methods based in the Art of Hosting movement and was a departure from traditional academic conferences and paper presentations.

Authors worked together in an "Open Space" format of structured discussions. In Open Space, each chapter author hosted three intense discussions with four or five other discussants. Keynote presentations were made at the beginning and end of the symposium by Gordon Rowland and Patrick Parrish, whose written versions are also included in this book.

Andrew Gibbons charts our investigation with a comparison of the design activity in other professional fields such as architecture and digital design to instructional design. He maps the theories and practices of instructional design to the broader fields of design and examines the range of scales present in design practice.

Building from the seminal work of Donald Schön in his examination of the architectural design studio, Monica Tracy and John Baaki examine the principle of Refection-in-Action in terms of theory, design practice, and our understanding of the design process, illuminating these examples through the lens of a case study of active designers.

How instructional designers learn and evolve as practitioners is examined by Elizabeth Boling and Kennon Smith in their delineating of critical issues in education through the studio. Central to their investigation is a connection with other fields of design and bringing common essential characteristics to the field of instructional design.

Design and narrative meet in two chapters. In the first, Katherine Cennamo relates her experiences in pairing two design forms in a multidisciplinary design studio. Not all design work is alike and different cultures exist in different disciplines. At the same time, there are lessons to be learned through this innovative studio environment. Subsequently, Wayne Nelson and David Palumbo present the crossover of an interactive design firm to engagement with instructional design.

Blending processes and ideas from product design and user-experience design informs their work, beginning from their entertainment-oriented experience and moving toward an educational product.

How people design—whether they are instructional designers, architects, or end users—is a valuable base for practice and education. Chapters by Lisa Yamagata-Lynch and Craig Howard examine the design process using different methods of inquiry, but both help us in our quest for understanding. While Yamagata-Lynch uses Cultural Historical Activity Theory to examine design from an end-user point of view, Howard builds on an extensive use of the case study method to examine our own practices of instructional design.

As we have seen in these chapters, instructional design is a diverse field and, while the specific subject matter is important, it is but one component of education. Wayne Nelson outlines the possible scope of research and practice and finds ways to integrate the field beyond traditional educational research. The qualitative and subjective aspects of instructional design must also be addressed. The specific elements of message design, judgment, and ethics are presented in chapters by M.J. Bishop, Nilufer Korkmaz and Elizabeth Boling, and Stephanie Moore. Each is critical in a holistic understanding of the field of instructional design, touching on such questions as how we convey meaning and information, our judgment of quality in our work, and our responsibilities as designers.

We began the symposium with the idea of the value of design thinking, and Gordon Rowland, in his chapter, presents a method for improving the use of design in learning and thinking. Design is "a unique and essential form of inquiry," and Rowland's method can advance the use of design as a full-fledged educational component.

Examining design and education encourages us to address larger, more systemic issues. Marcia Ashbaugh and Anthony Piña examine leadership thinking and how it could infuse and direct instructional design. How to improve the practice of design inquiry extends to the full field of education and to leadership in higher education. Paul Zenke's chapter examines the role of university leadership as designers. Challenges abound in the modern age for higher education, and the application of design thinking and transformation is sorely needed.

Our story, the chapters of this book, began with detailed views of the work of instructional design and with their inward reflections, and concludes with recognition of the role of instructional design existing in a complex and ill-defined world. Patrick Parrish identifies this "Half-Known World," a challenge that must deal with the learning experience as a whole: as designers, as subject matter experts, as parents, teachers, and learners. Recognizing the flow of the narrative is part of our fuller understanding of our responsibility to education.

This research symposium and this subsequent publication could not have been possible without the support of a great organization, and I must acknowledge the role of the Association for Educational Communications and Technology. The organization has always been very supportive of innovative and divergent ideas and was very receptive and encouraging to my initial concepts for the symposium. The staff was instrumental in organizing and smoothly presenting the symposium, matching the standards they set every year at the annual conference. I would also like to specifically thank Executive Director Phillip Harris for his encouragement, support, and humor in moving the symposium to reality. Jason Huett, Monica Tracey, and Greg Clinton served as the symposium advisory board and assisted in reviewing initial proposals with the symposium cochairs. I would also like to thank Stephen Peters for his editorial help. And specifically, I would like to thank my cochair, coeditor, and colleague, Andy Gibbons, for his great support and involvement.

Finally, the symposium participants are the ones who bring value to any such endeavor, and, in the end, are those who are bringing design to the world of educational technology. Thank you each for your participation as authors, as discussants, and as colleagues in a limitless field.

I hope you find this book as worthwhile and as interesting as it has been in its development.

St. Paul, MN, USA   Brad Hokanson

Contents

Design, Designers, and Reflection-in-Action

Monica W. Tracey and John Baaki

Keywords Design • Designers • Design thinking • Reflection-in-action • Designer self-reflection • Ill-structured problems • Design episodes • Design inquiry • Design exploration • Designer reflective conversation

Instructional designers are an integral part of successful design, and as a profession we are constantly looking to expand and improve our preparation methods in an effort to best prepare designers. Designers are active, influential change agents who work in a design space that includes interpersonal dimensions (Cross, 2011). They bring their own experience, perceptions, and interpretations of design to each project. Research on design in other disciplines indicates that aspects of the design process include research, reflection, conceptualization, and judgment (Nelson & Stolterman, 2003). Concepts including designer relation to design are superficially considered in some instructional design decision-making processes, but designers have yet to document their reflections during their design activities. Research on design seldom focuses on the designer while she is actually designing. Without deep understanding of what actually happens during design, we cannot prescribe improvements in design or preparing designers (Dorst, 2008). Reflection-in-action is one activity that may assist designers in improving their design activities.

M.W. Tracey (✉) • J. Baaki
Wayne State University, Detroit, MI 48202, USA
e-mail: monicatracey@wayne.edu

B. Hokanson and A. Gibbons (eds.), *Design in Educational Technology*,
Educational Communications and Technology: Issues and Innovations 1,
DOI 10.1007/978-3-319-00927-8_1, © Springer International Publishing Switzerland 2014

Design and Design Thinking

Depending on the context, design includes numerous definitions and descriptors. A summary of a study analyzing the most widely adopted textbooks and official definitions of the field of instructional design (Smith & Boling, 2009) indicated that design is a systematic process, represented by models, based on theory, and grounded in data while focused on problem solving (Tracey & Boling, 2013). When looking outside of the instructional design field, design is defined as "both a noun and a verb and can refer either to the end product or to the process" (Lawson, 2006, p. 3). In general, design is referred to as a generic activity (Lawson, 2006), a process, and a topic of study across disciplines that addresses complex human situations. Design is also defined as a space rather than a process, and design thinking is abductive (Cross, 2011; Dorst, 2011).

Design thinking incorporating abductive reasoning forces a designer to shift and transfer thoughts between the required purpose or function and the appropriate forms for an object to satisfy the purpose (Cross, 2011). In essence, designers move back and forth between an analysis space (required purpose or function) and a synthesis space (appropriate forms for an object to satisfy the purpose). The core challenge of design thinking is, in parallel, creating a complex object, service, or system and making it work (Dorst, 2011). Designers come up with the "what" and "how" and then test both in conjunction (Dorst, 2011, p. 5). Within a design space, designers need to tolerate uncertainty, interact with external representations (sketches, models, and other materials), rely on intuition, and take stock and reflect on the what and the how (Cross, 2011).

As instructional designers begin to look to the design worlds of architects, engineering designers, product designers, industrial designers, and software systems designers to truly understand what happens during design, instructional designers stand to gain much from reflective practice within design thinking. Cross (2011) indicates "there has been a significant history in design research of theoretical analysis and reflection upon the nature of design ability" (p. 5). Instructional designers can embrace best practices from reflection-in-action to assist them in developing their designer ability (Fig. 1).

Designers and Reflection-in-Action

As a specific type of reflective practice (how professionals think during practice), reflection-in-action emphasizes that unique and uncertain situations are understood through attempts to change them, and changed through the attempts to understand the situations (Schön, 1983). Reflection-in-action helps designers deal well with situations of uncertainty, instability, uniqueness, and conflicted values that are inherent in ill-structured problems (Schön, 1983).

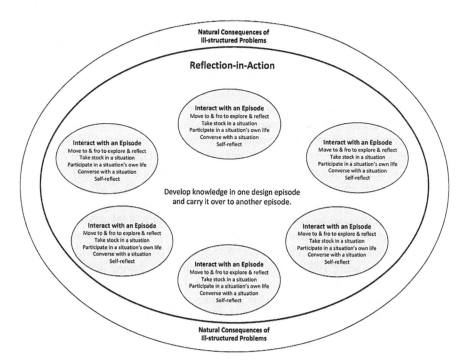

Fig. 1 A conceptual view of reflection-in-action

The second author headed a team that designed and developed an Internet Marketing web course for a major automaker's dealership sales consultants. The team's design ideas began to form when the team realized that customers who use the Internet should lead the 60-min web course. Using a whiteboard, the team sketched, interpreted, and developed three different Internet customers that would act as learning agents and present the course. Through biweekly, collaborative 60- to 90-min sessions that included quick interface sketching and storyboarding, the design team began to reflect on how the three Internet customer-learning agents would interact with learners through the web course interface. Through reflection-in-action, the team continued to design by digging into the Internet Marketing course secondary challenges: keeping ever-changing digital information current, choosing learning agents that are relevant across all dealerships, and developing current and useful Internet Marketing resources.

Working in a design thinking space (Cross, 2011), designers from different design fields, in the midst of the natural consequences of an ill-structured problem (Guindon, 1990), interact with a situation by having a reflective conversation with it. Designers are reflective participants in the design process (Scott, Shurville, Maclean, & Cong, 2007; Valkenburg & Dorst, 1998). To understand designers interacting with design episodes and having a reflective conversation with the situation, design thinking literature points to reflective practice ideas (Adams, Turns, &

Atman, 2003; Atman, Cardella, Turns, & Adams, 2005; Atman, Chimka, Bursic, & Nachtmann, 1999; Ball, Onarheim, & Christensen, 2010; Goel & Grafman, 2000; Guindon, 1990; Scott et al., 2007; Valkenburg & Dorst, 1998), especially to reflection-in-action (Schön, 1983, 1988). The idea of reflection-in-action is that unique and uncertain situations are understood through attempts to change them, and changed through the attempt to understand them (Schön, 1983, 1988).

Several researchers have indicated that reflection-in-action is best appreciated within the context of design activity. A design process has four aspects of design activity: (1) designer, (2) process, (3) content, and (4) context. Of the four aspects, designer is the most straightforward. Process is looking at design in two different ways: (1) rational problem solving and (2) reflective practice (Brown, 2008; Cross, 2011; Dorst, 2008; Schön, 1983). Content involves complex and uncertain design problems and the emerging solutions (Dorst, 2008; Schön, 1983). In general, a designer works in a particular context. A specific aspect of context is how designers draw from a repertoire of precedents inside and outside of the project (Brown, 2008; Cross, 2011; Dorst, 2008; Guindon, 1990; Schön, 1983). Studying and sharing design precedent has been gaining traction in the field of instructional design through journals, such as *The International Journal of Designs for Learning,* where designers share their designs plus detailed descriptions of their decision-making activities during design.

Theoretical Foundations of Reflection-in-Action

Theoretical foundations of reflection-in action include Donald Schön's (1983) theory of reflective practice and Kolb's (1984) work on experiential learning theory. Schön's (1983) theory of reflective practice or how professionals think in practice was developed to counter the rationality or scientific theory and techniques applied to practical problems (Cross, 2011). Schön attempted to explain how practitioners actually engage with their practice and discovered that designing appears to include a reflective conversation during and with the situation. When a designer is presented with a complex problem or situation, the designer shows a series of questioning, making a decision, reflecting on the consequences of the decision, then making another move. Main concepts are the notions of reflection-in-action, which refers to allowing one to experience the feelings and emotions inherent in a situation, and reflection-on-action, which refers to reflecting on something after it has happened through various methods, such as recording one's thoughts or talking about an event after it has taken place (Schön, 1983). This chapter focuses specifically on reflection-in-action, the reflection that occurs during design.

Kolb's (1984) experiential learning theory, although based on the experiences learners have, has value when looking at designers during designing. Kolb described experiential learning, grounded in experience, as a four-stage cycle based on the experiences learners encounter. The designer therefore observes and reflects on the design during the design experience. The designer then forms concepts, and perhaps rules, based on how the experience has been understood by observation and the reflection process. Finally, the designer tries out this new understanding in the next design situation. Experiential learning theory states that these four stages occur as part of the natural learning process. Designers as learners in every design experience engage in these four stages and, if observation and reflection are allowed and encouraged, can bring new insight to the next design experience, either working alone or with a team of other designers. Each designer brings his or her experiences to every new design experience.

Perspectives of Reflection-in-Design

Reflection-in-design can occur when designers deal with the natural consequences of ill-structured problems (Jonassen, 1997). Designers also interact with design episodes, including the movement between exploration and reflection, taking stock of a design situation, and participating in an episode that takes on a life of its own (Cross, 2011), each embracing reflection-in-action. Designers also have reflective conversations with the design situation and participate in a self-reflection process. One perspective of reflection is looking at the natural consequences of ill-structured problems.

Natural Consequences of Ill-Structured Problems

In the complex world of design, Guindon (1990) uses an interesting phrase to describe deviations in the design process. He notes from his study of software systems designers, "The analyses show that these deviations are not special cases due to bad design or performance breakdowns but are, rather, a natural consequence of the ill-structuredness of problems in the early stage of design" (p. 307). Ill-structured problems make design problems particularly difficult because ill-structured problems are incomplete and have ambiguous goals, have no predetermined solution path, and require an integration of multiple knowledge domains (Guindon, 1990).

As software systems designers reflected on an ill-structured problem involving the lift systems control of an elevator, Guindon (1990) observed systems designers drawing on multiple knowledge domains like design, software systems architecture, and computer science and found the designers weighing pros and cons of alternative solutions. As solutions began to evolve, designers reflected on the internal consistency, correctness, and completeness of a solution with respect to requirements, whether given, inferred, or added. An interesting consequence of the ill-structuredness of the problem was that when reflecting on an external representation of the solution, the software systems designers would change goals and immediately fix a newly discovered bug (Guindon, 1990). This closely ties to the idea of interacting with episodes (discussed later) by taking stock of the situation and making improvements.

It is this fixing the bugs now as a consequence of the ill-structured problem that provides a relevant introduction of Schön's (1983) reflection-in-action process. Reflection-in-action helps designers deal well with situations of uncertainty, instability, uniqueness, and conflicted values, which are inherent in ill-structured problems (Schön, 1983). Because design is complex and full of ill-structured problems, designers treat design cases as unique since they cannot deal with situations of uncertainty by applying standard theories and techniques.

Schön (1983) emphasizes reflection-in-action, rather than reflection-on-action. For Schön (1983), unique and uncertain situations are understood through attempts to change them, and changed through the attempt to understand them. In order to change the situation and understand the situation, designers reframe a situation by asking five questions: (1) Can I solve the problem I have set? (2) Do I know what I get when I solve the problem? (3) Have I made the situation coherent? (4) Have I made it congruent with my fundamental values and theories? and (5) Have I kept inquiry moving? (Schön, 1983).

Schön (1983) contends that much of reflection-in-action centers on the experience of surprise. Adams et al. (2003) connect reflection-in-action to this notion of surprise. For the Internet Marketing web course design team, surprises stemmed from the unpredictability of complex design situations like how to ensure sales consultants use critical thinking skills as they apply to best practices, how to present nonlinear content in a SCORM-compliant course, and how to quickly provide context around each learning agent through a combination of animation and narration. In these situations, Schön (1983) brings to light that the situation talks back and this back talk helps designers engage in a reflective conversation with the materials. Adams et al. (2003) conclude that this reflective conversation can help designers develop deeper understanding of the design problem.

What is important to take from the natural consequences of ill-structured problems is that designers design under conditions of complexity and uncertainty (Schön, 1988) and that designers analyze why actions do not lead to expected consequences and then form new plans for action and trying out new steps (Holmquist, 2007). Before any script, motion sample, and interface design were shared with the automaker, the Internet Marketing web course design team reflected quickly on four rounds of interface design sketches, two rounds of motion samples, and one script version 1.0. Each round triggered a new round of designing where a different sort of designing began. In the Internet Marketing web course design and development, an interesting outcome from the natural consequences of ill-structured problems is that the design team began to break down the overall design assignments into smaller situations or moves. The team would break down an 8-min module into the specific 20–30-s scenes than make up the module. Through reflection, designers can "rationally" make a decision to start a new activity (Valkenburg & Dorst, 1998). Using "rationally" is interesting as designers begin to make sense of ill-structuredness. Reflection within a situation of uncertainty and complexity leads designers to interact with an episode and participate in a reflective conversation with the situation.

Interaction with Episodes

The design process is episodic, which has strong implications for reflection from three perspectives: (1) Designers move to and fro between exploration and reflection,

(2) Designers take stock of a design situation, and (3) Designers participate in an episode that takes a life of its own (Cross, 2011). The Internet Marketing web course team often interacted with episodes by drawing on its knowledge of learning routines used in a previous course or a favorite practice item that emphasizes critical thinking skills. For example, the subject matter expert wanted to ensure that sales consultants understand what makes up a good follow-up email to a customer. Drawing on a drag-and-drop learning routine, the design team emphasized critical thinking skills by designing a practice item where sales consultants actually composed a follow-up email. The scriptwriter, the graphic designer, and instructional designer engrossed themselves in frame experiments as they moved to and fro between exploration and reflection. Taking stock of the design situation, the design reflected on many ideas to clarify vague ideas and move forward to a follow-up email practice routine.

Designers treat each design episode as unique (Schön, 1988). Designers build up knowledge in a cumulative and contemplative way, develop knowledge in one design episode, and carry it over to the next episode. Episodes can be complex and have lives of their own which may foil a project and create new meaning (Schön, 1983). As an external representation, design is constructed in public so other people can read and comment on it (Cross, 2011). Designers draw and sketch as a means of thinking out loud and as a process of criticism and discovery.

Move To and Fro Between Exploration and Reflection

Schön (1983) makes it clear that when reflecting in action a designer can think about doing and can think about doing something while doing it. In the midst of performance, reflection-in-action is bounded by an "action-present" zone of time (from minutes to months) in which action can still make a difference to the situation. For example, in looking at architects designing a lab configuration, Goel and Grafman (2000) conclude that designers generate a single idea or fragment and develop it through transformations where it is complete and can be evaluated. Even though these episodes were sometimes short, averaging between 1.2 and 1.6 min, actions like lab circulation patterns and placement of printers and workstations made a difference in the final design. The movement back and forth between exploration and reflection keeps the project moving forward as design transformations continue.

Take Stock of a Design Situation

Schön (1983) would argue that *action-present* is really actually taking stock of the design situation. Here, a designer takes account of unintended changes by framing new appreciations and understandings by making new design moves. Why take stock of the design situation? From multiple studies of engineering design students participating in design activities, Adams et al. (2003) conclude that reflection-in-action provides a means to fill gaps. The authors surmise that reflection-in-action allows designers to see new design requirements emerge and subsequently designers synthesize these new requirements into solution development. What is important in the process is that designers do not identify the requirements until they have designed and reflected on portions of the system.

In designing a web course, it is essential to ensure that learners find consistency in how they interact with the course. When reflecting on script version 1.0 and the initial motion sample, the Internet Marketing web course design team realized that the initial course designs did not consistently identify differences between content, examples, practice items, and feedback. New design requirements emerged from these designed portions of the web course. The design team decided that content would use the entire user interface, while sales consultants would trigger examples and practice items by interacting with a cell phone or computer screen interface. Through reflection-in-action, the design team participated in an in-depth exploration of solution ideas. The design team assessed the viability of uncertain ideas like no distinction between course content and examples and practice items and then gained confidence in the idea of presenting different interfaces for content and practice.

Participate in an Episode That Takes a Life of Its Own

In his study of architects, Schön (1988) asserts that skilled designers tend to treat each design situation or episode as unique. From this, designers build up knowledge in a cumulative way, develop knowledge in one design episode, and carry it over to the next episode. Although a designer may see each episode as unique, a good designer sees an episode as something that is part of a designer's repertoire (Schön, 1983). In other words, a designer sees a current episode as an episode from before so that a designer may pull from the earlier episode and use something in the new episode. Even though a designer contributes to an episode, episodes can be complex and have lives of their own, which may foil projects and create new meanings (Schön, 1983). Interacting with an episode means participating in a reflective conversation with the situation.

Reflective Conversation with the Situation

Because ill-structured problems are dynamic and complex, Schön (1983) explains that in good design processes designers engage in a reflective conversation with the design situation, answer the situation's back talk, and reflect-in-action on the construction of the problem, strategies of action, or models of the phenomena. When absorbed in a reflective conversation with a design situation, reflection-in-action has three critical dimensions: (1) a designer's language as she describes and appreciates the particular consequences of design moves, (2) the implications that are discovered and followed, and (3) the changing stance toward a design situation (Schön, 1983). In a situation's back talk, a designer can discover a whole new idea, which generates a system of implications for more moves. In other words, answering a situation's back talk results in a shift in a designer's stance. Keeping in mind that the design situation is engulfed in complexity and uncertainty, a designer shifts from "What if?" to do something with the episode, and a designer's stance shifts from exploration to commitment (Schön, 1983).

Adams et al. (2003) concur with Schön that reflection is critical to practice. A designer reflectively converses with a situation by framing the problem, naming things a designer attends to do within the frame, generating moves toward a solution, and reflecting on outcomes of the moves (Adams et al., 2003). The result is coupled iterations (Adams et al., 2003) where a designer revises problem understanding in the context of developing or revising solution elements. This is what Schön (1983) describes as a designer engaging in a conversation across problem and solution spaces where solution spaces are not yet fully developed.

In a study that really brings to light reflective conversation with a design situation, Valkenburg and Dorst (1998) examined engineering teams who competed in designing and building remote-controlled robots that had to transport as many balls as possible from a ball bin into a basket. Using episodes as raw data instead of traditional protocol analysis time intervals, Valkenburg and Dorst (1998) visualized four activities—naming, moving, reflection, and resetting the frame—in 30 min of the protocol. The first activity of the design team was naming relevant objects within the design situation: shooting the ball, collecting the balls, and driving the robot. In the second activity, the design team chose the most important relevant object to handle first. During reflection-in-action, the competing team asked and discussed: (a) What do we do now? (b) What do we have now? (c) Is this all? and (d) Does the robot have to shoot? The result was resetting the frame into getting balls into a basket as the most important problem issue.

What is significant is that in this design competition the team that spent the most time on reflection won. For the winning team, reflection occurred early and often. The winning team's reflected moments always occurred in relation to the design task. For the losing team, reflection happened at the end where it was too late to intervene with the project. The losing team's reflected moment was the team's last activity. In this design competition, early and multiple reflective conversations with the design situations affected which design team won the competition.

Designer Self-Reflection

Reflection should occur individually as well as within a design team during design. Self-reflection is the process of looking at one's self to understand feelings and emotions. Self-management may follow the process as a way to manage those feelings and emotions (Bradberry & Greaves, 2005). Based on their research, Hixon and Swann (1993) suggest that self-reflection, a meta-emotional activity, is essential to self-knowledge. It is through self-knowledge that designers are able to self-evaluate (a metacognitive function) and move deeper into expert status. Studying medical physicians and the need for and measurement of self-reflection, Aukes,

Geertsma, Cohen-Schotanus, Zwierstra, and Slaets (2007) discovered that self-reflection is considered a *mental hygiene* component to a physician and creates the ability to develop professionally, particularly in solving problems (Aukes et al., 2007). Educational theories focus on reflection as part of the process of active learning and learning through inquiry. Reflection is considered "metacognition" because it refers "to a response that considers the action itself and its relationship to the knowledge structure, that generated it, as well as the extent to which it achieved the intended goal" (Laurillard, 2012, p. 76). Designer self-reflection can provide the opportunity for a designer to look at design actions, the learning that resulted from those actions, and how the actions helped or hindered the ultimate goal along with building the designers' repertoire in design.

Throughout the Internet Marketing web course design, the instructional designer and lead project manager met periodically to discuss what was going well with the reflection-in-action approach, what was not going well, and what needed to change. This was particularly helpful when the design team faced design obstacles like the subject matter expert's desire to change the module sequence and when milestones had to be adjusted because the subject matter expert and the automaker team missed feedback deadlines.

In other fields—for example, psychotherapy—it is common knowledge that therapists can alter therapy outcomes through their behavior and reactions; therefore, supervisory sessions where self-awareness occurs and is articulated are considered critical to therapist development (Moffett, 2009). Novice therapists are asked to reflect upon their thoughts and feelings before, throughout, and/or after patient sessions (Fauth & Williams, 2005). Methods of implementation vary but often include structured questions that ask how the therapists *would* think/feel, what they *are* thinking/feeling, or what they *previously* thought/felt during client sessions. The process of self-awareness comprises both self-reflection and self-management. Self-awareness for the purpose of this discussion is the extent to which one can identify how one is feeling and how these feelings may be affecting, for example, client interactions, design decision-making, and design team interfaces. Self-management is the level at which an individual can direct actions and perceptions in such a way that more effective outcomes are possible.

After the subject matter expert's and automaker team's first review of script version 1.0, the interface look and feel, and the initial motion sample, some design team members felt frustrated and disappointed with the amount of feedback received. Should the design team have fleshed out more design details before presenting such early design "sketches"? After some self-reflection, the design team concluded that in the reflection-in-action spirit, it was important for the subject matter expert and automaker team to take stock in and react to the early design episodes. This early feedback was essential to designing script versions 2.0 and 3.0 and the experience design document that visually presented all learning routines.

Self-reflection provides an opportunity for designers to measure their thoughts, understandings, and actions. Concepts including designer self-awareness, introspection, self-insight, and interpersonal choices are superficially considered in some design decision-making processes, but an in-depth look at these activities is often neglected in studying instructional designers during the process of design. This may in part because of the nature of instructional design models embodying the design process, not the designer as a part of that process.

Implications on Design and Designers

Design involves dealing with uncertainties and designers must not only learn to deal with uncertainty but embrace and use uncertainty as a tool to propel optimal design solutions. Design is a complex activity most often involving ill-structured problems (Jonassen, 1997). Instructional designers should be prepared to deal with ill-structured problems and the complexity design inherently brings. It is time to prepare instructional designers in a similar fashion to other design professions. Cennamo et al. (2011) state that "the education of engineers, instructional designers, architects, landscape designers, and the like must, by necessity, prepare students to solve the very complex and ill-structured design problems with which they must grapple as professionals" (p. 13). Design thinking (Cross, 2007; Lawson & Dorst, 2009) and reflective designing (Lowgren & Stolterman, 2004) explain how no single approach to designing can address every future situation effectively, so the designer must be prepared to appreciate design situations subtly and with discipline, invent and reinvent processes, and take personal responsibility for the effects of their designs rather than handing off responsibility for quality outcomes to a single process or theory (Nelson & Stolterman, 2003).

Instructional designers bring different backgrounds and abilities to the classroom, studio, and/or workplace along with very different understandings of what design is and their role in it. Those who view design as a tradition distinct from science and who study how it occurs in practice present design not as a smooth systematic process. In addition, designer's values, belief structures, prior experiences, knowledge and skills, and their approach to design affect the final outcome (Nelson & Stolterman, 2003). Lawson and Dorst (2009) present a three-dimensional model of the constraints on designs, a view not intended to represent all facets of designing but one which "casts the designer not as a traveler along a winding process path, but as an actor in a space shaped both externally by constraints and internally by the designer himself" (p. 131). In this view, designers have to appreciate and impose constraints, and they have to manipulate the conceptual space in which they are working in response to those constraints (Tracey & Boling, 2013). Reflection-in-action during design can assist the instructional designer to acknowledge the uncertainty, identify the ill-structuredness of the design problems, and embrace the complexity inherent in the design solution.

Conclusions

Reflection-in-action is just one element of a design thinking approach to instructional design. Within a design thinking approach, instructional designers can learn much from how reflection-in-action can help solve design problems, align a designer's fundamental values with the design solution, ensure design situations are coherent, and, maybe most importantly, keep inquiry moving. Cross (2011) suggests that a considered and reflective approach to design and consideration of alternative solution concepts might save time and effort in the long run. Schön (1983) agrees as he discusses that reflection early on with pencil and paper, and well before a build, is a lot cheaper. Design moves that are costly during a build can be "…tried at little or no risk in the world of drawing" (Schön, 1983, p. 158).

Schön (1983) considers how reflection-in-action in a unique case may be generalized to other design cases. This occurs not by forming general principles, but adding to a designer's repertoire of important themes from which a designer can pull in future design projects. But, how can instructional designers become efficient and effective in reflection-in-action? Instructional designers can learn from design disciplines as design students are exposed to complex design problems. For example, Atman et al. (2005) note that as part of homework engineering design students are given complex design problems with varying task environments.

Dorst (2008) believes that designers can only foster a deeper understanding of design activity when all aspects of design activity are considered. Although there is research regarding the process of design activity, what research lacks are the other three aspects of design activity: (1) designer, (2) context, and (3) content (Dorst, 2008). Dorst (2008) advocates a new type of design research, "…in which the process and content of design activity are connected with a model of designer and the context in which designing is taking place" (p. 7). In regard to a reflection-in-action approach to improving a design while it is fluid, interesting research opportunities could include how individual designers reflectively converse with design situations as compared to how design teams converse; how levels of designers—novice, advanced beginner, competent, real expert, master, and visionary (Dorst, 2008)— reflect differently from one another; how context affects reflective practice; and how the design project's content affects reflection.

A reflective conversation with a design situation can be an effective way to judge the strengths and weaknesses of a design project while it is fluid. This has critical implications for most design projects, as they are complex, uncertain, and ill structured. A reflection-in-action approach is designed to operate in a complex world. It is this complex world where instructional designers engage in actual design practice.

References

Adams, R. S., Turns, J., & Atman, C. J. (2003). Educating effective engineering designers: the role of reflective practice. *Design Studies, 24,* 275–294. doi:10.1016/S0142 694X(02)00059-X.

Atman, C. J., Cardella, M. E., Turns, J., & Adams, R. (2005). Comparing freshman and senior engineering design processes: An in-depth follow-up study. *Design Studies, 26,* 325–357. doi:10.1016/j.destud.2004.09.005.

Atman, C. J., Chimka, J. R., Bursic, K. M., & Nachtmann, H. L. (1999). A comparison of freshman and senior engineering design processes. *Design Studies, 20,* 131–152.

Aukes, L. J., Geertsma, J., Cohen-Schotanus, J., Zwierstra, R. P., & Slaets, P. J. (2007). The development of a scale to measure personal reflection in medical practice and education. *Medical Teacher, 29*(2–3), 177–182. doi:10.1080/01421590701299272.

Ball, L. J., Onarheim, B., & Christensen, B. T. (2010). Design requirements, epistemic uncertainty, and solution development strategies in software design. *Design Studies, 31*, 567–589. doi:10.1016/j.destud.2010.09.003.

Bradberry, T., & Greaves, J. (2005). *The emotional intelligence quick book: Everything you need to know to put your EQ to work.* New York: Fireside.

Brown, T. (2008). *Change by design.* New York: Harper Business.

Cennamo, K., Brandt, C., Scott, B., Douglas, S., McGrath, M., Reimer, Y., et al. (2011). Managing the complexity of design problems through studio-based learning. *The Interdisciplinary Journal of Problem-Based Learning, 5*(2), 12–36.

Cross, N. (2007). *Designerly ways of knowing.* London: Springer.

Cross, N. (2011). *Design thinking: Understanding how designers think and work.* London: Berg.

Dorst, K. (2008). Design research: A revolution-waiting-to-happen. *Design Studies, 29*, 4–11. doi:10.1016/j.destud.2007.12.001.

Dorst, K. (2011). The core of "design thinking" and its application. *Design Studies.* doi:10.1016/j.destud.2011.07.006.

Fauth, J., & Williams, E. N. (2005). The in-session self-awareness of therapist trainees: Hindering or helpful? *Journal of Counseling Psychology, 52*(3), 443–447. doi:10.1037/0022-0167.52.3.443.

Goel, V., & Grafman, J. (2000). Role of the right prefrontal cortex in ill-structured planning. *Cognitive Neuropsychology, 17*(5), 415–436. doi:10.1080/026432900410775.

Guindon, R. (1990). Designing the design process: Exploiting opportunistic thoughts. *Human Computer Interaction, 5*, 305–344.

Hixon, J. G., & Swann, W. B., Jr. (1993). When does introspection bear fruit? Self reflection, self-insight, and interpersonal choices. *Journal of Personality and Social Psychology, 64*, 35–43.

Holmquist, M. (2007). Managing project transformation in a complex context. *Creativity and Innovation Management, 16*(1), 46–51. doi:10.1111/j.1467 8691.2007.00416.x.

Jonassen, D. (1997). Instructional design model for well-structured and ill-structured problem-solving learning outcomes. *Educational Technology Research and Development, 45*(1), 65–95.

Kolb, D. A. (1984). *Experiential learning: Experience as the source of learning and development.* Englewood Cliffs, NJ: Prentice-Hall.

Laurillard, D. (2012). *Teaching as a design science: Building pedagogical patterns for learning and technology.* New York: Routledge.

Lawson, B. (2006). *How designers think: The design process demystified* (4th ed.). Oxford, UK: Elsevier.

Lawson, B., & Dorst, K. (2009). *Design expertise.* Oxford, UK: Elsevier.

Lowgren, J., & Stolterman, E. (2004). *Thoughtful interaction design: A design perspective on information technology.* Boston, MA: MIT Press.

Moffett, L. A. (2009). Directed self-reflection protocols in supervision. *Training and Education in Professional Psychology, 3*, 78–83.

Nelson, H. G., & Stolterman, E. (2003). *The design way: Intentional change in an unpredictable world: Foundations and fundamentals of design competence.* Englewood Cliffs, NJ: Educational Technology Publications.

Schön, D. A. (1983). *The reflective practitioner: How professionals think in action.* Boston: Basic Books.

Schön, D. A. (1988). Designing: Rules, types, and worlds. *Design Studies, 9*(3), 181–190.

Scott, B., Shurville, S., Maclean, P., & Cong, C. (2007). Cybernetic principles for learning design. *Kybernetes, 26*(9/10), 1497–1514. doi:10.1108/0368 4920710827445.

Smith, K. M., & Boling, E. (2009). What do we make of design? Design as a concept in educational technology. *Educational Technology, 49*(4), 3–17.

Tracey, M. W., & Boling, E. (2013). Preparing instructional designers and educational technologists: Traditional and emerging perspectives. In M. Spector, D. Merrill, J. Elen, & M. J. Bishop (Eds.), *Handbook of research on educational communications and technology.*

Valkenburg, R., & Dorst, K. (1998). The reflective practice of design teams. *Design Studies, 19*, 249–271.

Eight Views of Instructional Design and What They Should Mean to Instructional Designers

Andrew S. Gibbons

Keywords Design process • Design methods • Design studies • Architecture • Professional

Introduction

The chapters in this volume are evidence of a new drive toward more robust and valid descriptions of design: better descriptions of design for novices and advanced concepts and methods for experienced designers.

A number of scholars are revitalizing the discussion of design within instructional technology, viewing design from different perspectives. Jonassen (2008) asserts the problem-solving nature of design. Rowland (2008) describes how we learn by designing. Bannan-Ritland (2003) places instructional design in context with design research in other fields. Bichelmeyer (2003), Reigeluth (1999), Reigeluth and Carr-Chellman (2009), and Yanchar and his colleagues (Yanchar, South, Williams, Allen, & Wilson, 2010) place stress on the nature of theory and its relation to design. Hokanson and Miller (2009) examine the multiple roles of the designer. Parrish (2005, 2006) explores the aesthetic nature of designing and of the designed artifact. Gibbons and Rogers (2009) propose how an architecture of designed things applies to instructional design. Wilson (2005) reexamines the practice of design. This energetic discussion of design echoes an interest in design which has been rising for decades outside of the instructional technology field, producing a rich literature that informs our own.

The backdrop to this discussion is a tradition of over 50 years of reliance on increasingly simplified descriptions of design in the form of design models. Smith

A.S. Gibbons (✉)
Brigham Young University, Provo, UT 84604, USA
e-mail: andy_gibbons@byu.edu

B. Hokanson and A. Gibbons (eds.), *Design in Educational Technology*,
Educational Communications and Technology: Issues and Innovations 1,
DOI 10.1007/978-3-319-00927-8_2, © Springer International Publishing Switzerland 2014

and Boling (2009) review the assumptions and misconceptions of design models that have evolved over that period. There is room to question whether the notion of a design model adequately describes what we know about design (Gibbons, Boling, & Smith, 2013; Gibbons & Yanchar, 2010). Gibbons and Yanchar (2010) identify a wide range of topics that would be included in a more robust description of design.

Placing Instructional Design in Perspective

Some of these issues can be addressed by viewing instructional design from different perspectives of scale that include its historical context, the environment of designing, the nature of the thing being designed, the thinking processes of the designer, and the conceptual tools the designer wields during design. Figure 1 illustrates eight different views of design that describe it from multiple scale perspectives. Describing these views bridges the conceptual and practical worlds of design at different levels of scale, yielding new questions for exploration.

Organizational View

The first view of instructional design describes the relationship of the designer to the larger organization. Instructional design consumes time, money, and resources. Making quality instructional products requires specialized skills, equipment, and collaboration among members of a team. For this reason, instructional design is

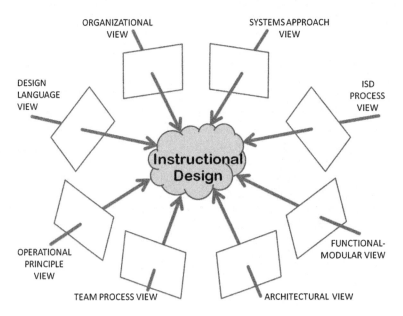

Fig. 1 Design viewed from many perspectives from Gibbons (2013)

normally carried out by a team under organizational sponsorship—a business, a school, the military, a government organization, or a client. When an organization considers funding and staffing a design project, it usually asks the designer what value it can expect as a return on its investment. Instructional designers, therefore, are becoming aware of the value they add to the organization.

The placement of instructional designers within organizations is changing. In the traditional pattern, designers operated in relative isolation within a training department, separated from the operational and administrative functions of the organization, disconnected from everyday operational concerns.

In this scenario the training department was an appendage to, and not really part of, the organizational fabric. Designers were told what to make—not consulted and not included in key organizational decisions. When there was a downturn in the organization's fortunes, the training department was a first candidate for cutting. The training function was most often placed under separate, nonoperational management.

A new pattern is evolving. Organizations are increasingly realizing that training is an important part of their product: something that enhances its value to customers. Organizations realize that there is value in training that supports the product or service, making it easier to use. The value of a workforce that is well trained in product skills and customer relations is being recognized, so organizations are using training to unify their workforce and focus their energies by increasing collaboration among employees. The value of these collaborations for creative problem solving is another value that does not escape organizational notice. As a by-product, organizations are seeing that training and education can help to create and maintain corporate morale through employee buy-in. In short, organizations are recognizing the function of training in creating organizational culture.

Training is increasingly viewed as a fundamental process of a competitive organization: a function essential to the organization's growth and adaptation within a changing environment. Designers must see themselves as creators of value within the organization. To do that, they must understand the values of the organization and how their products and services support them. The designer must understand how value is measured to the organization and what elements of a design lead to value. Designers must sometimes make calculated trade-offs between practical concerns and theoretical issues. The training designers receive must prepare them for this.

Organizations are interested in designers who can speak their language and who understand the rules of the new knowledge economy and the new information-based organization (Kahin & Foray, 2006; see also Drucker, 1989). Research on the value added of the designer and the new role of the designer within the new organization is badly needed.

Systems Approach View

A second view of instructional design—the systems approach view—is historical (Ramo & St. Claire, 1998). The practice of formal instructional design became a topic during World War I, but it became an imperative during World War II.

With the emergence of complex man-machine systems, time needed for training increased just at the time when it was becoming more scarce. Efficiency became the goal of training, and the systems approach became the means of designing training to reach that goal.

The systems approach is a problem-solving process for highly complex problems. It is not a single procedure but a set of problem-solving tools and techniques used by multidisciplinary teams of scientists and engineers. There is no set order, but as problems are solved, new problems appear, demanding the selection of appropriate tools. The first problem attacked by a team using a systems approach is to ascertain the real problem, which involves in most cases gathering large amounts of data for extensive data analysis. The systems approach is difficult to describe because it is a family of problem-solving methods rather than a formula.

The systems approach involves solving a complex problem viewed in terms of multiple complex interacting systems. The problem is broken down into independent solvable subproblems that involve the coordinated behavior of multiple subsystems. Analyzing problems and testing solutions normally involve quantification of variables.

In the systems approach, a multidisciplinary team consisting of both scientists and engineers works toward a solution. Decisions are based on the best data obtainable, using a wide range of problem-solving methods. Methods are selected according to problem status, not an orderly process. Multiple alternative solutions are explored and evaluated on the basis of multiple, sometimes conflicting, criteria that account for the needs of many stakeholders. System modeling and simulation are often used to test solutions.

Innovation is the goal because problems solved often have few precedents, and the context of problems introduces new variables. The systems approach is a rational approach to finding a practical, usable solution that implements existing theory as well as developing new theory along the way. Life cycle planning is always included in calculations, and human factors are used to fit the solution to the user's needs and abilities.

Robert Gagné edited a seminal work, *Psychological Principles in System Development* (1965), in which processes for engineering the human side of human-machine systems were described in great detail, with specific attention to the training function necessary to prepare humans to operate within a system environment. Soon after *Psychological Principles* was published, Gagné's associates, especially Leslie Briggs, began to popularize the systems approach among instructional designers. This set off a trend in which the systems approach was simplified through several generations of instructional design models (see the next section).

The systems approach was evolved to solve very complex problems. It is closely related to what is practiced today as design-based research (Bannan-Ritland, 2003; Collins, Joseph, & Bielaczyc, 2004; Reeves, Herrington, & Oliver, 2005). The systems approach cannot be equated with the procedural or formulaic process approach represented by existing instructional design models. Problems suitable for the systems approach include many unknowns and uncertainties, which make the problem unique and which influence the order of problem solving, so that one of the major activities of the solver is always to decide which part of the problem to attack next. This is a quality in the solving of instructional design problems that might be reclaimed, as described later.

Bannan-Ritland (2003) suggests that design leading to educational interventions should "move past isolated, individual efforts of design research" and undertake research "that considers both field studies and experimental research methodologies" (p. 21) in programmatic rather than piecemeal studies. What this means to the instructional designer is that every design is an opportunity to learn something from having designed and that chained design efforts over time can be used to create new knowledge, about instruction and about design, much as would occur in an application of the systems approach.

The tendency in instructional design to reduce the systems approach to a process or a model can be reversed by considering each new project and each new design problem as a type of small-scale research and an opportunity to learn about designing. What has been learned from past projects can be chained with what is learned from the present project. Bannan-Ritland (2003) proposed that the challenge to instructional designers is to "draw[s] from traditions of instructional design...product design...usage-centered design...and diffusion of innovations...as well as established educational research methodologies...." (p. 21). Design-based research restores a larger perspective that is lost when the scope of reference is the single project. Bannan-Ritland's comparison of instructional design with research and development processes from several other fields defines a trail of breadcrumbs for researchers in instructional technology.

ISD Process View

A third view of instructional design is the one most familiar to most designers—instructional design models. Instructional technologists at first enthusiastically embraced the systems approach, but it was so complex as a process that designers interested only in creating a product found the tool too large for the job. Not every designer had the goal of creating new knowledge on every project, and most worked under heavy resource constraints and client product expectations.

A process of simplification began to temper the demands of the systems approach and create a design process that fit the hand of this more practically oriented designer, who often worked alone or with a small team. This set off a trend toward instructional design models that bore the title "systems approach" but that increasingly lost resemblance to it. In this melee the original aims, methods, and spirit of the systems approach were largely lost, though the title of "systems approach" was retained. In the hands of average users, design models nominally based on the systems approach became more like formulas to be followed than a method of robust and unpredictable interdisciplinary problem solving (Gibbons et al., 2013; Smith & Boling, 2009). Figure 2 gives a composite view of the core elements that were explicitly part of or implied by design models proposed during this period.

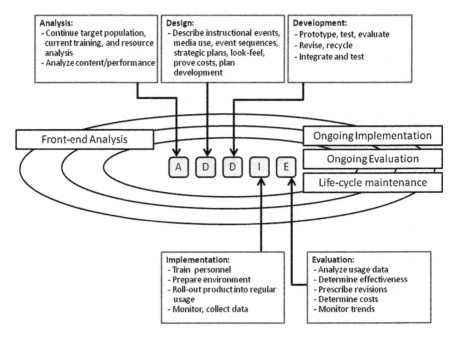

Fig. 2 A composite instructional design model showing the relationship to front-end analysis and after-project implementation, evaluation, and life cycle maintenance processes from Gibbons (2013)

The elements of this model should be sufficiently familiar not to need enumeration for this audience. What is important is that the model concept became so prevalent that for almost 50 years it was regarded as the orthodox approach to instructional design.

Numerous textbooks were written—at first for practicing designers, but eventually for novices and school teachers—describing a mostly standard process. What tended to vary from model to model was the grouping of design tasks. In this way, what was originally promoted in the name of the systems approach began to look little like its namesake. Design models became associated with the designations instructional systems design/development (ISD) and ADDIE. Gibbons et al. (2013) give a more detailed description of model proliferation.

The introduction of instructional design models was a major step forward for what had been a relatively disorganized instructional design world. But no sooner had the innovation of design models become popular than some problems became apparent. Many designers began to notice that what the ISD model told them to do didn't match what common sense and expediency told them they had to do to get the job done. The ISD narrative didn't describe what they really had to do in the real world (Cox & Osguthorpe, 2003; Rowland, 1992; Yanchar et al., 2010). Often designers found that the models led them to certain kinds of solution more easily, and over time design solutions began to look more and more similar.

At the same time, it became harder to design other kinds of things, such as simulations, collaborative learning, and games. Designers also found ISD models hard to apply in projects for culture, attitude, learning in informal settings, and other socially contexted and learner-centered methods.

Designers noticed that design projects were accompanied by decisions that had already been made, which seemed to eliminate the need for some design processes, but models didn't explain how to adapt themselves to these unexpected situations. Some model builders (mostly large organizations) took the specification of ISD processes to the extreme, defining processes in such great detail that the documentation of the process stood taller than the designer who used it. Some organizations insisted that the model processes be applied exactly as specified, leaving the designer no latitude for invention, innovation, or adjustment. Designers following process models discovered that it was hard to know how to inject theory into their designs, especially since many models came to include built-in theoretical commitments. Finally, some designers felt that ISD described how to carry out administrative and managerial functions at the periphery of the design without telling them how to actually determine the structures and details of a design.

Over time, the design model became recognizable as a special case of a general engineering model, adapted for application within instructional design and not an instance of the systems approach. Models from the very beginning (with Gagné and later with Briggs) incorporated domain-specific assumptions that limited their generalizability. For example, task analysis appeared in Gagné's original man-machine process formulation, despite the fact that not all design problems yield appropriate results when task analysis is used. Over time, highly simplified models created for use by untrained designers became the most well known. For example, the Interservice Procedures for Instructional Systems Development (IPISD; Branson et al., 1975) promulgated by the Army Training and Doctrine Command. Simplified models became used by constraint by a large number of novice military and government designers as cookbooks, so they became the most familiar face of instructional design to a large number of practitioners, many of whom later decided to make a career of instructional design in the growing commercial world.

The history and prevalence of instructional design models is one of the reasons for a conference on the future vision of instructional design such as this symposium. Placing design models in perspective with other design descriptions is one of the purposes of this paper, and that requires elevating other views of design, since models have been the predominant theme in the instructional design process literature for over 40 years.

Functional-Modular (Layer Design) View

A fourth view of instructional design can be termed a functional-modular view. This view is based on analyzing the functions of the designed artifact. It is based on the philosophy that designed artifacts can be characterized in terms of decomposable functional "layers" within which the designer addresses more detailed design questions (Gibbons & Rogers, 2009).

To obtain the benefits of layered design, one does not give up ISD design principles, since a general engineering process still raises important questions during design creation, especially at the higher levels of design project management. However, the order of design decision making changes at more detailed design levels.

The functional-modular view of design assumes a distinction between scientific and technological theory and that there are at least two types of technological theory: design theory and domain theory (Gibbons & Rogers, 2009). Instructional theory is a type of domain theory. Instructional theories are instances of domain theory; they pertain to the design of instruction and supply the elements incorporated into designs.

Functional-modular (layer) theory, on the other hand, is a design theory. It creates an architectural framework within which multiple domain theories pertaining to each layer can populate the design.

Functional-modular theory is applied in fields other than instructional design: in business, computer design, software design, architecture, and engineering. Examples of this include:

- Donald Schön (1987), in *Educating the Reflective Practitioner*, describes how an architectural design problem consists of numerous subproblems, each having its own principles, standards, and design terms, specialists, and domain theories.
- Stewart Brand (1994) likewise describes the layers of a building's design, noting that when a designer uses layering deliberately, a building's usable lifetime is extended because as layers aged unevenly they can be changed independently without destroying the entire edifice.
- Baldwin and Clark (2000) describe how the principle of modularity, which is based on the principle of design layers, is the economic factor that made the modern personal computer, with its replaceable functional modules (boards, drives, etc.), possible. Early computers were monolithic in their designs, so changing one part of the system meant disrupting the whole system design. Functional-modular separation changed that irreversibly.
- Fowler (2003) describes the enterprise architecture of software that increasingly forms the core mechanism that businesses use to carry out their essential functions. He explains the structure of this software in terms of three main layers which can be changed independently: "most nontrivial enterprise applications use a layered architecture of some form...." (p. 2).
- The software that forms the Internet is structured in terms of functional layers. Software protocols, the bits of software by which the Internet works, carry out their functions within the structure of multiple functional layers. Competing layer models have been proposed, some with four layers, some with five, and some with seven.
- Ericsson and Erixon (1999) describe the concept of *modular product platforms*, a design principle that considers a marketable product to consist of a family of reconfigurable components that can be assembled in different combinations to form different versions of the product. Separation of modules is a layering process. A module, or layer, may be defined for many different reasons, based either on conceptual or practical concerns.

Uyemura (1999) describes the value of thinking in terms of design domains with reference to digital system design:

> The detail of interest to you at a particular time depends on the level where you are working. Sometimes you will be interested only in the overall function of a complex unit, whereas at other times you may need to understand every element that goes into making a basic unit. The power in this approach derives from the fact that the important aspects vary with the level.... (p. 18)

There is evidence that instructional designers tend to think of designs in monolithic, unsubdivided terms. Frequently designers will refer to the configuration of their design in terms of a dominant school of thought, such as "this is a constructivist design" or "this is direct instruction." As Uyemura shows, this is not true in other, more mature design fields. Automotive and aeronautical designers think of their designs in terms of the systems and subsystems they incorporate. An auto designer might be expected to describe several subsystem influences on the design: "This model has rack and pinion steering, a V-6 overhead cam engine, manual transmission, and is equipped with the stabilizer package."

The instructional design field will gravitate toward more detailed descriptions of designs as the field matures and it becomes commonly understood that many subsystems are required to complete a design, each part of the design being dominated by its own design theories and philosophies. This evolution, which is already underway, has escaped notice. Instructional design teams today consist of multiple specialists representing multiple specialized domains, including artists of specialized kinds, writers, assistant designers, subject-matter experts, programmers, assessment experts, evaluators, and implementation specialists. Each of these roles contributes expertise to one or more layers of a design using principles and theories that pertain to just their specialty. The more complex the design, the larger the number of specialists required.

Layer design theory as described by Gibbons and Rogers (2009) names seven design layers, or domains, of an instructional design explaining that there may be more or fewer layers, depending on the insight of the designer. These layers represent major functions carried out by an instructional artifact. Each layer represents a subproblem of the original design problem, and each layer in turn decomposes into sub-layers that have all of the properties of a layer. Figure 3 illustrates the following layers named by Gibbons and Rogers:

- *Content layer.* An instructional design contains—implicit or explicit—a description of the structural nature of that which is to be taught. There are implicit or explicit units into which the subject matter and performances are divided. Teachers divide subject matter into parcels that associate with units, lessons, and activities. Instructional designers identify facts, concepts, tasks, rules, and so forth, and associate them with behaviors to form instructional objectives, but the content structure is only one element of an objective.
- *Strategy layer.* An instructional design must specify the physical organization of the learning space, the social organization of participants, their roles and responsibilities, instructional goals that consist of a content element and a performance element, the allocation of goals to time structures called "events," and strategic patterns of interaction between the learner and the instruction. These things are

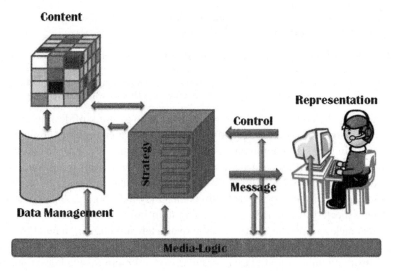

Fig. 3 The system of major layers proposed by Gibbons and Rogers (2009). Different designers perceive different layers, and layers subdivide as new technical and theoretical knowledge emerges or according to practical considerations from Gibbons (2013)

the concerns of the strategy layer. This layer has many sub-layers, each one corresponding to the concerns just listed and more.

- *Message layer*. A design must specify the units of tactical communication — the elements of the instructional conversation. These are the message structures through which the instruction communicates with the learner in a conversational manner. The units identified within the message layer are chosen because of their ability to carry out the larger strategic plan at a detailed exchange-by-exchange level.
- *Control layer*. A design must specify the control devices through which the learner expresses messages and actions to the instruction, along with a language that attaches meaning to inputs from the controls so that the learner's meaning can be analyzed and interpreted.
- *Representation layer*. A design must specify the representations that make message elements visible, hearable, and otherwise sense-able: the media representation channels to be used, the rule for assigning message elements to media channels, the form and composition of the representation, the synchronization of messages delivered through the multiple channels, and the concrete, tangible representations of content.
- *Media-logic layer*. A design must specify the rules and mechanisms for executing the functions of *all* of the other layers as well as the rules and mechanisms for communications with the environment outside of the instruction.
- *Data management layer*. A design must specify data to be captured, archived, analyzed, interpreted, and reported.

Layers are a natural result of the evolution and maturation of a design field. Layers emerge as new technological knowledge accumulates. The list above does not constitute a single, "standard" set of layers, because not only are designers' perceptions of useful layers in a state of constant change at the detailed level, but every layer is subject to splitting into sub-layers, modifying, and growing as technical knowledge and theoretical insight grow.

Moreover, different designers can "see" different layers. They may see the layers that other designers see, but some designers "see" additional layers that others have difficulty discerning. To that extent their layer definitions are different from those of other designers, and to the extent that these are useful and productive layers, they constitute the designer's competitive advantage: a value-added. Private layers allow a designer to think about design in more detail and nuance, and they lead to new design experiences, new experiments, which lead to new design insight and understanding.

Shared or public layers give a designer the ability to subdivide large design problems into smaller, solvable problems without losing the integrity and coherence of the larger design. They give a design team a common set of languages for describing the entire design as well as its constituent sub-designs.

Architectural View

A fifth view of design is the architectural view, as described by Blaauw and Brooks (1997). The architectural view describes how a designer can bring abstract ideas into a design in a way that gives coherence to the design, and this happens at the finest level of detail, at the heart of the design.

Blaauw and Brooks, who are computer designers, distinguish three stages in the evolution of a design: *architecture, implementation,* and *realization.* These are stages of *design,* not *manufacture,* and they are accomplished in parallel, interacting with each other, with the designer moving from one to the other as understanding of the design emerges. These stages involve design decisions at different levels of abstraction. They attempt to describe how a vague idea emerges from the fog in a designer's mind, takes shape, and eventually hardens into a plan—a design. The designer's mind moves back and forth between these stages, and they mutually influence each other.

The three stages of the evolution of a design are described using the example of designing an analog clock (one with hands):

- *Architecture.* The architecture of an analog clock consists only of (1) pointers or indicators to register the current hour and minute and (2) the spatial positions on the clock that correspond with hours and minutes—spatial positions that the pointers or indicators can be made to designate at a given moment.

- This specifies the clock's (1) conceptual structure and (2) functional behavior as seen by the user, but nothing more. Notice the things that are not mentioned in this description of the architecture: not the size and shape of the hands, their placement, their pattern of motion, their direction of motion, their color, the material they're made of, nor their style, not the placement of the numerals, or whether there will even be numerals. The architecture describes the clock only in terms of those abstract functions essential to time-telling. Moreover, the description of the elements of the architecture is completely free of detail. There is no mention of dimension, physical structure, nor any property.

- *Implementation.* The implementation describes the mechanisms of the clock and how they operate together. It describes how the clock's functions (described in the architecture) are made to happen. These mechanisms are described in terms of energy and information transmission.
- Blaauw and Brooks show several ways the abstract architecture could be implemented for a clock. They point out that the key elements of this particular implementation problem are (1) how to power the movement of either the pointers or the things pointed to and (2) how to transmit that power through a mechanism that causes the pointer or pointed-to to be in the correct position at any given time. Notice that this divides the clock design problem into two fairly independent subproblems—the power mechanism and the motion mechanism. Notice also that there are again no surface details specified. Blaauw and Brooks explain: "the implementation…is the *logical* organization of the inner structure of a designed object" (p. 5, emphasis added). That is, how the clock is made to tell time. Consider at this point how many different surface designs of clock could be generated from this level of abstract description. This is the generative kernel of the design. Together, the architecture and the implementation embody the operational principle of the design as it is described by Polanyi (1958) and Vincenti (1990).
- *Realization.* The realization describes all of the remaining details of the design. (Remember that this is still *just design*, not manufacture.)

Blaauw and Brooks call these the design's "geometries, strengths, tolerances, and finishes" (p. 5), which includes the physical placements of individual design elements, their connections with each other, their material specifications, their size, shape, color, texture, and appearance. Blaauw and Brooks point out that if the clock is to be handmade, some of these realization decisions may be left undefined and be allocated to the craft worker (who is both a detail designer and a manufacturer). If the clock is to be mass-produced, however, the realization of the design is completed to the minutest detail and fully documented, ready to be sent to manufacture.

Both the architecture and implementation stages of a design are abstract. A novice designer does not normally think in abstract terms, but an expert designer is able to. It is, in fact, one of the indicators of an expert instructional designer to be able to see below the surface of the design into its interior—to the abstract parts of the design that represent why it works. These inner workings operate by conveying energy and information. They determine how energy and information are transferred, transformed, stored, regulated, and delivered to where they are to be applied. This idea is elaborated below in the discussion of operational principles.

Team Process

A sixth view of design can be called the Team Process view. Most instructional design is carried out by multidisciplinary teams. Just as there are private design skills, there are also team design skills.

Team design is a method for disciplining and coordinating the creative efforts of design team members across several phases of activity. Bucciarelli (1994) describes the challenge of coordinated effort and shared mindset within a design team:

> Shared vision is the key phrase: The design is the shared vision, and the shared vision is the design—a (temporary) synthesis of the different participants' work within object worlds. Some of this shared vision is made explicit in documents, texts, and artifacts—in formal assembly and detail drawings, operation and service manuals, contractual disclaimers, production schedules, marketing copy, test plans, parts lists, procurement orders, mock-ups, and prototypes. But in the process of designing, the shared vision is less artifactual; each participant in the process has a personal collection of sketches, flowcharts, cost estimates, spreadsheets, models, and above all stories—stories to tell about their particular vision of the object.... The process is necessarily social and requires the participants to negotiate their differences and construct meaning through direct, and preferably face-to-face exchange. (p. 159)

The team innovation process can be described as repeating cycles of activity for (1) the conceptual unfolding of the design and (2) the day-to-day management of schedules, people, resources, and client relationships. These come together to define a process that alternates between (1) periods of specialty design activity carried out by individuals and (2) periods of team-led integration, refactoring, and fitting of sub-designs together and then evaluating the design by the team as a whole. Judging takes into account the changing environment of the design, including stakeholder criteria and resources.

The alternation between specialty design and joint fitting of the design elements with each other takes place in a constant cycle of low-stakes specialty-to-specialty collaborations and high-stakes integration and judging events. This reverberating process refines, focuses, disciplines, and eventually produces a final design. Part of project planning involves deciding the frequency of these cycles. Informal events may take place daily, but design team leadership sets schedules for major design coordination and integration points. Projects using virtual teams must pay more careful attention to the timing and scheduling of formal design coordination events.

Operational Principle View

A seventh view of design pertains to abstract concepts called operational principles and how they are incorporated into designs. The best way to see operational principles at work is to examine a Rube Goldberg machine at work. Goldberg machines are seen more commonly of late—from elaborate contraptions in music videos to serious educational use of them in teaching STEM subjects, where learner-produced contraptions are used in design and problem solving.

In a Goldberg machine a trigger event sets off a chain reaction of other events, until some trivial action occurs—a plate is washed, or a shoe is polished. Though Goldberg machines involve concrete things like wood, metal, and animals, these are concrete manifestations that hide inside something more abstract and invisible: the transfer of energy and information through a chain of events to a final destination where they accomplish some desired outcome. In physics terms, these physical machines deal with potential and kinetic energy and their transfer through the interaction of mechanisms.

At each point in an event chain, energy is supplied at a mechanical part and passed along the chain. What you see in a Goldberg cartoon is a physical embodiment, but what you don't see is the invisible transfer of energy and information that occurs as springs pull trap doors open and levers are pressed. Ironically, though we feel we see how the machine does its work, a physicist would say that it is the *invisible* transfers of energy in Goldberg machines that actually do the work.

A Goldberg machine can use basic principles like lever, spring, and inclined plane in multiple places in the same contraption; in one place it looks like a trap door, and in another it looks like a teeter-totter. The *abstractions* behind the surface manifestations are referred to as *operational principles.* Operational principles exist in every energy-using system. Operational principle is a term proposed by Michael Polanyi (1958) to describe how things can be made to work. It is not a scientific concept but a technological one. An operational principle is an abstract germ of an idea used at the   of a design to generate a hundred or a thousand different surface designs, all based on the same underlying principle of operation.

For example, designs of virtually all airplanes today are based on a single operational principle identified by George Cayley in the early 1800s. Cayley refined the challenge of flight into a single solvable problem statement: "to make a surface support a given weight by the application of power to the resistance of air" (Vincenti, 1990, p. 208). Note that Cayley's principle does not specify the size, shape, material, or relative dimensions and proportions of the surface or size of the power source.

What Cayley devised was not the design for a single airplane but the essential pattern for a million airplane designs—a basic pattern of the distribution and balancing of forces from which an endless number of specific designs could be generated. When the Wright Brothers flew successfully, they credited Cayley's idea, which they incorporated into all of their machines. When Curtiss improved the concept of flight controls, it was on a plane designed according to Cayley's operational principle for flight. As the variety of specific flyable designs multiplied, virtually all of them incorporated Cayley's operational principle. Today, thousands and thousands of specific airplane designs exist, all based on Cayley's principle, from the smallest experimental craft to the largest passenger liner.

Different values can be assigned to the variables of a Cayley design:

- The placement of the engine (forward or backward-facing, centered or distributed on the wings)
- The placement of the wing surface (above the body, below the body, forward, aft)

- The shape of the wing (flat, thick, tapered)
- The type of power used (reciprocating, turbine, jet)
- The means of propulsion (propeller, jet exhaust)

Everything is free to vary that does not nullify the central operational principle. This is what makes the number of possible combinations multiply.

Rube Goldberg machines and airplane designs are relevant to a discussion of instructional design because every human-made artifact incorporates one or more operational principles. Therefore, designed instructional products have their effect through an operational principle that defines the transfer of energy and information through actions and artifacts and the sensations they produce. Clark (2009) describes the operational principle concept, calling it the "active ingredient." Clark describes a systematic, four-stage research and development cycle that can be used to isolate "active ingredients" of instruction through experiments and then apply them in real-world settings: "...Active ingredient analysis...yields a recipe for constructing [a new] intervention that reflects the critical elements of the [laboratory] intervention that worked under controlled conditions" (p. 17).

Clark says that caution "must be exercised so that we do not simply group the treatments that share the same name" (p. 13). He warns against using common labels of things that resemble each other on the surface. What we should learn to see, he says, is "both novel and critical" and "we must look more deeply" (p. 13).

> Effective intervention design requires identifying the "active ingredients" or the key structural elements of the interventions or research treatments that have been found in...experiments to influence our chosen outcomes.... There are no rules yet for conducting this kind of analysis, but it is clear that we must look beyond the labels researchers give to their treatments in published articles and analyze the operations they implemented and their presumed impact on people and organizations.... The active ingredients we need as the core of a new technology are the causal agents in the experiments that were surveyed in [research]. We have evidence that these ingredients influence the problems we want to solve at the deepest structural level and so they must be the centerpieces in a solution. (pp. 13–14, emphasis added)

An instructional design incorporates an operational principle. It can transfer, transform, and conduct energy and information through a series of physical and intellectual mechanisms invisibly to bring about a desired result. When designs work, it is not by chance, it is because there is an operational principle active. Every design that achieves its intended results does so through an operational principle. If a designer designs without awareness of operational principles, an effective design will still achieve its effect through the operational principle incorporated into the design without the designer's explicit knowledge of it.

It is possible to discover the operational principles of a working artifact through a method of subtraction. A design that works can be whittled down in successive trials until it breaks and no longer works properly. At the point of breakage, something essential has been lost and has to be restored. The boundary of a principle has been crossed. Then trials continue, dissecting out other features until they break. This method works in a practical setting—usually over the span of multiple trials, such as in rapid prototyping or multiple evaluation and revision cycles. If designers can identify the operational principles they use in advance and apply them in a deliberate manner, the number of required cycles can be reduced.

An example of applying an operational principle would be represented by adopting "conversation" as the most basic design commitment and causing all other design considerations to revolve around it. Everyday conversations represent a dynamic and temporary structure held together by invisible forces of attraction and repulsion. Attraction is analogous to a magnetic or gravitational attraction between people. The opposing force of repulsion consists of anything that reduces commitment to the conversation: boredom, conflicting goals, or discomfort. There are many ways of establishing and maintaining attraction during an instructional conversation. At the same time, the opposite forces of repulsion are in competition, tending to drive the conversation apart. These forces—attraction and repulsion—hold the conversation together in a kind of dynamic tension so long as the feelings of attraction are sufficiently strong on both sides of the conversation.

If we were to compare this with the operational principle of Cayley and the variables that influence aircraft design, we would search for force-creating instructional acts that can be substituted into the attraction and repulsion sides of the equation. In a separate publication (Gibbons, 2013), I propose an extensive list of actions that create attractive and repulsive forces that can exert sustaining influence on an instructional conversation. A shorter list of these is provided in Table 1, which shows how they pertain to holding together a conversation at the beginning, in the middle, and at the end.

How does the operational principle concept relate to stock literature terms such as "motivation," "engagement," "participation," and "interaction"? These terms are used to describe goals and methods of instruction. They represent ideals. Operational principles describe the actions and therefore the forces behind these terms that allow them to be realized. They describe the inner working of emotional and intellectual forces that influence moment-by-moment changes in the learner and sustain the learner's commitment to exercise the agency to remain in the conversation or refuse it.

The entries included in Table 1 do not constitute a philosophical or theoretical statement beyond a commitment to the concept of conversation as the metaphor of instruction. They illustrate how individual actions during instruction introduce pulses of energy or information into an instructional conversation, either strengthening its attractive force or reducing it. For example, substituting "invite" for "compel" gives a much different dynamic to the conversation. A designer of "problem-based learning" may use "compel" rather than "invite," but it can be seen that different forces are set in motion by this choice.

It is no wonder, then, that with many such substitutions possible during the design of problem-based learning, there is great variability in problem-based learning research findings. It seems worthwhile, therefore, to consider describing instructional treatments in research reports in sufficient detail to allow the reader to discover firsthand the operational principles embedded in the treatments as easily as we read a Rube Goldberg contraption.

Table 1 Representative actions on both sides of an instructional conversation that either increase attraction or increase repulsion during different stages of an instructional conversation

Possible instructional action			Possible learner actions		
Initiating the conversation					
Invite	Contact	Rouse	Desire	Show interest	Attend
Tantalize	Welcome	Entice	Continue	Respond	Refuse
Announce	Entreat	Startle	Ignore	Answer	Notice
Approach	Puzzle	Offer			
Wake	Appeal				
Securing commitment to continue					
Propose	Challenge	Persuade	Counter	Accept	Refuse
Suggest	Bargain	Counter	Decline	Trust	Contract
Promise	Retract	Request	Consent	Continue	Join
Agree	Contract	Specify	Bargain	Propose	Request
Pester	Offer	Require	Ask		
Fascinate	Enlarge	Excite			
Conducting the conversation					
Display	Respect	Exhibit	Plan	Analyze	Deduce
Assist	Scaffold	Anticipate	Imagine	Suggest	Deliberate
Reason	Aid	Praise	Produce	Act	Choose
Counsel	Adjust	Provide	Meditate	Use	Ask
Debate	Encourage	Judge	Practice	Exercise	Consider
Charge	Reassure	Cooperate	Interpret	Invest	Respect
Argue	Portray	Feedback	Debate	Trust	Digest
Honor	Serve	Set stage	Theorize	Notice	Discover
Adapt	Comfort	Explain	Decipher	Connect	Try
Introduce	Cite	Measure	Respond	Explore	Observe
Dare	Discern	Test	Question	Cooperate	Converse
Inspire	Uplift	Critique	Dispute	Experience	Disregard
Dramatize	Collaborate	Guide	Cooperate	Reflect	Anticipate
Model	Socialize	Refer to	Articulate	Collaborate	Investigate
Transferring responsibility to the learner and terminating					
Culminate	Agree	Evaluate	Assess	Celebrate	Award
Finalize	Rate	Certify	Validate	Reminisce	Commit

Design Language View

The eighth view of design can be referred to as a design language view. Design is in one sense a linguistic exercise, but the terms of designing do not necessarily exist in written language. They exist in the many public and private design languages in the mind of the designer and in the shared, public concepts of a profession.

An observer watching an animated robot dressed as Abraham Lincoln can maintain detachment, realizing that the robot consists of individual joint articulations, each of which has only a few position states. An animated fountain likewise is made up of perhaps 300 identical water jets, each of which has only about ten distinct spurt patterns. The observer realizes that what seem to be moving walls of water are simply the coordinated actions of patterns of jets which have been timed precisely. Likewise, the robot's seemingly human postures and movements are synchronous, timed sequences of relatively uncomplicated joint motions.

These examples provide an insight into one aspect of design languages: Designers join together relatively simple primitive elements into structures whose enacted experiences convey information and produce emotions. At one end of the spectrum of abstraction are design language terms that define composite effects: "walls" of water, moving "shapes," playful "randomness," and awe-producing "order"—all calculated to produce an emotional reaction. The viewer recognizes these as symbols seen in the everyday world, and so they are gross terms the designer uses to convey a message to and evoke an emotion in the viewer.

The designer may have a name for each effect. But the designer may also have names for the individual elements—abstractions at a different level of detail—that lead to these effects: the crooking of a finger, the lifting of an eyebrow, and the rotation of the neck joint. These are much more detailed and mechanical terms in a design language for robots. The creation of the grand effects from small mechanical motions involves the conscious use of design language abstractions at multiple levels—terms that can be given names so that a team of designers can express and talk about an evolving design both in detail and in broad terms. In the process of calculating an effect, there may be *translations* required between languages at these different levels.

The value of design languages is found as much in their translation uses as in their communication uses. The mechanical acts of the robot do not create the desired effect when they are performed randomly. Only when they are part of a larger pattern do they come to have impact. In order to achieve this impact, the designer must translate the terms of a grand effect—the sweeping gestures, the expressions—into individual robotic motion acts and sequences of acts. In the end, the robot has no idea of the experience it produces for the user, but it faithfully performs its individual acts, and the effect of the suite of acts produces the effect: Viewers feel emotion and obtain information.

Design languages evolve as a technology matures. One measure of the maturity of the design field is the precision with which designers can discuss their designs in design language clearly and unambiguously. Design languages not only allow professionals to communicate generally about their work, but individual teams use design languages by inventing additional terms shared only by the team. Sometimes design languages are used in a closed circle to describe trade secrets which constitute a source of advantage. In the past such languages provided the basis for craft guilds to protect against competition and retain economic advantage.

A design language is a set of conceptual building blocks for describing designs and the conduct of designing. The vocabulary of a design language exists in two senses: (a) as thought structures in the mind of an individual and (b) as named entities that have verbal or symbolic identifiers that make them public. Every designer possesses and uses a number of design languages, though few designers are conscious of them as languages. Not all design languages have specific verbal terms. That becomes evident when two designers are conversing about a possible alternative and one or the other begins to use hyphen-connected phrases (e.g., "that-thing-we-did-on-the-last-project"). Many language terms born as hyphenated phrases are later given a single-word name as usage of the innovation catches on and people need to talk about it more often.

Public design languages use the syntax of a native language, substituting design language terms—which are nouns, verbs, and modifiers—into standard sentence patterns. When this happens, a conversation between two professionals becomes hard to interpret. Multiple design languages are required in designing an artifact. When Edison first began to invent, he had no idea of the number of design languages this would eventually entail:

> ... Technologists [like Edison] are tied into less obvious meaning systems [professional worlds] for the development, appreciation, production, funding, operation, maintenance, social control, evaluation, and distribution.... These...functions are likely to be distributed among different groupings in society.... Paper must be filed with financial backers, government regulators, technical R&D departments, sales forces, material suppliers, production machinery producers, and shop floor designers. (Bazerman, 1999, pp. 336–337)

Edison's light bulb invention spawned hundreds of design language terms: bulb, filament, base, contacts, and so forth. These of necessity found their way into the documentation of many other team members responsible for placing the light bulb on the market and into homes, offices, and workshops. As the technology continued to develop, additional terms perforce crept into usage because additional new parts of the invention also had to be named: socket, lead, terminal, connector, switch, and so forth. In the end, an entire electrical generation and distribution system had to be created, along with a multitude of new design language terms.

New design languages and language terms come into being in many ways, including the following examples:

- With the introduction of a new theory
- As growing expertise creates new technical concepts
- As new instructional techniques are developed
- As new hardware and software concepts are introduced
- As new kinds of artifact evolve
- As authors invent new terms in the literature
- As new theories are developed
- As professional cultures develop
- As new patterns of product usage are invented

Some design language terms are not shared with others, either because they are subtle and we find it hard to articulate them or because we choose not to share them in order to preserve an advantage. The continuous evolution of design languages, expressed and unexpressed, is the key to continued learning and improvement in any field.

Conclusion

The views of design in this paper join other views described in this symposium. Together they suggest how conceptual tools from multiple design disciplines can inform the thinking of the instructional designer. Instructional design can and should begin to tap into the relevant literature from other design fields.

A shift can be seen toward design processes that make use of traditional, classical concepts while encouraging the inclusion of new, imaginative processes and structures not suggested by traditional approaches. This paper encourages us to consider design as a bridge between a completely conceptual world of vague theoretical ideas on the one hand and a completely practical physical world of results and goals on the other.

Design by its nature begins with fuzziness. It is the process of drawing out of nowhere solutions to practical problems through the creation of artifacts, processes, and experiences. It is in this respect an act of magic. This sleight of hand becomes possible only as the designer begins to see things that others can't see or didn't see and learns to manipulate invisible structures of experience.

Seeing, to a designer, must take place at different levels of scale. It must employ gigantic levers in the form of experiences that last days, weeks, or even years. At the same time, it must be sensitive to minute forces set in motion by a glance, a word, or a motion.

The designer's seeing must also encompass the very abstract and the very concrete without being seduced by the very concrete. The history of technology in general, and in individual fields specifically, records in every case a journey from robust concrete concepts to wispy, ethereal abstractions. The progress of a technology depends on this journey. The digital computer as a concept began with the quest for mechanical devices to perform mathematical calculations. Who would have in those days imagined that the concept of a computer would ultimately be expressed in device-less terms: in the form of a model whose many subsequent realizations in device form would outlast generations of changes in device technologies, with little need for revision of the original conceptual model?

The imaginations of instructional designers, especially novice designers, are so easily captured by the allure of the "bright lights and loud noises" offered by today's production technologies that it takes experience to see beyond these things to the invisible qualities of a design that really matters. Nor is this descent into the rabbit hole of abstraction one where a designer ever touches bottom. Hence, the reason for every designer to be taught from the beginning that design expertise is not a destination but a lifelong commitment to constant refinement of the ability to observe and notice things that didn't seem to be there before.

Add to this the complication that an advancing technology of design is no longer a singles sport. The lone designer who could do it all is an extinct species. The social nature of designing makes it therefore, in one view, a linguistic exercise in which the dual challenge is to bring the thinking of a team into focus—both to allow the cross-specialty communication of technical aspects and to allow the sharing of visions and imaginations that lie entirely within no one's particular domain. Instead, new domains are invented as designers see more.

This paper began by describing a need for better, more robust descriptions of design to feed the growth of experienced designers as well as educating novices. Perhaps by teaching richer views of design, simplistic conceptions of design can be avoided among new designers, and the lifelong growth can become an expectation. Perhaps also experienced designers can find questions to advance their personal insights that will lead them on and on throughout a career of discovery that gives them the value as a professional rather than as a craft worker. For instructional designers of both types, it may be that this fascinating journey is just beginning.

References

Baldwin, C., & Clark, K. (2000). *Design rules: The power of modularity*. Cambridge, MA: MIT Press.

Bannan-Ritland, B. (2003). The role of design in research: The integrative learning design framework. *Educational Researcher, 32*(1), 21–24.

Bazerman, C. (1999). *The languages of Edison's light*. Cambridge, MA: MIT Press.

Bichelmeyer, B. (2003). Instructional theory and instructional design theory: What's the difference and why should we care? *IDT Record*. Retrieved February 17, 2010, from http://bit.ly/9HkisA.

Blaauw, G., & Brooks, F. (1997). *Computer architecture: Concepts and evolution*. Reading, MA: Addison Wesley Longman.

Brand, S. (1994). *How buildings learn: What happens after they're built*. New York: Penguin Books.

Branson, R. K., Rayner, G. T., Cox, J. L., Furman, J. P., King, F.J., & Hannum, W. J. (1975, August). *Interservice procedures for instructional systems development* (5 vols.) (TRADOC Pam 350–30). Ft. Monroe, VA: U.S. Army Training and Doctrine Command (NTIS Nos. AD-A019 4860-AD-A019 490).

Bucciarelli, L. L. (1994). *Designing engineers*. Cambridge, MA: MIT Press.

Clark, R. E. (2009). Translating research into new instructional technologies for higher education: The active ingredient process. *Journal of Computing in Higher Education, 21*(1), 4–18.

Collins, A., Joseph, D., & Bielaczyc, K. (2004). Design research: Theoretical and methodological issues. *The Journal of the Learning Sciences, 13*(1), 15–42.

Cox, S., & Osguthorpe, R. (2003). How do instructional design professionals spend their time? *TechTrends, 47*(3), 45–47.

Drucker, P. (1989). *The new realities*. London, UK: Mandarin.

Ericsson, A., & Erixon, G. (1999). *Controlling design variants: Modular product platforms*. Dearborn, MI: Society of Manufacturing Engineers.

Fowler, M. (2003). *Patterns of enterprise application software*. Boston: Addison-Wesley.

Gagné, R. M. (Ed.). (1965). *Psychological principles in system development*. New York: Holt Rinehart & Winston.

Gibbons, A. S. (2013). *An architectural approach to instructional design*. New York: Routledge.

Gibbons, A. S., Boling, E., & Smith, K. M. (2013). Instructional design models. In M. Spector, M. D. Merrill, J. Elen, & M. J. Bishop (Eds.), *Handbook of research on educational communications and technology* (4th ed.). New York: Springer.

Gibbons, A., & Rogers, P. C. (2009). The architecture of instructional theory. In C. M. Reigeluth & A. Carr-Chellman (Eds.), *Instructional-design theories and models: Vol. 3. Building a common knowledge base*. New York: Routledge.

Gibbons, A. S., & Yanchar, S. (2010). An alternative view of the instructional design process: A response to Smith and Boling. *Educational Technology, 50*(4), 16–26.

Hokanson, B., & Miller, C. (2009). Role-based design: A contemporary framework for innovation and creativity in instructional design. *Educational Technology, 49*(2), 21–28.

Jonassen, D. (2008). Instructional design as design problem solving: An iterative process. *Educational Technology, 48*(3), 21–26.

Kahin, B., & Foray, D. (2006). *Advancing knowledge and the knowledge economy.* Cambridge, MA: MIT Press.

Parrish, P. (2005). Embracing the aesthetics of instructional design. *Educational Technology, 45*(2), 16–25.

Parrish, P. (2006). Design as storytelling. *TechTrends, 50*(4), 72–82.

Polanyi, M. (1958). *Personal knowledge: Towards a post-critical philosophy.* New York: Harper Torchbooks.

Ramo, S., & St. Claire, R. K. (1998). The systems approach, anaheim, CA: KNI Incorporated. Retrieved from http://www.incase.org/productspubs/doc/systemsapproach.

Reeves, T., Herrington, J., & Oliver, R. (2005). Design research: A socially responsible approach to instructional technology research in higher education. *Journal of Computing in Higher Education, 16*(2), 97–116.

Reigeluth, C. (1999). *Instructional-design theories and models: Vol. 2. A new paradigm of instructional theory.* Mahwah, NJ: Lawrence Erlbaum Associates.

Reigeluth, C., & Carr-Chellman, A. (2009). *Instructional-design theories and models: Vol. 3. Building a common knowledge base.* New York: Routledge.

Rowland, G. (1992). What do instructional designers actually do? An initial investigation of expert practice. *Performance Improvement Quarterly, 5*(2), 65–86.

Rowland. (2008, March 27). Design and research: Partners in educational innovation. Keynote address to the Design and Technology SIG, American Educational Research Association, New York City.

Schön, D. A. (1987). *Educating the reflective practitioner.* San Francisco, CA: Jossey-Bass.

Smith, K., & Boling, E. (2009). What do we make of design? Design as a concept in educational technology. *Educational Technology, 49*(4), 3–17.

Uyemura, J. (1999). *A first course in digital systems design: An integrated approach.* Belmont, CA: Brooks/Cole.

Vincenti, W. (1990). *What engineers know and how they know it: Analytical studies from aeronautical history.* Baltimore, MD: Johns Hopkins University Press.

Wilson, B. (2005). Broadening our foundation for instructional design: Four pillars of practice. *Educational Technology, 45*(2), 10–15.

Yanchar, S. C., South, J. B., Williams, D. D., Allen, S., & Wilson, B. G. (2010). Struggling with theory? A qualitative investigation of conceptual tool use in instructional design. *Educational Technology Research and Development, 58*, 39–60.

Critical Issues in Studio Pedagogy: Beyond the Mystique and Down to Business

Elizabeth Boling and Kennon M. Smith

Keywords Action research • Critique • Design fixation • Design tensions • Instructional graphics • Novice practice • Precedent • Primary generator • Problem framing • Signature pedagogy • Studio pedagogy • Tool use

Enthusiasm is growing within the field of instructional technology for the adaptation of knowledge and approaches from other fields of design into our efforts to prepare instructional designers for practice. Among this knowledge and these approaches, there is particular interest around studio pedagogy (Shulman, 2005). This enthusiasm accompanies concerns that design is not sufficiently well understood within our field (Smith, 2008), taught in ways that do not address the realities of practice (Bichelmeyer, Boling, & Gibbons, 2006; Cox & Osguthorpe, 2003; Rowland, 1992; Tracey & Boling, 2013) and, while different in many ways across domains, similar in its fundamental nature across domains (Cross, 2006; Goel, 1997; Nelson & Stolterman, 2003; Brandtet al., 2013) are studying studio pedagogy across several domains of design education—including instructional design and technology—and identifying its critical characteristics, including surface features, pedagogy and epistemology, studio habits, and professional practice. Many of these are implicit in discussions of design pedagogy in fields outside ISD (Lawson & Dorst, 2009) and perhaps assumed to be universally understood, but a recent panel on studio approaches in the field of ISD (Hokanson et al., 2011) illustrates that the understanding and enactment of studio pedagogy also differs a good deal from one institution to another. Differences include variations in facilities and technologies, structure of design briefs (assignments), use of and approach to critique, and guidance in projects.

E. Boling (✉) • K.M. Smith
Indiana University, Bloomington, IN, USA
e-mail: eboling@indiana.edu

B. Hokanson and A. Gibbons (eds.), *Design in Educational Technology*,
Educational Communications and Technology: Issues and Innovations 1,
DOI 10.1007/978-3-319-00927-8_3, © Springer International Publishing Switzerland 2014

Those who use studio approaches in traditional domains of design have also addressed some of its shortcomings. Some key concerns have included questions about the efficacy, consistency, and transparency of critiques (Anthony, 1991; Webster, 2007; Wilkin, 2000), the tendency to emphasize the physical characteristics of design solutions while minimizing or ignoring social and political issues (Salama, 1995), and the development of a disciplinary culture which focuses inward instead of on clients and their concerns (Nicholson, 2000), including counterproductive stress, difficulties adapting to new technologies, cost of facilities, and more (Mewburn, 2010). As budgets at academic institutions tighten and the range of desired competencies for designers expand, design educators who utilize the traditionally time- and space-intensive studio models face pressures to justify costs of facilities and to increase student–teacher ratios (Morgado, 2009), while also struggling to develop and maintain the expertise necessary to respond to the unpredictable nature of studio teaching (Salama, 1995). In many programs instructors observe barriers to learning that their students face as they learn in a studio-oriented mode (Mathews, 2010; Siegel & Stolterman, 2009). Conclusions reached by scholars and teachers have been echoed and added to by students who report encountering difficulties as they navigate the traditional studio learning environment (Chen, 2011; Willenbrock, 1991). These kinds of observations suggest that, while studios have a long and rich tradition, and bring with them many benefits, they should not be adopted in (or adapted to) instructional design classrooms uncritically. This signature pedagogy should be utilized only with a clear-eyed view of its short-comings in other settings, and implementations should be studied rigorously so as to fine-tune adaptations in ways that maximize potential benefits and minimize potential problems. This chapter is based on the ongoing study of one such implementation and uses the lens of action research to reflect upon 7 years of data, surfacing specific questions about traditional assumptions in studio design pedagogy.

The authors of this chapter are engaged in a multi-year study (2005–2011) on the design and implementation of, and activities in, a studio-based instructional graphics course (Boling & Smith, 2009, 2010a, 2010b). The authors both learned in the studio tradition at the college level, one in architecture and the other in fine arts printmaking. Together with several authors, they have described their experiences (Boling, 2005), which share a number of common features. These include easily available and plentiful precedent (representations of designs), flexible workspaces shared with other students, and available extended hours if not round the clock; public display of work and public discussion or critique as a primary mode of instruction; intensive practice in hands-on work; under-defined briefs (assignments with minimal definition) for projects; and intense relationships with fellow students, both more experienced and less experienced than each other. As described, these features all interact with each other. Student relationships include competition, self-reliance, and peer support—all fueled by the transparency inherent in public displays of work and the minimal definition of assignments. Students manage assignments in part by the availability of precedent and by interaction (modeling and direct instruction) with peers. Individual experiences are characterized by a conscious effort to establish an identity within the group of studio students and gain respect for design skill or acceptance from the group for some recognized contribution. These experiences provide access to peer support and are intensified by long hours of practice in common spaces.

At the launch of the course, our explicit intention was to infuse a studio experience into the 2-year masters program in instructional design. We chose the instructional graphics course for several reasons: It was an elective course and there were no broader curriculum implications from tinkering with it; it could be taught in the summer as an overload and therefore be offered whether minimum enrollments were met or not; and it could be offered in the second summer term when a classroom was available round the clock—not possible for any classroom available to us during the other terms of the year.

When the elective instructional graphics class was re-launched as a studio course in 2005, there already existed conditions within the larger instructional design department that some educators might view as being consistent with, or even evidence of, a studio approach to design pedagogy. For example, the required introductory instructional design course was oriented around team projects intended to be similar to authentic work. In some previous terms it had included a few critique sessions (although more often these were presentation sessions at the end of the course), and the department provided workrooms for student teams from 8:00 a.m. to 10:00 p.m. However, the inclusion of some "studio-like" surface features in the existing introductory class were not sufficient for us to consider it a studio course in the sense of our own experiences, and neither was the rest of the program. Furthermore, the class included a number of features that were distinctly unlike many of the studios we had experienced and observed in other design fields: Class time included a good deal of lecture and, in spite of the authentic-style projects, course activities were sequenced with easier tasks preceding harder ones and according to a single process model. We never thought that revamping the elective graphics course with the intention of providing students an 8-week, more thoroughly studio-like experience would instill all the skills and habits of thought needed by designers, nor that it would or necessarily should entirely replace the approaches learned in other courses, but we did discuss the possibility that students would recall the studio experience after the class was over and rely on that experience as a base for extending their skills and their conceptions of designing.

The study described in this chapter is based on data from seven iterations of the course, including student work and reflections, field notes (326 pages of notes covering years 2008–2011), and course documents. Over the course of the ongoing study, the researchers have utilized a series of lenses with which to interrogate the data for different kinds of insights. These have included the design activity framework of Lawson and Dorst (2009), activity analysis (Yamagata-Lynch & Smaldino, 2007), and critical reflection (Carspecken, 1995) by the researchers. At the conclusion of its 2011 implementation, 52 students have taken the course, with 51 participating in the study.

Year	Students
2005	9
2006	12
2007	5
2008	5
2009	10
2010	5
2011	6

Number of students enrolled in graphics course by year
Total students = 52; students participating in study = 51

As we enacted the course, we made revisions from one iteration to another. These changes were in direct response to our own discussions and cycles of action and reflection, informed by our intensive readings in the areas of design philosophy, theory, and pedagogy, and based on documented activities of the instructor and the students. In the first year, the course looked somewhat similar to our existing instructional design courses. Major features included lectures on design principles, demonstrations of techniques, multiple assignments focused on practicing individual skills, and specific deadlines for specific stages of projects. Its key studio components included a large shared workspace with a worktable assigned to each student; regular and public critique of work in progress; ample precedent material in the form of images covering all the walls and contained over 100 design books in an in-class library; and the requirement to collect instructional graphics (physically or photographically) during the 8-week session. Over the seven iterations to date, our revisions have resulted in a course design much closer to our conception of a traditional studio class. No scheduled lectures or demonstrations are held. Fewer assignments, defined in less detail are presented to the students with the open requirement to make progress from one session to the next instead of any prescription regarding project milestones or process. The instructor spends the entire work period moving from one table to another confronting the problems that arise for each student designer as their projects take shape, and the critique period guiding discussion. Short, impromptu talks occur when a key principle comes up in the context of work, or when multiple students have reached a similar impasse or insight. Students spend a good deal of time showing each other practical skills, giving each other design suggestions, establishing their credentials within the group and assessing their own work in the light of everyone else's work. In addition to the tremendous sense that these changes freed the instructor to address each student's development effectively, and that the individual elements of studio worked best when all were employed together, we saw positive outcomes in the later iterations of the course (Boling & Smith, 2010a). Students assessed their own work critically, reframing it on their own initiative and reworking projects drastically without complaining about the additional work. They chose and learned new tools strategically, again without undue regard for the "extra" time this would take. Their use of precedent matured over the 8 weeks, during which time they moved from seeing the images covering the classroom walls almost as decoration, to standing and studying images that offered affordances for the problems they had at hand in their work. They developed an appreciation of the impact one decision in design might have on those made previously and those yet to come, showing this in their reflective notes as well as in the caution with which they undertook decisions later in the session.

At the same time, we are seeing that some of the basic assumptions and perspectives in studio education may not be as we have assumed; our experiences are raising questions for us regarding the way we work with students to develop their expertise in design. The most salient of these we recognize as coming from our own experiences as students, as design instructors, and as participants in conversations with peers who also teach in studio settings. We have made the assumptions addressed by these questions ourselves, been taught according to the assumptions, and heard the assumptions expressed many times by our peers.

1. What is "the novice"? Can we teach to the general model of a novice? Beginning design courses address novice designers—obviously, and we probably all know that these novices come to class with varying levels of experience in design. Here we are asking not about their experience, but about the character each may exhibit as a developing designer.

2. Is it necessary to ask students to generate many alternative concepts early in a project? As students we have both experienced exercises that required us to propose multiple concepts before we were allowed to choose one and pursue it; as instructors we have made the same requirement and we have observed our peers doing so as well. For us, this has been intended to stimulate divergent thinking and demonstrate to students that design ideas do not derive automatically from problem statements. However, our reflective practice is suggesting questions for us regarding the assumption that this staple of studio assignments is always appropriate.

3. Can we separate tool learning from learning concepts and habits of thought? Should we? In our own practice, tensions regarding how we use the limited time available within a course—particularly in a masters level program. Do we teach specific, and sometimes complex, skills with tools (which can be time consuming), or focus on the conceptual aspects of designing, which feel as though they are more enduring contributions to our students' educations? We have seen, and practiced, multiple versions of courses in which tool learning has been disconnected from concepts in one way or another on the assumption that tools are called into play only after ideas have been generated.

What Is "the Novice"? Can We Teach to the General Model of a Novice?

Studies involving novice designers and design pedagogy (Christaans & Venselaar, 2005; Lawson & Dorst, 2009; Siegel & Stolterman, 2009; Welch & Lim, 2000), rigorous as they are, may not take sufficient account of the differences between those novices; these are not just differences in their relevant experience, but in the kernel of their developing professional design character, which plays out in their approaches to problems and habits of work. We may be working counterproductively if we view novices as a group primarily sharing characteristics of novices and heading for a shared, idealized state of expertise, rather than as individuals developing along differing, legitimate paths.

Each Student as an Individual Versus "the Novice"

Analyzing the design activities of students in one iteration of the studio course (Boling & Smith, 2010a), we saw clearly that they each displayed a unique pattern of activity across the multiple projects and weeks of the course. While we cannot say definitively what gives rise to these patterns, in working with the students a strong impression arises that their personal proclivities toward action and their general work/study experiences—including those that occur in this course—influence them.

Mark, a student who stated openly that he was lacking technical skills and felt he needed to catch up to younger students in the program, approached the Draw 100 Things project in a deliberate manner. He established that he could complete the project using altered photos instead of drawings, searched for photos that he thought would work, and then applied Photoshop filters to those images, working down the menu from the top and trying each in turn (Fig. 1).

He did the same with the layout for the 100 images, working through the options offered by his chosen layout tool until he found one that he thought would work. During this process we talked explicitly about the time remaining in the summer session and the amount of work he still needed to do. He recognized that other projects might suffer if he did not turn his attention to them in parallel with the 100 things, but he could not begin on one of them until he had completed the first one. While he did characterize himself as "that kind of person," it was also possible to observe that the frustrating challenges presented to him by the production tools absorbed his attention to the exclusion of other concerns. As it happened, he had to finish his projects after the session ended and he was not able to make some of the changes he wanted to before he had to turn his attention to the demands of the fall term (Fig. 2a, b).

In contrast, George started all his projects at once. He was more comfortable with some tools than Mark was, but he did not have complete confidence in his ability to draw. He tried out tools, but not in a systematic way; he was driven by the direction that his concepts were taking and chose tools he could manage to support those concepts. George repeatedly reframed his projects. He was having difficulty with the different scales of the vehicles he had chosen for his 100 things and sacrificed the hours of work he had put into creating details for them when he decided to depict them in silhouette. For one of his individual graphics, he planned to show proper form for a golf swing. After photographing a model brought into class and creating simple images from those photos, he recognized that the form of the model had not been accurate. He went to a golf course and met with a pro, who agreed to

Fig. 1 Martin used one color plus black and highly simplified, although descriptive, forms to depict 100 kitchen implements. His layout was a finely judged exercise in visual balance

be photographed, then redrew his images based on those photos. The pro explained the concept of the "striking plane," and George reframed his approach to incorporate this concept visually into the image (Fig. 3a, b).

In their patterns of activity during the course, George's profile as a novice contrasts strongly with Mark's. It would be tempting to view George's approach as a better one; he was more flexible and his parallel work style left him time to make changes on a larger scale than Mark did. However, George also ran into some problems because he was so willing to reframe his projects that he fell into difficulty with two of his graphics—changing his approach on them until he had to scramble at the end to finish them and in the process make choices he wasn't entirely happy with the process. Mark practiced making some fine distinctions between the effects that tools were giving him as he worked through the options methodically,

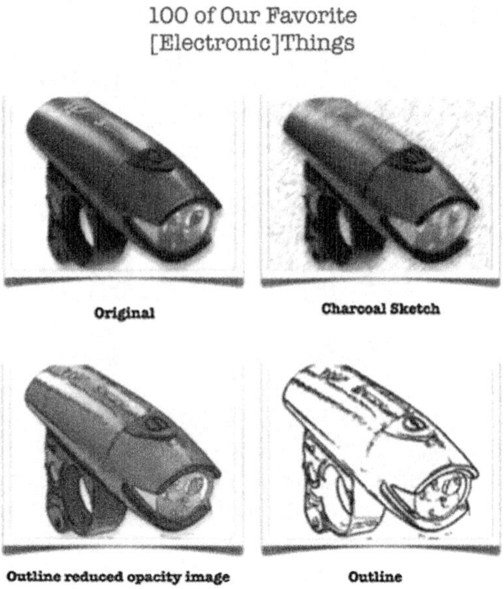

Fig. 2 Mark not only tried all the filters and combinations available, he laid them out next to each other to decide which he might choose for the final treatment

100 of Our Favorite [Electronic]Things

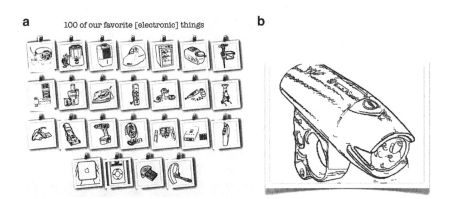

Original   Charcoal Sketch

Outline reduced opacity image   Outline

a   100 of our favorite [electronic] things   **b**

Fig. 3 (**a**) Using a feature he had found while trying all the menu items in a layout tool, Mark arranged and rearranged his 100 things into a catalog format. (**b**) Close-up of a single image in Mark's layout

increasing his appreciative abilities over his starting point. They were not entirely equal in their performance as students and George did sacrifice some richness in his experience through running out of time. However, we consider each of their profiles as a legitimate starting point for the development of design expertise and anticipate that differing patterns of work forms only one among perhaps multiple dimensions along which individual novices are likely to differ from one another.

Is It Necessary to Ask Students to Generate Many Alternative Concepts Early in a Project?

The issue of getting students to generate "alternative concepts" is reported as a persistent problem in design pedagogy (Chen, 2011; Darke, 1984; Siegel & Stolterman, 2009). However, our study suggests that, with an appropriate learning experience, design novices behave similarly to experts when they are supported in working with their first ideas through a project's legitimate constraints and possibilities. In recent iterations of the graphics course, students *not* pressured to produce "ten very different ideas" for tackling a brief were demonstrated to reframe their projects radically over the course of 8 weeks and to be quite willing to abandon aspects of a design that were obviously not working—a judgment that an instructor could have made in advance of their efforts, but which they probably could not have made before they tried to work the ideas through to fruition. If these early student ideas, instead of being put on hold until multiple alternatives are generated, were viewed as growing from a "primary generator" (Darke, 1984), they might be recognized as a necessary launching point for the student to engage in the conjecture-analysis approach often employed by professional designers to test and expand their early ideas (Roozenburg & Cross, 1991). The early idea might be a student's best effort for the point of development where she is at that moment; even if it does not represent the best of which she could be *made* to be capable at that time, it may represent the one she is best equipped to work with. While an experienced designer might be working from the *parti* described by Nelson and Stolterman (2003) as a subconscious and malleable, but disciplined, template for what will be the conscious design, and a student from something more like a nascent concept with even less form and dimensionality, treating that first idea as if it could be made viable might allow us to:

- Stop wasting time requiring students to generate multiple non-viable ideas from an experience base which they do not yet have.
- Avoid the opportunity costs involved in redirecting students from ideas they can own, with all their problems, to ideas we implicitly, perhaps unconsciously, "approve" through discussion or critique following the generation of alternatives.
- Respect and encourage one of the habits that students display which they hold in common—at least to a degree—with experts (pursuing an initial idea and using it to surface issues in the design space)
- Avoid giving students the impression that experienced designers do, in fact, generate multiple alternatives for their own sake at the start of a project.
- Avoid assuming that our students will necessarily achieve better results on a given project if they have been required to generate multiple concepts and choose from among them.
- Maintain motivation, or refrain from squashing enthusiasm, early in students' experiences with design.

Supporting the Students' First Concepts

Andrea came to the class with no graphics background and comparatively low confidence in her skills, although she did not lack confidence as a learner. As many students do, she considered the challenge of a required project, *Draw 100 Things* (in which students are required to create images of one hundred common objects and present them as a set), first in terms of where in her life she might find a hundred things to draw. Quite early she hit on the idea that, since she worked as a bartender, she might draw a hundred different drinks—specifically, one hundred different cocktails. This was not a fully formed idea; Andrea thought she might draw a hundred different shapes of glasses or perhaps a hundred different colors of liquor in mixed drinks. The definition of the idea seemed to shift for her from one discussion to another, and she was distinctly dissatisfied with her early sketches. I (the first author, who has carried out most of the direct instruction for the studio course) was skeptical about the idea myself, thinking about the difficulties of representing glass and liquid and of choosing a frame for the project that would allow one hundred small variations to play out for her. I was also concerned that she seemed fixated on this idea, and worried that if it did not work out for her she would become discouraged (Fig. 4).

By the time of this iteration of the course we were not requiring students, as part of the assignment, to generate multiple ideas at the beginning of a project, so the choice came down to working with Andrea to develop this idea, talking her out of it, or requiring that she do something else. I sensed that anything but the first option would divert Andrea's commitment in learning from something she felt she owned to something owned by me. So I suggested tools that might help (French curves, markers, vector tools) and encouraged her to seek out precedent materials to help sharpen her idea. She did not embrace every idea with equal enthusiasm, and sometimes she turned to other students for technical help instead of trying the methods I suggested. When an idea made sense to her, though, she pursued it and she gradually focused her concept more tightly (Fig. 5).

As she worked on the project, Andrea encountered many of the difficulties that a more experienced designer might have been able to anticipate at the outset. These included difficulty in managing the abstraction required in producing a 1" by 1" representation of an object significantly larger in real life while maintaining enough detail to make the 100 similar items visually distinct and recognizable. Furthermore, her expertise in drink-mixing pushed her to initially focus on realistic representations of color gradients of each drink, without fully recognizing that such fine-grain distinctions could not be represented in the small final images.

Once she had found a visual voice that satisfied her, Andrea was willing and able to reframe her project to match the constraints of time and production skill that she faced. Using a general approach drawn from precedent gathered through online searches and a new tool that afforded the treatment she wanted (colored brush pens), she settled on drawing four groups of glasses, two with color and two without. Her treatment was minimalist; black lines for the glasses and simple colored shapes to represent liquors and garnishes. Given her starting point, Andrea was not going to leave the course a fully accomplished visual designer. In the end, she also did not leave the course having produced a product that appeared fully professional.

a   **b**   **The Backswing**
Keep your hands on the striking plane throughout the backswing

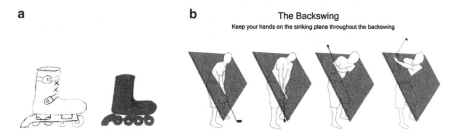

Fig. 4 (**a**) At the sketch stage George has produced many images with details included. When he reframed the project, all the detail was subsumed into silhouettes. (**b**) George took a big step forward in his ability to visualize and manipulate form in the service of explanation when he reframed his poster project after meeting with a golf pro

Fig. 5 Andrea's early sketches for differently shaped glassware

wine glass   Margaritta glass

She did, however, make her decisions as a designer would, choosing an approach that was graphically satisfying by exploiting the production skill she had acquired, rather than trying for effects she could not accomplish at her level of skill. Although not polished, her project was internally consistent and satisfying visually in an intentional way, rather than as a matter of chance (Fig. 6).

From the teaching perspective, it was difficult to watch Andrea's frustration as she pursued that first idea, which I had doubts about from the start. It was sometimes difficult to think of another way to support her efforts when a current method was not productive. I was also worried that allowing Andrea to pursue just one idea might narrow her learning, but I do not now believe that it did—in the span of 8 weeks she reached a point at which she was able to consider and manage multiple dimensions of a visual idea that had been beyond her ability to shape when she began. She had engaged in repeated manipulations and judgments of form, gaining an appreciation of those forms as she went. She had also experienced, in returning by the end of the project to a much-refined version of her earliest idea, the demands that a concept inevitably places on a designer as it becomes tangible. Had I insisted at the beginning that she pursue an idea that I deemed more within her scope and free of some of the predictable obstacles she ultimately faced, Andrea might have had time to produce a more "polished" final project. However, such a pedagogical approach may have cut short opportunities for her to engage larger issues which

Fig. 6 Andrea used a marker and light table, a smaller and more regular format, and an idea from precedent material to work out a trial run at 100 different glass shapes

shaped this critical experience. Her personal commitment to, and ownership of, her initial concept motivated her to push through the challenges and explore many different conceptual and production paths for completing the project. I did not leave Andrea to explore aimlessly. I worked with her collaboratively, modeling designer norms by thinking through her problems aloud with her and by asking her questions which turned the design problems back to her, so that she built her own expertise instead of relying on mine (Cennamo et al., 2011). Her explorations were therefore guided by me along a path similar to that of an experienced designer, but they did not take a single course—or *my* expected course—to a predetermined outcome. In addition, having brought very little background in design to the class, Andrea also demonstrates what we consider to be an instance of individual success even though other students brought more relevant experience with them and advanced further.

Martin, in contrast to Andrea, came to the course with several years' professional experience in a job combining graphic design and instructional design, both of which he had studied previously at the college level. His plan for the course was to challenge himself by defining his projects to address areas in which he had not had much experience, a plan that the design of the course accommodated. An avid cook, he decided quickly to draw 100 kitchen implements and to simplify them radically. It did not surprise me that he stayed with this core idea throughout the project. He was working the way an experienced designer does—envisioning the central concept of a work, then refining and reworking the concept in response to constraints as they emerge. He sought out precedent almost immediately to inform his approach, recognized at the outset the core challenge that would be presented in the extreme simplification he was

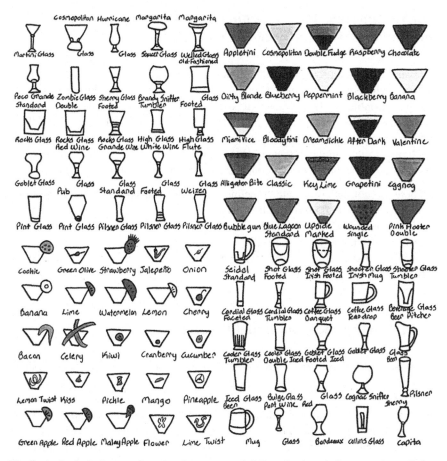

Fig. 7 Andrea's final poster featuring the two sets of differently-shaped glasses, and two distinct color segments created with brush pens

pursuing, and introduced constraints early on to guide his decision-making (such as limiting views to profiles and overhead shots instead of three-quarter views). I did not see a valid learning goal to be served in requiring him to produce multiple additional concepts before he began to work, and I anticipated that such a request would diminish the project for him, so I supported him as he pursued his early idea.

Martin had a broader range of skills than Andrea did, so he did not struggle finding a production path for this project. Instead, his challenges with the project took place at a different level. He wrestled with the fact that the extremely minimalist style he wanted to produce was unforgiving of the smallest details that did not fit in. He had also conceived of a color scheme that would identify for viewers the "working parts," or surfaces, of each implement. After trying out this scheme on multiple implements, it became clear that the color coding interfered with the descriptive shapes for too many of them. Both of these factors resulted in his reworking individual items repeatedly until he had a well-defined set of formal rules worked out and could, like Andrea, proceed efficiently to complete the project (Fig. 7).

Can We Separate Tools Learning from Learning Concepts and Habits of Thought? Should We?

At several documented points in the literature, and in our own study, we see a phenomenon whereby design students coming into their studies with little tool knowledge have trouble tackling conceptual issues in design (Clinton & Reiber, 2010) or trouble distinguishing conceptual issues from process issues (Brown, 1999). This problem does not go away until a minimum competency has been established, which runs counter to views that hold "tool issues" and "concept issues" to be separate. We see the need for special consideration in this area in programs where:

- There are not undergraduate "pipelines" in which students have mastered tools before arriving at graduate studio courses.
- We establish studios with emphasis on "design thinking" and place potentially insufficient emphasis on tool skills.
- We do not have sufficient technical expertise ourselves to diagnose and/or teach these skills.

Tool Expertise and Conceptual Progress

Kylie started the course with a strong background in tool use; in fact, she led a short session on *Adobe Illustrator* for her peers on the second day of class and ended up helping fellow students with related tool questions during the course. On presentation of the briefs, which were deliberately low in detail, she was able to test several different themes for *Draw 100 Things* by using a production path with which she was already familiar. Her initial ideas, first to draw 100 chairs, and then to draw 100 lamps, were quickly put aside when she mocked up samples and felt that they were not working well when presented in the required format of one square inch per image. She then rapidly settled on the theme of 100 designer coffee cups and applied her production path to testing and developing her concept. It was clear at the outset that she understood, not every move she would make for individual items (and she did reframe her selection of coffee cups partway through), but the process moves that would afford an imagined outcome. Her skills with tools were an integral part of the way she thought about and framed this project (Figs. 8 and 9).

For her instructional booklet project, Kylie started with her known production path to translate existing photographs into line art. Once she had created the images, she extended the previously mastered technique to refine her concept based on what she saw emerging from her early moves. Her ability to conceptualize a project was enhanced by her tool knowledge in two ways: first, she could envision a route—not to a known end point, but to a stage from which she could engage in dialogue with her concept; and second, she gained time with which to explore her ideas and to identify which of several approaches would best allow the finished images to communicate the pertinent information at the center of her concept. Specifically, she

Fig. 8 Kylie's tool skills were integral to her ability to envision the approach she took to Draw 100 Things

Fig. 9 A variant of the production path she used for Draw 100 Things allowed Kylie to translate photos she already had into an illustrated process booklet

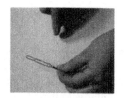

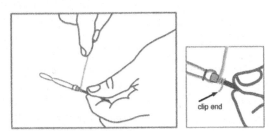

Step 1: Starting the wire wrap
Use wire cutters to cut wire 18 inches in length. Open barrette and begin to wrap wire tightly around one end 3-4 times to secure a base for the beads. Clip extra visible wire from the end.

explored different ways of focusing attention on the relatively small, detailed tools and materials used in the jewelry-making, while still showing a portion of the hands to provide context and enhance probable understanding. Incidentally, her tool expertise turned out to be of great use when a major portion of her work was lost in a hard drive crash and she was able to quickly reproduce it.

Fig. 10 After producing the first set of instructions for using chopsticks, Yin realized that she had asked the model to hold the chopsticks at an angle not appropriate for eating. Tools were not a barrier for her at this point; she was willing to discard all four illustrations in the set and start over from scratch to take and trace new ones

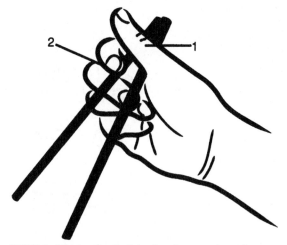

STEP3: Hold point 2 tight, but keep point 1 loose, at the same time, try to expand your palm, but keep the top end of chopsticks close together

Yin joined the class with some confidence in her hand drawing skills and photography skills, but without extensive experience using digital tools to create graphics. In response to the brief requiring an instructional graphic that included one or more depictions of hands, she decided tentatively that she wanted to create some kind of instruction combining two of her interests—food and her Chinese culture. She had a wrapper from a pair of restaurant chopsticks, but had trouble moving from there to a project idea that she could carry forward. Her ideas at this point were vague and shifted somewhat unproductively over several class periods.

One day in class, she watched a peer using the vector-based brush tool in Photoshop to trace over a photograph and was captivated. The other student showed Yin how to use this tool and Yin practiced a short time before declaring that she knew how she would carry out her project. She took photos of the hand model supplied to the class, traced over them with the brush tool, and was on her way to completing this graphic. This small increase in tool skill opened the conceptual door that allowed Yin to envision her project. The example of Andrea, who produced the 100 images of mixed drinks discussed previously in the context of following an initial design idea, can also be viewed as an obvious example of the interplay between tool skills and conceptualization. Yin's example is subtler than Andrea's, but we believe it demonstrates the same dynamic. Tool skills do not seem to be required simply to bring a concept to fruition, but to be able to generate and facilitate the concept in the first place. From this perspective, we have begun to question curriculum design in which tool skills are separated from concept generation, or seen as something that students will pursue on an "as needed" basis (Fig. 10).

Discussion

As we launched the studio course described in this chapter, we discussed several times the difficulties of teaching a studio class without having experienced one as a student. Shulman (2005) discusses the efficiency of signature pedagogies, pointing to the fact that neither the students nor the instructors in domains where they are established have to consider how classes will be structured or what the facilities, interactions, and strategies for instructions are going to have to be. Seen from a generational perspective, a pedagogy like the studio ensures the preparation of new instructors who know how to enact that pedagogy when and if they begin to teach within themselves. For domains in which studio pedagogy is a new option, not previously established, at least one or two generations of instructors may have to start from the ground up. They may operate on vague notions of studio instruction, or on long-standing misconceptions enacted within studio instruction, in well-intentioned efforts to develop instructional expertise to adopt or adapt studio to their needs.

As graduates of multiple studio programs ourselves, the authors recognize further that our own assumptions about studio education need to be revisited. In carrying out a longitudinal, reflective study of this one course, we have created a situation in which we are consciously recording and observing the progress of every student, every student's work, and our own intentions and moves as instructors. As researcher-instructors, we cannot enact patterns within the studio on the assumption that they work the way we think they do without confronting instances in which they do not. Those have given rise to the questions entertained in this chapter and will undoubtedly present us with more in the future.

While the course we have been studying and discussing here addresses instructional graphics, making it—on the surface—similar to design fields with an obvious visual focus (graphic design, architecture, product design), we see the underlying design orientation of all such fields, instructional design included, as broadly the same (Goel, 1997) and therefore amenable to the use of studio pedagogy. Since the inception of the course described in this study, the larger program has evolved and the two basic instructional design courses, taught for decades as hands-on, project-based courses, are now taught in a nascent studio format with persistent space for the students and a single project carried across two semesters.

In addition to the issues we discuss here, design tensions at the level of the organization (Tatar, 2007) continue to challenge us (Boling & Smith, 2009). The space designated at the department level for the core studio courses was recently absorbed back into the traditional classroom inventory, meaning it will see a rotation of classes all day and not be available for persistent use by the studio students. A smaller space will be available for them instead, and it remains to be seen what functions this space will support. For example, unless course enrollment is very small, it is not clear that the new studio will provide space for projects to be laid out and revisited over time, or offer wall space for sufficient precedent samples to be displayed. Only one of our active faculty members has experienced studio education as a student, or taught previously in this format, making the ramp into this form of teaching steep. Resourceful educators can always work around these kinds of limitations eventually, but the complications of design tensions like these must be taken into account as we ask ourselves which aspects of studio are necessary, which are adaptable, and which are deserving of skeptical scrutiny.

Conclusion

We view the effective preparation of instructional designers as a critical issue in the field, particularly at a time when discussions of design and design thinking are exploding around us with widely varying commitment to specificity and rigor. If we borrow ideas like studio pedagogy from other disciplines without sufficient critical examination, we run the risk of wasting time and—potentially—of substituting new misconceptions concerning design for our current ones (Smith, 2008). Our reflective study suggests that we need to pay careful attention to what is actually happening in our courses rather than designing solely from theory or, worse, from our assumptions regarding studio education.

References

Anthony, K. H. (1991). *Design juries on trial: The renaissance of the design studio.* New York: Van Nostrand Reinhold.

Bichelmeyer, B., Boling, E., & Gibbons, A. (2006). Instructional design and technology models: Their impact on research, practice and teaching in IDT. In M. Orey, J. McLendon, & R. Branch (Eds.), *Educational media and technology yearbook 2006.* Westport, CT: Libraries Unlimited.

Boling, E. (Ed.). (2005). *Design cultures. IDT record short papers.* Retrieved from http://www.indiana.edu/~idt/shortpapers/documents/design_cultures.html

Boling, E., & Smith, K. M. (2009). *Design tensions: Adapting a signature pedagogy into instructional design education.* San Diego, CA: American Educational Research Association.

Boling, E., & Smith, K. M. (2010a). *Intensive studio experience in a non-studio masters program: Student activities and thinking across levels of design.* Design and Complexity: Design Research Society Conference 2010. Montreal, QC, Canada: School of Industrial Design.

Boling, E., & Smith, K. M. (2010b). *Design education in the studio: Iterations in the work of students studying instructional graphics design.* Denver, CO: American Educational Research Association.

Brandt, C., Cennamo, K., Douglas, S., Vernon, M., McGrath, M. & Reimer, Y. (2013). A theoretical framework for the studio as a learning environment. *International Journal of Technology and Design Education, 23*(2), 329–348

Brown, A. (1999). *Strategies for the delivery of instructional design coursework: Helping learners develop a professional attitude toward the production process* (Doctoral dissertation). Retrieved from ProQuest (731845241).

Carspecken, P. (1995). *Critical ethnography: A theoretical and practical guide.* New York: Routledge.

Cennamo, K., Brandt, C., Scott, B., Douglas, S., McGrath, M., Reimer, Y., et al. (2011). Managing the complexity of design problems through studio-based learning. *Interdisciplinary Journal of Problem-based Learning, 5*(2), 11–36.

Chen, W. (2011). A study of the learning problems of undergraduate industrial design students in studio courses. In N. F. M. Roozenburg, L. L. Chen, & P. J. Stappers (Eds.), *Diversity and Unity: Proceedings of IASDR2011 4th World Conference on Design Research*, October 31–November 4, 2011, Delft, The Netherlands.

Christaans, H., & Venselaar, K. (2005). Creativity in design engineering and the role of knowledge: Modeling the expert. *International Journal of Technology and Design Education, 15*(3), 217–236.

Clinton, G., & Reiber, L. (2010). The studio experience at the University of Georgia: An example of constructionist learning for adults. *Educational Technology Research and Development, 58*(6), 755–780.

Cox, S., & Osguthorpe, R. T. (2003). How do instructional design professionals spend their time? *TechTrends, 47*(3), 45–47, 27.

Cross, N. (2006). *Designerly ways of knowing*. London: Springer.

Darke, J. (1984). The primary generator and the design process. In N. Cross (Ed.), *Developments in design methodology* (pp. 175–188). New York: Wiley.

Goel, V. (1997). *Sketches of thought*. Boston: MIT Press.

Hokanson, B., Clinton, G., Boling, E., Martindale, T., Rieber, L., Kinzie, M., et al. (2011). *Comparing instructional design studio programs*. Presentation at the Association for Educational Communications and Technology Convention, Jacksonville, FL, November 8–12.

Lawson, B., & Dorst, K. (2009). *Design expertise*. New York: Taylor & Francis.

Mathews, J. M. (2010). Using a studio-based pedagogy to engage students in the design of mobile-based media. *English Teaching: Practice and Critique, 9*(1), 87–102.

Mewburn, I. (2010). Lost in translation: Reconsidering reflective practice and design studio pedagogy. *Arts and Humanities in Higher Education*. Retrieved June 20, 2011, from http://ahh.sagepub.com/content/early/2011/06/15/1474022210393912

Morgado, P. (2009). From passive to active learners: Implementing the pedagogy of "learning by doing" in a design foundation course with large enrollment. *Proceedings of the Conference on the Beginning Design Student*, Baton Rouge, LA, March 12–14, 2009.

Nelson, H. G., & Stolterman, E. (2003). *The design way: Intentional change in an unpredictable world: Foundations and fundamentals of design competence*. Englewood Cliffs, NJ: Educational Technology.

Nicholson, R. (2000). Foreward. (Is this the spelling of the piece?). In D. Nicol & S. Pilling (Eds.), *Changing architectural education: Towards a new professionalism* (pp. xvi-xix). London: Spon Press.

Roozenburg, N. F. M., & Cross, N. G. (1991). Models of the design process: Integrating across the disciplines. *Design Studies, 12*(4), 215–220.

Rowland, G. (1992). What do instructional designers actually do? An initial investigation of expert practice. *Performance Improvement Quarterly, 5*(2), 65–86.

Salama, A. (1995). *New trends in architectural education: Designing the design studio*. Releigh, NC: Tailored Text & Unlimited Potential Publishing.

Shulman, L. S. (2005). Signature pedagogies in the professions. *Daedalus, 134*(3), 52–59.

Siegel, M. A., & Stolterman, E. (2009). Metamorphosis: Transforming non-designers into designers. *Undisciplined! Design Research Society Conference 2008*, 16–19 July 2008. Sheffield, UK: Sheffield Hallam University.

Smith, K. M. (2008). Meanings of "design" in instructional technology: A conceptual analysis based on the field's foundational literature (Doctoral dissertation, Indiana University, 2008). *Dissertation Abstracts International, 69–08*, 3122A.

Tatar, D. (2007). The design tensions framework. *Human Computer Interaction, 22*(4), 413–451.

Tracey, M. & Boling, E. (2013). Preparing instructional designers. In M. Spector, D. Merrill, M. J. Bishop, & J. Elen (Eds.), *Handbook for research in educational communications and technology* (4th ed.). New York, NY: Springer.

Webster, H. (2007). The analytics of power—Re-presenting the design jury. *Journal of Architectural Education, 60*(3), 21–27.

Welch, M., & Lim, H. S. (2000). The strategic thinking of novice designers: Discontinuity between theory and practice. *Journal of Technology Studies, 26*(2), Retrieved from http://scholar.lib.vt.edu/ejournals/JOTS/Summer-Fall-2000/welch.html

Wilkin, M. (2000). Reviewing the review: An account of a research investigation of the "crit."
   A case study. In D. Nicol & S. Pilling (Eds.), *Changing architectural education: Towards a new
   professionalism* (pp. 100–107). London: Spon Press.
Willenbrock, L. L. (1991). An undergraduate voice in architectural education. In T. A. Dutton
   (Ed.), *Voices in architectural education: Cultural politics and pedagogy* (pp. 97–120). New
   York: Bergin & Garvey.
Yamagata-Lynch, L. C., & Smaldino, S. (2007). Using activity theory to evaluate and improve
   K-12 school and university partnerships. *Evaluation and Program Planning, 30*, 364–380.

In Education We All Want to Be Nice: Lessons Learned from a Multidisciplinary Design Studio

Katherine Cennamo

Keywords Creativity • Innovation • Multidisciplinary • Transdisciplinary • Studio • Studio-based learning • Collaboration • Design disciplines • Design • Design culture • Qualitative research

Following Parrish's suggestion (see Chap. 15) that we think of design, teaching, and, by extension, research, in terms of a narrative, I'm going to present this research project as a story. In many ways, research itself is a classic story of the hero's journey: We are presented with a challenge, we look for mentors and guides, we encounter obstacles along the way, and, if all goes well, we emerge from the journey wiser than before.

The purpose of this investigation was to identify factors that might foster and sustain innovative design thinking through a qualitative examination of a multidisciplinary student team charged with the design of an immersive museum experience. In this chapter, I describe the experience that piped my curiosity, the exploration that ensued, and the picture that emerged at the end. In this process, I not only learned how multidisciplinary design projects can foster innovation but also gained insight into the differing cultures in which various design disciplines are educated.

The Story Begins

This journey, like many journeys, began a few years ago. At that time, I was serving as an educational advisor on a project, funded by the National Science Foundation (NSF), to design an immersive museum experience to introduce the scientific principles of fields to middle-school-aged children. The purpose of this planning grant was to lay the foundation for a second grant to the NSF to construct the exhibition.

K. Cennamo (✉)
Virginia Tech, Blacksburg, VA, USA
e-mail: cennamo@vt.edu

B. Hokanson and A. Gibbons (eds.), *Design in Educational Technology*,
Educational Communications and Technology: Issues and Innovations 1,
DOI 10.1007/978-3-319-00927-8_4, © Springer International Publishing Switzerland 2014

As part of this project, a two-semester special studies course sequence was offered through industrial design in which student groups were charged with designing the exhibit concepts. The first course consisted of 12 undergraduate and graduate students from industrial design, architecture, computer science, mechanical engineering, and education. In the second semester, 7 out of the original 12 chose to continue with the course and two additional students joined the team.

Students and faculty worked in the context of what the course instructor described as a design studio environment. Although the students neither met as a class for the extended hours typical of many studio courses nor were provided with dedicated desk space available to them at all times, the pedagogy and epistemology of these courses was consistent with that of the industrial design studio (Brandt et al., 2011).

The emphasis of the courses was on ideation, presentation, and critique. Students were provided with abbreviated project "briefs" to start their design work; they were expected to work independently and in groups to solve the design problems; and students periodically presented their evolving designs to faculty and students, with advisors joining the team on three separate occasions to see and discuss progress (see course timeline in Table 1). All in all, the students were responsible to ten project advisors (five consultants, one contractor, and four principle-investigators that included experts in educational technology for children, science exhibition design, and mechanical and electrical engineering) as well as architecture and education faculty. Course deliverables included two presentations to members of the advisory

Table 1 Course timeline

August	• Teams formed and introduced to the task
September	• *Field trip* to visit an exhibit fabricator and innovative museum
	• Students asked to individually explore the various types of scientific fields that we might consider in the overall exhibition, and then to propose *unrefined concepts* to the whole team
	• Then team was asked to select the stronger proposals to take forward to the next level of refinement. It was critical that the selection process be open and group-driven. We used a *system of Post-it® notes* for this process, where students were asked to rank their choices of concepts
	• Once we had narrowed the concepts down to a manageable group, the students then *named the concepts* in order to put us all on the same page when communicating about these still ill-defined ideas
	• Once titles were established, each individual was asked to *rank his/her top ten* on a list to be posted side by side for discussion and critique. *Parallel Planes* was one such concept that drew considerable support. Like most of the ideas at this stage, *Parallel Planes* lacked details, but we shared an understanding of the meaning of the name, which was an idea about technologically "smart" floors and ceilings that are interactive with visitors as they moved through the exhibit
	• We realized that there was some hierarchy and overlap among the top ten concepts. As a group, we reorganized and merged these ideas into four more general domains. From these four, we created *small work teams* that now focused on the more focused field and exhibit types
	• Teams then worked independently on presentations for the first *advisory board meeting*, in October

(continued)

Table 1 (continued)

October	• During the first advisory board meeting, the advisors pushed for a clear identification of the concepts that would be taught within the exhibit. The fundamental way that the student design team, mostly nonscientists, maintained a focus on the science was through the development of an inventory of characteristics of fields, which we later called our *Field Principles*
December	• Planning for second meeting with advisors. The team still struggled with how to organize the visitor's experience through each of the field exhibits. Consequently we introduced a *theater-based exercise* where the students were required to enact a visitor's experience through their concepts. This work illuminated where some of the key problems were in the design concepts, and it suggested how the students would present to the advisors, using a theatrical demonstration and rough prototypes
	• Second meeting with advisors. In this meeting the students were able to present ideas that were now more focused and shaped by the Field Principles
January	• At the beginning of the second semester, several changes occurred as the design team composition and venue changed. We moved the meetings to a conference space where all students met at a table to present and exchange ideas. We met on various agreed dates for longer spans of time rather than for shorter weekly meetings, which made charrettes more possible
March	• One month before the final presentation to the advisors, we held an all-day charrette on a Saturday (*Design charrettes* are short, intense, time-limited exercises that force participants to make decisions quickly and render these designs in expressive, understandable, and meaningful drawings.)
	• A charrette brief was sent out to all participants the day before, which gave them a mission statement, a list of deliverables for the charrette, and any background theory or information that had been formulated throughout the planning phase (for example, the Field Principles, project mission statement, reminders about parallel models, and conceptual change)
April	• Final presentation to the advisory board in New York City
May	• Entire group presented to the NSF program officer
	• Students created a project book and 130-panel exhibition of the project book, both of which were the final deliverables for the year's work

board on campus, a presentation to the advisory board in New York City, a project book to which all the students contributed, and a multimedia exhibit on campus for the assigned NSF program officer.

The Call to Adventure

As an educational advisor on the project, I did not begin this project with the intent of collecting data. However, early in the project, I became quite impressed with the innovative nature of the students' work and their resilience, drive, and motivation. As I observed their initial meeting with the advisors in October, I was struck by the quality and originality of their work. The presentations were well researched and many hours had been put into the visual and conceptual presentations. However, the advisors proceeded to critique the work to the extent that few of the original ideas were retained. Following the advisors' critiques, I was even more impressed at the way the students simply resumed work reconceptualizing the project, returning a few weeks later with a new set of well-researched, well-presented, and innovative design ideas. A similar thing happened at the December meeting, although in many ways it was more severe. Whereas at the October meeting, the class was exploring multiple ideas for the exhibit, in December, the group had coalesced around one idea. Each student team was responsible for one part of the design. Students presented to a large group of advisors and visitors that included many who had not attended the previous meetings. Once again, key ideas that represented hours and hours of work were discarded based on an advisor's comment.

As I reflected on times in which my former students in instructional design had their work rejected by clients, I recalled how demoralized they often became. I wondered what inspired this particular group of students to create such innovative, high-quality work and to persist in the face of rejection. I recognize that instructional design students need to learn to accept, perhaps embrace, criticism as a natural part of improving a design solution. During the formative evaluation process, they need to solicit input from both experts and learners in order to refine the instructional products. They need to accept feedback from clients and subject matter experts as well. Feedback—and criticism—is a necessary part of the instructional design process.

Thus, I began my investigation of the case in an attempt to discover characteristics of the group, task, or process that might inform future teaching and research endeavors. Like instructional designers, industrial designers are expected to be adept at process—identifying and resolving design problems given the unique parameters of any discipline or situation. For this reason, it seemed that an examination of this particular course experience might be especially applicable to the education of instructional designers.

A Guide Appears

As is typical in the hero's journey, I looked for guidance from those who had gone before me. The literature on group creativity has identified several factors that have been shown to facilitate creative outcomes, primarily though studies of professional work groups, and appeared to offer insight that could inform my research.

The ability to generate a wide *variety of potential solution ideas* is generally accepted as a key precursor to creative design outcomes. Researchers in the area of creativity (e.g., Combs, Cennamo, & Newbill, 2009; Raths, Wasserman, Jonas, & Rothstein, 1986; Starko, 2005) have identified several techniques that contribute to the generation of multiple original ideas. Creative thinkers are able to examine ideas from various perspectives, often exploring a challenge using a variety of raw materials, stimuli, and experiences to provide alternative perspectives on a challenge. As they explore ideas from various perspectives, they observe carefully, make inferences, and elaborate on their thinking. In addition, creative thinkers use analogies or metaphors to think through novel problems, reasoning from examples or similar situations to consider multiple possible courses of action.

The development of creative products also requires *reflective judgment* to select the best ideas to move forward. Reflective judgment requires analysis, synthesis, and evaluation skills (e.g., Combs et al., 2009; Paul & Elder, 2004; Sternberg & Spear-Swerling, 1996). Analysis involves questioning and comparing new ideas to previous ones (Black, 2005; Marzano et al., 1988). Ideas are synthesized through organizing, interpreting, sorting, and summarizing. Finally, ideas are evaluated by making judgments as to their logic, value, and worth, and generalizing to new situations (Nickerson, 1984; Paul & Elder, 2004; Raths et al., 1986).

However, it must be recognized that this is an iterative process. Creative thinkers do not simply generate a variety of ideas and then select the best one to move forward. Instead they cycle through the process multiple times—generating ideas, judging those ideas, using the outcomes of their reflective judgment to generate more and different ideas, and so forth until a desired solution is reached.

When examining *group composition*, studies of creative work groups reveal that a diversity of participants positively influences creative outcomes (Nijstad & Paulus, 2003). Diversity of detectible characteristics such as age, race, and gender are of less importance than attributes such as education, opinions, and values (Milliken, Bartel, & Kurtzberg, 2003; Nemeth & Nemeth-Brown, 2003). Stasser and Birchmeier (2003) indicated that it is the diversity of information that is important to generating a variety of original ideas. Diversity of preferred problem-solving strategies within the group also contributes to creative outcomes (Kurtzberg, 2005). The effect of newcomers is generally positive in that it increases the information diversity (Choi & Thompson, 2005; Katz, 1982). When existing members orient new members to the group, they may further analyze, synthesize, and evaluate their ideas as they revisit and clarify their original decisions for the newcomers (Levine, Choi, & Moreland, 2003). Not surprisingly, the addition of newcomers that are creative has an especially positive effect (Choi & Thompson, 2005).

Group process factors that have been shown to contribute to group creativity include, among others, a critical group process (Nemeth, Personnaz, Personnaz, & Goncalo, 2004; Tjosvold, 1998), intrinsic motivation (Hennessey, 2003), and adequate time for the members to all contribute their unique knowledge (Larson, Chrisietnesen, Abbott, & Franz, 1996). When group members have the opportunity to compare their ideas to those of others, this comparison can result in beneficial competition that increases the number and originality of ideas generated (Michinov & Pimois, 2005). However, pressure to conform has a negative effect on creativity (Chirumbolo, Livi, Mannetti, Pierro, & Kruglanski, 2004).

Group climate factors found to be important include interpersonal trust (West, 2003), the perception by members that their contributions are valued (Stasser & Birchmeier, 2003), challenging tasks (Amabile, Conti, Coon, Lazenby, & Herron, 1996), high standards (Hooker, Nakamura, & Csikszentmihalyi, 2003), support for innovation (Amabile, 1983), and participants' perceptions of safety (Nijstad & Paulus, 2003). Groups in which the members identify with the team, have a stake in the teams' success, and are encouraged to take risks produce products that are more innovative than groups who lack these characteristics (Sethi, Smith, & Whan Park, 2001). Support for communication among team members also has a positive effect on innovation (Sethi et al., 2001).

The Challenge

Using the factors identified in the literature on group creativity as a guide to data analysis, we sought to determine the presence of those factors, as well as others, in the student group charged with developing a viable museum exhibit design. The primary data were collected through two open-ended surveys and a focus-group interview. Questionnaires were completed by the student team in February and by all project participants (student teams, advisors, PIs) in April. The question prompts that yielded data for this case study, along with the way that they are noted in the coded data, are listed in Table 2. Other questions on the surveys addressed facets of the class unrelated to the design process. In early June, all of the students and the course instructor participated in a focus-group interview of one- and one-half hours in length. During the focus group, students were asked to discuss the process through which they developed the museum exhibit design. The discussion was recorded and the data transcribed for analysis. Secondary data, used to provide insight on the primary data set, included written summaries of the project prepared for various reasons such as journal articles, conference and grant proposals, case study competitions, and the project book.

Factors that had emerged from the literature on creative groups were used to establish an initial set of data-coding categories (see Table 3). The primary researcher and an independent reviewer both searched the data to identify instances of each characteristic during a joint-coding session. Differences in coding were discussed until both reviewers agreed upon the meaning of each coding category. Following this orientation to establish shared meaning for each coding category, the

Table 2 Questions from survey used for data collection and how indicated in coded data

Coded	Question from survey
February survey of students	
Q, S, 5	5. Describe your initial expectations of the Phoebe's Field Exhibition course when you first started
Q, S, 6	6. Describe your view of the process and method undertaken for the course and how it is similar or different from other classes that you have participated in
Q, S, 7	7. Describe one or more experiences interacting with the team members in terms of the challenges as well as benefits of working with people from other disciplines
Q, S, 9	9. In regards to the planning process, identify one or more things that could be improved, in your opinion
Q, S, 10	10. Describe any significant obstacles and/or breakthroughs that the team encountered in the design process thus far. Why do you think this occurred?
April survey of whole team	
Q, W, 6	6. How has the project developed over time, in your opinion?
Q, W, 7	7. Describe one or more experiences interacting with the team members in terms of the challenges as well as benefits of working with people from other disciplines
Q, W, 9	9. In regards to the planning process, identify one or more achievements, in your opinion
Q, W, 16	16. At this point, what are your expectations for the future of the Phoebe's Field Exhibition?

Table 3 Characteristics of creative work groups and example data

Characteristics	Example quotes from the data
Membership	
Diversity of knowledge and expertise	"The different disciplines not only brought more opinions and different ideas because of their different lives but they have knowledge of subjects that other did not."
Benefits of newcomers	(In reference to the two new class members in the spring) "… and you know and I think a lot of us were feeling a little fried in terms of ideas, and what it does is confirms what you thought before or it twists it differently and suddenly you can get re-energized about it and that's the beauty of having a fresh voice come in."
Intrinsic motivation	"You get projects where you design something for this imaginary purpose, and then we have, you know, well, we wanna help middle school aged girls learn about science and get them interested and it's like, 'This is *really* cool.' This is worthwhile and if this actually happened and we did a good job and you might get more kids interested in science, you know. It's something that's, you know, you can actually grab a hold of it and, like, make it important to yourself."
Group processes	
Accepting of diverse opinions	"Allowing for and considering input from all team members (there is no wrong answer)."
Supportive climate where group members help train each other	"I think you guys [the industrial design students] were patient too … We kind of had to be coached. Like when Janice sat with Karen and I, she was like 'Look, this is how it goes.' {laughter!} 'You do this because you are asked to do this and, you know, let it go.' And I think, you know, among the group there were definitely coaches that were kind of like 'In ID [industrial design], this is kind of how it is.'"
Trust	"It goes back to that, you know, a lot of that trust issue that every single one of us would probably agree that we just felt that the group was capable of this. We trusted in the project and everybody's capabilities."
Openness	"Open ideation and discussion is definitely a must have. Being able to freely voice opinions and bounce ideas around was extremely generative."
Reflect on group processes	"The final booklet I believe was a major break through. It really spoke about all the project as it developed."
Critical group norm	"From a design perspective, critique is a delicate proposition for students outside of the typical design studio culture. So, the distillation of ideas could seem abrupt to some students. However, I never witnessed any serious withdrawal of students as we needed to narrow from many ideas to a few."
Avoidance of premature consensus	"The fact that so many ideas were pursued and improved only to be replaced by another idea is very good in my opinion. It shows that the group and the design process are broader than simply finding a solution but dedicated to finding the best solution. I feel lucky to be a part of the design even though it is in the later part of the process."
Creativity valued	"This design process is much different than what I am used to. There is a lot more free thinking allowed and creation of new ideas."
Group contexts/environment	
Freedom/autonomy	"The class was more 'freestyle' than others. It evolved as the semester proceeded. Almost everyone had an equal say in how things were done or had to be done (with the exception of certain executive decisions that had to be taken). Though it seemed a little chaotic at times, I think it was a really good learning experience."
Supervisory encouragement	"One thing was that Mitzi was with us at every step …. She was there for every meeting."
Adequate time to generate/ contribute a variety of ideas	"Even though it was outside of my expectations, I really thought the long process to develop many concepts and really think about why we were designing this exhibit was crucial to the overall design. What I thought should have been a quick design solution, turned out to be a detailed, thought through idea. And I think that was a positive aspect to making the project a success."
Support for communication	"The open flow of communication in the meetings, through emails and on the wiki has been great."

independent reviewer coded the remaining data, while remaining open to data that did not conform to the preestablished categories.

Following the coding of the data, the primary researcher reviewed the coded data to determine the most salient features of the case and to gain insight into the group characteristics and processes that contributed to the success of this multidisciplinary design effort. The data were further analyzed using the constant comparative method (Merriam, 1998) to illuminate the story that emerged in the data set. This method required an iterative process of identifying major and recurring themes in the data, developing categories for these themes, working with and coding the data to reveal representations of the identified categories, and synthesizing categorized data within a larger context that identified essential relationships and processes. And finally, the course professor and student project manager were invited to review the findings as a means of member-checking the results of the analysis.

Insight Is Gained

Although almost all of the characteristics of creative groups identified in the literature were present to some degree in the class structure (see Table 3), the data indicated that group diversity, a critical group norm, intrinsic motivation, and strong leadership were prevalent themes within the case. In the following narrative, notice how these key factors are interrelated.

Diversity of knowledge and expertise was of primary importance. When asked in a questionnaire to describe one or more experience interacting with the team members in terms of the challenges as well as the benefits, one student responded, "The different disciplines not only brought more opinions and different ideas because of their different lives but they have knowledge of subjects that other did not" (#10, Q, S, 7).[1] The addition of newcomers midway through the project was also seen as a positive force. One student stated,

> While the core team had the advantage of already knowing each other's skills and the project scope, the newcomers were a welcomed addition. Not only did they provide the team members with the opportunity to explain and reiterate the project scope, they brought in a fresh perspective, providing both a new look on the previous work as well as bringing original concepts to the table. (AIA, p. 30)

---

[1] Key to data notation:

- #8, Q, W, 6 refers to the response of participant 8, on the questionnaire to the whole group, question number 6.
- #10, Q, S, 7 refers to the response of participant 10, on the questionnaire to the students, question number 7.
- Lynn, FGT, p. 30 refers to Lynn's (pseudonyms used) comment, found in the focus group transcript on page 30.
- AIA, p. 16 refers to page 16 of a project summary prepared by the student project manager for the American Institute of Architects case study competition.

At the same time, *navigating this diversity was not always smooth*. One student commented,

> There is definitely a disconnect between the scientists and the designers and those involved with social or human development. Sometimes it seemed as though people just weren't getting each other and the same idea was communicated over and over again. (#1, Q, W, 7)

Part of this disconnect was due to *communication challenges* among disciplines. One industrial design student commented,

> When I was working with team members whose area is in computers and engineering, we did not always speak the same language. For example, one team member and I talked around and around for some time about desired technology vs. design practicality without resolution. Some of the time I could see that there were non- [industrial] design folks who didn't get some of the [industrial] design terminology being thrown around. (#1, Q, S, 7)

Of particular note were the differences in design cultures among the group members. This disconnect was felt by both the industrial design students and the students from other design disciplines. On one hand, there were differences in aspects of the problem to which the students attended. When asked to describe the process and method used in the class, one engineering student commented,

> This design process is much different than what I am used to. There is a lot more free thinking allowed and creation of new ideas. With my engineering courses things were very concrete and variation from the norm was never usually looked upon very well. If something met the needs of the problem and did it inexpensively it was considered well done. There was very little room for creativity. (#8, Q, S, 6)

An industrial design student commented,

> For the interactive theater, I was grouped with two engineers. While they had a lot to offer on the project, it was a challenge to, see, work together and collaborate—the different angles we were coming from. I was thinking design and aesthetics, while they were thinking technical and details on the science aspect. (#9, Q, S, 7)

Differences were often due to deeply embedded conventions of the various design cultures. One industrial design student commented,

> At first it was challenging working with one individual that does not come from an [industrial] design background ... if he had an idea that other members of the group did not like, he thought that must be because we did not understand him, and he would continue explaining the same idea over and over again. People with [industrial] design backgrounds are less attached to their ideas, and are okay with it when ideas get thrown out. (#3, Q, S, 7)

As alluded to in this quote, many of these differences centered around the way industrial design students had been taught to view the idea generation and selection process. One student explained it succinctly during the focus group:

> I think that [industrial] designers learn to let things go as part of their education and the whole process. I always wondered how people from other disciplines would deal with that, because, you know, we are used to just throwing ideas out there and you know you have to. Especially a professional world, you are selling them. But you know they might not work. You have to believe in them because you want them to work. If they don't, well, if they don't make it, they don't make it. You let it go. (Lynn, FGT, p. 30)

Another student commented:

> ...the second I put something out there it's not mine ... and that's how you have to give your ideas vitality: by letting them be themselves. When you have people that come into a group that—I think most of us pretty well understood that in the spring you know, but in the fall you could definitely see we had people in the group that weren't willing to just cut it and let it go. (Carl, FGT, p. 25)

The culture of criticism was not familiar to all students. When referring to the challenges of working in interdisciplinary groups, one industrial design student commented, "They also didn't seem to get the process of spending lots of time coming up with design ideas and going through open forum critiques only to have the ideas thrown out and having to start from scratch again" (#1, Q, S, 7). When the focus-group discussion turned to the meetings with advisors, one student from education stated, "In education, it's not that stressful. It's like we all want to be nice and collaborate and care about people's feeling" (Jen, FGT, p. 2).

In contrast, the industrial design students spoke of the importance of critique and discarding ideas. Students who were familiar with the culture discussed why they were not bothered by criticism (FGT, p. 33):

Jay: The way I look, with my projects in studio, when (the professor) tears apart my work, it's like, when (the professor) actually deigns to look down on my crappy little work and go "Hmm, that's interesting enough for me to form a thought and give you feedback." [laughter!] It's like, "Yes!" She's saying something negative, but yes that gives me something to build on.

Mona: That's how I am. I'm like, well, at least she's taking the time to tell me what I should do.

Carl: It's fired her up in some way.

Those who were familiar with the culture took aside those who were not and let them know how it was done. As one student from education noted in the focus group,

> We had no idea. We kind of had to be coached. Like when Janice sat with Karen and I, she was like "Look, this is how it goes." [laughter!] "You do this because you are asked to do this and, you know, let it go." And I think, you know, among the group there were definitely coaches that were kind of like, "In ID [industrial design], this is kind of how it is." (Jen, FGT, p. 25)

Despite differences in perspectives and cultures, students repeatedly acknowledged the benefits of working with other disciplines. This was true for both the industrial design students and those from other backgrounds. One industrial design student, commented,

> The challenges of working in interdisciplinary teams is that other disciplines follow a vastly different design process than what I have been taught—fail early to reach the better design and don't get too attached to any one idea because it can always be done better. Although this was at times frustrating, the expertise members of the team from other disciplines provided broadened my scope of understanding and their knowledge base allowed for them to generate ideas that I would not have. (#4, Q, S, 7)

A nonindustrial design student commented,

> Working with other disciplines provided me with a broader way of thinking, and resulted in a much larger pool of ideas to pick from. ... The challenges mostly arose when it became apparent that those in the majors who focused on creativity, focused very little on whether or not the final idea agreed with the physics behind it. In a way, having both types of majors present provided for a sort of check on each other. (#11, Q, S, 7)

Eventually, trust and comfort was built up. When asked about significant breakthroughs, one student commented,

> I think once the teams started thinking like other team members thought, and really started listening to everyone's input, things started to take off. The engineers were beginning to think like [industrial] designers and [industrial] designers understood more of the engineer's or computer science side. (#10, Q, S, 10)

Students began to work as a team rather than individuals. In the focus group, one student commented,

> ... there's not too much about this that's individual. It's not really about, you know, doing well within the group, you know, being better than anyone. It's about the group doing better, and then because the motivation isn't really, you know, in the grade or whatever. It's in the group doing well in this thing that we have all worked so hard on, actually working at some level that all, you know, I should say most aspects of competition disappear. (Dan, FGT, p. 22)

The unity of thought was evident in the focus group, where students were completing each other's sentences. This unity of thought is illustrated in the following passage:

Carl: I don't think there is, you would be hard pressed, even if there were little pieces of things, oh, this is this person's idea, it's been re-thought...
Jen: ... massaged and polished ...
Jay: ... worked over so much ...
Carl: ... that ownership is dissolved. (FGT, p. 22)

They also learned to appreciate each other's strengths and weaknesses, as illustrated in the following passage: "... at the same time we were comfortable with, say, if I have something to ask about layout, I definitely need to go to Carl. Or if I have a science question, Aaron was there" (Jay, FGT, p. 9).

The deadlines for presenting to the advisory board provided a key impetus for pulling together as a group:

> You know we had these big presentations where you get there, the first one, and you sort of immediately started to lose a little bit of that like "I am not sure if we can get this all done." You start to develop that trust, not just in what you are capable of, but as the group moves through these things, you trust that, you know, everything is going to get done and everything is going to get done really well. It's not to be full of ourselves or pompous or anything, but if you move through it, you know that you can trust everybody else in the group to get their part of it done so that as a whole it looks a lot stronger. When it comes to panic, you know, you are really concerned about getting things done, but it's not sort of a panic in this sort of global idea that we are just not gonna finish this or it's gonna turn into complete crap or something. (Carl, FGT, p. 2–3)

They spoke of their "panic calendar," where they were meeting constantly in order to meet the deadlines:

Carl: It's where we went from meeting every two weeks to meeting every two hours. [laughter!]

Ben: So, we never really left the meeting. [laughter!] It was just like this table in the studio.

Carl: It was almost like a continual meeting with people kind of coming in and going out, coming in and going out. [laughter! Several speaking at once]

MP: Break for a shower.

Ben: Break for Starbucks.

Mitzi: It really was that way the last two weeks before New York. I mean we were either meeting in the conference room or meeting downstairs in the studio. (FGT, p. 13)

Students looked at these presentations as "high stakes," yet repeatedly spoke of it being an "honor" and a "privilege" to work on the project. In the focus group, one industrial design student commented, "We got to present it in front of a board of professionals. What other student gets to do that? We had the possibility of what we designed maybe someday making it in some form into reality and no students get to do that" (Dan, FGT, p. 16).

As alluded to in the previous quote, the group culture existed simultaneously with a strong degree of intrinsic motivation on the part of the individual students. In the focus group, one student explained,

> There's nothing really academic at all about the motivation. The motivation is that this is a real thing and what it takes at that point is somebody going out on a limb and trusting all this money to your work as a student—free to say, "Wait a minute, there's something really important about this," and that's not something that can really be, ah, faked and it's obvious to everyone here that this is an enormous privilege, you know, and when it becomes an enormous privilege all these other things fall into place because we care. (Dan, FGT, p. 16)

Students repeatedly talked about the fact that it was "real" rather than an academic exercise. They also viewed it as an opportunity to work on something that could be of potential benefit to future generations. One student explained that, "The fact that it is a very real and legitimate project is a huge motivation to do the very best work on it. I liked both that it was something unique and that it was something important and might someday be a reality" (#6, Q, S, 5). Another student succinctly stated his expectations of the project in the questionnaire: "I hope to take my children to it and say daddy did that, that is, when I have children" (#12, Q, W, 16).

This project was also unique in that the course professor was heavily invested in the success of the project. In a summary of the project, one student stated, "There was no question that this was Mitzi's brainchild and the team quickly grew to feel mutually responsible for the life of the project" (AIA, p. 16). She further stated that, "Mitzi expected a lot from the students but gave even more. Her impassioned and charismatic leadership balanced by high expectations and strong criticism brought the team to a new level of performance from the previous semester" (AIA, p. 32). In the focus group, one student commented,

> One thing was that Mitzi was with us at every step—not like other classes where you meet with them once a month to do their progress reports and say, "Okay, I want this by this date" and they don't care whether we sleep, whether we do it. When we were not sleeping, Mitzi was there not sleeping along with us. [laughter!] She was there through all of us at the same time. She was there for every meeting. We'd go into teams, meet, and then we'd work overnight and then come the next day morning and present it. It's not just class projects. (Aaron, FGT, p. 18)

Returning Home

So what can we derive from this case study of a multidisciplinary student group's experience in designing a museum exhibit that can help us better prepare students of instructional design to be innovative, resilient professionals?

This case study reinforced many of the findings from experimental research on factors that contribute to creative group outcomes. Students were intrinsically motivated by the perceived benefits of the project to society. The time constraints and the high-stakes deadlines of presenting to the advisors left the students little choice other than to pull together and trust each other. The variety of expertise within the group contributed to the diversity of ideas generated (Stasser & Birchmeier, 2003). In addition, a diversity of problem-solving strategies was exhibited in the composition of the group. While some group members were initially more comfortable with highly structured, process-oriented approaches, others were more comfortable with unstructured, broad, idea generation approaches. Students who were familiar with the design studio-like environment of the course mentored those who were less familiar with it. Kurtzberg (2005) found that groups containing a mix of problem-solving types generated more creative outcomes than those consisting of members who were homogenous. Although the literature suggests it is important that groups exhibit openness to multiple ideas during the idea generation phase, criticism that maintains high standards is valuable during the idea selection phase (Nijstad & Paulus, 2003). A critical, yet open and supportive group norm has been shown repeatedly to facilitate creative outcomes. A "somewhat critical but open climate, in which new ideas are valued, but in which there is no excessive consensus seeking, appears to be most beneficial for creative performance" (Nijstad & Paulus, 2003, p. 330). From the data, it was obvious that the transformational leadership style of the course professor contributed to a group process characterized by trust, high standards, and openness, as well as a critical group norm. West (2003) argued that, "Such leaders use emotional or ideological appeals to change the behavior of the group, moving them from self-interest in work values to consideration of the whole group and organization" (p. 266).

Yet it was the education student's comment on the culture of American schools of education, in which most programs of instructional design are situated, that provided the most interesting insight on why my students were unprepared for the criticism that is a natural part of the instructional design process. Recall the student from education who stated that, "In education, it's not that stressful. It's like we all want to be nice and collaborate and care about people's feelings" (Jen, FGT, p. 2). Contrast this with the view of students from industrial design who stated, for example, that,

> ... when (the professor) actually deigns to look down on my crappy little work and go, "Hmm, that's interesting enough for me to form a thought and give you feedback." [laughter!] It's like, "Yes!" She's saying something negative, but yes that gives me something to build on (Jay, FGT, p. 22).

Or another student who commented, "We are used to just throwing ideas out there ... But you know they might not work ... If they don't, well, if they don't make it, they don't make it. You let it go" (Lynn, FGT, p. 30). Or another student who commented, "... the second I put something out there it's not mine ... And that's how you have to give your ideas vitality: by letting them be themselves" (Carl, FGT, p. 25). Whereas the industrial design students accepted criticism as a natural part of the idea selection and refinement process, the education student recognized a very different environment than the one in which she normally functioned.

More than once, I have observed faculty in education who otherwise incorporate the studio method avoid the critique for fear of hurting students' feelings. In describing one of the most well-known instructional design and development studios, Clinton and Reiber (2010, p. 763) have noted that their studios, by design, do not include, "one notorious element of art studios—merciless public critiques of student work." I acknowledge that, historically, schools of architecture have documented negative practices that can result from the norms and expectations surrounding the studio critique (Koch, Schwennsen, Dutton, & Smith, 2002). Yet, as the design faculty interviewed by Dannels (2005) noted, the ability to separate work from self is an important element of professional communication that is cultivated during the studio critique.

In discussing the benefits and challenges of the studio critique, Hokanson (2012) notes the value of the critique for conveying design knowledge while acknowledging the need to establish appropriate social structures and norms to ensure quality critiques. He states that the "development of the skills of critique among faculty, adjuncts, visiting critics, and students may be one of the lynchpins of [a] successful critique system" (p. 80), especially in disciplines without a long history of studio-based pedagogy. In other research, we have found that even when students have prior experience with studio-based learning, instructors and students must actively work to establish the rights and duties of a respectful, productive studio environment (Cennamo et al., 2011). It was obvious that the students who participated in the interdisciplinary group charged with designing a museum exhibit benefited from a design studio culture that valued generating, critiquing, and discarding ideas within the context of a real project with perceived benefits to society, as well as the diversity of the group membership.

Although we will seldom be able to replicate the conditions found in this particular course experience—students from a variety of design disciplines coming together to work on a well-funded project with perceived benefits to society—there are other lessons learned from this case that we can incorporate into our classes more easily. We can attempt complex projects that extend across multiple semesters, recognizing that some students may leave the project and others may join, but that changes to group composition can be beneficial. We can require students to present to professionals from various fields and advisory groups to raise the stakes. We can work to establish social norms that value generating and discarding ideas freely. We can prepare our students to welcome critiques as valuable to the idea selection process as opposed to seeking consensus. We can always treat students with respect and invest resources in them. And as professors, we can fully participate as members of the design team.

In some fields, creativity is represented through aesthetic expression. However, creative thought is also of value in professions that focus on problem solving, such as instructional design. Whether the goal is to develop an aesthetically pleasing product or to solve a challenging problem that requires thinking in new ways, the literature on creativity and innovation reveals that the development of creative design solutions is an iterative process, involving idea *refinement* as well as idea generation. This investigation has revealed several ways that we, as teachers, can create a classroom culture that supports both the innovative thought that is needed to generate ideas and the resilience that is needed to refine them.

Acknowledgments This work was supported by Grant No. ESI-0442469 from the National Science Foundation. Any opinions, findings, and conclusions expressed in this chapter are those of the authors and do not necessarily reflect the views of the National Science Foundation or the entire research team. Other project team members were Margarita McGrath, Associate Professor of architecture in the School of Architecture + Design at Virginia Tech, and Mitzi Vernon, Professor in the Industrial Design Program in the School of Architecture + Design at Virginia Tech team members who contributed to the data collection and analysis include Leigh Lalley and Phyllis Newbill.

References

Amabile, T. M. (1983). The social psychology of creativity: A componential conceptualization. *Journal of Personality and Social Psychology, 45*, 357–376.

Amabile, T. M., Conti, R., Coon, H., Lazenby, J., & Herron, M. (1996). Assessing the work environment for creativity. *Academy of Management Journal, 39*, 1154–1184.

Black, S. (2005). Teaching students to think critically. *Education Digest: Essential Readings Condensed for Quick Review, 70*(6), 42.

Brandt, C. B., Cennamo, K., Douglas, S., Vernon, M., McGrath, M., & Reimer, Y. (2011). A theoretical framework for the studio as a learning environment. *International Journal of Technology and Design Education, 23*(2), 329–348.

Cennamo, K., Brandt, C., Scott, B., Douglas, S., McGrath, M., Reimer, Y., et al. (2011). Managing the complexity of design problems through studio-based learning. *Interdisciplinary Journal of Problem-Based Learning, 5*(2), Article 5. Retrieved from http://docs.lib.purdue.edu/ijpbl/vol5/iss2/5

Chirumbolo, A., Livi, S., Mannetti, L., Pierro, A., & Kruglanski, A. (2004). Effects of need for closure on creativity in small group interactions. *European Journal of Personality, 18*, 265–278.

Choi, H. S., & Thompson, L. (2005). Old wine in a new bottle: Impact of membership change on group creativity. *Organizational Behavior and Human Decision Processes, 98*, 121–132.

Clinton, G., & Reiber, L. P. (2010). The Studio experience at the University of Georgia: An example of constructionist learning for adults. *Educational Technology Research & Development, 58*, 755–780.

Combs, L. B., Cennamo, K. S., & Newbill, P. L. (2009). Developing critical and creative thinkers: Toward a conceptual model of creative and critical thinking processes. *Educational Technology, 49*(5), 3–14.

Dannels, D. P. (2005). Performing tribal rituals: A genre analysis of "crits" in design studios. *Communication Education, 54*(2), 136–160.

Hennessey, B. A. (2003). Is the social psychology of creativity really social? Moving beyond a focus on the individual. In P. B. Paulus & B. A. Nijstad (Eds.), *Group creativity: Innovation through collaboration* (pp. 181–201). New York: Oxford.

Hokanson, B. (2012). The design critique as a model for distributed learning. In L. Moller & J. B. Huett (Eds.), *The next generation of distance education: Unconstrained learning* (pp. 71–83). New York: Springer. doi:10.1007/978-1-4614-1785-9-5.

Hooker, C., Nakamura, J., & Csikszentmihalyi, M. (2003). The group as mentor: Social capital and the systems model of creativity. In P. B. Paulus & B. A. Nijstad (Eds.), *Group creativity: Innovation through collaboration* (pp. 225–244). New York: Oxford.

Katz, R. (1982). The effects of group longevity on project communication and performance. *Administrative Science Quarterly, 27*, 81–104.

Koch, A., Schwennsen, K., Dutton, T. A., & Smith, D. (2002). *The redesign of studio culture: A report of the AIAS Studio Culture Task Force*. Washington, DC: American Institute of Architecture Students.

Kurtzberg, T. R. (2005). Feeling creative, being creative: An empirical study of diversity and creativity in teams. *Creativity Research Journal, 17*(1), 51–65.

Larson, J. R., Jr., Chrisietnesen, C., Abbott, A. S., & Franz, T. M. (1996). Diagnosing groups: Charting the flow of information in medical decision making teams. *Journal of Personality and Social Psychology, 71*, 315–330.

Levine, J. M., Choi, H.-S., & Moreland, R. L. (2003). Newcomer innovation in work teams. In P. B. Paulus & B. A. Nijstad (Eds.), *Group creativity: Innovation through collaboration* (pp. 202–224). New York: Oxford.

Marzano, R. J., Brandt, R. S., Hughes, C. S., Jones, B. F., Presseisen, B. Z., Rankin, S. C., et al. (1988). *Dimensions of thinking: A framework for curriculum and instruction*. Alexandria, VA: Association for Supervision and Curriculum Development.

Merriam, S. B. (1998). *Qualitative research and case study applications in education*. San Francisco: Jossey-Bass.

Michinov, N., & Pimois, C. (2005). Improving productivity and creativity in online groups through social comparison: New evidence for asynchronous electronic brainstorming. *Computers in Human Behavior, 21*, 11–28.

Milliken, F. J., Bartel, C. A., & Kurtzberg, T. R. (2003). Diversity and creativity in work groups: A dynamic perspective on the affective and cognitive processes that link diversity and performance. In P. B. Paulus & B. A. Nijstad (Eds.), *Group creativity: Innovation through collaboration* (pp. 32–62). New York: Oxford.

Nemeth, C., & Nemeth-Brown, B. (2003). Better than individuals? The potential benefits of dissent and diversity for group creativity. In P. B. Paulus & B. A. Nijstad (Eds.), *Group creativity: Innovation through collaboration* (pp. 63–84). New York: Oxford.

Nemeth, C. J., Personnaz, B., Personnaz, M., & Goncalo, J. A. (2004). The liberating role of conflict in group creativity: A study in two countries. *European Journal of Social Psychology, 34*, 365–374.

Nickerson, R. S. (1984). Kinds of thinking taught in current programs. *Educational Leadership, 42*(1), 26.

Nijstad, B. A., & Paulus, P. B. (2003). Group creativity: Common themes and future directions. In P. B. Paulus & B. A. Nijstad (Eds.), *Group creativity: Innovation through collaboration* (pp. 326–339). New York: Oxford.

Paul, R., & Elder, L. (2004). Critical thinking and the art of close reading (Part III). *Journal of Developmental Education, 28*(1), 36–37.

Raths, L. E., Wasserman, S., Jonas, A., & Rothstein, A. (1986). *Teaching for thinking: Theory, strategies, & activities for the classroom*. New York: Teachers College Press.

Sethi, R., Smith, D. C., & Whan Park, C. (2001). Cross-functional product development teams, creativity, and the innovativeness of new consumer products. *Journal of Marketing Research, 38*(1), 73–85.

Starko, A. J. (2005). *Creativity in the classroom: Schools of curious delight* (3rd ed.). Mahwah, NJ: Erlbaum.

Stasser, G., & Birchmeier, Z. (2003). Group creativity and collective choice. In P. B. Paulus & B. A. Nijstad (Eds.), *Group creativity: Innovation through collaboration* (pp. 85–109). New York: Oxford.

Sternberg, R. J., & Spear-Swerling, L. (1996). *Teaching for thinking.* Washington, DC: American Psychological Association.

Tjosvold, D. (1998). Co-operative and competitive goal approaches to conflict: Accomplishments and challenges. *Applied Psychology: An International Review, 47,* 285–342.

West, M. A. (2003). Innovation implementation in work teams. In P. B. Paulus & B. A. Nijstad (Eds.), *Group creativity: Innovation through collaboration* (pp. 245–277). New York: Oxford.

When Design Meets Hollywood: Instructional Design in a Production Studio Environment

Wayne A. Nelson and David B. Palumbo

Keywords Project management • Production processes • Rapid prototyping • Interactive media • Production studios • Team roles • Design research • Learning experience design

This chapter tells the story of an interactive new media design firm in Austin, TX, that successfully integrated instructional design processes with management and production processes based on a Hollywood film studio model. In the process of this integration, user experience design methods adapted from fields like product design and human–computer interaction were also incorporated into the instructional design processes used in the company. We also tell the story of how this integration created an approach to instructional design that focused on learning experiences rather than traditional instructional design methods and concerns. Along the way, much was discovered about how designers work in the context of a creative company, how creative design is managed, and how characteristics of design practice in this setting might be brought to universities to help students learn to be effective learning experience designers.

The story is based on what happened during an ethnographic research study at the company (we'll call the company HC), where the first author acted as participant observer on more than a dozen projects over the course of 2 years. His roles included being a subject matter specialist, an instructional designer, and an evaluator (see Notes for details about data collection and analysis). The first author was challenged by the second author (the Vice President of the Learning Division at HC) to study and capture the processes being used to design learning experiences within the

W.A. Nelson, Ed.D. (✉)
Southern Illinois University Edwardsville, Edwardsville, IL, USA
e-mail: wnelson@siue.edu

D.B. Palumbo, Ed.D
National Heritage Academies, Austin, TX, USA

B. Hokanson and A. Gibbons (eds.), *Design in Educational Technology*,
Educational Communications and Technology: Issues and Innovations 1,
DOI 10.1007/978-3-319-00927-8_5, © Springer International Publishing Switzerland 2014

organization. As leader of a group that included more than 15 producers, designers, and production specialists, the second author's focus was on how to design high quality products while maintaining profits. As the capturing unfolded, the first author noticed how different the language, roles, and design approaches were from the traditional instructional design that is presented in the literature and taught at many universities. After 2 years, his analysis and reflections resulted in attempts to transform how instructional design and development could be taught at a university. The differences in approach to design, along with the transformation of teaching that resulted from the analysis and reflection, are described below.

Background

New media design companies are often organized based on their historic roots in the film industry. These firms are the latest evolution of an industry that has grown and changed for more than 100 years. Films, television, and digital media are created in production studios for a variety of reasons that are based in the history of Hollywood and the technology of filmmaking. Hollywood became the dominant location for movie production during the 1920s (Lampel & Shamsie, 2003), as the industry evolved along with the development of various film technologies that blended capabilities of scientific inventions with many art forms (theater, art, etc.). The earliest, pre-Hollywood films were produced by the people who developed and patented the technologies, such as Lumiere and Edison, but as Hollywood was established and grew to as many as 30 film studios in the early 1900s, organizational and physical structures called studios were established to efficiently manage the creative talents and to house the technologies.

By the 1920s movie production was streamlined to the point where large numbers of creative people with a variety of skills were employed under contract to a single studio. At the same time, studio sound stages evolved so that sound could be recorded and synchronized with the film, requiring large sets that were flooded with light. Following antitrust litigation, the studio system was dismantled in the 1940s, replaced by a contract system where independent production firms contract with studios for distribution of the films. In the 1960s, Hollywood met another threat from the television industry, which used similar production practices and organizational structures. But even though the medium had shifted from film to broadcast television signals, the approach to production remained very similar. And later, as new media firms emerged in the 1990s, they grew naturally from the Hollywood production model of film/television that had been established for nearly a century (Seidel, 2011). But the interesting thing for this chapter is that the Hollywood production model has also been adapted to other kinds of project-based activities, including e-business, learning (Lamos & Parrish, 1994), and consumer entertainment products such as video games. It should be noted, however, that the Hollywood production studio model described here is not the same as the design studio model that is currently being promoted as a pedagogical approach to teaching instructional design. The design studio model is based on the notion of an atelier (Brown, 2006) as commonly employed in architecture and art education, and more recently adapted for teaching instructional design (Clinton & Rieber, 2010) and computer science (Brandt et al., 2011).

HC was one of the companies that successfully adapted a Hollywood production model to its interactive multimedia product design. Established in the late 1990s, HC was founded by two graduates of industrial design schools. The company was highly successful from the outset, with their first product winning awards for its interactive achievements (PRNewswire, 1997). Soon, the company grew and prospered to the point where 200+ employees worked in a large office building in downtown Austin. HC had acquired venture capital that allowed them to expand in Austin, as well as to merge with other studios in Tokyo and San Francisco, and, at the time the author visited, the company was preparing for a public stock offering. This fast growth was typical of the dot-com industry at the time, but unfortunately, the company did not make it through the bursting of the bubble (Abramson, 2005). It did not fail as a business. Rather, its success allowed it to fall prey to the merger and acquisition strategies so common in business.

The Context

The Austin "studio" (that is the term HC used when referring to its organization in conversation or in marketing publications) divided itself into divisions named Learn, Work, and Play, referring to the kinds of projects that were sought and completed. Supporting the three main groups of designers, producers, and associate producers (their terminology) were groups labeled Internet Design Group (everyone called them "the programmers," split between network specialists and interactive authoring experts), the Graphics Group (both 2D and 3D artists), and the Audio/Video Group. Additional support groups focused on business (marketing, sales, and management), legal (contracts and copyrights, etc.), all with the help of a limited clerical staff. In addition, there was a group of four or five individuals (led by one of the founders of the company) that focused on emerging technologies research to guide future projects and business opportunities.

Everything that happened in the business was associated with a project, either to produce a product or to provide a service for clients. In this sense, the studio model was ideal in that it provided the flexibility to reconfigure project-specific resources in a nimble fashion, which allowed the company to pursue a wide variety of clients. Even though there were Learn, Work, and Play divisions, project teams were assembled that often crossed these division lines. For example, one client brought several projects to the firm at the same time. Some of the projects involved consumer entertainment, while others were educational products. The studio executives assigned people to teams based on the nature of the product to be developed, but also cross-pollinated the teams with expertise from both Learn and Play groups so that the various teams could respond to client expectations, and so that both divisions could remain in a communication loop that kept everyone informed and updated, regardless of the project on which they worked.

Table 1 Categories and roles of project teams

Category	Role and typical activities
Producer	Engage with client; coordinate design, development, implementation, and evaluation processes; manage budget and team roles
Experience designer	Analyze opportunities, determine goals, conduct research with target learners, write proposal, requirements, and design docs
Associate producer	Assist producer and designer as needed
Graphics Group	Provide digital art as needed for docs and interactive products
Internet Design Group ("programmers")	Utilize interactive tools to develop systems to function as specified, including prototyping, testing, debugging, and quality assurance; provide web and server functions as specified; coordinate with client for implementation on client networks

The central person in the design and production of projects was the producer, who filled a combined role as a project manager and design team leader, with responsibilities that included budget, task scheduling, client engagement, facilitation of design meetings, and producing documentation. The producer also provided an important focus for teams by facilitating dialog around innovation and creativity in the projects and products under their supervision.

The producers often utilized assistant producers to help, especially on projects with a large scope or short time lines. The work was completed in teams, with personnel whose selection depended on the nature of the project requirements. Teams typically consisted of a producer (project and design team manager), a lead designer (specializing in interactive design and/or learning design), a graphic artist (responsible for the "look and feel"), and a programmer (responsible for programming the interactions for the interface and/or creating the functionality for web-based products). Depending on the scope, an associate producer might be added to assist the producer, or an audio/video media production specialist might be included on projects that emphasized a variety of multimedia. Other personnel configurations were created as needed because of the "flat" organizational structure of the studio that was both flexible and communicative (Meyer & Marion, 2010). People generally worked on two or three projects at a time, while producers generally worked on only one project until it was completed. Table 1 shows the various personnel categories and the roles they filled in the design and production process.

The managers of these groups of creative, design-oriented individuals were the executive producers (three individuals) and the group vice presidents (three individuals). They effectively built work cultures where a sense of pride in the work was highly evident. On many occasions, managers in meetings gave glowing compliments to the design or the product under consideration. Teams were encouraged to pin their work to the studio's "war wall" so that people on other teams could see the current state of work across the whole studio. There was a constant push for "spectacular" learning environments (a term used consistently by the second author to communicate his vision for the work) with a high production quality in terms of media and user experience.

In addition, producers and interactive designers were encouraged to pitch new ideas for products using a "green light" proposal process similar to what happens in Hollywood filmmaking. If the ideas were seen as viable and marketable, the company would support the idea through design, production, and marketing. This was an achievement that was coveted by the designers and producers in the firm, as most work came from outside clients. A green light for an internal project indicated a willingness to support innovation from within the organization, and helped to shape the creative culture of the organization (Fleming & Marx, 2006).

A driving part of the value proposition of HC was the repeatable convergence of creativity, innovation, and design. Through an operational structure that was highly blended across the various design and production groups, a scalable development process emerged. This process, led by the producer, always sought to delight the customer and the end users in the experiences provided by the product. Rather than solely relying on needs assessments and requirement analysis, the team would consider these data along with boundary-stretching ideas drawn from other experiences and disciplines, helping to position HC as a premium development studio. To warrant above-market pricing in a highly competitive space, the company needed to provide additional value to customers. This came by delivering more than what was asked for by the client. Much like Christensen's central thesis in *The Innovator's Dilemma* (1997), HC resisted implementing a process that was too customer-intimate. Instead, the project leadership was charged to drive design and development conversations that were always looking for creative and innovative solutions.

Like the customer-value proposition, the people-value proposition found in HC also focused on attracting, retaining, and engaging the very best people from a variety of disciplines to combine for a unique design solution. This approach allowed people from various backgrounds to contribute and continue to grow over time. Such creative expectations prevented burn out and attrition, and created a highly stable team that continued to push the design envelope again and again over multiple projects, multiple clients, and multiple years.

The project orientation of media production studios and other design firms supports and promotes creative activities while still allowing for discipline in project management, budget, and other business concerns (Meyer & Marion, 2010). HC exhibited many of the characteristics identified by those who study business management for creative industries (e.g., Pratt, 2009; Seidel, 2011). In particular, HC focused on user-centered design to understand the user (or learning) experience at deep levels. There was an alternating focus on both the overall system being designed and the details of subsystems. Teams were highly active and developed various communities of practice as well as knowledge sharing techniques. Development was agile, iterative, and began early in the process through a rapid prototyping strategy. Finally, management was "light-handed" (Meyer & Marion, 2010, p. 27), allowing teams to exercise limited autonomy to make decisions in consultation with the client, as long as the decision did not impact the budget significantly. This differs from other top-down management approaches that would have the team wait for a review meeting by executives in order to continue design and development.

The Design and Production Process

Unlike what is typically taught in universities using traditional instructional design models, the design practices of HC were first and foremost driven by business goals (Rhodes, 2000). The approach to design and development did not resemble the typical linear, circular, or waterfall design processes espoused by instructional design texts or taught in many instructional design courses. For one reason, HC was a for-profit company that emphasized product design for clients seeking their own profits from the product. As such, this was a different business model than many instructional design firms that are organized to provide a service to clients. For example, the first phase of any project was business development, and since HC was a new media company, only certain kinds of projects were pursued, and only certain kinds of clients sought the company's expertise. This meant that the media to be employed were determined before the project began, not after instructional strategies and objectives had been established, which is contrary to many traditional instructional design process models. The executive VPs, in collaboration with the executive producers, the sales staff, and the clients, developed a vision for the end product early in the process. The focus of design was not on needs or problems; instead, it was on opportunities. One executive described the process of envisioning and proposing solutions and products to the clients as an A, B, C, … Q approach:

> We work with the client to see what they think they want, and what success criteria they desire. Then we go away and meet to create a proposal that presents several options. The A option basically spits back to the client what they said they wanted. The B and C options go a bit further, adding some elements that are a bit flashy, but not significantly different other than in production values and costs. Then we hit them with the Q version that blows them out of the water. It meets all their criteria, and is spectacular to boot. It's something they would never have thought of, and they usually go for it, even if it costs more. (Rory, Company President, HC in Austin)

Once the client had accepted the proposal and contracts were signed, the VPs and executive producers assembled a design and production team. As mentioned earlier, members of the team were assigned based on their expertise and ability. Design and development followed an iterative process that had very interesting characteristics, including an emergent approach to design based on rapid prototyping processes, client input and approvals, management that was motivating to creative types, and open and frequent communication between team members, executive managers, and clients. The processes employed for design were very nimble, as indicated by one executive producer:

> We have to be ready for anything. The initial ideas presented in the proposal we send to clients are just the starting point. We have to nimble, and ready to change at any point in the process. We always tell clients that the design doc is a living document. It can change based on how we begin to understand the situation, how they react to our ideas, and how the prototype testing goes. (DeAnne, Producer in HC Learning division)

Other emergent design characteristics were apparent in the distribution (geographically, or even virtually) of many design ideas and decisions. A project web site was the center of communication and documentation for the design process, storing project management plans and timelines, archives of all communications, and various files for approval of documentation or production elements (e.g., graphic treatments, scripts for video). The mission and vision documents for HC even expressed commitment to the "development of shared values to support effective client experience management." Such a dedication to experience, even at the level of managing client experience, reveals a desire to foster creativity at all levels of the organization, not just in design activities (McDonald, 2011; Sun, Williams, & Evans, 2011). This focus on experience went both directions: from HC to clients and from clients to HC. In one case, a client continued to contribute design ideas as the project unfolded. During the kickoff meeting, the client made evident his/her desire for effective and "magical" learning experiences that engaged children in playful activities and wonderment. He/she even went so far as to provide copies of Pine and Gilmore's *The Experience Economy* (1999) to everyone on the HC team. During the kickoff, the vice president used the theme of "841" to illustrate the ways in which "29 squared" could be remembered by children playing with the toys being designed. His presentation included magic tricks and other engaging play activities to drive home his experiential vision. Later, even though the design work had been turned over to HC designers, the client suggested in one communication: "I have some more ideas for our 841 games. How about hot potato with the toy? Or maybe a game where a story is told, and math facts have to be correctly recalled in order to move through the story?" (George, XXX Toys)

Overlapping design phases or layers (Gibbons & Duffin, 2001) that increased in detail were common. For example, rapid prototyping with significant client input and approval points was the common design and development strategy. In addition, information architecture was the primary concern for design decisions. In order to learn, HC designers expected learners to navigate through a variety of information organization and interaction schemes (spaces, categorizations, or people) to get to the desired or discovered materials and activities. Accessing information was for the purposes of solving problems or following a story, and information navigation strategies supported problem solving or narrative elements in the context of narrative situations.

Methods of contextual inquiry, including some of those suggested by Garrett (2003), were employed as design research methods. Task analyses, content identification and organization, as well as interviews with potential learners guided this form of design research (Beyer & Holtzblatt, 1999). A variety of possibilities for learner experience, presented in the form of scenarios, were distilled from learner stories, and used to design and develop detailed learning activities (Forlizzi & Ford, 2000). The use of principles of learning experience design appeared in many instances throughout the various projects. In particular, the four principles espoused by Parrish (2009) were common to many of the designs (e.g., plots, learners as protagonists, theme established through activity, and immersion in context). In fact, experiential world descriptions, complete with context, scenarios, characters, and storyline were established early in the process of the design, serving as a guide for further design activities and revisions (Wellings, 2008). For example, in one project designed to ready undereducated workers for positions in the high-tech industries in Texas (Russell & Bednar, 2001), an early form of "blended" classroom and computer-based interactive learning was created. The learning experiences utilized stories, role playing, challenge-based learning activities, and collaborative learning to help prepare the learners.

Finally, the people who designed and developed the learning experiences greatly influenced the nature of the product through their personalities, beliefs, and philosophies about design and learning. They came from different backgrounds that didn't always involve education. The first author noticed early in his observations that these folks talked differently. It was apparent from their terminology and language that their approach diverged from traditional instructional design in important ways. One example was the intermingling of the terms user, learner, and audience. These terms all meant the same thing, and referred to the people who were the target users/learners for the design projects. In many cases, beliefs about how to create meaningful and engaging learning experiences were the main influences on their decision-making (Lang, 2008). Some of the quotes from interviews indicate the commitment of individuals within the organization to designing innovative and effective learning products, regardless of their backgrounds:

> It is amazing that we can engage with clients who are interested in developing rich learning environments that have not been feasible before the advent of the computer and web technologies. (Layla, trained as product designer)
>
> We want the users of our products to feel connected to a community of learners outside their particular location and setting. (Gina, trained as instructional designer)
>
> The interactive experiences that we design are always a part of a larger experience that enhances individual experience through group experiences. (Marshall, trained as a programmer)
>
> We can provide so many experiences that learners wouldn't be able to do, like going back in time or building a bridge. (Sam, trained as a graphic artist)

In summary, the work at HC broadened the focus of instructional and learning design to include considerations of life patterns, goals, activities, contexts, repeated use, sharing, emotion, and much more. Rather than focusing on discrete events or product functions, design decisions were made from the perspective of enhancing the person's experience with the product or situation (Pine & Gilmore, 1999). Experiences include both internal and external events, from individual cognitive experiences (Carlson, 1997), to engagement in situations that take place between an individual and the world (Dewey, 1934), to co-experiences that took place in social contexts (Forlizzi & Battarbee, 2004). The design process that was captured at HC revealed some of the principles of learning experience design that have been suggested more recently by various scholars. These included:

- Thinking of learning as transactions that enable transformative experiences, including the personal qualities and temporal dimensions that influence learning experiences (Krishnan & Rajamanickam, 2004; Parrish, Wilson, & Dunlap, 2010).
- Aiming toward higher levels of experiential learning that feature aesthetic (Parrish, 2009) and powerful learning experiences (Rowland & Divasto, 2001).
- Creating worlds (situations and contexts) in which the experience will take place (Wellings, 2008).
- Theming the experience (Pine & Gilmore, 1999).
- Considering a "bigger picture" involving transformational and aesthetic outcomes (Doering & Veletsianos, 2008).

Not only did these folks talk differently, they worked differently in terms of how they focused on design and production models that created spectacular and effective learning experiences.

Bringing the Hollywood Studio to the University

Implementing the approach to design and production described above to enhance learning at a university is not as simple as it may seem. But the first author tried with some degree of success (Nelson, 2003) to create a production studio environment for learning. This was not a design studio with a particular approach to pedagogy (e.g., Clinton & Rieber, 2010); it was a production studio with design processes based in real world contexts.

As such, this studio approach brought a large degree of authenticity to the learning experiences of the students who were involved. A focus on learning experience design and production was integrated into three graduate courses in instructional technology: an instructional design class, a software development class, and a project management class. In the past, these courses were taught using traditional approaches, including in-class exercises based on decontextualized examples, readings from texts and journals, minimal collaboration, and individual final projects as a basis of student evaluation. This approach created huge limitations for the students, as the courses and students were isolated from each other, and taught in silos even when offered in the same semester. Moreover, the courses were removed from practical and authentic contexts, forcing students to see the content of courses as isolated stages of a process, not as integrated activities within a single process.

In an attempt to transform these classes, several problem scenarios were compiled that included possibilities for real and simulated interaction with clients. The instructor sought out clients, and in cases where none were available, the instructor took on the role of client without telling the students he was doing so (a little e-mail trickery sufficed to keep students believing a real client was on the other end of the messages, but after the semester was over, the instructor revealed his actual role as a pseudo-client). A set of performance expectations for various roles in the scenarios was created, along with major deadlines and ideas regarding the various working relationship among the three classes. As various problem scenarios were introduced by the clients to students at the beginning of the semester, each class member was invited to volunteer for problem scenarios that were personally appealing, although this process was monitored to ensure that at least one student from each class was on each project team. Once all students had volunteered for a team, the performance expectations document was distributed. Members of each team collaboratively worked to devise processes of design and production that would result in suitable artifacts as their part in the scenario unfolded.

Because each team was autonomous, no single description of the events that semester could fully capture each team's approach to design. In general, members of the project management class were in charge of the various projects. The project managers worked with the clients to establish project goals and then worked with their teams to identify and sequence project tasks. Members of the design class assisted project managers in completing a needs assessment and analysis. Members of the design class also developed a design plan that members of the project management class presented to the client for approval. After the clients approved the various design plans, members of the software development class produced prototypes based on the plan created by the design class. The prototypes were tested with target audiences. The project management class then produced an evaluation report and held a culminating meeting with the design team to reflect on the process and outcomes of the design project.

The distribution of students who were enrolled in three different courses that met on three different nights created challenging issues for communication within each team. Project managers maintained Web sites for each project. These Web sites allowed all team members to view work schedules, drafts of design plans, and prototypes. Team members could communicate with each other and the client through e-mail. An important feature was that, using the Web sites as guides, each group, for the most part, was self-directed and self-sufficient. The professor's role was to serve as a consultant to the teams at various points of difficulty, as a client when quick decisions were necessary regarding project goals or vision, and as a team member when production problems arose. By the end of the semester, the classes had successfully completed seven projects, and students remarked that the process, while arduous, was also meaningful, fun, and afforded them opportunities to learn in ways that were different from those in traditional graduate classes.

Although the experimental approach to teaching these courses had some problems, it was also encouraging to see some of the differences in learning that students experienced. First, the curriculum was composed of problems, not topics. Even the idea of teaching design skills and sensibilities as a topic in a curriculum is problematic because design is not an object of study; design is a mode of inquiry and exploration (Davis, Hawley, McMullan, & Spilka, 1997). Instead of a contrived curriculum presented through an artificial context, it was particularly effective for students to learn in an environment where design tasks and learning goals emerged from the situation at hand, along with constraints and challenges. So while a predetermined curriculum may not be essential, the adoption by a professor of a new pedagogical role is necessary and vital to students' success. Professors serve as facilitators and share their expertise as experienced designers. They can help students establish individual and small-group goals through the use of performance contracts (Rieber, 2000). They can moderate design evaluations, helping and encouraging learners to offer feedback to their peers. Professors can also model design expertise by helping students formulate alternatives for various student decisions as the design process unfolds.

Conclusions

The story told in this chapter has two endings: one for HC and the other for the teaching and learning of a professor and his students. While the ending for HC was a business merger, and eventual closing of the office in Austin, it was not without a lasting impact. Former employees moved on to continue creating spectacular learning environments at other companies. Some have become or are studying to become college professors, specializing in games for learning and other emerging instructional technologies that emphasize learning experience design. Questions of how designers use principles of learning experience design, and what processes they follow, were answered. The effects of organizational and management factors on creative design and production activities were observed and experiments in teaching with such a metaphor were conducted. These results suggest that a studio approach to support learning experience design is appropriate for a number of reasons, many of which have been argued by others (Brandt et al., 2011; Clinton & Rieber, 2010; Simpson, Burmeister, Boykiw, & Zhu, 2002).

In a teaching model that emphasized authentic learning experiences over direct instruction with exercises, students became designers and developers in many authentic ways. They worked collaboratively, using conversation, argumentation, and persuasion to achieve consensus about perspectives and actions that might move projects forward. Conflicting viewpoints were debated, and differences of opinion were negotiated. In this way, dialog transformed individual thinking, creating collective thought and socially constructed knowledge within the team (Sherry & Myers, 1998). Beyond working collaboratively, the student designers tended to be self-organized both individually and within their collaborative groups (Thomas & Harri-Augstein, 1985). They largely accepted responsibility for their own learning by identifying their own purposes, setting goals for learning, implementing learning strategies, and identifying appropriate resources and tools.

The most noticeable difference observed between learning experience design and more traditional instructional design was the focus of the design teams on larger, more powerful outcomes beyond simple learning objectives (Chen, 2010). If we can accept the challenge to think in broader terms as we approach instructional design opportunities (Wilson, Parrish, & Veletsianos, 2008), then perhaps we can attain the level of aesthetic, transformational learning experiences that many scholars have envisioned, as suggested by Toshiko Mori:

> We have to create an atmosphere and a space where students and teachers can do their most creative work. I compare it to being a film producer instead of a director. ... You produce a body of work ... by putting people, ingredients, and stories together to make things happen. Education is invisible really. So you have to make certain intellectual, aesthetic, and spiritual investments. (Szenasy, 2003)

Notes

The bulk of the research data described here consisted of field notes (more than 150 handwritten pages in a design journal), along with transcripts of structured interviews with 25 producers, designers, associate producers, and production specialists. In addition, meeting minutes and action lists from design and production meetings, and documentation produced by the participants during various design and production activities were used as part of the data set. Written documentation of information used by managers for business planning, training, and managing the various design and production teams was also included in the data collection process.

Data was analyzed using a qualitative lens as described by Eisner (1998), following a data reduction process advocated by Miles and Huberman (1994). Data from the interview transcripts, field notes, and documents were coded into categories using a qualitative data analysis software tool. The data were initially parsed to remove any references to common work functions, business logistics, office support, or other non-project information not directly related to design and production (e.g., timesheet, xerox, memo).

Fictional names for people and companies are utilized to maintain the anonymity of participants in the projects described.

About the Authors

Wayne Nelson is currently University Fellow for Online Learning and Assessment at Southern Illinois University Edwardsville, after more than 25 years of teaching educational psychology and instructional technology, as well as serving as a Department Chairman. His research interests have included investigations of the characteristics of learning with various interactive media, and the processes utilized to design learning activities and environments. In addition to teaching and research, he has maintained extensive involvement in efforts to integrate technology into the classrooms and curricula of schools, and as a consultant to a variety of companies about learning, training, and design processes.

David Palumbo has built a career around the creation of profitable and effective learning systems that bridge the paradoxes of learning in a digital age. From his current position as Chief Academic Officer at National Heritage Academies, he concerns himself with leading and managing a corporation devoted to challenging each child to achieve personally in more than 80 charter schools across the nation. As a teacher, research scholar, academic administrator, entrepreneur, consultant, salesman, and corporate executive, Dr. Palumbo has carved a unique global position in the business of learning.

References

Abramson, B. (2005). *Digital phoenix: Why the information economy collapsed and how it will rise gain.* Cambridge, MA: MIT Press.

Beyer, H., & Holtzblatt, K. (1999). Contextual design. *Interactions, 6*(1), 32–42.

Brandt, C. B., Cennamo, K., Douglas, S., Vernon, M., McGrath, M., & Reimer, Y. (2011). A theoretical framework for the studio as a learning environment. *International Journal of Technology and Design Education, 23*(2), 329–348.

Brown, J. S. (2006). New learning environments for the 21st century: Exploring the edge. *Change, 38*(5), 18–24.

Carlson, R. (1997). *Experienced cognition*. New York: Lawrence Erlabaum Associates.

Chen, P. (2010). Experience design: A framework for e-learning design and research. In D. Gibson & B. Dodge (Eds.), *Proceedings of Society for Information Technology & Teacher Education International Conference 2010* (pp. 2580–2582). Chesapeake, VA: AACE.

Christianson, C. M. (1997). *The innovator's dilemma*. New York: Harper Business.

Clinton, G., & Rieber, L. P. (2010). The studio experience at the University of Georgia: An example of constructionist learning for adults. *Educational Technology Research and Development, 58*(6), 755–780.

Davis, M., Hawley, P., McMullan, B., & Spilka, G. (1997). *Design as a catalyst for learning*. Alexandria, VA: Association for Supervision and Curriculum Development.

Dewey, J. (1934). *Art as experience*. Carbondale, IL: Southern Illinois University Press.

Doering, A., & Veletsianos, G. (2008). What lies beyond effectiveness and efficiency? Adventure learning design. *The Internet and Higher Education, 11*(3–4), 137–144.

Eisner, E. (1998). *The enlightened eye: Qualitative inquiry and the enhancement of educational practice*. Upper Saddle River, NJ: Merrill.

Fleming, L., & Marx, M. (2006). Managing creativity in small worlds. *California Management Review, 48*(4), 6–27.

Forlizzi, J., & Battarbee, K. (2004). Understanding experience in interactive systems. In *Proceedings of the 2004 conference on designing interactive systems processes, practices, methods, and techniques—DIS '04* (pp. 261–268). New York, NY: ACM Press.

Forlizzi, J., & Ford, S. (2000). The building blocks of experience: An early framework for interaction designers. In *Designing Interactive Systems 2000 Conference Proceedings* (pp. 419–423). New York, NY.

Garrett, J. J. (2003). *The elements of user experience*. Indianapolis, IA: New Riders.

Gibbons, A. S., & Duffin, J. (2001). Understanding designs and improving the design process through a layered approach. In *17th Annual Conference on Distance Teaching and Learning*. Madison, WI: The Board of Regents of the University of Wisconsin System.

Krishnan, L. R., & Rajamanickam, V. (2004). Experience-enabling design: An approach to elearning design. *elearningpost Blog*. Retrieved June 4, 2010, from http://www.elearningpost.com/articles/archives/experience_enabling_design_an_approach_to_elearning_design.

Lamos, J. P., & Parrish, P. (1994). *What Hollywood can teach us about producing multimedia instruction*. Nashville, TN: Association for Educational Communications and Technology.

Lampel, J., & Shamsie, J. (2003). Capabilities in motion: New organizational forms and the reshaping of the Hollywood movie industry. *Journal of Management Studies, 40*(8), 2189–2210.

Lang, M. (2008). The influence of disciplinary backgrounds on design practices in Web-based systems development. *Central European Conference on Information and Intelligent Systems*. Retrieved from http://www.ceciis.foi.hr/app/index.php/ceciis/2008/paper/view/131.

McDonald, J. K. (2011). The creative spirit of design. *TechTrends, 55*(5), 53–58.

Meyer, M. H., & Marion, T. J. (2010). Innovating for effectiveness: Lessons from design firms. *Research Technology Management, 53*(5), 21–28.

Miles, M., & Huberman, A. M. (1994). *Qualitative data analysis*. Thousand Oaks, CA: Sage.

Nelson, W. A. (2003). Problem solving through design. In D. Knowlton & D. Sharp (Eds.), *Problem-based learning in the information age* (pp. 39–44). San Francisco: Jossey-Bass.

Parrish, P. (2009). Aesthetic principles for instructional design. *Educational Technology Research and Development, 57*(4), 511–528.

Parrish, P., Wilson, B. G., & Dunlap, J. (2010). Learning experience as transaction: A framework for instructional design. *Educational Technology, 51*(2), 15–21.

Pine, J., & Gilmore, J. (1999). *The experience economy*. Boston: Harvard Business School Press.

Pratt, A. (2009). Situating the production of new media: The case of San Francisco (1995–2000). In A. McKinlay & C. Smith (Eds.), *Creative labour: Working in creative industries* (pp. 195–209). London: Palgrave.

PRNewswire. (1997). Human code publishes upgrade to classic edutainment CD-ROM: The cartoon history of the universe. *The Free Library*. Retrieved August 21, 2012, from http://www.thefreelibrary.com/Human+Code+Publishes+Upgrade+to+Classic+Edutainment+CD-ROM,+The...-a019309063.

Rhodes, S. (2000). Learning code. In J. Bourdeau & R. Heller (Eds.), *Proceedings of World Conference on Educational Multimedia, Hypermedia and Telecommunications 2000* (pp. 1784–1785). Chesapeake, VA: Association for the Advancement of Computers in Education.

Rieber, L. P. (2000). The studio experience: Educational reform in instructional technology. In D. G. Brown (Ed.), *Best practices in computer enhanced teaching and learning* (pp. 195–196). Winston-Salem, NC: Wake Forest Press.

Rowland, G., & Divasto, T. (2001). Instructional design and powerful learning. *Performance Improvement Quarterly, 14*(2), 7–36.

Russell, M. G. & Bednar, D. K. (2001). Entertech: An engine for personalized, collaborative training. In C. Montgomerie & J. Viteli (Eds.), *Proceedings of World Conference on Educational Multimedia, Hypermedia and Telecommunications 2001* (pp. 1601–1602). Chesapeake, VA: AACE.

Seidel, S. (2011). Toward a theory of managing creativity-intensive processes: A creative industries study. *Information Systems and e-Business Management, 9*(4), 407–446.

Sherry, L., & Myers, K. (1998). The dynamics of collaborative design. *IEEE Transactions on Professional Communication, 41*(2), 123–139.

Simpson, M., Burmeister, J., Boykiw, A., & Zhu, J. (2002). Successful studio-based real-world projects in IT education. In T. Greening & R. Lister (Eds.), *Conferences in research and practice in information technology* (Vol. 20). Adelaide: Australian Computer Society.

Sun, Q., Williams, A., & Evans, M. (2011). A theoretical design management framework. *The Design Journal, 14*(1), 112–132.

Szenasy, S. S. (2003). Class notes: Tschumi and Mori on the education of architects. *Metropolis Magazine*. Retrieved July 22, 2010, from http://www.metropolismag.com/story/20030801/class-notes.

Thomas, L., & Harri-Augstein, S. (1985). *Self-organised learning*. London, UK: Routledge.

Wellings, P. (2008). Create the world, the interface will follow. *Adaptive Path Ideas Blog*. Retrieved July 13, 2010, from http://www.adaptivepath.com/ideas/create-the-world-the-interface-will-follow.

Wilson, B. G., Parrish, P. E., & Veletsianos, G. (2008). Raising the bar for instructional outcomes: Toward transformative learning experiences. *Educational Technology, 48*(3), 39–44.

Understanding and Examining Design Activities with Cultural Historical Activity Theory

Lisa C. Yamagata-Lynch

Keywords Cultural historical activity theory (CHAT) • Vygotsky • Activity theory • Activity systems analysis • Leontiev • Engeström • Corporate training • Instructional design • Design models • Mediated action • Sociocultural • Qualitative research

The goals of this chapter are to discuss the need in instructional technology to understand design within the context of complex real-world human activities and identify methods for examining these activities. I will build a case for cultural historical activity theory (CHAT) as one suitable theoretical framework for this examination. In building this case, I will describe how my experience as a corporate instructional design intern 17 years prior to writing this chapter affected my identity as an instructional designer and my future interest in both research and practice. I will share my perspective on the challenges that the field of instructional technology has historically encountered when examining design. I will then introduce CHAT and activity systems analysis as the framework and analytical lens that I now rely on since my instructional design intern experience. As an example analysis, I will share a real-life design scenario that was published in a *New York Times* article about a family's experience designing and building a passive home in Vermont, United States. I will present an activity systems analysis of the design scenario from a CHAT perspective. The example is not necessarily an instructional design activity, but is a complex real-world design situation that is well suited to a CHAT analysis. I will conclude the chapter with discussions on future implications to instructional design when designers conceptualize their work as a complex in-the-moment transactional activity.

L.C. Yamagata-Lynch, Ph.D. (✉)
Educational Psychology and Counseling, University of Tennessee,
A532 Bailey Education Complex, Knoxville, TN 37996, USA
e-mail: LisaYL@utk.edu

B. Hokanson and A. Gibbons (eds.), *Design in Educational Technology*,
Educational Communications and Technology: Issues and Innovations 1,
DOI 10.1007/978-3-319-00927-8_6, © Springer International Publishing Switzerland 2014

My Encounter with Corporate Culture Training

I was a corporate instructional design intern immediately after I completed my master's degree. In this experience, I encountered a situation where I found a series of complex human activities critical to my design project that was inseparable from the sociocultural context of the project and myself. At the time, I did not have any formal training in how to capture the interactions described above among the sociocultural context, the design activities, and myself. Since then, based on the research and practice I have engaged in, I have a better understanding of the nature of human activity and its relation to design, which I will share in this chapter. When I introduce the design project, I will share information about myself to the extent that is useful for the reader to gain an insider perspective on my experience. Due to the nondisclosure agreement with the company, my discussion about the context of the design activity will be kept anonymous and fairly limited. Nevertheless, my reflections will help the reader understand why it became critical to my work that as a designer I understand complex real-world human activities and how that affected who I became as a researcher and a practitioner.

Personal Background

Much like other students who enter an instructional technology graduate program, I did not know much about the field until I started my coursework. I obtained my master's degree in instructional technology at a large Midwestern university in the mid-1990s. This was my first experience living in the United States and pursuing a degree at a public coeducational institution. I spent an intensive 2-year period completing my degree as a full-time student while I learned real-world English rather than in a classroom in Japan while I studied the language and adapted my cultural norms to better blend into the predominant Midwestern culture.

Prior to coming to the United States, I spent my entire life in Japan, where I was born and raised as an Irish-American and Japanese biracial person. I grew up at a time that was less than 30 years after World War II, when Japan was transforming itself into an economic superpower while healing from the crippling effects of the previous government making large investments in a war they lost. At that time there were not a whole lot of biracial children or foreign individuals living in Japan, so, needless to say, I always stood out as "the minority."

My parents enrolled me in a K-12, international girl's Catholic school, where all subjects were taught in English. However, my home language was Japanese, so I never considered English my native language. After graduating high school, I went to a Japanese Catholic women's university and completed my degree in cognitive experimental psychology. Soon after, I moved to the United States because it was customary in Japan to start graduate work shortly after graduating from college, especially in the field of psychology. I was 22 years old at the time, entering adulthood, and part of my goal in coming to the United States was to find out who I was becoming as an adult working to embrace my biracial background. I had worked so hard my entire life up to that point to fit into the Japanese community, when I had no chance to blend in because I looked too White. Once I finished my master's degree, it was time for me to decide whether to stay in the United States or go home to Japan. To help my decision-making process, I accepted a position as an instructional design intern for an American global company at their Japanese training division.

Instructional Design Intern Experience

When I arrived at the corporate office in Japan, which I will refer to as Global Communications Company from here on, I was given two tasks to complete during the 3-month internship. One task was to evaluate a vendor course on creativity in the workplace following Kirkpatrick's evaluation model (Kirkpatrick & Kirkpatrick, 2006) and to redesign the course from a 3-day event to a 2-day event with the intention to cut costs. My second task, which greatly affected the choices I made for the rest of my career, was to create a prototype of an eight-hour training on corporate culture following Gagne's nine events of instruction (Gagne, 1985). My Caucasian American expat supervisor explained to me that the Japanese employees of the Global Communications Company were not behaving in a manner that their employees from any other part of the world would. He further explained to me that

> The Japanese employees do not act like they are Xxx-ans [corporate name with "ans" to show membership in the group]. When I go to the corporate office in Korea or Singapore I know the moment I walk in that I am at our company because the employees act and do business like they are Xxx-ans. (Conversation with my supervisor, in May 1996)

When I heard what my supervisor explained to me, I had a strong reaction that this was not an eight-hour training problem. My supervisor agreed with me but reminded me that my job was to treat it as an eight-hour training problem and make my best attempt at designing the prototype because that was the starting point for the corporate headquarters investing their time in examining the problem.

As far as a first assignment in the real-world went, this project quickly became complicated when compared to projects in my graduate program that were usually about designing and developing training materials about procedural tasks like what to do when you have a flat tire. This project made me examine myself as a person and what role I took as a designer in the situation at hand. I realized that my graduate training gave me all the tools I needed to treat the corporate culture problem as an eight-hour training problem, which meant that I knew how to systematically approach design in a seemingly sequential manner. However, I did not know how to capture data about complex human activities that I so desperately wanted to understand in this situation.

At this point, I had no formal training in qualitative research, but I started the project by collecting survey data among Japanese employees. I then interviewed employees in Japan in person and then, on the phone, non-Japanese employees from the corporate headquarters and other Asian offices. I even had an email transaction related to this topic with the corporate CFO, who was the grandson of the founder of the company. I then reviewed documents, including popular press publications written about the company; business journal articles about the company; and both print and video materials the corporate press produced for public distribution. I was impressed by how my supervisor enabled me to gain access to people higher up in the corporate hierarchy and that they were willing to spend their time talking to me about corporate culture.

I learned from these experiences that many employees at the company were proud of the corporate culture set in place by the founder. There were several stories about how the founder took care of his employees during the depression era in the United States and fiercely disapproved of compromising quality in product development based on decisions driven by cutting costs. These stories were typically introduced to employees as informal narratives shared by experienced employees, but as the company became bigger and global, there were some challenges in managing the oral history tradition for developing and maintaining corporate culture.

During interviews with Japanese employees, I learned that several of them envied how American employees acted as true Xxx-ans and how they longed to become Xxx-ans themselves. However, this was difficult because of how the Japanese office was deliberately set up differently than most of the other offices in other parts of the world in hopes to make it easier for the company to enter the traditional and tight Japanese market. With my own background being bicultural and with a mixed race appearance, I had tried for most of my life desperately to find a place for myself as a unique individual in a highly homogenous culture. When I encountered the design project at the Global Communications Company, I felt compassion for the Japanese employees. I suddenly realized that there were similarities between the design situation for which I was charged to develop a prototype and the core of my personal struggles. With this realization, I became determined that my job as an instructional designer had to include being an advocate for my target audience and ensuring that their voice was heard though nobody else might even notice. The design solution I propose had to provide opportunities for the learners to become empowered Xxx-ans. Audience advocacy was something I had never encountered during my training as an instructional designer, and once again I had no way to deal with this overwhelming need to serve the learners.

Design Solution and Where It Took Me

At the end of the 3-month internship, the eight-hour training I designed consisted of several stories that had been traditionally passed on from one generation of employees to another as cases for participants to analyze and reflect. I saw that my job was to become a storyteller of the corporate culture and give opportunities for Japanese employees to reflect on how to conduct business as Xxx-ans. I did not know it then, but I was approaching design in a manner that was much closer to developing a story of learner experiences as discussed by Parrish (2006) as a result of my overwhelming empathy towards them. I chose this approach in place of what

I was taught in my graduate program, which led me to believe that design was a simple sequential process once the analysis was complete. Additionally, I prepared a document for my supervisor that outlined issues beyond the eight-hour training that need to be taken into consideration by the corporate headquarters for the problem to find a resolution. At that point, I chose to go to the United States once again to pursue a doctorate degree and learn more about methods for capturing complex human activities in a manner that can be insightful to designers. In this process I moved away professionally from being a cognitive experimental design researcher to a social constructivist qualitative researcher and practitioner.

The Challenging Task of Conceptualizing Design Activities: The Struggles I Resonate With

Instructional technologists would agree that they belong to a field in which theory and practice intersect through design of human learning and performance. However, it has been unclear how to go about making a contribution to this theory and practice intersection because the theoretical discussions are typically isolated from the culturally embedded practice of design. Historically, scholars in this field have been predominantly influenced by the traditional scientific method and experimental design approach for pursuing generalizable claims within research settings where variables are purposefully broken down to their simplest forms with the intention to remove bias from observations and the likelihood of the observations being accounted to error.

There have been significant efforts put into interpreting, applying, and testing theories related to human learning and performance with the hope of uncovering useful, objective, and, at times, generalizable design theories/principles/strategies (e.g., Reigeluth, 1983). In another line of well-circulated work, there have been scholars who disseminate design models/procedures that are aimed to help instructional designers, especially novices, to engage in design work with a systematic approach (e.g., Dick, Carey, & Carey, 2008; Smaldino, Lowther, & Russell, 2011). While efforts such as the above are methods of interpreting and developing understandings of design, they have contributed to the development of a vigorous line of research that does not examine learning and design as it takes place in real-world situations. In fact there is a lack of focus on asking the very question of how people design in instructional design situations (Bichelmeyer, Boling, & Gibbons, 2006).

While it was not the original intentions, the proliferation of the theory-driven and systems-driven approach to design promoted instructional technologists to focus their energy on contributing to the development of theories and models that are far removed from practice. These types of works have promoted the oversimplification of design as a human activity. It has contributed to stunting opportunities for instructional technology researchers and practitioners to examine design activities in real-world settings.

Design, as I understand it now in the real-world, can be described as a goal-driven, problem-solving activity with the purpose of identifying solutions while developing both intangible design artifacts in the form of mental representations and tangible artifacts (Jonassen, 2000a). Design is an ill-defined and ill-structured human activity defined by its goals, constraints, and criteria for measuring its success for addressing the problem at hand (Cross, 2006, 2008). This type of approach to design requires designers to engage in a complex reflective process in real-world contexts while they explore various modes of thinking beyond the sequential structure (Lawson & Dorst, 2009).

In the field of instructional technology, there may be an agreement that design is an ill-defined activity, but the structure associated with design is treated as an oversimplified, at times non-reflective sequential event. This has led to a situation where design as practiced by instructional designers in real-world settings has become a mystical activity. Additionally, there is yet to be any agreed upon method to study or communicate findings about design activities. Over time, researchers in instructional technology have become more or less irrelevant to practitioners because practitioners find that theory development and research are disseminated in forms that are inaccessible to them and difficult to contribute their practical knowledge (Lynham, 2000), and they find that theories do not address design questions in real-world situations (Yanchar, South, Williams, Allen, & Wilson, 2010).

I am not the first researcher/practitioner to point this out. For example, there were heated exchanges surrounding how to conceptualize learning in practice and how that affects instructional design in the 1990s. Several authors at the time were interested in examining learning in practice both from situative and constructivist perspectives. Some of these representative works include, but are not limited to, Duffy and Jonassen (1992); Duffy, Lowyck, and Jonassen (1991); and Duffy and Cunningham (1996). In these works, some of which were edited volumes, numerous authors introduced constructivism as an alternative epistemology for understanding how people learn and engage in everyday activities. They often made a point about how most instructional design models are primarily based on the positivist epistemology that inevitably identified design as a set of procedures to be followed rather than an activity that instructional designers engage in real-world settings (see Duffy & Jonassen, 1992). The efforts made by these authors became the foundational works for introducing and legitimizing non-positivist frameworks in instructional technology, such as situated cognition, legitimate peripheral participation, community of practice, and social constructivism.

More recently the professional conversations regarding development research brought some attention to design and development relevant to practice (e.g., Reeves, Herrington, & Oliver, 2004). This growing interest is highlighted in an *Educational Technology Research and Development* (ETR&D) two-volume special issue (see ETR&D volume 52 numbers 3 and 4). These works identified how to engage in development research while addressing real-world design questions especially related to online learning environments. As part of this discussion, Wang and Hannafin (2005) pointed out that while theoretical frameworks based on non-positivist epistemologies have become popular in instructional technology, methodologically we tend to rely on the experimental design approach that cannot fully address the complexities involved in research questions that are raised from a non-positivist standpoint.

When I initially encountered both of the above exchanges that unfolded in front of my very eyes, my reaction was "Yes, I am a constructivist" and "Yes, I am a development researcher." However, in both cases, I realized that aligning myself to constructivist epistemology with a development research methodology did not help change my practice as a researcher and practitioner of design. These exchanges helped me think through who I was as a scholar and practitioner, but I realized that there is much more work to be done on my part for being able to work with the ill-defined and ill-structured nature of design. I now see that a designer's work requires him/her to create a manageable structure within ill-defined and ill-structured situations to be able to understand, communicate, evaluate, and address the design problem. Aligning myself to an epistemology and a methodological approach did not provide me with a solution for how to go about addressing design; it provided me a guide for my ongoing development as a researcher and practitioner of design.

In its current state, research and practice of instructional design continue to stay removed from one another because the professional conversation has not moved beyond epistemological and methodological discussions. As a field, instructional technology needs to develop new understandings about design activities in real-world settings. Our work needs to transition from uncovering oversimplified universal principles, which may or may not be relevant to unique design situations, to identifying how we can examine design in action. In this process there needs to be more time spent on understanding and describing real-world design activities rather than being content with the false assumption that prescription-based works related to design that are detached from everyday contexts are intellectually superior to understanding practice itself.

This will require many scholars in instructional technology to embrace and make use of works that emphasize particularization as practiced in qualitative research and explained by Stake (1995, 2010). In these works the complexities involved in who, what, when, where, why, and how of design activities need to be addressed to identify how our investigations would help understand the transformations that the designed artifacts, designers, stakeholders, users, and the social context of the designed artifacts undergo. We need to collectively work on this reconceptualization of design as a lived experience and engage in further conversations about methodologies for observing, examining, and understanding this phenomenon.

Instructional Technology and Cultural Historical Activity Theory: The Way I See the World

CHAT is a framework that is based on Lev Vygotsky's work during the 1920s and 1930s. Vygotsky passed away in his late 30s after a long battle with tuberculosis, and his work did not have the time to fully develop. Vygotsky's original works can be difficult to locate in the present time because there are no centers that collect his entire work and make them available to scholars (van der Veer, 1997). Furthermore, many of his works were affected by censorship during the Soviet era, and since then some of his works encountered translation problems from Russian to English.

Fig. 1 Vygotsky's basic
mediated action triangle
(adapted from Cole &
Engeström (1993))

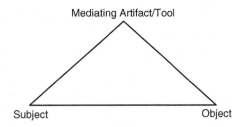

Contemporary scholars who study Vygotsky are charged with the work of interpreting his work and finding relevance to current issues (van der Veer, 2008). Despite the difficulties associated with reading Vygotsky's works in English, he has influenced many North American scholars who are moving away from a positivist theoretical and methodological framework.

Among instructional technologists, CHAT has been identified as one framework for scholars to take when examining design (Jonassen, 2000b; DeVane & Squire, 2012; Yamagata-Lynch, 2010) because it can accommodate to real-world complexities. While CHAT has not necessarily been used in our field consistently to examine design, it has been warranted as a viable topic entry in the second Handbook of Educational Communications and Technology (see Barab, Evans, & Baek, 2003). Additionally, there has been various studies related to instructional technology using this framework for analytical purposes to (a) summarize organizational change related to an online community (Barab, Schatz, & Scheckler, 2004), (b) identify guidelines for designing constructivist learning environments (Jonassen & Rohrer-Murphy, 1999), and (c) follow moment-to-moment developments in learning environments (Barab, Barnett, Yamagata-Lynch, Squire, & Keating, 2002; Yamagata-Lynch, 2003).

From a CHAT perspective, human psychology is conceptualized as a series of activities involving individuals engaging with the environment and artifacts in the environment while they coevolve (Cole, 1996; Cole & Engeström, 1993; Wertsch, 1991). This dialectical human learning/developmental process is often explained by interpretations of Vygotsky's (1978) work on mediated action made by contemporary authors such as Michael Cole and James Werstch. In mediated action individuals take the role within an activity as the subject, while they engage with artifacts in the environment that take the role of a tool for the subject to attain the object of the activity. Researchers and practitioners can start to conceptualize the phenomenon they are examining in action rather than a set of static variables when the focus of analysis is mediated action.

Mediated action as a process involves an object that can be defined as the goal and motive for subjects to participate in an activity while they take advantage of the mediating artifact or the tool (Cole, 1996; Leontiev, 1978) (Fig. 1). Most CHAT scholars agree that the "object" is the reason why individuals and groups of individuals, as the subject, choose to participate in an activity (Kaptelinin, 2005; Nardi, 2005). Therefore, the object is what holds the elements in an activity together (Hyysalo, 2005).

Fig. 2 Engeström's activity
system (adapted with
permission from Engeström
1987)

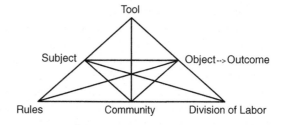

Discussions on mediated action among North American authors over the last 4 decades have focused on observational data in real-world settings. However, CHAT authors in Russia, who worked closely with Vygotsky, have embraced the assumption that human activity involves both observable experiences and mental activities (El'konin, 1993; Galperin, 1989). The lack of discussion on mental activities among North American scholars was not a deliberate choice made by authors such as Michael Cole and James Wertsch, who made Vygotsky's work accessible to the English speaking community throughout the 1960s until the present. Instead, it was a reflection of how the professional dialogue and interest among educational scholars who read Cole and Wertsch's works were developing at the time. When Cole and Wertsch's works on Vygotsky were first published, many North American scholars had doubts about the cognitive revolution. There was a growing interest in understanding how human learning took place in naturalistic environments. In response to the cognitive perspective, the situative perspective did not emphasize cognitive processes that coupled the observed experiences. As a result, there is currently a void in discussions on how to analyze both observable human experiences and mental activities among North American CHAT scholars.

Leontiev (1978) made further distinctions between actions and activities. According to him, actions are temporary and can be characterized as steps within activities. He further explained that actions are often focused on individual participants and may not have collective implications. In my work, I have found that the outcomes of actions taken within activities may bring reasons for the overall activity to be modified and transformed with the individuals participating in the activity while the objects stay constant.

Engeström (1987) expanded the concept of mediated action from a sociocultural perspective and included contextual components into the model derived from Vygotsky's work and introduced a new model as activity systems (Fig. 2). In an activity system the top triangle is identical to the mediated action triangle including the subject, object, and the tool (Fig. 1). The new components included rules, community, and division of labor. Both formal and informal rules can be included in the rule component of an activity system that affects the subject's experiences. The community can be the group of individuals that affect the subject's experience in the activity. The division of labor is any task that may be shared among the community members while the subject is engaging in an activity.

Engeström (1987, 1993) discussed how human activity can be affected by systemic contextual contradictions that bring tensions into the subject's ability to attain the object. Within the model, he uses a diagonal line to represent these tensions. Tensions arise when the conditions in the context of the activity put the subject in contradictory situations and make it difficult to achieve the object or impact the nature of participation in the activity (Yamagata-Lynch, 2010). At the same time, tensions can drive the subject to change how to engage in an activity (Engeström, 1993).

In more recent discussions regarding CHAT, Stetsenko has introduced the Transformative Activist Stance (TAS) (Stetsenko, 2005, 2008, 2010). From a TAS perspective, CHAT scholars need to pay attention to how human beings not only engage in learning through a dialectical process of interacting with the environment and social others but also are transforming themselves and the environment while they develop a new identity through experiences and their reflections on those experiences. As a developmental process, learners are changing themselves as well as the environment when they engage in learning activities.

CHAT as a theoretical framework works with complexities involved in human activity, unlike other frameworks often referred to in instructional technology, and CHAT does not disregard complexities to fit its work into a process of building a generalizable model. CHAT affords designers a rich appreciation of human learning and design activities. CHAT is not a design model, but, as it will be demonstrated in the sample case that follows, it provides a framework for designers to analyze, understand, and communicate complex design situations while developing an understanding of ill-defined and ill-structured problems.

Sample Case Description

The sample case is from a 2010 *New York Times* article by Tom Zeller Jr., located at http://www.nytimes.com/2010/09/26/business/energy-environment/26smart. html?_r=1&pagewanted=1&ref=general&src=me. The article and the accompanying video on *The New York Times* website describe the Landau family's experience building an energy-efficient passive home in the state of Vermont, United States, which is a rather cold area of the country. The article is written to showcase an interesting and unique home construction project one family chose to experience for the purpose of ultimate energy conservation. It also showcases the difficulties they encountered in the design and construction process.

According to the article, passive homes are more popular in Europe than the United States and are designed in a manner that takes advantage of the sunlight, extremely thick insulation, and materials that allow the construction of an airtight home that requires minimal heat. In the United States, building a passive home is far more costly than building a conventional home; however, it is said that passive homes can save up to 90% of heating and cooling energy compared to conventional homes. Passive home standards in the United States are not well established or well known, but the article noted a growing interest in this type of home in the United

States and mentioned that Habitat for Humanities was exploring passive home construction for future projects.

In the video segment of the newspaper article, Mr. Landau reflects on how awe struck he was when he read a book about a European passive home that was heated by the body heat of the occupants and a teakettle in the kitchen. As a family, the Landaus had prior experience building and living in a home that was certified as energy efficient in the United States, but they were curious about how they could design and build a home that was even more efficient. They decided for their new home they would take on the challenge of building a passive home in the United States. They were aware that in the United States their experience would not necessarily follow the ideal scenario that was presented in the book Mr. Landau read because architects and builders were not familiar with passive home construction or the standards provided by the European Passive Home Institute.

The Landau family began their design and building process by hiring an American architect and builder, who did not have experience building passive homes but was willing to learn about its particularities and had access to a passive home design architectural software. In the design and construction process, the family quickly found that, without a large demand in the US market for building passive homes, materials for their new home had to be special ordered and custom made. This made the project significantly more costly than what can be expected in Europe. Furthermore, ironically, because passive homes are not part of the United States government's federally supported green building program, the Landau family found that they could not meet the standards set by the Energy Star or Leadership in Energy and Environmental Design (LEED) programs even though their new home was going to be far more energy efficient and environmentally responsible than conventional homes that met the above requirements. If they were to meet the requirements of federally supported programs, it was going to compromise the efficiency of their home. As a result, the Landau family did not qualify for several of the tax incentives provided to homeowners that met green building requirements.

The reporter further discusses how the Landau family had difficulties in managing expectations related to building a home in Vermont. For example, they experienced social pressure from friends questioning why on Earth they wanted to spend so much money on constructing a passive home and why they could not build a conventional home instead. The explanations the family provided to their friends did not seem to help their friends to gain a better understanding of the Landaus' motives. In another example, included in the video segment, Mrs. Landau describes how she and her family realized that their expectations of common design features in a conventional home in Vermont were at times incompatible with passive home construction. Mrs. Landau wanted a wood-burning fireplace in her new passive home. Living in Vermont, she could not imagine a house without a fireplace. The architects initially told her that it would overheat the house and that it could not be accommodated into the passive home design, but after several negotiations they were able to come to a conclusion that they could strategically locate insulation to prevent the home from overheating and the family could open a window; however, the family was informed that this could jeopardize the likelihood of meeting the passive home certification requirements. Finally, the family experienced difficulties finding an insurance company that would insure their home because they did not have plans for installing a furnace. Insurance companies were concerned that the plumbing would burst during the cold winter months and refused to insure their home.

The New York Times article was written during the construction process of the Landau family home and does not provide information on how the process finalized. It does state that the family was able to keep working on the construction because they had the financial ability to do so. The family fully intended to have the home certified through the Passive Home Institute in Europe. However, in the process of building a home that met the building codes in the United States with typical design features in a conventional home that the family could not give up, it was unclear whether their home would meet the European certification requirements.

Sample Case Analysis: How I Would Go about It

In this section I will present an activity systems analysis of the sample case described in the previous section to address the complex design situation from a CHAT perspective. Please note that while I am the primary and sole author of this case analysis, participants in a course on activity systems analysis methods I taught in 2010 contributed their ideas while we used this case in class. Each member of the course, including myself, engaged in a thematic analysis of the data, using the constant comparative method (Corbin & Strauss, 2008). Then we shared our thematic analysis and individually constructed activity systems based on the thematic analysis. I took the lead and presented a series of activity systems that followed the narrative scenario in the newspaper article, and participants shared their model. We jointly modified my model and generated a composite model. The activity system I am presenting in this paper is the modified model based on course participant input (Fig. 3).

The activity systems model for this case includes the Landau family experience as the main activity and an ideal activity nested into the tool component of the main activity. This ideal activity is based on what Mr. Landau read about building a passive home in Europe. This nested activity was based on a book that Mr. Landau read that excited him and his family to become motivated to build a passive home in Vermont. This ideal activity was not necessarily an activity that the Landaus experienced or observed in action, but became a cognitive tool that they referred to while engaging in the subsequent design-related actions and the activity.

In the ideal activity, European homeowners are the subject with the object to build a passive home. They have access to tools such as off-the-shelf material, experienced builders and architects, and a clear expectation for certification requirements. In this activity homeowners work with clearly set guidelines for building a passive home for certification purposes. Homeowners do not have to explain their motives for building a passive home to their friends because there are other passive homeowners who share a common set of values for building this type of home. Thus, in general, there is a supportive community of other homeowners and builders.

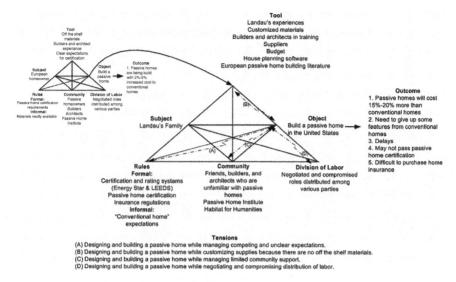

Tensions
(A) Designing and building a passive home while managing competing and unclear expectations.
(B) Designing and building a passive home while customizing supplies because there are no off the shelf materials.
(C) Designing and building a passive home while managing limited community support.
(D) Designing and building a passive home while negotiating and compromising distribution of labor.

Fig. 3 Activity systems analysis of Landau family experience building a passive home

As part of the community in this activity, the Passive Home Institute provides information and guidelines to homeowners and contractors. There is a clear division of labor in this activity between the architect, builder, and homeowner because they are familiar with the common design features and processes involved in designing and building a passive home. The outcome of this activity is that passive homes in Europe can be built with 2–5 % increase in cost compared to conventional homes.

The Landau family experience building a passive home in Vermont was far from the ideal activity. The ideal activity became a cognitive tool within the Landau family activity while they pursued their object of building a passive home in the United States; they experienced several tensions due to the nature of the various components within their design and construction activity. The tools available to the Landaus were not as conducive for attaining the object as described in the ideal activity. These tools included the previously described ideal activity, the family's past experience building an energy-efficient home, customized material that had to be special ordered, architects and builders who were in training during the design and construction activity, the supplier, the family's budget, passive home design software, and European passive home building literature. The rules that affected the activity were difficult to maneuver in the design and building process. Formal rules such as the Energy Star and LEEDS certification requirements were not compatible with the passive home standards, and insurance regulators could not see past the regulations for conventional homes regarding risks involved in insuring a home without a furnace in Vermont. Informally, friends scrutinized the Landau family's choice for engaging in an activity that they had difficulty valuing. The community consisted of their friends, builders, and architects who were not familiar with passive homes. At times the community of this activity, such as family and friends, did not necessarily understand or share the Landaus' passion for pursuing the object of this activity. Other community members in this activity included the Passive Home Institute in Europe and Habitat for Humanities in the United States. In this activity the division of labor was not clearly identified and was modified as the activity unfolded through actions that involved negotiations among the various parties involved in the activity. The tensions in this activity included designing and building a passive home while (a) managing competing unclear expectations, (b) customizing supplies because there are no off-the-shelf materials, (c) managing limited community support, and (d) negotiating and compromising the division of labor. The overall outcome of this activity included that the construction of the Landau family home would be 15–20 % more costly than a conventional home, that there were some features considered standard in a conventional home the family had to give up, that the new home might not meet passive home standards, and that it was difficult to purchase home insurance.

Discussion of the Data Relevant to Design Activities

The Landau family experience in designing and building a passive home is not an instructional design activity, but it helps to identify characteristics of real-world design and how activity systems analysis from a CHAT perspective can uncover the complexities involved in the design activity. The Landau family's activity was chaotic and an emotional roller coaster ride that was driven by their object of designing and building a passive home. Their activity was transformative during the design and construction process. Each individual involved in the activity affected the other individuals' contribution to the activity and the outcome. Throughout this process, the activity and the expectations of the end product were continually modified while addressing contextual elements related to attaining the object, and at times individuals in the activity had to modify their desired outcome in order to attain the object.

The activity consisted of multiple, unique tensions brought upon by contextual contradictions that in the design and building process could not be ignored or eliminated as extraneous variables. These contradictions and tensions, especially prevalent in the tools and rules component of the activity, had to be addressed one way or another and incorporated into the design and building of the home. The Landau family's overall object remained constant throughout their activity while they addressed the contextual contradictions and tensions. In this process, there were several instances when the family, architect, and the builder had to maintain a balance between modifying the design and construction of the passive home in response to the contradiction and tensions while at the same time avoid severely compromising the integrity of the desired outcome. When watching the video on *The New York Times* website, it is evident that these tensions stirred an emotional response and challenged the Landau family's conviction to attain the object and affected the collective design decisions that were made as a team. This process cannot be explained with a one-word label, but by examining the whole activity and following how the activity evolved it becomes possible to conceptualize design as a transformative process, where it is not a series of variables waiting to be manipulated. Instead, it is an organic process shared among all individuals involved. Furthermore, designers can become much more aware and deliberate when they address how the transformative experiences of various individuals affect the final product.

Going back to my experience at the Global Communications Company, as an instructional design intern, I was experiencing for the first time the responsibilities associated with how my design decisions could affect employees. I yearned for a framework to guide my design actions and activities that helped me become more aware and deliberate about them in the context of the problem I was charged to address. I wanted to be able to assess how my decisions had potential transformative consequences. At the end of my 3-months internship, it felt awful to leave a designed prototype behind with no method for communicating to the next designer, who would be taking over the project, the complexities involved in the real-world phenomenon I attempted to address. It felt like without being able to communicate these complexities, my audience advocacy stance was washed down the drain. Now I see how an appreciation of CHAT and activity systems analysis can guide the analysis stage of a design activity and also guide a communication process about design decisions and modifications to clients, stakeholders, researchers, and other designers. It helps me build a strong case for why I came to specific decisions while addressing the various tensions and contradictions involved in the situation and how to be sensitive to them. It also helps me understand and document the transformational consequences that unravel after a designed artifact is implemented in its intended context.

Implications

Design activities are ill-defined and ill-structured while in a continual flux as individuals involved and the environment coevolve within the boundaries of the design motives. Therefore, real-world design situations are a collection of complex transactional actions and activities, but in the field of instructional technology, we do not necessarily have tools or methods for examining and communicating these transactions. The type of communication that is currently lacking among researchers and practitioners of design is the moment-to-moment capture and analysis of complex human design activities. When design researchers and practitioners take on the role of a design storyteller to share these moment-to-moment design situations, CHAT can provide the conceptual tools and methods for examining these transactions and point out how design activities influence the designed artifact, design goals, design processes, designers, stakeholders, and individuals who engage with the designed artifact. Through this framework we can examine design as a whole activity, as a tool, or as the object of an activity and capture how in real-world situations it is not a static phenomenon.

As a next step, there needs to be significant effort in instructional technology put into identifying methodologies for capturing, examining, and analyzing design data that can lead to findings that are relevant to both researchers and practitioners. When taking a CHAT approach, naturalistic inquiry (Lincoln & Guba, 1985) that relies on qualitative data collection and analysis methods can provide rich data necessary for conducting an analysis of particular situations. An in-depth understanding of these activities from a CHAT perspective may not generate generalizable claims that can be disseminated to researchers and practitioners, but can be a data source for examining trends across design situations that have implications relevant to current and future research and practice. This will help future designers when approaching their own complex design situations and help future researchers gain a better understanding of design as a complex activity and develop new methods for analyzing and communicating findings.

Acknowledgements I would like to thank the editors of this volume and reviewers assigned to comment on my work. There were several reviewers, but I would like to particularly thank Dr. Craig Howard who poured attention to this chapter when it was not one of the chapters he was assigned to review. His comments challenged my thinking and had influence on its final development. I would also like to thank my colleague Dr. Trena Paulus who volunteered and took time reviewing this work.

References

Barab, S. A., Barnett, M., Yamagata-Lynch, L., Squire, K., & Keating, T. (2002). Using activity theory to understand the systemic tensions characterizing a technology-rich introductory astronomy course. *Mind, Culture, and Activity, 9*(2), 76. doi:10.1207/S15327884MCA0902_02.

Barab, S. A., Evans, M. A., & Baek, E. (2003). Activity theory as a lens for characterizing the participatory unit. In D. Jonasen (Ed.), *Handbook of research for educational communication and technology* (2nd ed., pp. 199–214). New York: Simon & Schuster.

Barab, S. A., Schatz, S., & Scheckler, R. (2004). Using activity theory to conceptualize online community and using online community to conceptualize activity theory. *Mind, Culture, and Activity, 11*(1), 25–47. doi:10.1207/s15327884mca1101_3.

Bichelmeyer, B., Boling, E., & Gibbons, A. S. (2006). Instructional design and technology models: Their impact on research and teaching in instructional design technology. In R. M. Branch, M. Orey, & V. J. McClendon (Eds.), *Educational media and technology yearbook* (Vol. 31, pp. 33–73). Littleton, CO: Libraries Unlimited.

Cole, M. (1996). *Cultural psychology: A once and future discipline.* Cambridge, MA: Harvard University Press.

Cole, M., & Engeström, Y. (1993). A cultural-historical approach to distributed cognition. In G. Salomon (Ed.), *Distributed cognitions: Psychological and educational considerations* (pp. 1–46). New York: Cambridge University Press.

Corbin, J., & Strauss, A. C. (2008). *Basics of qualitative research: Techniques and procedures for developing grounded theory* (3rd ed.). Los Angeles: Sage.

Cross, N. (2006). *Designerly ways of knowing.* Basel: Springer.

Cross, N. (2008). *Engineering design methods: Strategies for product design* (4th ed.). Chichester: Wiley.

DeVane, B., & Squire, K. (2012). Activity theory in the learning technologies. In D. Jonassen & S. Land (Eds.), *Theoretical foundations of learning environments* (2nd ed., pp. 242–267). New York: Routledge.

Dick, W., Carey, L., & Carey, J. O. (2008). *The systematic design of instruction* (7th ed.). Boston: Allyn & Bacon.

Duffy, T. M., & Cunningham, D. J. (1996). Constructivism: Implications for the design and delivery of instruction. In D. H. Jonassen (Ed.), *Handbook of research for educational communications and technology* (pp. 170–198). New York: Simon & Schuster/Macmillan.

Duffy, T. M., & Jonassen, D. H. (Eds.). (1992). *Constructivism and the technology of instruction: A conversation*. Hillsdale, NJ: Lawrence Erlbaum Associates.

Duffy, T. M., Lowyck, J., & Jonassen, D. H. (Eds.). (1991). *Designing environments for constructive learning: NATO ASI Series*. New York: Springer.

El'konin, B. D. (1993). The nature of human action. *Journal of Russian and East European Psychology, 31*(3), 22–46.

Engeström, Y. (1987). Learning by expanding: An activity-theoretical approach to developmental research. Retrieved November 30, 2009, from http://lchc.ucsd.edu/MCA/Paper/Engestrom/expanding/toc.htm.

Engeström, Y. (1993). Developmental studies of work as a testbench of activity theory: The case of primary care medical practice. In S. Chaiklin & J. Lave (Eds.), *Understanding practice: Perspectives on activity and context* (pp. 64–103). New York: Cambridge University Press.

Gagne, R. M. (1985). *The conditions of learning and theory of instruction* (4th ed.). Belmont, CA: (Need city) Wadsworth.

Galperin, P. I. (1989). Mental actions as a basis for the formation of thoughts and images. *Soviet Psychology, 27*(3), 45–64.

Hyysalo, S. (2005). Objects and motives in a product design process. *Mind, Culture, and Activity, 12*(1), 19. doi:10.1207/s15327884mca1201_3.

Jonassen, D. H. (2000a). Toward a design theory of problem solving. *Educational Technology Research and Development, 48*(4), 63–85. doi:10.1007/BF02300500.

Jonassen, D. H. (2000b). Revisiting activity theory as a framework for designing student-centered learning environments. In D. H. Jonassen & S. M. Land (Eds.), *Theoretical foundations of learning environments* (pp. 89–121). Hillsdale, NJ: Lawrence Erlbaum Associates.

Jonassen, D. H., & Rohrer-Murphy, L. (1999). Activity theory as a framework for designing constructivist learning environments. *Educational Technology Research and Development, 47*(1), 61–79.

Kaptelinin, V. (2005). The object of activity: Making sense of the sense-maker. *Mind, Culture, and Activity, 12*(1), 4–18. doi:10.1207/s15327884mca1201_2.

Kirkpatrick, D. L., & Kirkpatrick, J. D. (2006). *Evaluating training programs: The four levels* (3rd ed.). San Francisco: Berrett-Koehler.

Lawson, B., & Dorst, K. (2009). *Design expertise*. London: Architectural Press.

Leontiev, A. N. (1978). The problem of activity and psychology. In A. N. Leont'ev (Ed.), *Activity, consciousness, and personality* (pp. 45–74). Englewood Cliffs: Prentice Hall.

Lincoln, Y. S., & Guba, E. G. (1985). *Naturalistic inquiry*. Beverly Hills, CA: Sage.

Lynham, S. A. (2000). Theory building in the human resource development profession. *Human Resource Development Quarterly, 11*(2), 159–178. doi:10.1002/1532-1096(200022)11:2<159::AID-HRDQ5>3.0.CO;2-E.

Nardi, B. A. (2005). Objects of desire: Power and passion in collaborative activity. *Mind, Culture, and Activity, 12*(1), 37–51. doi:10.1207/s15327884mca1201_4.

Parrish, P. (2006). Design as storytelling. *TechTrends, 50*(4), 72–82. doi:10.1007/s11528-006-0072-7.

Reeves, T. C., Herrington, J., & Oliver, R. (2004). A development research agenda for online collaborative learning. *Educational Technology Research and Development, 52*(4), 53–65. doi:10.1007/BF02504718.

Reigeluth, C. M. (1983). *Instructional-design theories and models: An overview of their current status*. Hillsdale, NJ: Lawrence Erlbaum Associates.

Smaldino, S. E., Lowther, D. L., & Russell, J. D. (2011). *Instructional technology and media for learning* (10th ed.). Boston: Allyn & Bacon.

Stake, R. E. (1995). *The art of case study research*. Thousand Oaks, CA: Sage.

Stake, R. E. (2010). *Qualitative research: Studying how things work*. New York: The Guilford Press.

Stetsenko, A. (2005). Activity as object-related: Resolving the dichotomy of individual and collective planes of activity. *Mind, Culture, and Activity, 12*(1), 70–88. doi:10.1207/s15327884mca1201_6.

Stetsenko, A. (2008). From relational ontology to transformative activist stance on development and learning: Expanding Vygotsky's (CHAT) project. *Cultural Studies of Science Education, 3*, 471–491. doi:10.1007/s11422-008-9111-3.

Stetsenko, A. (2010). Standing on the shoulders of giants: A balancing act of dialectically theorizing conceptual understanding on the grounds of Vygotsky's project. In W. M. Roth (Ed.), *Re/structuring science education* (Vol. 2, pp. 69–88). Dordrecht: Springer, Netherlands. Retrieved from http://www.springerlink.com/content/m871956518271w66/.

van der Veer, R. (1997). Some major themes in Vygotsky's theoretical works: An introduction. In R. W. Rieber & J. Wollock (Eds.), *The collected works of L.S. Vygotsky: Volume 3: Problems of the theory and history of psychology* (pp. 1–7). New York: Plenum Press.

van der Veer, R. (2008). Multiple readings of Vygotsky. In B. Van Oers, W. Wardekker, E. Elbers, & R. Van der Veer (Eds.), *The transformation of learning: Advances in cultural historical activity theory* (pp. 20–37). New York: Cambridge University Press.

Vygotsky, L. S. (1978). *Mind in society: The development of higher psychological processes.* Cambridge, MA: Harvard University Press.

Wang, F., & Hannafin, M. (2005). Design-based research and technology-enhanced learning environments. *Educational Technology Research and Development, 53*(4), 5–23. doi:10.1007/BF02504682.

Wertsch, J. V. (1991). *Voices of the mind: A sociocultural approach to mediated action.* Cambridge, MA: Harvard University Press.

Yamagata-Lynch, L. C. (2003). Using activity theory as an analytical lens for examining technology professional development in schools. *Mind, Culture, and Activity, 10*(2), 100–119. doi:10.1207/S1532-7884MCA1002_2.

Yamagata-Lynch, L. C. (2010). *Activity systems analysis methods: Understanding complex learning environments.* New York: Springer.

Yanchar, S. C., South, J. B., Williams, D. D., Allen, S., & Wilson, B. G. (2010). Struggling with theory? A qualitative investigation of conceptual tool use in instructional design. Educational Technology Research and Development, 58(1), 39–60. doi:10.1007/s11423-009-9129-6.

Zeller, T. Jr. (2010, September 25). In passive-house standards: A brighter shade of green. *The New York Times.* Retrieved from http://www.nytimes.com/2010/09/26/business/energy-environment/26smart.html?_r=1&pagewanted=1&ref=general&src=me.

The Rhetoric of Instructional Design Cases: Knowledge Building Via Examples of Process and Product

Craig D. Howard

Keywords Design case • Case studies • Design process • Instructional design • Design methods • Pedagogical design • Publication • Precedent

Introduction and Background

Until recently, the field of instructional design did not collect and share actual completed instructional designs and designers' reflections on the creation of those designs (Howard, Boling, Rowland, & Smith, 2012). Knowledge built in the process of instructional design was trapped in the designers who created them. This chapter tells the story of efforts to make the sharing of that knowledge open, accessible, and a widespread aspect of our practice. I start with where we are now in that process.

The *International Journal of Designs for Learning* (IJDL) is in its fifth year of publication. The journal documents designed instruction and attempts to distribute knowledge garnered through the artifacts and processes that produced these designs via *rigorous design cases* (Boling, 2010; Smith, 2010) that have undergone scholarly peer review.

IJDL emerged from recognition by a group of members at the Association of Educational Communications and Technology (AECT) that rigorous instructional design cases contain valuable insights that often escape other forms of scholarly expression. This group, many of whom became advisory board members of IJDL, saw a need for a scholarly venue to solicit, develop, and distribute this type of design research. The effort to create the venue was led by Elizabeth Boling at Indiana University Bloomington, who had previously been the editor-in-chief at

C.D. Howard (✉)
Texas A & M University, Texarkana, TX, USA
e-mail: craig.howard@tamut.edu

B. Hokanson and A. Gibbons (eds.), *Design in Educational Technology*,
Educational Communications and Technology: Issues and Innovations 1,
DOI 10.1007/978-3-319-00927-8_7, © Springer International Publishing Switzerland 2014

Tech Trends, another AECT publication. In the years leading up to IJDL's first issue, Elizabeth and the editorial staff at *Tech Trends* had taken a column that was titled the "Instructional Design (ID) Portfolio" and converted it to a peer-reviewed feature. The ID Portfolio focused on representations of specific designs and the process which lead to their creation. However, the "ID Portfolio" had limited space (3,000–4,000 words), and the expression of each design was limited by the print medium—static images and text only. It was decided that multimedia capabilities were essential to allow authors to fully express their designs and that design cases were more valuable when rigorous. Rigor required more elaboration (Smith, 2010) because of the prevalence of multimedia approaches in the field and because many designs need the full length of a scholarly article to present a rigorous case. IJDL was created to overcome these obstacles. It was created to publish design cases that would have value to the field of instructional design in both their presentation and rigor. IJDL is open-access, capable of supporting audio, video, and interactive formats of expression. Print articles are generally 9,000–11,000 words in length.

The vision for the journal was complex, but not without consensus (Boling, 2010; Howard et al., 2012; Smith, 2010). Design cases to be published in IJDL had to meet various standards of rigor (Smith, 2010). However, these standards of rigor did not equate to a formal structure because each case is unique. The presentation of each case depends on the precedent the designer wants to express through the discussion of final product and the process of design (Boling, 2010). For the first two issues of the journal, all articles were reviewed by members of the advisory board who shared this vision.

Developing Reviewers for the International Journal of Designs for Learning

It quickly became apparent that having each article reviewed by a member of the advisory board or the editorial staff was not sustainable. The number of submissions doubled from each year to the next, and interest in reviewing for the journal also increased. However, many of those interested in reviewing for the journal were not fully versed in the vision of the journal, nor were they precisely sure how the journal approached rigor. A member of the advisory board put forward the notion of a critical friend in the process of review (Costa & Kallick, 1993). The *critical friend* is an editorial process whereby a trusted person asks the writer provocative questions, offers critiques without judgments, and takes the time to understand the context of the work and how it relates to the manifest product (Costa & Kallick, 1993). Critical friends are advocates rather than evaluators. IJDL's process began using critical friends with reviewers, not authors. In 2011, members of the advisory board began coaching first-time reviewers in the spirit of a critical friend relationship. The discussion between the reviewer and the review coach was meant to support and elicit rigor through transparency in the case, and keep to the vision of the journal in-tact as new reviewers came in.

These critical friends to the reviewer, or *review coaches*, have made specific observations about the process of being a critical friend. Namely, that coaching a review is fundamentally different from giving an article a second review. The purpose of coaching a review is not to develop the subject of the discussion, the design case under review, but rather to develop the reviewer's understanding of the knowledge building process of the design case. That understanding is greatly influenced by the experience of writing a design case yourself (Exter, Gibbons, & Rowland, personal communication). Examples a from coached reviews elucidate this change in focus when a critical friend supports a new reviewer:

> You compliment the authors appropriately in a number of areas and make reasonable suggestions in several. I agree that the information on the artifact is good, and having the artifact embedded in the case for the readers to be able to try it out is great. As you point out, the user experience is missing. I suggest that we request more details. (Rowland, used with permission, 2011, no page)
>
> You state a desire for "useful, generalizable information." I'd reconsider the wording, as this isn't really what we seek in an IJDL design case. (Rowland, used with permission, 2011, no page)

The examples above bring up recurring topics that appear in reviews of design cases. However, there are more. I have collected and categorized these recurring topics as I have seen them through for the "ID Portfolio" and 2 years coordinating reviews for *IJDL*. At the same time, I include related first-hand experience from my own design case (Howard & Myers, 2010). I include my observations because the experience of creating my own case and experiencing the review process has influenced how I have perceived these areas common among reviewers. As others have mentioned, the experience of writing a case influences how other design cases are understood.

The Perspective After Having Written a Design Case

As those who have coached reviews have pointed out, the experience of having written a design case influences the direction and empathy when reviewing another's instructional design case. My design case was about a pedagogical intervention I created for a blended undergraduate education class. The design used videos of practicing teachers posted to YouTube to facilitate discussions among preservice teachers. I had given the learners the task of viewing the videos in conjunction with asynchronously discussing teaching practices via annotations placed atop the video (Howard & Myers, 2010).

Like other cases I had read, mine was also a complex design. Even after having read a number of design cases and having seen authors struggle to verbalize the complexity of their own designs, I failed to truly recognize the complexity of my own. Components of my design needed to be presented clearly, concisely, and, most importantly, separately in order to be useful for other designers. I had initially written my case as I had lived it, in a narrative of the experiences and struggles of many tasks, many overlapping each other. In doing so, I had trapped myself in an untenable situation of having to toggle between parts of the design which were created in tandem—in sequences sometimes contingent on the completion of other tasks and sometimes not. Step x was completed before step y, but components of y had to be decided upon before z could be finished, and so on.

The narrative, like many other components of design cases, had limited utility in explaining the complexity of a design to another designer. Despite having read many cases and reviews of cases, I struggled with explaining the complex design in a simple way that other designers could use. This experience forced me to confront my own understanding of design cases, and brought me to the task of grouping the questions I was facing with the questions and comments I had seen on other manuscripts.

I grouped the questions and comments into five categories. In this chapter, I have sequenced these categories of reviewer concerns to loosely mirror a plausible rhetorical structure that an instructional design case might take, but these categories are not meant to dictate a perspective to others. The last category contains items that are often selected by knowledgeable reviewers for removal from design cases. In each category, I include some rationale about how reviewers come to these questions in hopes that this article will help other authors create rich precedent that designers can use to effectively share their insights.

Situating the Design

What Were Changes in Context Which Motivated the Design or Re-design?

Readers' understanding of the rationale behind design decisions and the trustworthiness of the entire design case may hinge on a clear presentation of the context of the design. Even after offering a rich description of the context of my learning design, I had failed to come out and say that my intervention was replacing another one. I am not alone in failing to recognize all the aspects of the context which motivated the redesign. All the changes in context may not be relevant, or even known to the author of the design case, but rarely does a design take place in a completely new context (Cross, 2007). The context was new to me, but not altogether new. Even repurposed designs can be worthy of a written design case, provided the author includes the rationale that linked his or her choice to the new context. A thorough description of context, which the reader needs in order to grasp a conceptual image of the case, could contain any number of foci: the learners, the school or institution, agendas of people in pivotal positions driving action, available technologies, sources of support, other resources, and one aspect of context which I missed—a discussion of the relevant stakeholders.

In my case, I was a new stakeholder equipped with new tools. The designer (me) was a new aspect of the context, but there were also new media available that had not been available when the initial design had been created. My position as teacher/ designer and a new media opportunity (video annotations) initiated the redesign. I created the YouTube videos because I (1) believed in shared teacher observation discussions and (2) I could. I also brought to the situation an interest in online discussions. I had planned the discussion to take place on top of the video via annotations because I was curious about how people use new media to communicate. One reviewer wrote, "So the change in the teacher-stakeholder motivated the design?" I had recognized the new affordances of the media, but I hadn't seen myself as a stakeholder. Authors new to writing design cases for pedagogical interventions, including myself, can easily overlook the fact that the reason we design something is often because another design has failed to live up to new desires or expectations of new stakeholders.

While changes in stakeholders can be the impetus behind redesigns, authors new to design cases may be reluctant to identify these changes — especially if the changes in context have to do with their own personal decisions. Reviewers of design cases often ask about stakeholders, and, in a section where the context is discussed, this is key information. In my case, the previous design had been created by a colleague. I was reticent to state my perspective for fear that it might highlight shortcomings of the previous design and seem to blame previous teachers of the course. But in truth, a previous stakeholder was now absent, and my own goals had become a new aspect of the context. While I still identified the context in the legacy of someone else, the reviewer did not. I was redesigning another designer's work to fit my own goals and how I interpreted the goals of the course. Identifying aspects of context which did not exist for the previous designer(s) helped me make the case that I built on that previous design, rather than tore it apart. By noting changes in stakeholders, new goals, or other contextual changes, such as the desires of a new stakeholder / designer, you can give credit to previous designs and previous designers while at the same time introducing the motivators behind the redesign.

Who Was the Design Team and What Were Their Influences?

Rigorous design cases include all the descriptions needed to characterize context, and this includes descriptions of the people who were involved in the design process. Reviewers requested more information about the design team, but I felt awkward describing myself in a scholarly publication despite my having been the primary designer. I reasoned the influences I brought to the design were more important than a description of me. I described my background rather briefly in one line, but I expanded on other factors which influenced the design. Since my design was closely tied to my research, I had been doing a large amount of traditional scholarly reading, and this was working on me while I was designing the intervention. This discussion of influential readings was far more complex and became 2:25 min of audio in the final multimedia design case, much more in depth than the self-description. I had also sought out the help of a colleague at a critical incident during the design. He provided a description of his previous experience and background to explain what brought him to his design decisions in solving the problem I had brought to him. We placed the description of his experience in the narrative of that aspect of the design, but the description of my influences closer to the beginning of the design case. Providing these descriptions gave reviewers the information they needed to understand the influences relevant to the design. Reviewers were open to how we wanted to frame that information and where in the case we felt it was needed.

Discussions of readings, previous designs, theoretical perspectives, and training influential in the designers' thinking can elucidate the perspectives of the designers, in turn helping readers grasp the perspective of the case. This practice is closer to practices in naturalistic research than it is to forms of scientific writing that report experimental research (Boling, 2010). In most cases a team has come together to create the design. Reviewers are often curious to know how the design team was comprised, especially if it was specifically recruited for the project. The narrative about how I recruited my colleague to solve the critical incident was brief but important, because the solution he chose was very much related to his experiences and training. The experiences and perspectives that are brought to the design are a crucial part of a design case because readers need to know what skills sets were brought to the design in order to follow the rationale and see the relationships between the design team and the choices the design team came up with. A designer working alone may frame a problem differently than a designer working in a team with diverse perspectives and approaches, thus leading to different design decisions (Cross, 2011).

Why Might Readers Find This Design Case Interesting?

It is important to acknowledge why you want to write the case and to understand, and provide for, unanticipated interest from readers. The aspect of my design which I found most interesting was the resulting discussion among preservice teachers, but the reviewers were more interested in how I created the total design. This question has challenged other authors as well. Like a number of other authors, I did not state how the case might prove useful to another designer in my original submission. During the revisions I found myself moving a number of statements about possible audiences from the conclusion to the introduction and then putting something forward which was relatively vague, ". . . for those who want to see learners in engaging discussions about pedagogy." Uncomfortable as it is, authors must state why they feel their case is worth reading and who they envision finding it useful, even though they cannot pinpoint the most valuable part of their case for readers.

We cannot pinpoint who will find the case most useful because the utility of a case is determined by those who use it, not the writer of the design case (Smith, 2010). Design cases serve very different purposes for different readers (Rowland, 2007). Identifying what insights readers might find useful puts focus behind the presentation of the case right from the opening paragraphs. An excellent example is Mulcahy's (2011) design case focused on a simulation design. He was driven to write the case because of a disjoint between what he felt was a design failure and the accolades the project received. Readers will surely find precedent in his design decisions, but his design choices are not what drove him to write the design case. What made the story of the design worth telling for Mulcahy were the questions his design case raises, and these questions guide the themes within his case, allowing the reader to experience one train of thought in an otherwise complex narrative. This approach allows readers to take precedent where they find it within the narrative, but also allows the case to be a single, unified statement.

It is not expected that the aspects of a design case which excite the authors are precisely what reviewers see as the case's true points of merit. I was excited to write my design case because I felt it was novel, but novelty is not necessarily an asset to a design case. A design that is unusual or new forces the author to explain its complexity with more precision. Reviewers of my design case were less interested in the new aspects of the design (viz., video annotations) than they were in how I had addressed recurrent issues that plagued the design genre (viz., asynchronous discussions). In other words, reviewers were interested in what new ways old problems could be tackled. The media choices were less important than the rationale behind them and the design's ability to address larger and recurrent issues. Newby, Ertmer, and Kenny (2010) experienced the same when they discussed strategies they used to overcome obstacles in making groups for international group work. By creating a system of tiers of project managers within smaller groups, they facilitated work across nonoverlapping semester schedules at different universities in dramatically different time zones. This was a complex but new solution to a problem always faced in international group work. Reviewers focused in on these discussions in their design case but were less concerned with explanations of their end product, a wiki.

Describing the Design

Would Other Modalities Express Your Design Directly? Images? Video? Audio? Interactions?

Without mode-appropriate assets supporting the presentation, the design itself might be hard to imagine, even with rich textual descriptions. Naturalistic media, such as photographs, are full of detail; many of these details are inexpressible in verbal communication (Kress & van Leeuwen, 2006). Photos are not the only option and perhaps not the most desirable option for cases that focus on other modalities. I first proposed the article in storyboard form with clear indications that much of the design case would be a narrated video and would include user navigation. I chose an interactive format with video assets to present my design because understanding the design depended on experiencing the two different kinds of videos. The first video

Fig. 1 A design case presentation of audio development for the *chill out song*. Frank, Z. (2010) the chill out song. Interactive Multimedia (http://www.zefrank.com/chillout/)

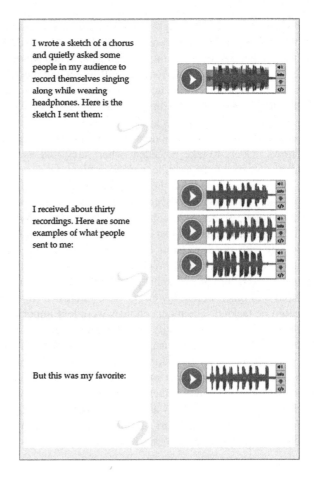

asset was unannotated, and the second contained annotation. Only through seeing both could the audience of the design case appreciate that the experience of watching the two was fundamentally different. A design case which focused on other modes would need to make use of different modalities to express the design.

In a design case written to describe how a collaborative internet-mediated song was created using emailed recordings made with basic software, Frank (2008) uses audio to compliment his text. Figure 1 presents an excerpt from the design case where the author presents audio artifacts across from his reflections. He describes what he was thinking when the artifact was created, but the audio impacts our understanding of his language. Notice in the upper left-hand box that he has described the audio track as a "sketch." It might be difficult for readers to imagine an audio sketch until they listen to the track. His meaning becomes clear through the audio asset. The author also uses the term "favorite" (bottom left), which is valuable because it drove design decisions. The author cannot express the contrast between

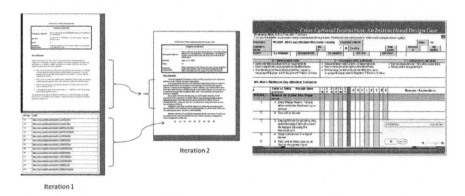

Fig. 2 Two visual artifacts made from developed texts for use in design cases (Howard & Myers, 2011; Tracey & Unger, 2010)

voices without the audio clips, and the meaning of "favorite" here is specific within the context of the design. These nuances which tie the design case together are only accessible through the audio.

Alternative modality assets do not have to be restricted to pictures of a design, people using a design, or to multimedia products. Design components which are texts themselves, such as rubrics, can be shown through their progression, with changes visually highlighted or highlighted through audio narration. I included graphics developed from textual artifacts because I had read a number of reviews asking for graphics, even when the designs being discussed were embodied in texts. Figure 2 shows two graphics which depict textual documents. The textual artifact on the left was made using simple visual indicators while in the artifact on the right, audio narration highlighted developments in the document (Howard & Myers, 2011; Tracey & Unger, 2010).

Can You Present a Concrete Illustration of the Finished Design, Including the Complex and Intangible Parts?

Presenting a design for learning often includes figuring out how to present intangible aspects of the design in conjunction with tangible parts. When a reviewer asked after the initial submission, "So what exactly are the components of this design?" it led me to think of the intangibles as components rather than as aspects of the development narrative. I created a diagram by showing the intangibles as icons and created relations between them using arrows. Intangible aspects of my design could not be captured in perfectly appropriate icons. For example, *the assessment tool*, a php script, was simply represented by a cube with lines, reminiscent of a computer tower. The relations were a little easier to represent with arrows. In Fig. 3, *the*

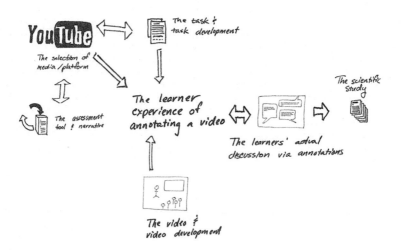

Fig. 3 A graphic organizer artifact developed to help conceptualize a design

assessment tool, an intangible, impacts and is impacted by *the section of media* — so this relationship is represented by a bidirectional arrow. On the other hand, *the learners' actual discussion* impacts the scientific study but the scientific study did not impact the discussion. Therefore, that relationship is represented by a single direction arrow.

The diagram also served to facilitate the narrative of development. Following the diagram, I discussed each component separately in its totality. Presenting a design's development purely chronologically appears the logical choice until the complexity of the relationships between design tasks forces the author to organize the presentation in some other way. I found creating a *concrete illustration* the most difficult aspect of writing the design case because my lived experience of creating the design was a sequence of interrelated events, not separate parts. Reorganizing the narrative by components provided a more straightforward approach. From the perspective of the reader, when decisions about different aspects of a design are presented in tandem as they were lived, the complex narrative becomes hard to follow. Dependencies between parts are hard to remember when following the text of an extended narrative. The bidirectional arrows between components signify joint development or repeated toggles between design tasks. Single arrowheads signify completion of one component feeding into another component's development or into the learning experience itself. Workflow on multiple tasks in this design, as in many others, was not necessarily linear, but often codependent between tasks. A chronological recount would present the false impression that one area was the starting point when actually I did not want to suggest that. In my case, a diagram of the total design was the strategy I used to conceptualize the whole. How to holistically express the design beyond the narrative is something every complex design case must grapple with. A diagram is one strategy to talk about intangibles, process and unify different aspects of a design.

Depicting the Experience of the Design

Can You Describe the User Experience?

The learner experience is "imagining the journey of a learner's experience in engaging with a finished design" (Parrish, 2006, p. 74). Of course individual learners experienced my design differently; however, reviewers asked me direct questions, such as "What does the learner actually see? Can they stop? Who do they talk to?" I imagined the typical learner's experience and described what I guessed was likely to be seen, felt, and done during the course of the experience. Including the user experience in a design case provides the reader with a perspective which the author can use to show where different features of a design interact with the learner. It can also be used to draw distinctions between features to explain how they support learning.

Describing the user experience provided a clarification of the nature of design features. Users will not interact with all the components of a design all the time. In fact, some components may not be meant to interact with the learners at all but are still essential to the design. In my own design case, the user never experienced the assessment tool (see Fig. 3), a php script which the coauthor of the design case created to record and time-stamp participation in the video-annotated discussion. While the assessment tool was essential to the efficacy of the design because it supported the teacher and provided a key affordance—data collection—it was not part of the learner experience. Because it made grading possible, my final design hinged on the assessment tool, even though it did not directly impact the learner experience. Components such as these have been called soft scaffolds if they are meant to support the teacher rather than directly supporting the student (Brush & Saye, 2002). A clear description of the user experience can help distinguish these components from others and expose relationships with more visible design components in a complex design.

Are You Confounding Performance Measures with "Results"?

While a transparent discussion of a design may well take into account the performances demonstrated during the task, these are not results in the sense that we have results in scientific, experimental studies. Thinking of performance measures this way led me, as well as a number of other authors, down a fruitless path. Like other authors new to design cases for learning, I was looking for results to document and present. I saw the final discussion as the "results," so I counted words and annotations and reported these using descriptive statistics. However, in truth, if there was any "result" from a design case, it would be the design itself, not the performance measures. In some traditional modes, the only interesting aspect of a design is the learning outcomes: Did people learn and, if so, how much? Building knowledge through design cases aims to answer a different question: How did this instantiation of an intervention come about, and what design resulted from the process? Data on the ultimate effectiveness may be interesting, but performance measures do not necessarily validate, or invalidate, the aspects of how that intervention was created.

Performance measures tell us a partial story of learners' experiences; they partially express what happened within the particular design in a particular context. Within the context of a design case, they do not tell us about a theory, nor do they tell us about how the design would function if recreated by another designer (Boling, 2010; Rowland, 2007). In a design case, performance measures are nontransferable and represent the ultimate particular (Stolterman, 2008). The statistics of the numbers of words produced, the numbers of annotations, and the amount of time spent on task in my discussion of the design described an aspect of the design (viz., the user experience) rather than measured the outcome of the design process. This realization came when I answered questions about my design case after it was published and I saw other authors struggle with writing results sections in their own cases. Performance measures may describe part of the user experience, but they are not essential to understanding a design.

From reading revisions and experiencing confusion myself surrounding how performance measures fit into a design case, a question arises about how new authors view design cases in relation to scientific experimental studies in education. Do designers, who are also researchers, recognize the difference in perspective between a design case and an experimental study which uses a design for teaching and learning? From my own experience, this was a subtle but important change in perspective. In a scientific experimental study used for educational research, there is often a design that generates data. The design is part of the study. In a design case, however, the study becomes a component of the design. In Fig. 3, the scientific study appears on the far right as a component of the design. It may have been because the production of scientific data was an essential affordance of my design that I had mistaken the performance measures for results. The requirements of the scientific study had a very limited role in impacting media choices, the development of the assessment tool, and certain features of the assignment, so I admit a soft line could be drawn from the study component to the others. However, the completed discussion directly provided data for the scientific study, but not for the design. It was the difference in perspective that I had not grasped which caused this confusion between performance measures and results. I had planned during the design that performance measures would be extractable from the learners' discussions to enable a scientific study, but this did not mean the result of the design case was the discussions. In the context of an experimental scientific study, the measures I used could be results. However, in the context of a design case, performance measures are not results; the result is the design.

Transparency in the Analysis

How Has the Design Failed?

Cases with no discussion of the failures of the design appear as advertisements rather than rigorous studies of real designs (Smith, 2010). Design failures may also be the most interesting aspects of the case for readers who share common dilemmas, constraints, goals, or contexts. Readers want to know what you uncovered when you looked critically at your design and your design process. Notes I had taken while I was creating the intervention helped in writing parts of the narratives that suggested process failures. I had noted that I should have saved video clips in a systematic order with labels that described the abstract concept the clip exemplified and that other software choices might have made the creation of the teaching videos more effecting and engaging. These provided for discussion of my process of designing, but they did not lend to the analysis of the design itself. Identifying failures in my design process was less challenging than identifying failures in the performance of the finished product. I felt my design had done what I wanted it to do. While it seemed reviewers could not foretell specific design failures from my initial submission, their probing questions suggested I had not asked other stakeholders about their experience of the design, and I could not yet know the failures. Just because the design had accomplished the task did not mean it was without need for improvement. They suggested I ask other people about the failures of the design.

Perspectives from outside the design team helped to uncover failures that I had not originally seen. Only after discussions with the other teacher who had used the design could I see where the design had failed. The other teacher of the course was a stakeholder I had not consulted in the initial write up of the case. Her contribution turned out to be essential to writing an honest discussion of design failures. The other teacher of the course had experienced not being able to give students quick, accurate directions on how to login and use the video annotation system. She also did not know how to collect the annotations and grade them using the tool. Where my design had failed was not in the user experience, but in providing the other teacher of the course with enough support to feel the product was a tool she could easily use. Essentially she was a stakeholder I had forgotten during the design and the design itself consequently overlooked. The probability that different stakeholders characterize success and failure differently is high; this tactic may serve other authors well in uncovering a design's shortcomings.

Like other manuscripts I have seen, a thorough discussion of design failures was the weakest part of my initial draft. Acknowledging outside perspectives lends to the transparency of the case. While we often envision the task of creating rigorous research a solitary one, the only route for me to see these other perspectives was dialogue.

Design failures may be an unfortunate, and sometimes misleading, term. The failure of a design to produce the expected results in one context may turn out to be a design's strength in another context (Krippendorff, 2006). Failures are not necessarily the fault of the designer, and the term is not meant to convey blame. Some reviewers have seemed to avoid the term design failures, presumably because educators sometimes interpret the term to imply failed teaching, which it does not. Other questions aimed at a transparent discussion of design failures are: How has the design manifested unexpected experiences? or In what ways might this design be improved? Authors of design cases should not be surprised if reviewers ask about design failures; they are the most common request I have seen in reviews.

Have You Done Justice to the Complexity of the Issues Related to the Design?

Strategies to uncover design decisions can expose complexities of the design which might have gone unnoticed. If the designer is the one writing the case, dialogue can expose curiosities the reader brings but the writer/designer simply has not thought to include. I was so deep in the design process that some decisions were taken as a matter of course. Assumed rules of practice can dictate choices almost unconsciously, even when the impetus of those practices has since disappeared (Fanselow, 1987). My coauthor recognized design decisions I had not deliberated on during the process of design and had left out of the initial draft. For example, I had not considered any other alternative to starting with an informal usability test. For me, this was not a design decision; for him it was. The observations from the usability test led me to creating a video tutorial which it turns out I may not have actually needed. YouTube changed the interface while my task was assigned, but learners managed to coach each other using the annotations themselves. My design case never questioned usability testing as a departure point, but perhaps it should have. A stakeholder, the reviewers, and my coauthor (who was the rest of the design team) helped uncover things I would have not thought to include as decisions. The dialogues revealed essential parts of the case which I had not initially considered, and brought up a larger issue. The learners' overcoming the change in interface midway through the task raised questions about my assumed one-size-fits all starting point.

Items Often Removed from Design Cases

The categories in this chapter up to this point have all included common questions knowledgeable reviewers have posed to me and other authors of design cases. This category is different. These subsections are not questions because reviewers do not ask questions on these topics. Rather, they often ask that these topics be removed or reworked into a different perspective.

Methods and Research Question Sections

Rich descriptions of the design moves that culminated in the finished design are the development narrative, not methods as the term traditionally implies. Some authors have titled the narrative "methods" to imply a method of design, but reviewers interpret the section as a statement of research method. Design cases are representations of knowledge which develop naturalistically as the designer or someone close to the design collects key artifacts and reflects on the reasoning behind decisions and the

Original submission	Revised text
We pinned our design efforts to a research question that we felt could be addressed over the course of a rigorous design and evaluation project: how do interactive visualization tools impact the instructor and student experience in military history education?	In the following design case, we describe how our design decisions were impacted by a central research question: how do interactive visualization tools impact the instructor and student experience in military history education? We state this question not because we intend to answer it fully here, but because it underpinned the entire TEMPO project, from conceptualization through design to implementation and evaluation.

Fig. 4 A revised passage from a design case submitted to *IJDL*, taken from Prestopnik and Foley (2012) p. 53

efficacy of those decisions (Boling, 2010). Rich descriptions describe the design process, and sometimes they include reference to process models the designers used. This does not make these rich descriptions research methods. I put references to scholarly publications in my description of the design team because the readings influenced my design. I actively avoided the term "methods" because I had read so many reviews and seen subsequent revisions grapple with finding a common under- standing of the term within the context of a design case.

The motives behind writing a design case are not the same as those for scientific studies. Scientific studies ask research questions, but research questions are awk- ward in a design case because design cases only ask one question: How did the design come to be as it is? (Boling, 2010; Howard & Myers, 2011; Smith, 2010). Authors have reworked what they originally thought of as research questions into problem statements (Hosack, 2010) or even statements that express the authors' desire to share the precedent they believe was created in the project (Paulus & Spence, 2010). The motive behind my case was a desire to share what I felt was a curious new medium, but Rowland, Hamilton, and Morales (2011) saw their design case as an opportunity to address the complexities brought up in a process which used systems principles for a complex real-world design. Design cases do not con- tain research questions of the sort we find in experimental studies.

Rather, what may seem to the author of a design case as a research question may actually be the manner in which the design problem was framed. Prestopnik and Foley (2012) provide an excellent example. After review and revision, the statement became a way to describe the design context, rather than a question that drove data collection and analysis (Fig. 4).

The concept that Prestopnik and Foley (2012) originally viewed as a research question became a way to provide greater transparency to the case by illuminating the perspective that the designers took while designing.

Design Guidelines, Lessons Learned, and Design Principles

It is hard to ignore the irony in prescribing to others that they should not write prescriptions. However, reviewers have suggested in my case, and in others, that blanket guidelines tend to oversimplify the design process and work against the transparency of a design case. The rationale behind this is presumably that it is difficult to draw probabilistic design principles from one single case, but prescriptions in design cases are on shaky grounds for other reasons as well. The goal of writing design cases is not to collect enough of them for "real research" to have data sets; rather, it is to share design knowledge that is so tightly connected to the complexities of particulars that it cannot be generalized to other cases. Design knowledge need not be generalizable to be valid. What may seem like a handy design guideline now may not stand the test of time, may be useful primarily in building your design judgment, or develop into part of your design philosophy (Boling & Smith, 2008). Since readers will take away the most useful precedent they find in a design case anyway, design guidelines, lessons learned, and prescriptions only obscure the trustworthiness of a design case, especially if the reader does not interpret the case as directly feeding into the stated prescription.

Conclusion

While I was used to having in-depth discussions about teaching, finding the tensions, and then weighing competing goals within interventions I had created, I was far less used to actually representing designs in all their complexity to someone removed from my own teaching context. Describing a total pedagogical design is difficult, and like many educators, I was not trained to talk about teaching and learning in this way. Teachers skip details in their descriptions, perhaps because there are often thousands of decisions being made during one instance of a learning design. Perhaps it is because other teachers share a knowledge base and some things are assumed. Perhaps I had been taught that only certain types of studies are pertinent to educational scholarship, such as studies which directly inform theories.

Design cases are knowledge building of a different sort. A large portion of educational research follows the scientific tradition; design cases follow the design tradition. Consequently, educators eager to share their designs often do not know where to start. This change of gears can be frustrating for seasoned authors who are comfortable in the scientific format (Ertmer, personal communication). A common misconception is that design cases are not *real* knowledge building at all. We need to be careful to consider rigorous design cases as true scholarly work, because they are. Design cases are empirical in the same sense that scientific studies are: They are based on observations. This does not mean design cases should appear in the same format as studies focused on creating scientific generalizable knowledge. This is the concept that Rowland is trying to support in his critical friend comment to a reviewer earlier in this chapter. Generalizable knowledge is not what design cases aim to create.

Since design cases build knowledge in a fundamentally different way than has been done in the past in education, we should expect them to look different. In many ways, the format of a design case is intrinsically linked to the larger mission of advancing knowledge via that case. The format of the case is another tool to express the precedent in the case. In the end, a case should be presented in the most reasonable way possible. This is especially important in a new journal where there is a vision, but not a tradition that has been tried, tested, and developed into a genre of research. As authors, reviewers, and readers craft the new discussion, the format of the design case for learning will surely develop. This is an exciting time to be part of building our collective knowledge about creating designs for learning.

Acknowledgements This study would not have been possible without the support of the many good-natured reviewers and authors of design cases at the *Tech Trends'* feature the "ID Portfolio," and the *International Journal of Designs for Learning (IJDL)*. Colin Gray, Nate Prestopnik, and Gordon Rowland graciously provided their communications from within the editorial process to help make this article possible. Portions of this article appeared in *IJDL* in 2011, and are reprinted here under the creative commons licence: Howard, C.D. (2011). Writing and rewriting the instructional design case: A view from two sides. *International Journal of Designs for Learning*, 2(1), 40–55. Retrieved from http://scholarworks.iu.edu/journals/index.php/ijdl/index. Copyright © 2011, Creative Commons http://creativecommons.org/licenses/by-nc-nd/3.0/ .

References

Boling, E. (2010). The need for design cases: Disseminating design knowledge. *International Journal of Designs for Learning*, *1*(1), 1–8. Retrieved from http://scholarworks.iu.edu/journals/index.php/ijdl/index.

Boling, E., & Smith, K. M. (2008). Exploring standards of rigor for design cases. Paper presented at the Design Research Society Conference Undisciplined! Sheffield Hallam University, Sheffield, UK.

Brush, T. A., & Saye, J. W. (2002). A summary of research exploring hard and soft scaffolding for teachers and students using a multimedia supported learning environment. *Journal of Interactive Online Learning*, *1*(2), 1–12.

Costa, A., & Kallick, B. (1993). Through the lens of a critical friend. *Educational Leadership*, *51*(2), 49–51.

Cross, N. (2007). *Designerly ways of knowing*. Basel, Switzerland: Birkhäuser.

Cross, N. (2011). *Design thinking: Understanding how designers think and work*. Oxford: Berg.

Fanselow, J. F. (1987). *Breaking rules: Generating and exploring alternatives in language teaching*. White Plains, NY: Longman.

Frank, Z. (2008). Chillout song. *Zefrank.com*. Retrieved September 23, 2011, from http://zefrank.com/chillout.

Hosack, B. (2010). VideoANT: Extending online video annotation beyond content delivery. *Tech Trends*, *54*(3), 45–49.

Howard, C. D., Boling, E., Rowland, G., & Smith, K. M. (2012). Instructional design cases and why we need them. *Educational Technology*, *52*(3), 34–38.

Howard, C. D., & Myers, R. D. (2010). Creating video-annotated discussions: An asychronous alternative. *International Journal of Designs for Learning*, *1*(1), multimedia: http://scholarworks.iu.edu/journals/index.php/ijdl/index.

Howard, C.D. & Myers, R.D. (2011, April). A design case: Creating a video annotated teaching observation. Paper presented at the annual meeting of the American Educational Research Association. New Orleans, LA.

Kress, G., & van Leeuwen, T. (2006). *Reading images: The grammar of visual design*. New York: Routledge.

Krippendorff, K. (2006). *The semantic turn: A new foundation for design*. Boca Raton, FL: CRC Press.

Mulcahy, R. S. (2011). Bottom line: Defining success in the creation of a business simulation. *International Journal of Designs for Learning, 2*(1), 1–17.

Newby, T. J., Ertmer, P. A., & Kenney, E. M. (2010). The INSITE Project: Engaging Students In International Team Collaborations to Create a Web 2.0 Tool Repository. *International Journal of Designs for Learning, 1*(1), 21–39. Retrieved from http://scholarworks.iu.edu/journals/index.php/ijdl/index.

Parrish, P. (2006). Design as storytelling. *TechTrends, 50*(4), 72–82.

Paulus, T., & Spence, M. (2010). Using blogs to identify misconceptions in a large undergraduate nutrition course. *TechTrends, 54*(5), 62–68.

Prestopnik, N., & Foley, A. (2012). Visualizing the past: The design of a temporally enabled map for presentation (TEMPO). *International Journal of Designs for Learning, 3*(1), 52–60. Retrieved from http://scholarworks.iu.edu/journals/index.php/ijdl/index

Rowland, G. (2007). Educational inquiry in transition: Research and design. *Educational Technology, 47*(2), 14–28.

Rowland, G., Hamilton, J., & Morales, M. (2011). The IICC project: Integration, insight, creativity, and character. *International Journal of Designs for Learning, 2*(1), 18–39. Retrieved from http://scholarworks.iu.edu/journals/index.php/ijdl/index.

Smith, K. M. (2010). Producing the rigorous design case. *International Journal of Designs for Learning, 1*(1), 9–20.

Stolterman, E. (2008). The nature of design practice and implications for interaction design research. *International Journal of Design, 2*(1), 55–65.

Tracey, M. W., & Unger, K. L. (2010). Cross cultural instruction: An instructional design case. *International Journal of Designs for Learning, 1*(1), multimedia. http://scholarworks.iu.edu/journals/index.php/ijdl/index.

The Many Facets of Design and Research in Instructional Design

Wayne A. Nelson

Keywords Design research • Instructional design • Research during design • Research about design • Research through design

Professors of instructional technology would say they "do research" as part of their career practice, if for no other reason than to gain tenure and achieve promotion. But would practicing instructional designers say that they do research in the same ways that designers in other fields characterize their design research activities? The view proposed in this chapter is that the answer lies in the ways that research is defined, taught, and conducted in the field of instructional design as compared to other design fields, and it is due to the purposes for which research is utilized in practice as opposed to academic settings. As Stappers (2007) notes:

> A lot of debate has been devoted to the relation between design and research, and a consensus outcome has not been established ... One problem in the debate is that ... [the debate] is often carried on a level of abstraction which tends to confuse rather than enlighten, because generic terms as "research" and "design" carry more implicit connotations than explicit denotations. (p. 81)

So, before going further, it is necessary to establish definitions of design and research in order to examine the various ways that design research is employed within the field of instructional design. In essence, research activities are undertaken to discover and utilize new knowledge, following a studious process in order to discover and interpret facts, revise theories, or apply new knowledge to practice. The National Science Foundation (2012) further describes different forms of research and development, including basic research (fuller understanding of the world without applications toward processes or products), applied research (gaining understanding to determine means by which a need may be met), and development

W.A. Nelson, Ed.D. (✉)
Southern Illinois University Edwardsville, Edwardsville, IL, USA
e-mail: wnelson@siue.edu

B. Hokanson and A. Gibbons (eds.), *Design in Educational Technology*,
Educational Communications and Technology: Issues and Innovations 1,
DOI 10.1007/978-3-319-00927-8_8, © Springer International Publishing Switzerland 2014

research, which is viewed as a systematic use of knowledge to produce useful materials, devices, and systems or methods. Given these definitions, it would appear that most research in instructional design is applied or developmental. But there are many nuances in terms of the various purposes to which research activities are undertaken, just as there are many research methods that can be employed for various design research activities. It is these purposes and methods that will be the focus of discussion in this chapter.

Even with all its nuances, it seems easier to formulate a definition of research than a definition of design. *To design* (verb) might mean to contrive, create, devise, fashion, execute, or construct, while *a design* (noun) might be defined as a mental scheme, a preliminary sketch, or an outline. These definitions can be a source of confusion (Hjelm, 2005), because the noun form of design involves a representation or a plan, while the verb form refers to human activity that results in a representation or plan (Love, 2002). For example, does the phrase "instructional design model" refer to a process (verb) or an object (noun)? While there is no widely accepted definition for instructional design, the majority of definitions and descriptions refer to it as a process, rather than a product (Dick, Carey, & Carey, 2009; Smith & Ragan, 2005). But a sketch, a document, or a flow chart can also represent a design and can be referred to as a design model because the artifact describes and represents the form and characteristics of what is being designed. Even this simple distinction points to the need for greater care and precision when using the term *design*.

In addition to the conceptual confusion caused by the terminology we use, there has long been a debate about the nature of design within the field of instructional technology. Is design a science, a practice, or an art? Can there be a science of instructional design (Kember & Murpby, 1995)? How should we define our field and its knowledge base (Reiser, 2001; Richey, Klein, & Tracey, 2011)? Some hold fast to the assertion that instructional design is a scientific field (Reigeluth, Bunderson, & Merrill, 1994; Richey et al., 2011) and research should be based in empiricism in order to develop sound educational theories. Others have objected to the notion of instructional design research as basic scientific research, suggesting instead that the field should focus on applied and development research activities (Reeves, 2000) in order to develop grounded theories based in practice. Reliance on empirical research to study design activities in order to validate models and provide disciplinary integrity is surely appropriate, but will there ever be such a thing as a general theory of or model for instructional design? If so, why are there so many published instructional design models (Gustafson & Branch, 2002)? While some argue that both *normal* and design sciences are necessary in education (Sloane, 2006), it may be more useful to view instructional design as a design field, not a scientific field (Murphy, 1992). In that way, we may be closer to studying the actual practice of designers and, therefore, gain a better understanding of what designers do and how they do it (Gibbons, 2003; Rowland, 1993).

Describing design is also made more difficult by the nature of thinking that is involved in the design process. Design thinking is not scientific thinking. While both kinds of thinking can be creative, design is concerned with *making*, while science is concerned with *finding* (Owen, 2007). It is widely accepted that design is a form of problem solving (Gibbons & Rogers, 2009; Jonassen, 2008; Nelson, Magliaro, & Sherman, 1988) with the special feature that design problems are complex or *wicked* (Rittel & Webber, 1973), requiring extensive effort to understand the problem to be solved and to identify constraints that guide solution possibilities (Dorst, 2004; Schon, 1983).

Designers generally collaborate on teams, or even if working individually, they are outer-directed as they work for others in a client-based relationship (Owen, 2004). They frequently partner with professionals from other disciplines, using a wide range of tools to collect and organize information as part of the process of developing the product that the client requests. Designers work by synthesizing ideas within real-world situations that involve creating artifacts and managing the environment, while scientists largely work analytically within an abstract, symbolic world. In this sense, design is the obverse of science in terms of the kinds of thinking that are involved in each endeavor. As Owen (1998) has noted:

> Design is not science, and it is not art—or any other discipline. It has its own purposes, values, measures and procedures ... .In short, there is little to point to as a theoretical knowledge base for design ... Knowledge is generated and accumulated through action. Doing something and judging the results is the general model. (pp. 10–11)

If we are going to do research in the field of instructional design, perhaps a better approach is to conceive of the important research questions and methods in light of design as it is practiced (Gibbons, 2003), in addition to pursuing basic scientific research. Given the academic traditions and conditions under which instructional design has evolved, it is not surprising that we have approached its study with traditional scientific thinking. But as some have noted, design can be both an object of study and a means of carrying out that study (Glanville, 1999). It is with this dual conceptualization that the remainder of this chapter will present descriptions and examples of various types of design research.

What, Then, Is Design Research?

Suggestions to view research within instructional design from broader perspectives are not unique to this chapter. Over the years, various types of design research have been described using many labels, including action research (Archer, 1995), design experiments (Brown, 1992), developmental research (Richey & Nelson, 1995), development research (van den Akker, 1999), design and development research (Richey & Klein, 2011), and engineering research (Edelson, 2006). Early attempts at describing developmental research within instructional design delineated several purposes for research activities and hinted at some of the different categories described in this chapter (Richey & Nelson, 1995). van den Akker (1999a) compared development research to other approaches typically used in the field of instructional design, suggesting that, while methods might be similar, the nature of the knowledge gained from development research is in the form of design principles and heuristics derived through formative evaluation of "successive approximations of interventions in interaction with practitioners" (p. 8). Edelson (2006) noted different kinds of thinking and research goals that are inherent in an engineering approach to design research in education, as opposed to a scientific approach that uses a theory-testing paradigm (Edelson, 2002).

This was all happening as the larger field of educational research was also moving toward forms of design research as accepted paradigms (Bannan-Ritland, 2003; Barab & Squire, 2004). Initial proposals using different labels have already been noted above (design experiments, developmental research, etc.). Much debate occurred in the process of defining, describing, and accepting design research in education (Bell, 2004; Collins, Joseph, & Bielaczyc, 2004; Shavelson, Phillips, Towne, & Feuer, 2003). Questions in the debate were centered on methodological validity, whether conclusions could be generalized, and whether *science* could be advanced using design research. The approach is now generally accepted, resulting in the addition of a new label for design research (e.g., *design-based research*) which utilizes similar activities for similar purposes than those already described above (Design-Based Research Collective, 2003).

So given the many approaches and labels for design research, not to mention the varying purposes and methods, some clarification would be helpful. In order to provide an alternative view of the kinds of design research that are possible within the instructional design field, a classification of research *during* design, research *about* design, and research *through* design is proposed. As shown in Fig. 1, these categories represent different reasons for conducting research within design settings that range from pure theory to pure practice. The first category, research during design, happens as part of a design process where research activities are utilized in support of design practices in a particular context (Stapleton, 2005). Research about design is undertaken in order to understand, inform, and improve design practices by generating knowledge about the effectiveness of design models, methods, and tools. Research through design is focused on meta-level questions with the larger objective of creating theoretical knowledge rather than creating a solution for a particular situation (Frankel & Racine, 2010). The categories roughly correspond to the mind-sets of designers suggested by Sanders (2008). Though not wholly precise, the descriptions in Fig. 1 are suggested to help clarify the potential purposes of the various forms of design research that are possible, following the frameworks suggested by Frayling (1993) and Friedman (2003).

This classification better meets what some have envisioned for design research in instructional design: that is, to study technology-based solutions in ways that are socially responsible (Reeves, Herrington, & Oliver, 2005), to develop new tools and methods that can facilitate better designs for learning (Mor & Winters, 2007), and to explore and refine theories of learning and curriculum (Nelson, Ketelhut, Clarke, Bowman, & Dede, 2005). The classification is also better aligned with design research in other fields where there is a deep connection between design and research (Stapleton, 2005), with skill sets in each area being necessary for successful innovation (Stappers, 2007). Focusing our conceptualization and communication about design research on the various small words that can connect design and

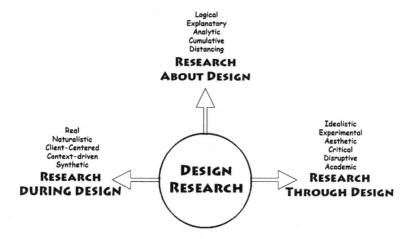

Fig. 1 Types of design research in a space of theory and practice

research (i.e., during, about, and through) can give designers an array of choices when designing, as well as develop critical understanding of what designers do.

Research During Design

This chapter contends that research activities that are an integral part of any design process as practiced should be viewed as design research. Further, it is assumed that design is occurring at all phases of a project, not just in one particular part of the design and development process labeled as design (see Bichelmeyer's, 2005 critique of the ADDIE model). As mentioned earlier, this assumes a broader definition of research as a systematic search or investigation to produce new knowledge, rather than scientific research as practiced by academic scholars. Instructional designers don't typically consider needs analysis, content analysis, learner analysis, etc. as research, even though research methods are employed (Boling, 2005). Some of the areas of design and development research described by Richey and Klein (2011) are similar to research during design—in particular, product development research that occurs during the design and development of an instructional product or program.

But while Richey and Klein's classification is similar to the notion of research during design as undertaken in other design fields, there are subtle but important differences. The major difference is that research during design would not be published. Instead, the findings of research during design serve the design process and the design decisions being made about project needs, requirements, conceptualizations, testing, etc. Results from such research may exist in some form of documentation to analyze what happened and why, but would never be publicly shared after the completion of the project. This is not to say that designers do not engage in such research activities in order to codify and share lessons learned. They definitely

Table 1 Some design research methods and tactics (Adapted from Bruseberg & Mcdonagh-Philp, 2000; Laurel, 2003; Roschuni, 2009)

Design phase	Methods or tactics
Up-front analysis	Product evaluations, usability testing (existing product), stakeholder interviews, focus group interviews, user interviews focused on existing situation/product, expert interviews, literature reviews, taxonomies, card sorting, observation, document analysis
Requirements definition	Personas, design workshops, dramatic/theatrical/narrative performance or document (scenarios), design games, experience cards, activity/task analysis, camera journal, empathy probes
Conceptual design	*Ideation*
	Design probes, use cases, layered elaboration, design in context
	Communication of ideas
	Storyboards, focus troupes, prototype trials, experience models and maps, conceptual design templates, content mapping, collaborative authoring (wikis)

utilize reflection-in-action (Schon, 1983) and post hoc reflection about their design activities (Shedroff, 2003). The point is that publishing results based on lessons learned in a particular project or with a particular tool is better considered research about design (as discussed below) rather than research during design, if for no other reason than for clarity in our discussions of the various types of design research.

One look at the contents of Brenda Laurel's book entitled *Design Research* (Laurel, 2003) reveals many ways that research activities are integrated into the design process in other design fields. There are specific tactics and design research methods (not models and not research methods) that are commonly employed in user experience design, product design, interactive design, etc. to help formulate design research plans for moving the design process forward from initial up-front considerations to design conceptualizations, prototype testing, and, finally, evaluation. The sampling of methods shown in Table 1 focuses on both products and process: The methods may examine existing products or situations in order to guide inquiry, but the methods themselves are processes. Settings for this research can be in labs, remote locations, or by using guerilla research tactics (Maier, 2011). The choice of design research method and location can also depend upon the type of data sources, research method (qualitative vs. quantitative), and context of use (Rohrer, 2008). Design research is a necessary part of design practice to complete design, production, product testing, and evaluation activities (Foshay & Quinn, 2005). Usability research is another common approach in interactive systems design and is becoming an important activity for research during design in the practice of instructional design as well (Baek, Cagiltay, Boling, & Frick, 2008).

The examples cited above are classified as research during design because the research is conducted with the intent to gather information, identify opportunities and constraints, understand the context, and make design, production, and evaluation decisions. It is research completed as part of the design process. Research during design might also be used to help bridge the gap between research and practice, if designers can be trained to act as translational developers (Norman, 2010).

Such individuals could "mine the insights of researchers and hone them into practical, reliable, and useful results. Similarly, translational developers must help convert the problems and concerns of practice into the clear, need-based statements that can drive researchers to develop new insights. Neither direction of translation is easy" (p. 12).

Research About Design

Some research in instructional design has focused on exploring and validating the effectiveness of design processes, developing and using new tools for design, and examining the characteristics and utility of various artifacts produced as part of design activities. This is research about design. The goal of such research is to " ... develop a detailed and unified understanding of the human activity of design or design related activities" (Forlizzi, Stolterman, & Zimmerman, 2009, p. 2892). It is a " ... form of design research that is exploratory of the process and the materials, it is through making ... that new ideas can be tested, to develop a critical understanding of what designers do and the objects that are created by design" (Burdick, 2003, p. 82). Research about design involves the analysis of design products and activities and operates from outside of the practice of design, conducting observations that keep the subjects and objects of design at a distance in order to produce "universally verifiable findings" (Schneider, 2007, p. 214).

When products are the focus of research about design, there may be a number of research questions regarding the efficacy of methods, models, or tools used to design and produce the products. The representations used by designers to document and communicate their design decisions and ideas can also have an impact as products on how a design is perceived by the design team and its stakeholders. Various representations or design sketches, written documentation, and other artifacts produced during design can be studied to determine the utility of the artifacts as design tools, as well as indicators of the nature and effectiveness of the design process and designer cognition (Baek et al., 2008; Purcell & Gero, 1998). There is also promise in the research about design being undertaken to study ways that a visual language for instructional design might be developed to express design elements as well as to document and communicate design features (Waters & Gibbons, 2004).

When process is the focus, the emphasis of research about design can involve models and tools as well as the activities of individual designers or collaborative design groups. There has been considerable research regarding instructional design automation with tools and with learning objects (e.g., see Richey, Klein, & Nelson, 2004, for a summary) and more recently with tools for learning design (Conole, 2010) and the use of design patterns (Frizell & Hübscher, 2002). New design models to guide learning experience design activities have been proposed (Chen, 2010; Cilesiz, 2010; Garrett, 2003; Park, 2008), while design culture and design communication processes have also been studied (Könings, Brand-Gruwel, & van Merriënboer, 2005).

Other related areas of research about design involve design cognition, the development of design expertise, and learning while designing. Designers learn as a result of their design activity, and design research in other fields suggests that design is inherently a learning process (Buchanan, 2001; Evenson & Dubberly, 2011). This is partly a function of designer cognition and expertise development (Lang & Fitzgerald, 2007; Lawson, 2006; Stolterman, 2008) and has been studied in the field of instructional design for some time (Wedman & Tessmer, 1992). It has been shown that disciplinary backgrounds and training of designers impact their decision making and influence the kinds of designs they create (Lang, 2008; Lawson, 2004). Development of instructional design expertise is enhanced by seeking a variety of design experiences, becoming familiar with capabilities of technological tools, learning to write well, and enjoying work. For success in an ever-changing landscape of instructional design practice, it is also necessary to develop a creative spirit for design work that features imagination, a product or production orientation, and facility in interdisciplinary activities (McDonald, 2011).

If our intent as professors of instructional technology is to help people learn to be instructional designers, how can we provide designers with learning environments that create the proper experiences and develop the appropriate expertise? One suggestion is to look at our culture of instructional design. Major differences exist between the design culture of instructional design and design cultures in other fields, and some believe that in order to develop a more robust design culture within instructional design, we should be teaching more than just design processes (Boling, 2005). Methods might include juries (Nelson, 2003), charrettes (Walker & Seymour, 2008), student-developed scenarios (Shambaugh, 2000), and desk *crits* (Shaffer, 2005).

Another suggestion that is a focus of current research in instructional design is teaching design in a studio format and using design pedagogies derived from other disciplines. Design studios provide a promising bridge between design practice and the academic concerns of schools, colleges, and universities (Brandt et al., 2011). This format has been shown to be effective in teaching instructional design (Clinton & Rieber, 2010), largely because the design context can be better represented and students gain experience in managing the complexities of design (Lawrence & Sharag-Eldin, 2000). Pedagogical practices that tend to be effective in the design studio include direct modeling and coaching, co-construction of problems through interaction and shared experiences between faculty and students, witnessing and critiquing, prompts, and reminders (Brandt et al., 2011). Such activities can occur in traditional face-to-face settings or in virtual, online studios.

The lines of inquiry mentioned above are all examples of research about design, which can help the field to develop not only new processes and tools for instructional design and development but also new understanding of ways to develop design expertise in students and new mind-sets for designers and researchers. When examining various examples of research about design, it is also clear that there is some overlap between this category and research through design, to be discussed below. This overlap is largely due to the purpose for the research. If the research focus is to learn more about design as it is practiced, then it is research about design, although new knowledge produced by research through design as a means of inquiry may also occur when studying design practice.

Research Through Design

In defining research through design, it is recognized that this is the kind of research that is generally referred to in the larger field of education as design research, design-based research (Barab & Squire, 2004; Design-Based Research Collective, 2003), or design experiments (Brown, 1992). But as Bereiter (2002) has noted, "… design research is not defined by its methods but by the goals of those who pursue it" (p. 321). The focus of this type of research is generally on academic questions rather than design practices. It provides an alternative perspective for theory development that can produce useful results that emerge from researchers working in contexts that directly impact educational practice (Edelson, 2002). Goals involve the study of learning in context, as well as progressive refinement of the design (Collins et al., 2004). Research through design typically utilizes participatory design processes, where the potential learners and teachers are an integral part of the design team (Könings et al., 2005). The emphasis in this form of design research is to produce and iteratively refine designed products that also advance the development of learning or instructional theories (Reeves et al., 2005). Such research is meant to develop theories, not to modify or *tune* what we already know to be working (Cobb, Confrey, DiSessa, Lehrer, & Schauble, 2003).

One way to distinguish research through design from other types of design research is by looking at the questions being asked by the researcher(s). Boess (2009) suggests that design questions that have concrete design goals, decisions, and evaluations, such as "Does X work?" where "X" is at the actual level of design practice, are a different question than meta-level questions involving research through design. She goes on to suggest that answers to these higher-level questions will be answered:

> … by systematically experimenting with the qualities of the materials. By creating a collaborative process in which domain knowledge from various experts is brought together to generate new avenues. Do these approaches work, and why? And what does this mean for the nature of internal and external processes in designing /the nature and process of collaboration/the use of objects made with the materials in specific situations? (p. 4541)

In a similar vein, Zimmerman, Forlizzi, and Evenson (2007), believe that the knowledge produced in research through design lies in the product, in the sense that the product "reflects a specific framing of the problem" that "provide[s] the catalyst and subject matter for discourse in the community" (p. 6). It is important to note here that research through design is situated in naturalistic contexts (Barab & Squire, 2004) where the products are being used, so that context is central to the goals of research (Kelly, 2006). One way of looking at product characteristics in order to compare designs is through the use of engagement curves which can assure that an instructional product possesses appropriate qualities of engagement (Parrish, 2008). Other forms of research through design that focus on product comparisons, validation, or effectiveness studies might benefit from an engineering research approach (Nieveen, McKenney, & van den Akker, 2006) where a variety of different studies using a variety of research methods are used to explore and confirm various aspects of the design (Sloane & Gorard, 2003).

There are also interesting trends in recent research through design that indicate new concerns for the quality of instructional products, not in the sense of effectiveness or professionalism of materials and activities, but in the sense of aesthetics (Parrish, 2009; Wilson, Parrish, & Veletsianos, 2008) and social impact (Campbell, Schwier, & Kenny, 2009; Yusop & Correia, 2011). The notion of aesthetic design (Parrish, 2009) can provide new lenses for research through design that is focused on transformative learning experiences such as adventure learning (Doering & Veletsianos, 2008) or consequential engagement (Gresalfi, Barab, Siyahhan, & Christensen, 2009), to name just a few new approaches to learning with technology tools.

Research through design supports the creation of emergent theory that can shape both the product being designed as well as the research methods and design processes being used, or as Joseph (2004) has noted: "The conjoined goals of developing effective designs and contributing to basic understandings create through their interactions a powerful engine for driving innovative work in education" (p. 241). Along with emergent theories, there may be "embodied conjectures" inherent in designs that offer ways to understand how designing educational interventions is inherently a theoretical activity where "the value of taking a theoretical stance toward design is that it then demands a methodology to confirm or disconfirm the conjectures embodied in design" (Sandoval, 2004, p. 26). But it is important to remember that though research through design might be seen as experimental, it is not a research experiment, nor does it generate and test hypotheses (Kelly, 2006). Instead, research through design can be used to both create "innovative learning ecologies" in local contexts, as well as "study the forms of learning that those learning ecologies are intended to support" (Gravemeijer & Cobb, 2006, p. 45).

Conclusions

This chapter has argued for a broader recognition of the interactions between research and design in the field of instructional technology. It has been noted that what has traditionally been called design research (or design-based research or development research or developmental research) is a different kind of endeavor than research meant to make decisions or draw conclusions (Rowland, 2007). It has also been suggested that research is an integral part of the design process, taking various forms and being used for various purposes (Rowland, 2008). As Bereiter (2002) has asserted, "Design research is part of the design process; if separated from it, it ceases to be design research p. 10." This chapter contends that the opposite is also true: if there is no research, there cannot be effective and successful design. This is true in all three categories proposed above. Similar to Fallman's (2008) analysis of research in interaction design, the types of research for instructional design described above serve different purposes. Research during design, as embodied in design practice, is meant to help understand and envision changes for situations, while research about design is meant to explain how and why design works the way it does. In contrast, research through design has a transcendent character with the goal of suggesting alternatives, identifying problems of practice, and criticizing the current state of affairs in order to provoke theoretical discussions.

A recent literature review has established the current state of design-based research (research through design) in education (Anderson & Shattuck, 2012), showing that 31 articles (66 % of all articles identified for the study) presented results of design-based research studies, with the remaining 16 articles focused on description and promotion of the approach. There was a "combined focus on theory building and practical, effective applications" (p. 24) that indicated design-based research was making a difference, but "mostly at the level of small-scale interventions and in the lives of individual teachers and schools" (p. 25). In order to move forward with the various research agendas that may comprise future instructional design research, new attitudes and conceptualizations about research and its role in instructional design will need to be established. Design has its own traditions and culture built from inquiry and action (Nelson & Stolterman, 2003), but that culture has not yet become pervasive in the instructional design field. We might get closer to a true design culture if we can acknowledge and accept that a designed instructional product is a work that can be "critically engaged as a vehicle of knowledge by a wide audience" (Chi, 2007, p. 7). This would require a different frame of reference, but might open up new opportunities for scholarly activities involving design criticism based on models of artistic research with an "enlightened eye" (Eisner, 1998).

We also need to continue to move conceptualizations of the field away from science and toward a design discipline (Owen, 2007). This will require a reexamination of our curricula, with an eye to clarifying for students the role of research in design. In particular, it may be useful to teach research during design to our bachelor's or master's students who plan to become design practitioners, while teaching research about design and research through design to our doctoral students who will continue to help expand the knowledge and theories for the field. This reconceptualization will also require new definitions and criteria for what is accepted as scholarship in our institutions and in our journals. If we continue to see design as a scientific field and require quantitative, basic research for our journals, we may not make the transition to a new design-based conceptualization of our field (Reeves, 2006).

Finally, through design research, significant innovation, and substantial improvement of educational outcomes can be achieved (Edelson, 2006). The evidence suggests that design research in the field of instructional design is becoming more common, but are we looking at the right questions and using the right methods compared to other design fields? Have we gone far enough in transforming our field from a science to a design discipline? Is design a form of research, or is research a subset of design? After all, we design research, don't we? It is time to envision new ways of doing research that can create and promote a more coherent culture for instructional design.

About the Author

Wayne Nelson is currently Faculty Fellow for Online Learning and Assessment at Southern Illinois University Edwardsville, after more than 25 years of teaching educational psychology and instructional technology, as well as serving as a department chairman. His research interests have included investigations of the characteristics of learning with various interactive media and the processes utilized to design learning activities and environments. In addition to teaching and research, he has maintained extensive involvement in efforts to integrate technology into the classrooms and curricula of schools and as a consultant to a variety of companies about learning, training, and design processes.

References

Anderson, T., & Shattuck, J. (2012). Design-based research: A decade of progress in education research? *Educational Researcher, 41*(1), 16–25. Retrieved from http://edr.sagepub.com/cgi/doi/10.3102/0013189X11428813.

Archer, B. (1995). The nature of research. *Co-Design, 1*(2), 6–13.

Baek, E.-O., Cagiltay, K., Boling, E., & Frick, T. (2008). User-centered design and development. In J. M. Spector, M. D. Merrill, J. van Merrienboer, & M. Driscoll (Eds.), *Handbook of research on educational communications and technology* (3rd ed., pp. 659–670). New York: Lawrence Erlbaum Associates.

Bannan-Ritland, B. (2003). The role of design in research: The integrative learning design framework. *Educational Researcher, 32*(1), 21–24. Retrieved from http://edr.sagepub.com/cgi/doi/10.3102/0013189X032001021.

Barab, S., & Squire, K. (2004). Design-based research: Putting a stake in the ground. *The Journal of the Learning Sciences, 13*(1), 1–14.

Bell, P. (2004). On the theoretical breadth of design-based research in education. *Educational Psychologist, 39*(4), 243–253.

Bereiter, C. (2002). Design research for sustained innovation. *Cognitive Studies, Bulletin of the Japanese Cognitive Science Society, 9*(3), 321–327.

Bichelmeyer, B. A. (2005). "The ADDIE Model"—A metaphor for the lack of clarity in the field of IDT. *IDT Record*. Retrieved August 2, 2012, from http://www.indiana.edu/~idt/shortpapers/documents/IDTf_Bic.pdf

Boess, S. (2009). Designing in research: Characteristics and criteria. *Rigor and Relevance in Design*. International Association of Societies of Design Research. Retrieved from http://www.iasdr2009.org/ap/Papers/Special Session/Assessing knowledge generated by research through design/Designing in research—characteristics and criteria—Research method, questions and programme.pdf

Boling, E. (2005). Teaching a design model vs. developing instructional designers. *IDT Record*. Retrieved September 2, 2012, from http://www.indiana.edu/~idt/shortpapers/documents/IDTf_Boling.pdf

Brandt, C. B., Cennamo, K., Douglas, S., Vernon, M., McGrath, M., & Reimer, Y. (2011). A theoretical framework for the studio as a learning environment. *International Journal of Technology and Design Education*, 1–10. Retrieved from http://www.springerlink.com/index/10.1007/s10798-011-9181-5

Brown, A. (1992). Design experiments: Theoretical and methodological challenges in creating complex interventions in classroom settings. *The Journal of the Learning Sciences, 2*(2), 141–178.

Bruseberg, A., & Mcdonagh-Philp, D. (2000). User-centred design research methods: The designer's perspective. In P. R. N. Childs & E. Brodhurst (Eds.), *Integrating design education beyond 2000 conference* (pp. 179–184). Sussex: University of Sussex.

Buchanan, R. (2001). Design research and the new learning. *Design Issues, 17*(4), 3–23.

Burdick, A. (2003). Design [as] research. In B. Laurel (Ed.), *Design research: Methods and perspectives* (p. 82). Cambridge, MA: MIT Press.

Campbell, K., Schwier, R. A., & Kenny, R. F. (2009). The critical, relational practice of instructional design in higher education: An emerging model of change agency. *Educational Technology Research and Development, 57*(5), 645–663.

Chen, P. (2010). From memorable to transformative e-learning experiences: Theory and practice of experience design. In H. Yang & S. Yuen (Eds.), *Handbook of research on practices and outcomes in e-learning: Issues and trends*. Hershey, NY: Information Science Reference.

Chi, L. (2007). Translations between design research and scholarship. *The Journal of Architectural Education, 61*(1), 7–10. Retrieved from http://doi.wiley.com/10.1111/j.1531-314X.2007.00120.x.

Cilesiz, S. (2010). A phenomenological approach to experiences with technology: Current state, promise, and future directions for research. *Educational Technology Research and Development, 59*(4), 487–510. Retrieved from http://www.springerlink.com/index/10.1007/s11423-010-9173-2.

Clinton, G., & Rieber, L. P. (2010). The studio experience at the University of Georgia: An example of constructionist learning for adults. *Educational Technology Research and Development, 58*(6), 755–780. Retrieved from http://www.springerlink.com/index/10.1007/s11423-010-9165-2.

Cobb, P., Confrey, J., DiSessa, A., Lehrer, R., & Schauble, L. (2003). Design experiments in educational research. *Educational Researcher, 32*(1), 9–13. Retrieved from http://edr.sagepub.com/cgi/doi/10.3102/0013189X032001009.

Collins, A., Joseph, D., & Bielaczyc, K. (2004). Design research: Theoretical and methodological issues. *The Journal of the Learning Sciences, 13*(1), 15–42.

Conole, G. (2010). Learning design—Making practice explicit. *ConnectEd 2010: 2nd International Conference on Design Education*. Sydney, Australia.

Design-Based Research Collective. (2003). Design-based research: An emerging paradigm for educational inquiry. *Educational Researcher, 32*(1), 5–8. Retrieved from http://edr.sagepub.com/cgi/doi/10.3102/0013189X032001005.

Dick, W., Carey, L., & Carey, J. (2009). *The systematic design of instruction* (7th ed.). Upper Saddle River, NJ: Merrill/Pearson.

Doering, A., & Veletsianos, G. (2008). What lies beyond effectiveness and efficiency? Adventure learning design. *The Internet and Higher Education, 11*(3–4), 137–144. Retrieved from http://linkinghub.elsevier.com/retrieve/pii/S109675160800047X.

Dorst, K. (2004). The problem of design problems. *The Journal of Design Research, 4*(3).

Edelson, D. C. (2002). Design research: What we learn when we engage in design. *The Journal of the Learning Sciences, 11*(1), 105–121.

Edelson, D. C. (2006). What we learn when we engage in design: Implications for assessing design research. In J. van den Akker, K. Gravemeijer, S. McKenney, & N. Nieveen (Eds.), *Educational design research*. New York: Routledge.

Eisner, E. (1998). *The enlightened eye :Qualitative inquiry and the enhancement of educational practice*. Upper Saddle River, NJ: Merrill.

Evenson, S., & Dubberly, H. (2011). Design as learning—or "knowledge creation"—the SECI model. *Interactions Magazine, 18*(2), 1–6.

Fallman, D. (2008). The interaction design research triangle of design practice, design studies, and design exploration. *Design Issues, 24*(3), 4–18. Retrieved from http://www.mitpressjournals.org/doi/abs/10.1162/desi.2008.24.3.4.

Forlizzi, J., Stolterman, E., & Zimmerman, J. (2009). From design research to theory: Evidence of a maturing field. *Rigor and Relevance in Design* (pp. 2889–2898). Korean Society of Design Science. Retrieved from http://www.iasdr2009.org/ap/index.html

Foshay, W. R., & Quinn, D. W. (2005). Innovations in instructional technology design science as a frame for evaluation of technology in education and training. In J. Michael Spector, C. Ohrazda, A. Van Schaak, & D. A. Wiley (Eds.), *Innovations in instructional technology: Essays in honor of M. David Merrill* (pp. 151–169). Mahwah, NJ: Lawrence Erlbaum Associates.

Frankel, L., & Racine, M. (2010). The complex field of research: For design, through design, and about design. In E. S. David Durling, Rabah Bousbaci, Lin-Lin Chen, Philippe Gauthier, Tiiu Poldma, Seymour Roworth-Stokes (Ed.), *Design & complexity: International conference of the Design Research Society*. Design Research Society. Retrieved from http://www.designresearchsociety.org/docs-procs/DRS2010/

Frayling, C. (1993). Research in art and design. *Royal College of Art Research Papers, 1*(1), 1–5.

Friedman, K. (2003). Theory construction in design research: Criteria, approaches, and methods. *Design Studies, 24*(6), 507–522.

Frizell, S. S., & Hübscher, R. (2002). Aligning theory and web-based instructional design practice with design patterns. In M. Driscoll & T. Reeves (Eds.), *Proceedings of world conference on e-learning in corporate, government, healthcare, and higher education* (pp. 298–304). Chesapeake, VA: Association for the Advancement of Computers in Education.

Garrett, J. J. (2003). *The elements of user experience*. Indianapolis: New Riders.

Gibbons, A. S. (2003). What and how do designers design ? A theory of design structure. *TechTrends, 47*(5), 22–27.

Gibbons, A. S., & Rogers, P. C. (2009). The architecture of instructional theory. In Charles M. Reigeluth & Alison A. Carr-Chellman (Eds.), *Instructional-design theories and models: Vol. 3: Building a common knowledge base* (pp. 305–326). New York: Routledge.

Glanville, R. (1999). Researching design and designing research. *Design Issues, 15*(2), 80–91.

Gravemeijer, K., & Cobb, P. (2006). Design research from a learning design perspective. In J. van den Akker, K. Gravemeijer, S. McKenney, & N. Nieveen (Eds.), *Educational design research* (pp. 45–85). New York: Routledge.

Gresalfi, M., Barab, S., Siyahhan, S., & Christensen, T. (2009). Virtual worlds, conceptual understanding, and me: Designing for consequential engagement. *On the Horizon, 17*(1), 21–34. Retrieved from http://www.emeraldinsight.com/10.1108/10748120910936126.

Gustafson, K., & Branch, R. (2002). *Survey of instructional development models*. Syracuse, NY: ERIC Clearing house on Information & Technology.

Hjelm, S. I. (2005). If everything is design, what then is a designer? *Nordes Conference*. Retrieved from http://www.nordes.org/opj/index.php/n13/article/view/234.

Jonassen, D. H. (2008). Design as problem solving: An iterative process. *Educational Technology, 48*(3), 21–26.

Joseph, D. (2004). The practice of design-based research: Uncovering the interplay between design, research, and the real-world context. *Educational Psychologist, 39*(4), 235–242.

Kelly, A. (2006). Quality criteria for design research: Evidence and commitments. In J. van den Akker, K. Gravemeijer, S. McKenney, & N. Nieveen (Eds.), *Educational design research* (pp. 166–184). New York: Routledge.

Kember, D., & Murpby, D. (1995). Research and the nature of design on ID fundamentals. In B. B. Seels (Ed.), *Instructional design fundamentals: A reconsideration* (Vol. 1, pp. 99–111). Englewood Cliffs, NJ: Educational Technology.

Könings, K. D., Brand-Gruwel, S., & van Merriënboer, J. J. G. (2005). Towards more powerful learning environments through combining the perspectives of designers, teachers, and students. *The British Journal of Educational Psychology, 75*(Pt 4), 645–660. Retrieved from http://www.ncbi.nlm.nih.gov/pubmed/16318683.

Lang, M. (2008). The influence of disciplinary backgrounds on design practices in web-based systems development. *Central European Conference on Information and Intelligent Systems*. Retrieved from http://www.ceciis.foi.hr/app/index.php/ceciis/2008/paper/view/131

Lang, M., & Fitzgerald, B. (2007). Web-based systems design: A study of contemporary practices and an explanatory framework based on "method-in-action". *Requirements Engineering, 12*(4), 203–220. doi:10.1007/s00766-007-0052-2.

Laurel, B. (Ed.). (2003). *Design research: Methods and perspectives*. Cambridge, MA: MIT Press.

Lawrence, A., & Sharag-Eldin, A. (2000). Reconstructing models of studio pedagogy in response to models of emerging professional practice. In L. V. Wells-Bowie (Ed.), *Proceedings of the ACSA 88th Annual meeting*. Washington, DC: Association of Collegiate Schools of Architecture.

Lawson, B. (2004). Schemata, gambits and precedent: some factors in design expertise. *Design Studies,* *25*(5), 443–457. Retrieved from http://linkinghub.elsevier.com/retrieve/pii/S0142694X04000328.

Lawson, B. (2006). *How designers think: The design process demystified* (4th ed.). Amsterdam: Architectural Press.

Love, T. (2002). Constructing a coherent cross-disciplinary body of theory about designing and designs: Some philosophical issues. *Design Studies, 23*(3), 345–361. Retrieved from http://linkinghub.elsevier.com/retrieve/pii/S0142694X01000436.

Maier, A. (2011). Complete beginner's guide to design research. *UX Booth Blog.* Retrieved from http://www.uxbooth.com/blog/complete-beginners-guide-to-design-research/

McDonald, J. K. (2011). The creative spirit of design. *TechTrends, 55*(5), 53–58. Retrieved from http://www.springerlink.com/index/10.1007/s11528-011-0528-2.

Mor, Y., & Winters, N. (2007). Design approaches in technology-enhanced learning. *Interactive Learning Environments, 15*(1), 61–75. doi:10.1080/10494820601044236.

Murphy, D. (1992). Is instructional design truly a design activity? *Educational and Training Technology International, 29*(4), 279–282.

National Science Foundation. (2012). Definitions of research and development: An annotated compilation of official sources. *Office of Management and Budget Circular A-11.* Retrieved February 22, 2012, from http://www.nsf.gov/statistics/randdef/fedgov.cfm

Nelson, B., Ketelhut, D. J., Clarke, J., Bowman, C., & Dede, C. (2005). Design-based research strategies for developing a scientific inquiry curriculum in a multi-user virtual environment. *Educational Technology, 45*(1), 21–28.

Nelson, H., & Stolterman, E. (2003). *The design way-intentional change in an unpredictable world. Foundations and fundamentals of design competence.* Englewood Cliffs, NJ: Educational Technology.

Nelson, W. A., Magliaro, S., & Sherman, T. M. (1988). The intellectual content of instructional design. *Journal of Instructional Development, 11*(1), 29–35.

Nelson, W. A. (2003). Problem solving through design. *New Directions for Teaching and Learning, 2003*(95), 39–44.

Nieveen, N., McKenney, S., & van den Akker, J. (2006). Educational design research: The value of variety. In J. van den Akker, K. Gravemeijer, S. McKenney, & N. Nieveen (Eds.), *Educational design research* (pp. 229–240). New York: Routledge.

Norman, D. A. (2010). The research-practice gap: The need for translational developers. *interactions magazine, 17*(4), 9–12. Retrieved from http://portal.acm.org/citation.cfm?doid=1806491.1806494

Owen, C. L. (1998). Design research: building the knowledge base. *Design Studies, 19*, 9–20.

Owen, C. L. (2004). What is design? Some questions and answers. Chicago, IL. Retrieved from http://www.herron.iupui.edu/sites/all/files/documents/whatisdes.pdf

Owen, C. L. (2007). Design thinking: Notes on its nature and use. *Design Research Quarterly, 2*(1), 16–27.

Park, J. Y. (2008). iLED: Interactive learning experience design. *MERLOT Journal of Online Learning and Teaching, 4*(3), 357–370.

Parrish, P. (2008). Plotting a learning experience. In L. Botturi & T. Stubbs (Eds.), *Handbook of visual languages in instructional design* (pp. 91–111). Hershey, PA: Information Science Reference.

Parrish, P. (2009). Aesthetic principles for instructional design. *Educational Technology Research and Development, 57*(4), 511–528.

Purcell, A. T., & Gero, J. (1998). Drawings and the design process: A review of protocol studies in design and other disciplines and related research in cognitive psychology. *Design Studies, 19*(4), 389–430. Retrieved from http://www.sciencedirect.com/science/article/pii/S0142694X 98000155.

Reeves, T. (2000). *Enhancing the worth of instructional technology research through "design experiments" and other development research strategies.* New Orleans, LA: American Educational Research Association.

Reeves, T. (2006). Design research from a technology perspective. In J. van den Akker, K. Gravemeijer, S. McKenney, & N. Nieveen (Eds.), *Educational design research* (pp. 86–109). New York: Routledge.

Reeves, T., Herrington, J., & Oliver, R. (2005). Design research: A socially responsible approach to instructional technology research in higher education. *Journal of Computing in Higher Education, 16*(2), 97–116.

Reigeluth, C. M., Bunderson, C. V., & Merrill, M. D. (1994). Is there a design science of instruction? In D. Merrill & D. G. Twitchell (Eds.), *Instructional design theory*. Englewood Cliffs, NJ: Educational Technology.

Reiser, R. A. (2001). A history of instructional design and technology: Part II: A history of instructional design. *Educational Technology Research and Development, 49*(2), 57–67.

Richey, R., & Klein, J. D. (2011). *Design and development research: Methods, strategies, and issues. Design.*. New York: Routledge.

Richey, R., Klein, J. D., & Nelson, W. A. (2004). Developmental research. In D. Jonassen (Ed.), *Handbook for research on educational communications and technology* (2nd ed., pp. 1099–1130). Hillsdale, NJ: Lawrence Erlbaum Associates.

Richey, R., Klein, J., & Tracey, M. (2011). *The instructional design knowledge base: Theory, research, and practice*. New York: Routledge.

Richey, R., & Nelson, W. A. (1995). Developmental research. In D. Jonassen (Ed.), *Handbook for research on educational communications and technology*. New York: MacMillan.

Rittel, H., & Webber, M. (1973). Dilemmas in a general theory of planning. *Policy Sciences, 4*, 155–169.

Rohrer, C. (2008). When to use which user experience research methods. *Jakob Nielsen's Alertbox*. Retrieved from http://www.useit.com/alertbox/user-research-methods.html

Roschuni, C. (2009). Design research methods. Retrieved from http://roschuni.com/wiki/index.php/Design_Research_Methods

Rowland, G. (1993). Designing and instructional design. *Educational Technology Research and Development, 41*(1), 79–91.

Rowland, G. (2007). Educational inquiry in transition: Research and design. *Educational Technology, 47*(2), 14–23.

Rowland, G. (2008). Design and research: Partners for educational innovation. *Educational Technology, 48*(6), 3–9.

Sanders, L. (2008). An evolving map of design practice and design research. *Interactions Magazine, 15*(6), 13. Retrieved from http://portal.acm.org/citation.cfm?doid=1409040.1409043.

Sandoval, W. (2004). Developing learning theory by refining conjectures embodied in educational designs. *Educational Psychologist, 39*(4), 213–223. Retrieved from http://www.informaworld.com/openurl?genre=article&doi=10.1207/s15326985ep3904_3&magic=crossref||D404A21C5BB053405B1A640AFFD44AE3.

Schneider, B. (2007). Design as practice, science, and research. In M. Ralph (Ed.), *Design research now: Essays and selected projects* (1st ed., pp. 207–218). Basel: Birkhauser Verlag.

Schon, D. (1983). *The reflective practitioner*. New York: Basic Books.

Shaffer, D. W. (2005). *Studio mathematics: The epistemology and practice of design pedagogy as a model for mathematics learning*. Madison, WI: Media.

Shambaugh, N. (2000). Using student-developed scenarios to couple design and reflection. *TechTrends, 48*(3), 26–31.

Shavelson, R. J., Phillips, D. C., Towne, L., & Feuer, M. J. (2003). On the science of education design studies. *Educational Researcher, 32*(1), 25–28. Retrieved from http://edr.sagepub.com/cgi/doi/10.3102/0013189X032001025.

Shedroff, N. (2003). Research methods for designing effective experiences. In B. Laurel (Ed.), *Design research: Methods and perspectives* (pp. 155–163). Cambridge, MA: MIT Press.

Sloane, F. (2006). Normal and design sciences in education: Why both are necessary. In J. van den Akker, K. Gravemeijer, S. McKenney, & N. Nieveen (Eds.), *Educational design research* (pp. 19–44). New York: Routledge.

Sloane, F., & Gorard, S. (2003). Exploring modeling aspects of design experiments. *Educational Researcher, 32*(1), 29–31. Retrieved from http://edr.sagepub.com/cgi/doi/10.3102/0013189X032001029.

Smith, P. L., & Ragan, T. J. (2005). *Instructional Design* (3rd ed.). Hoboken, NJ: Wiley.

Stapleton, A. J. (2005). Research as design-design as research. *Proceedings of the DiGRA 2005 Conference: Changing Views—Worlds in Play.*

Stappers, P. J. (2007). Doing design as a part of doing research. In R. Michel (Ed.), *Design research now: Essays and selected projects* (pp. 81–97). Basel: Birkhauser Verlag.

Stolterman, E. (2008). The nature of design practice and implications for interaction design research. *International Journal of Design, 2*(1), 55–65. Retrieved from http://www.ijdesign. org/ojs/index.php/IJDesign/article/view/240/148.

van den Akker, J. (1999). Principles and methods of development research. In J. Van Den Akker, R. Branch, K. Gustafson, N. Nieveen, & T. Plomp (Eds.), *Design approaches and tools in education and training* (pp. 1–14). Dordrecht, The Netherlands: Kluwer Academic.

Walker, J. B., & Seymour, M. W. (2008). Utilizing the design charrette for teaching sustainability. *International Journal of Sustainability in Higher Education, 9*(2), 157–169. Retrieved from http://www.emeraldinsight.com/10.1108/14676370810856305.

Waters, S. H., & Gibbons, A. S. (2004). Design languages, notation systems, and instructional technology: A case study. *Educational Technology Research and Development, 52*(2), 57–68. Retrieved from http://www.springerlink.com/index/10.1007/BF02504839.

Wedman, J., & Tessmer, M. (1992). Instructional designers' decisions and priorities: A survey of design practice. *Performance Improvement Quarterly, 6*(2), 43–57.

Wilson, B. G., Parrish, P. E., & Veletsianos, G. (2008). Raising the bar for instructional outcomes: Toward transformative learning experiences. *Educational Technology, 48*(3), 39–44.

Yusop, F. D., & Correia, A.-P. (2011). The civic-minded instructional designers' framework: An alternative approach to contemporary instructional designers' education in higher education. *British Journal of Educational Technology, 43*(2), 180–190.

Zimmerman, J., Forlizzi, J., & Evenson, S. (2007). Research through design as a method for interaction design research in HCI. *Human-Computer Interaction.* Retrieved from http://repository. cmu.edu/hcii/41

Reconceptualizing Instructional Message Design: Toward the Development of a New Guiding Framework

M.J. Bishop

Keywords Instructional design • Message design • Instructional message design • Communication theory • Learning theory • Information-processing theory • Multimedia learning • Redundancy • Communication noise • Attention • Retrieval • Theoretical framework

According to Pettersson (2002, 2007), message design in the broadest sense comprises the analysis, planning, presentation, and understanding of the content, language, and form of messages that are created for the purpose of satisfying the aesthetic, economic, ergonomic, and subject matter information needs of the intended receivers. More specifically within the educational context, message design has been defined as the manipulation and planning of signs and symbols for the purpose of modifying the cognitive, affective, or psychomotor behavior of one or more persons (Fleming & Levie, 1978, 1993; National Council for Accreditation of Teacher Education (NCATE), 2000, 2005; Seels & Richey, 1994). As a part of the overall instructional design process, instructional message design is the point at which generalized specifications about the nature of instruction are translated into the specific plans for the instructional materials to be used and how they should be designed in order to enhance learning from them (Grabowski, 1991; Reigeluth, 1983). And, like the field of instructional design generally, perspectives on instructional message design have changed as the theoretic orientations of psychologists and educators have changed over the years about how people learn.

Berry (1995) thoroughly reviewed this evolution within instructional message design, beginning with the early behavioral emphasis on realistic, direct experiences (Carpenter, 1953; Dale, 1969; Gibson, 1954; Morris, 1946), through the cognitivist interest in designing messages to overcome mental processing limitations in

M.J. Bishop (✉)
Lehigh University, Bethlehem, PA 18015, USA
e-mail: mj.bishop@lehigh.edu

B. Hokanson and A. Gibbons (eds.), *Design in Educational Technology*,
Educational Communications and Technology: Issues and Innovations 1,
DOI 10.1007/978-3-319-00927-8_9, © Springer International Publishing Switzerland 2014

attention, perception, and filtering of information and to facilitate the basic processes and structures associated with storage and retrieval of information (Hannafin
& Hooper, 1989, 1993; Hannafin & Rieber, 1989a, 1989b; Hooper & Hannafin,
1988). Berry's historical review noted further that, by the early 1990s, a philosophical shift toward constructivism and the creation of learner- and context-centered
environments was causing some to argue that traditional instructional design and
instructional message design orientations were antithetical to this new educational
approach—stirring considerable debate in the field.

The concern was essentially that the systems approach had led to mechanistic
notions of learning driven largely by cause-and-effect/input–output analyses of
effectiveness. Further, cognitive psychology's reliance on "an objectivist conception of knowledge" meant its constructs were fundamentally no different than traditional behaviorist notions (Jonassen, 1990, p. 32). According to constructivists such
as Cooper (1993), Jonassen (1990, 1991), and Kember and Murphy (1990), knowledge does not exist independently of learners but, rather, is actively constructed
through interactions between learners' prior understandings and new, authentic
experiences with the world. Duffy and Cunningham (1996) argued, therefore, that
the notion we can create an optimally effective instructional communication system
resulting in wholly shared meaning between the sender and receiver is misguided.
Jonassen (1990) contended the field should, instead, be seeking ways to support
learners' active knowledge construction. Hannafin (1992) agreed and argued further
that "external agents" such as teachers or instructional materials should be recast
"as activators for learning rather than mediators of knowledge" (p. 53).

Despite Grabowski's (1991) and others' efforts to clarify the role message design
might still play within a more learner-centered paradigm (see Bednar, Cunningham,
Duffy, & Perry, 1991; Winn, 1993), use of the term *instructional message design*
appears to have fallen out of favor since the mid-1990s. Further, as Molenda and
Boling (2007) observed, instructional message design research has been fairly
sparse since Dwyer's visual literacy studies in the early 1990s, with recent compila-
tions of research-based principles for instructional media designers still relying
principally on earlier empirical work (see Lohr, 2008; Morrison, Ross, Kalman, &
Kemp, 2011). It appears that, while instructional design has philosophically moved
away from "the design of pre-specified instructional routines" to be delivered in a
variety of communication formats and toward "the design of environments to facilitate learning" (Januszewski & Molenda, 2008, p. 2), little attention has been paid
over the last 20 years on what Fleming (1993) viewed as the "linking science"
between learning theory and instructional practice (citing Dewey, 1900). In its
place, research in this area has focused increasingly on highly constrained comparison studies of multimedia learning and its effects on cognitive processes (see work
by Mayer, 2001, 2003, 2005, 2008, 2009, 2011; and his colleagues Clark, Johnson,
Moreno, and others).

Advocating for the revitalization of instructional message design as an area of
inquiry, I recently traced the field's theoretical and historical foundations at the
intersection of communication and learning theory, explored the current issues discussed above, and recommended three paths to future relevance: (a) a revised

theoretical framework based in a *transactional* rather than *transmission* model of communications, (b) a broader definitional focus that looks at more than just optimizing cognitive processing, and (c) a new systems view of our approach to research in this area (Bishop, 2013). This chapter takes the next step toward creating a guiding framework for thinking about message design in learner-centered environments by revisiting a model I actually created more than 10 years ago as I was exploring sound's potential to facilitate learning within the instructional communication system (see Bishop, 2000; Bishop & Cates, 2001). In the sections that follow, I will trace my development of this framework within the context of the research over the last 10 years on multimedia learning. I will then discuss how the framework's recommendations might be applied to inform the design of instructional messages to facilitate learning.

Research on Multimedia Learning

At about the time research on instructional message design trailed off, Mayer and his colleagues began very systematically exploring a line of research they have called *multimedia learning* (Mayer, 2001, 2003, 2005, 2009). Grounded in cognitive load theory (Paas, Renkl, & Sweller, 2003; Sweller, 2005), the three goals of this program of inquiry have been to identify for designers how they might (a) reduce cognitive processing that is extraneous (does not serve the instructional goal), (b) manage cognitive processing that is essential (builds a mental representation of the presented material), and (c) foster cognitive processing that is generative (exerts effort to make sense of the presented material and integrate with existing knowledge structures) (Mayer, 2013). Over the years, multimedia learning research has been scientifically rigorous and intentionally rooted in authentic learning situations and materials.

For example, to test the *arousal theory* notion that more learning will occur when instructional materials are added that arouse learners' emotions (Berlyne, 1960; Eysenck, 1982; Yerkes & Dodson, 1908), Mayer and his colleagues conducted a series of eleven studies to see what effects adding "interesting but irrelevant" text, images, and sounds would have on recall and retention of instructional content (see Harp & Mayer, 1997, 1998; Mayer et al., 1996; Mayer, Heiser, & Lonn, 2001; Moreno & Mayer, 2000). The researchers added materials that, while interesting and tangentially related to the topic under study, were almost entirely irrelevant to the intended learning outcome. In a scientific lesson on how lightning forms, for instance, the researchers added short vignettes on how many Americans are killed and injured each year by lightning (Harp & Mayer, 1997, 1998). In another study utilizing the same lightning content, they added a "synthesized and bland" 20-s instrumental musical clip that looped in the background (Moreno & Mayer, 2000). The findings from these studies clearly indicated that student learning does not increase, and in many regards actually decreases, when these sorts of "seductive details" are added to instructional presentations. The problem with arousal theory,

Mayer (2001) concluded, is that it too was based on an outdated, objectivist view of message design. He argued further that when we instead view learning as a process of knowledge construction—"involving selecting relevant information, organizing the information into a coherent structure, and integrating material with existing knowledge" (p. 119)—it follows that including these extraneous materials may hinder rather than facilitate learning.

The *coherence principle* derived from this research, therefore, unilaterally recommends that designers of instructional materials "delete extraneous material from multimedia instruction" as it competes for cognitive resources in working memory (Mayer & Moreno, 2010, p. 137). But, while this and other principles derived from research on multimedia learning tell us how not to design instructional messages, they do not yet provide much guidance on how to design instructional messages (Boling, 2010; Krippendorff, 2006). How do we determine what is likely to be extraneous material versus what is likely to be essential and/or generative material? What models should we be using to make these message design decisions and on what information about the learner and the learning context should we be basing those decisions?

Development of the Framework

Like the evolution of instructional message design generally, my framework for thinking more systematically about the design of instructional messages emerged from the juxtaposition of communication and cognitive processing theories. This section supplies those theoretical foundations for the framework, describes my application of communication theory to learning, and demonstrates how the much-maligned concept of redundancy might be recast to inform the design of instructional communications systems that facilitate knowledge construction.

Theoretical Foundations in Communication Theory

Early communication theorists—engineers such as Shannon and Weaver (1949), Lasswell (1948), and Gerbner (1956)—emphasized the process of communication. Concerned with efficiency and accuracy in the various stages of mechanical message transmission, proponents of process considered misunderstandings between the sender and receiver simply to be technical breakdowns among the system elements. These researchers not only proposed a particularly linear causality in terms of sender, message, channel, and receiver but also suggested that a complete understanding of the system might be possible by studying each system element separately. Therefore, the process school focused its research primarily on individual elements and isolating the component processes of communication (Krippendorff, 1975).

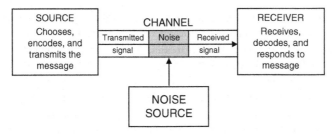

Fig. 1 The communication system (Adapted from Shannon & Weaver, 1949)

For example, the Shannon–Weaver model depicts a simple linear system (see Fig. 1). A source (far left) chooses information to communicate, encodes the message in a way appropriate for the size of the communication channel, and transmits a signal. The transmitted signal (middle left) begins making its way through the limited-capacity channel. As the transmitted signal moves from left to right, it encounters noise that has been introduced into the system by an external noise source (illustrated here as a box located below the channel). As the transmitted signal passes through channel noise, it is potentially altered into what will ultimately be the signal received (middle right). The receiver receives the altered signal, decodes it as well as possible, and is potentially affected by the message in some way.

At the time he developed this model, Claude Shannon was employed by Bell Telephone Company as a research scientist working to minimize the distortion and maximize the capacity of telephone lines. The complex formulas for signal transmission presented in his original paper, "The Mathematical Theory of Communication," were never intended to be applied to anything but mechanistic communication channels. As such, his paper did not discuss the semantic meaning of a message or its pragmatic effects on the listener. It was Warren Weaver's supplemental paper, which accompanied Shannon's original description of the model in the 1949 publication, that explained Shannon's complicated ideas in layman's terms and applied the model to communication more broadly.

In his elaboration, Weaver (Shannon & Weaver, 1949) divided the analysis of communication problems into three levels. The simplest and closest to Shannon's original intent for the model, Level A, deals with how accurately the symbols can be transmitted. Here, technical errors introduced into the communication from competing external or internal stimuli overpower all or part of a transmission, preventing the receiver from being able to select the communicated signal for decoding. Level B concerns how precisely the transmitted symbols convey the desired meaning. Problems at this level arise from semantic errors that occur when the receiver has no interpretive framework for analyzing an incoming signal and none is supplied by the source, preventing accurate decoding. Level C addresses how effectively the received meaning affects conduct in the desired way. At this level, problems arise when the connotative meaning of a message—such as aesthetic appeal, style, execution, and other psychological and emotional factors—fails to match the receiver's own relevant beliefs, cultural values, and experiences, resulting in conceptual errors that can prevent the communication from producing the desired outcome.

According to the Shannon–Weaver model, these three communication levels are interrelated and interdependent. It becomes very difficult for a signal to convey its message (Level B) when there are errors in the signal's transmission (Level A). Similarly, a message is unlikely to produce the desired outcome (Level C) if misinterpreted (Level B) or received inaccurately (Level A). But, while the Shannon–Weaver model acknowledged that communication problems can occur in the interpersonal aspects of conversation as well, they neither depicted these transactions in their model nor explored these processes further. That said, they did suggest that efforts to find solutions to problems at Levels B and C might be guided, at least analogically, by the same techniques that have proven effective at Level A.

Over the years since the Shannon–Weaver model was published, however, Jackson (1969) and others have argued that because human communication systems are dynamic functional systems, understanding the communication of meanings and the ultimate effect a message has on its receiver is much too complicated for linear, cause-and-effect approaches (see Fisher, 1975; Newcomb, 1953; Schramm, 1955; Westley & MacLean, 1957). Rather than view communication as a straight line, these theorists contended that the key to systematic understanding is viewing communication as circles of influence. By tracing these circles of influence, one can see the patterns that repeat themselves, making problem situations better or worse, and can detect how this feedback can be used to control the process.

For this reason, communication theorists like Peirce (1931), Osgood (1967), Ogden and Richards (1956), and Saussure (1913/1986), who viewed communication as the production and exchange of meanings, have emphasized the structure of communication. These theorists pursued the science of signs and meanings, or semiotics, and focused on the relationships among the elements of a message that enable it to signify something to particular receivers. Proponents of semiotics consider misunderstandings to be the result of any number of problems within the communication system. Semioticians maintain that because communication has holistic qualities that are more than the sum of its parts, a research strategy that only observes each unit separately cannot possibly explain the entire system. In addition to studying individual system elements and component processes, the semioticians focus their research on discovering the outcomes of communication and understanding the underlying dynamics of the process as a whole.

Application of Learning Theory to the Framework

Clearly there is a good deal of synergy between the Shannon–Weaver model and its development over time and the classic information-processing model first suggested by Atkinson and Shiffrin (1968). Understanding the complex "circles of influence" in instructional communication—the important elements, component processes, associated problems, and potential solutions to problems—might, therefore, begin

Fig. 2 Receiver's component knowledge-construction processes (Bishop, 2000)

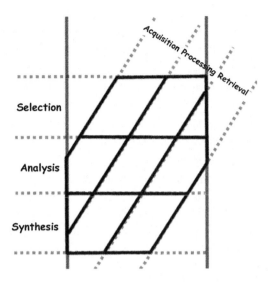

by adding the receiver's information-processing transactions to the Shannon–Weaver model. Figure 2 depicts the receivers' component processes in more detail, illustrating an idealized representation of the three levels of communication as three knowledge construction phases (the selection, analysis, and synthesis rows) (Mayer, 1999; Wittrock, 1990, 2010). To attain each of these learning levels, one cyclically applies to a greater or lesser extent the three information-processing operations (the acquisition, processing, and retrieval columns) (Neisser, 1976). The dividing lines between acquisition, processing, and retrieval dissect the illustration diagonally in order to depict how each operation is applied in varying amounts as information flows through the system during learning (Driscoll, 2005). Processing is depicted as the middle of the three because it relies on acquisition and retrieval to supply the information and memories it acts upon. During selection, processing calls upon acquisition heavily; in contrast, only the most salient memories are retrieved during selection. During analysis, processing is central, although acquisition and retrieval are also relatively active. During synthesis, processing calls upon retrieval most heavily, while only the most salient new stimuli are acquired. Whether conscious (strategic) or unconscious (automatic), executive control processes within the information-processing system make decisions about information flow and processing priorities as learning progresses through the selection, analysis, and synthesis phases (Atkinson & Shiffrin, 1971; Gagné, 1985; Phye & Andre, 1986).

Messages that have entered the sensory registry are processed within this grid of interacting and interdependent levels and operations. However, this rarely occurs without information-processing noise entering the system. As we know from research on the limitations of human perception and cognition, instructional communication systems can fail because of errors induced by excessive noise within any of the three information-processing operations. Table 1 depicts these potential problems in instructional communication. *Acquisition noise* (first column) is the sum of

Table 1 Problems in instructional communication (Adapted from Bishop, 2000; Bishop & Cates, 2001)

	Acquisition noise	Processing noise	Retrieval noise	Outcomes
Selection Technical difficulties Competing internal and external stimuli cause message-transmission problems	Learner has trouble directing attention to the instructional message	Learner does not identify patterns in the instructional message	Learner cannot locate existing schemas that relate to information contained in the instructional message	Learner fails to *select* message
Analysis Semantic difficulties Missing interpretive frameworks cause message-interpretation problems	Learner has trouble focusing attention on the instructional message	Learner cannot organize the information contained in the instructional message	Learner does not use the information contained in the instructional message to build upon existing knowledge	Learner fails to *analyze* message
Synthesis Effectiveness difficulties Prompt/schema mismatches cause message-understanding problems	Learner has trouble sustaining attention on the instructional message over time	Learner cannot elaborate upon the information contained in the instructional message	Learner does not use the information contained in the instructional message to construct transferable knowledge structures	Learner fails to *synthesize* message

competing external and internal stimuli that disrupt learners receiving instructional signals at all. These errors in the channel often cause the learner to fail to attend to the communicated instructional material throughout the knowledge construction process. Individuals remain essentially unaware of information not selected for attention. *Processing noise* (second column) is the sum of errors that distort instructional message decoding in each level of knowledge construction. These errors can cause the learner to misinterpret the instructional signals. Information that does not get properly analyzed is quickly discarded or overwritten. *Retrieval noise* (third column) is the sum of errors that prevent the instructional message from being properly matched to larger conceptual structures. These errors can cause the learner to misunderstand the instructional signal and to misfile it in long-term memory, making later retrieval difficult if not impossible.

Following the cells vertically down the information-processing columns, the framework anticipates deepening attentional, organizational, and relational difficulties across the rows at each subsequent phase of knowledge construction (top to bottom). For example, Shiffrin (1988) suggested that while it can be difficult to overcome acquisition noise at selection in order to gain a learner's attention, it often is much harder to overcome acquisition noise in analysis in order to focus a learner's attention and harder still to hold a learner's attention over time for synthesis.

Following the cells horizontally across the rows, the framework depicts how, at each deeper phase of active learning, the relative strength of potential noise as well as the ultimate consequence of that noise increases. For example, if an instructional message does not direct attention, help the learner identify patterns, or access existing knowledge, the learner is not likely to select the material for further study. If the message does not focus attention, organize the new information, or build upon existing knowledge, then the learner is not likely to analyze the material. And if the message does not hold attention over time, elaborate upon the new information, or support new knowledge constructions, then the learner is not likely to synthesize the material. Fixing these problems in the instructional communication system involves revisiting another very useful but often misunderstood communications concept that was also first proposed by Shannon and Weaver: redundancy.

Redundancy in Communication

The Shannon–Weaver model makes a sharp distinction between the information contained in a message and the meaning of a message. Messages are ordered sets of perceptual elements or cues drawn from a particular pool and assembled in a deliberate way (Potts, 1977). The model defines information as the freedom that a source has in choosing and putting together those message cues. In this sense, the concept of information applies not to the messages themselves, as is the case with meaning, but instead to the degrees of freedom within the situation as a whole. In other words, information is what a source *could* communicate, whereas meaning is what a source *does* communicate. Sometimes called the *surprisal* factor, information is that aspect of a message that removes or reduces uncertainty in the situation (Pask, 1975).

For example, in a simplified situation where messages are paired elements taken from the pool ♣, ♦, ♥, and ♠, the maximum number of potential element combinations, or messages, is 16:

♣ ♦	♦ ♥	♥ ♠	♠ ♣
♣ ♥	♦ ♠	♥ ♣	♠ ♦
♣ ♠	♦ ♣	♥ ♦	♠ ♥
♣ ♣	♦ ♦	♥ ♥	♠ ♠

Assuming nothing is known of the source's intent, from the receiver's perspective, there is a one-in-sixteen chance the source will assemble a particular message for communication. One might say that this probability is a measure of the level of uncertainty in the situation. When the source communicates ♥♣, the message resolves that uncertainty. If the number of elements in the pool is increased to 5, the number of choices and, therefore, the level of uncertainty in the situation double to 32. That means the same ♥♣ message, when chosen from a five-symbol pool, clears up even more uncertainty. It is said to contain more information. Thus, the larger the pool of possible message elements from which to choose—that is, the greater the degrees of freedom in a situation—the smaller the probability that a particular message will be communicated. Stated differently, the more elements in the pool, the more uncertain is the situation and the more information-filled is the message ultimately communicated. While uncertainty suggests future events and information past events, the property in question is the same. In communication theory, that property is referred to as *entropy*.

As a measure of the predictability or certainty in a situation, *redundancy* is the opposite of entropy. Continuing the four-symbol example from above, consider a transmitted signal encountering noise that generates the following error-filled message:

Through the noise, the receiver can discern that the first cue is ♣. This information provides the receiver with enough certainty to eliminate three-quarters of the possible messages (all those that do not begin with the ♣ symbol). Nonetheless, because of the error, the receiver remains uncertain of the identity of the second cue and, hence, of the message. The second cue could be any one of the four symbolic possibilities. However, if the receiver knows that the source is combining only cues of the same color, the possibilities for the second cue are reduced to ♣ or ♠. Color redundancy between the message cues halves the receiver's uncertainty about the identity of the second cue. Assume further that the receiver knows that the source is combining only cues of the same color and the same shape. Now, receiving only the first ♣ through the noise is sufficient for the receiver also to know the identity of the second cue. Within this context, the message, despite its errors, resolves all of the receiver's uncertainty. In other words, the addition of a syntax, of sorts, for the message's structure added the redundancy necessary to defeat the adverse effects of noise in the system.

Fixing Problems in Instructional Communication Using Redundancy

In this way, Shannon and Weaver argued that increasing various types of redundancy between message cues can help to offset technical, semantic, and effectiveness noise in the communication system. Thus, redundancy, in the Shannon and Weaver sense, is a good thing for communication—it comprises the parts of a message that reduces or eliminates the receiver's uncertainty over the source's intent. And, while redundancy can be eliminated without sacrificing any information in the message, doing so is very likely to increase the receiver's uncertainty over the sender's intent behind the message, particularly in noisy communications channels. Fiske (2011) agreed and argued,

Table 2 Application of various types of redundancy to the solution of instructional communication problems (Adapted from Bishop, 2000; Bishop & Cates, 2001)

	Content redundancy	Context redundancy	Construct redundancy	
	Amplifies the content for message acquisition	Supplies the context for message processing	Cues appropriate constructs for message understanding	Outcomes
Selection Encourages noise-defeating learner selection states	1. Message cues help learners direct attention	2. Message cues help learners identify patterns	3. Message cues help learners tie into previous knowledge	Learner is interested
Analysis Encourages noise- defeating learning analysis strategies	4. Message cues help learners focus attention	5. Message cues help learners organize information	6. Message cues help learners build upon existing knowledge	Learner is curious
Synthesis Encourages noise-defeating learner synthesis schemes	7. Message cues help learners hold attention over time	8. Message cues help learners elaborate upon information	9. Message cues help learners prepare knowledge structures for transfer to new learning contexts	Learner is engaged

> The layman's use of the term [redundancy] to imply uselessness is misleading. Redundancy is not merely useful in communication, it is absolutely vital. In theory, communication can take place without redundancy, but in practice the situations in which this is possible are so rare to be non-existent. A degree of redundancy is essential to practical communication. (p. 9)

According to Fiske, redundancy in the Shannon–Weaver sense serves two purposes. First, redundancy is a technical aid that overcomes deficiencies of a noisy channel, facilitates the accuracy of decoding, and helps overcome the problems of transmitting a highly entropic message. "These problems may be associated with accuracy and error detection, with the channel and noise, with the nature of the message, or with the audience" (p. 11). The second function of redundancy, Fiske suggested, is to introduce shared patterns or "conventions" into a message structure, which helps to overcome message interpretation (Level B) and message effectiveness (Level C) problems. In this way, for example, "redundancy is a critical part of the satisfaction provided by the form or structure of a work of art" (p. 13). It appears various types of redundancy may help to overcome the noise that can raise barriers at each level of communication.

Table 2, therefore, applies *content, context,* and *construct* redundancy strategies for designing instructional message cues to facilitate information processing (see acquisition, processing, and retrieval columns) at each level of knowledge construction (see selection, analysis, synthesis rows). Thus, when one traces the first, selection-level row of cells horizontally across the information-processing stages, the framework suggests that instructional message cues should be employed that will help learners direct attention (cell 1), identify patterns (cell 2), and tie into previous knowledge (cell 3). Similarly, message cues should help learners to focus attention (cell 4), to organize information (cell 5), and to build upon existing knowledge (cell 6). Likewise, message cues should be combined to help learners hold attention over time (cell 7), to elaborate upon new information (cell 8), and to prepare knowledge for later use (cell 9).

When designed systematically into the instruction in this way, various redundancies used in the development of instructional messages might supplement learning environments with the additional content, context, and construct support necessary to overcome many of the acquisition, processing, and retrieval problems one might encounter at each level of knowledge construction. This more deliberate and theory-grounded approach to the selection and use of various modalities in instructional communications might, therefore, be the key to identifying *essential, generative,* and *non-extraneous* message cues aimed at facilitating the cognitive processing necessary for knowledge construction.

Application of the Framework

For example, to facilitate selection-level cognitive processes one might begin a lesson on lightning by including multimedia materials that enhance the lesson's curb appeal (cell 1), establish the communication syntax (cell 2), and make the content relatable (cell 3). An opening title sequence with The Doors' "Riders On the Storm" (and its accompanying stormy sound effects) playing softly in the background might depict a scene just outside a house window on a stormy night. Inside, the learner sees a shadowy young male/female couple fighting and hears their muffled verbal exchange. While their actual words are inaudible (like the way adults' voices were depicted in the *Peanuts* cartoons), it is clear from the sounds of their voices their frustration is mounting over an apparent disagreement that slowly builds both visually and auditorially until it erupts into an explosion of angry shouting—timed perfectly, of course, with a thunderous boom and clap of lightning.

To encourage analysis-level cognitive processing, the lesson might then incorporate materials that signal how to isolate and disambiguate information (cell 4), provide a means for organizing the material (cell 5), and suggest the ways the content might fit into existing knowledge structures (cell 6). After the opening sequence, the lightning lesson might then directly relate the building tension and eventual eruption of an argument to the processes involved in the formation of lightning. The closely cropped scene outside the couple's window backs away to depict a wide shot that still includes the house with the couple still in view in the window, but now the shot also allows the learner to see idealized illustrations of what is occurring in the sky as a storm develops and lightning forms. As each of the five discrete steps in the lightning formation process are depicted, a corresponding segment of the couple's opening animation is played and accompanied by discrete sound bytes of the initial conversation (perhaps with the woman's voice accompanying positive charges and man's voice accompanying negative charges), intensifying irritation (voices get louder, faster paced, and more highly pitched), and an eventual angry outburst (perhaps accompanied by thunder to make it clearly different from the other sounds).

At the synthesis level, appropriate cognitive processing might be facilitated by multimedia lesson materials that provide opportunities to play with ideas (cell 7), enable learners to organize the material in ways that make the most sense to them (cell 8), and allow experimenting with the ways the material fits into the learners' unique existing knowledge structures (cell 9). While the lesson's embedded practice opportunities would, at first, make use of the lesson's argument analogy and accompanying multimedia cues to reinforce content, the lesson might then also provide learners opportunities to consider other analogous models for mentally representing the material under study, allowing for the diversity of prior experiences and knowledge that learners bring to the learning context. For example, after reviewing the five lightning formation steps in conjunction with the couple's analogous building argument, learners might then be given the opportunity to explore the lightning formation steps further on a new screen. In a series of embedded practice items, learners could be asked to drag and drop icons representing the steps in the lightning formation process in the correct order while the analogous argument sound effects play again. As learners further explore these concepts by manipulating the lightning formation processes on an interactive screen, the initial sound effects might be altered to represent changes in the lightning components (woman's voice becomes higher pitched as positive charges build, erupting argument sounds different for cloud flashes versus cloud-to-ground lightning). This screen might then also provide learners the opportunity to select their own multimedia analogy for the lightning formation process, allowing them to relate these concepts more meaningfully to previously constructed knowledge.

Thus, tracing down the columns instead of across the framework's rows in this example, it appears that addressing attentional, processing, and retrieval difficulties throughout knowledge construction in a transactional instructional model of instructional communication might still begin the conversation with an opening message designed with cues aimed at piquing interest, but then allow a dialogic exchange that increasingly turns over the ownership for interpreting the material to the increasingly engaged learner. However, in order to design truly effective technology-based tools within a transaction-oriented communications perspective, instructional designers must begin by being more aware of the inevitable biases we introduce the instant we make our first design decision (Subramony, 2004).

Concluding Thoughts

Whether it is the examples we choose, the colors we use, the interactions we devise, or the feedback we supply, every design decision we make imposes something of our own understandings into the learning environment and runs the risk of circumventing the learner's own knowledge construction processes to some degree. At the same time there has also been growing recognition that—in addition to cognitive processes—emotions play a critical role in human learning as well (Pekrun, 2011). In light of these facts, Wilson (2005a, 2005b) has suggested we extend our "pillars of practice" beyond individual cognition/behavior and social/cultural learning to include the "often neglected aspects of design, particularly the moral and value layers of meaning, and the aesthetic side of our work" (p. 15). Extending our view of instructional message design in these ways will likely require moving beyond a cognitive theory of multimedia learning toward one that considers learner volition and affect as well.

While I believe the framework presented in this chapter has the potential to help us think more systematically about the design of messages in socio-constructivist learning environments, it will likely need to be further revised in order to resolve these and other apparent philosophical mismatches between the traditional transmission-oriented instructional *message* design inertia and the current transaction-oriented instructional design momentum of the field. As suggested by De La Cruz and Kearney (2008) and others, movement away from an objectivist, linear paradigm of instructional message design and delivery and toward creating technology-facilitated environments that support multiple two-way communication transactions will require that we find ways for participants, other than the initial source, to support and represent their thinking while engaged in the discourse (see Boyd, 2004; Gibbons, 2009; Gibbons & Rogers, 2009a, 2009b). I envision the design of these supports to be an important new line of inquiry in the area of instructional message design that this framework might help to guide in the future.

References

Atkinson, R. C., & Shiffrin, R. M. (1968). Human memory: A proposed system and its control processes. In K. W. Spence & J. T. Spence (Eds.), *The psychology of learning and motivation: Advances in research and theory* (2nd ed., pp. 89–195). New York: Academic.

Atkinson, R. C., & Shiffrin, R. M. (1971). The control of short-term memory. *Scientific American, 225,* 82–90.

Bednar, A., Cunningham, D., Duffy, T. M., & Perry, J. D. (1991). Theory into practice: How do we link? In G. Anglin (Ed.), *Instructional technology: Past, present, and future* (pp. 88–101). Englewood, CO: Libraries Unlimited.

Berlyne, D. (1960). *Conflict, arousal, and curiosity.* New York: McGraw-Hill.

Berry, L. H. (1995). Instructional message design: Evolution and future directions. In B. Seels (Ed.), *Instructional design fundamentals: A reconsideration* (pp. 87–98). Englewood Cliffs, NJ: Educational Technology.

Bishop, M. J. (2000). The systematic use of sound in multimedia instruction to enhance learning. *Dissertation Abstracts International, 61*(07), 2669.

Bishop, M. J. (2013). Instructional design: Past, present, and future relevance. In J. M. Spector, M. D. Merrill, J. Elen & M. J. Bishop (Eds.), *Handbook for research in educational communications and technology* (4th ed.). New York: Springer.

Bishop, M. J., & Cates, W. M. (2001). Theoretical foundations for sound's use in multimedia instruction to enhance learning. *Educational Technology Research and Development, 49*(3), 5–22.

Boling, E. (2010). The need for design cases: Disseminating design knowledge. *International Journal of Designs for Learning, 1*(1), 1–8.

Boyd, G. M. (2004). Conversation theory. In D. H. Jonassen (Ed.), *Handbook of research on educational communications and technology* (2nd ed., pp. 179–197). Mahwah, NJ: Lawrence Erlbaum.

Carpenter, C. R. (1953). A theoretical orientation for instructional film research. *AV Communication Review, 1*(38), 52.

Cooper, P. A. (1993). Paradigm shifts in designed instruction: From behaviorism to cognitivism to constructivism. *Educational Technology, 33*(5), 12–19.

Dale, E. (1969). *Audiovisual methods in teaching.* New York: Dryden.

De La Cruz, G., & Kearney, N. (2008). Online tutoring as conversation design. In R. Luppicini (Ed.), *Handbook of conversation design for instructional applications* (pp. 124–143). Hershey, PA: Information Science Reference.

Dewey, J. (1900). Psychology and social practice. *Psychological Review, 7*, 105–124.

Driscoll, M. P. (2005). *Psychology of learning for instruction* (3rd ed.). Boston: Allyn & Bacon.

Duffy, T. M., & Cunningham, D. J. (1996). Constructivism: Implications for the design and delivery of instruction. In D. H. Jonassen (Ed.), *Handbook of research for educational communications and technology* (pp. 170–198). New York: Macmillan.

Eysenck, M. (1982). *Attention and arousal.* New York: Springer.

Fisher, B. A. (1975). Communication study in system perspective. In B. D. Ruben & J. Y. Kim (Eds.), *General systems theory and human communication* (pp. 191–206). Rochelle Park, NJ: Hayden.

Fiske, J. (2011). *Introduction to communication studies* (3rd ed.). New York: Routledge.

Fleming, M. (1993). Introduction. In M. Fleming & W. H. Levie (Eds.), *Instructional message design: Principles from the behavioral and cognitive sciences* (2nd ed., pp. ix–xi). Englewood Cliffs, NJ: Educational Technology Publications.

Fleming, M., & Levie, W. H. (Eds.). (1978). *Instructional message design: Principles from the behavioral sciences.* Englewood Cliffs, NJ: Educational Technology.

Fleming, M., & Levie, W. H. (Eds.). (1993). *Instructional message design: Principles from the behavioral and cognitive sciences* (2nd ed.). Englewood Cliffs, NJ: Educational Technology.

Gagné, E. D. (1985). *The cognitive psychology of school learning.* Boston: Little, Brown.

Gerbner, G. (1956). Toward a general model of communication. *AV Communication Review, 4*, 171–199.

Gibbons, A. S. (2009). The value of the operational principle in instructional design. *Educational Technology, 49*(1), 3–9.

Gibbons, A. S., & Rogers, P. C. (2009a). The architecture of instructional theory. In C. M. Reigeluth & A. A. Carr-Chellman (Eds.), *Instructional-design theories and models* (3rd ed., pp. 305–326). New York: Routledge.

Gibbons, A. S., & Rogers, P. C. (2009b). Coming at design from a different angle: Functional design. In L. Moller & D. M. Harvey (Eds.), *Learning and instructional technologies for the 21st century* (pp. 15–25). New York: Springer.

Gibson, J. J. (1954). A theory of pictorial perception. *Audio-Visual Communications Review, 2*, 2–23.

Grabowski, B. L. (1991). Message design: Issues and trends. In G. J. Anglin (Ed.), *Instructional technology: Past, present and future* (pp. 202–212). Englewood, CO: Libraries Unlimited.

Hannafin, M. J. (1992). Emerging technologies, ISD, and learning environments: Critical perspectives. *Educational Technology Research and Development, 40*(1), 49–63.

Hannafin, M. J., & Hooper, S. R. (1989). An integrated framework for CBI screen design and layout. *Computers in Human Behavior, 5*, 155–165.

Hannafin, M. J., & Hooper, S. R. (1993). Learning principles. In M. L. Fleming & W. H. Levie (Eds.), *Instructional message design: Principles from the behavioral and cognitive sciences* (2nd ed., pp. 191–231). Englewood Cliffs, NJ: Educational Technology.

Hannafin, M. J., & Rieber, L. P. (1989a). Psychological foundations of instructional design for emerging computer-based instructional technologies: Part II. *Educational Technology Research and Development, 37*(2), 102–114.

Hannafin, M. J., & Rieber, L. P. (1989b). Psychological foundations of instructional design for emerging computer-based instructional technologies: Part I. *Educational Technology Research and Development, 37*(2), 91–101.

Harp, S. F., & Mayer, R. E. (1997). The role of interest in learning from scientific text and illustrations on the distinction between emotional interest and cognitive interest. *Journal of Educational Psychology, 89*, 92–102.

Harp, S. F., & Mayer, R. E. (1998). How seductive details do their damage: A theory of cognitive interest in science learning. *Journal of Educational Psychology, 90*, 414–434.

Hooper, S. R., & Hannafin, M. J. (1988). Learning the ROPES of instructional design: Guidelines for emerging interactive technologies. *Educational Technology, 28*(7), 14–18.

Jackson, D. (1969). The individual and the larger context. In W. Gray, F. J. Duhl, & N. D. Rizzo (Eds.), *General systems theory and psychiatry* (pp. 390–415). Boston: Little, Brown.

Januszewski, A., & Molenda, M. (Eds.). (2008). *Educational technology: A definition with commentary*. New York: Routledge.

Jonassen, D. H. (1990). Thinking technology: Toward a constructivist view of instructional design. *Educational Technology, 30*(9), 32–34.

Jonassen, D. H. (1991). Objectivism versus constructivism: Do we need a new philosophical paradigm? *Educational Technology Research and Development, 39*, 5–14.

Kember, D., & Murphy, D. (1990). Alternative new directions for instructional design. *Educational Technology, 30*(8), 42–47.

Krippendorff, K. (1975). The systems approach to communication. In B. D. Ruben & J. Y. Kim (Eds.), *General systems theory and human communication* (pp. 138–163). Rochelle Park, NJ: Hayden.

Krippendorff, K. (2006). *The semantic turn: A new foundation for design*. Boca Raton, FL: CRC–Taylor Francis.

Lasswell, H. D. (1948). The structure and function of communication in society. In L. Bryson (Ed.), *The communication of ideas, a series of addresses* (pp. 61–89). New York: Harper.

Lohr, L. (2008). *Creating graphics for learning and performance: Lessons in visualliteracy* (2nd ed.). New York: Prentice Hall.

Mayer, R. E. (1999). *The promise of educational psychology*. Upper Saddle River, NJ: Prentice Hall/Merrill.

Mayer, R. E. (2001). *Multimedia learning* (1st ed.). Cambridge: Cambridge University Press.

Mayer, R. E. (2003). The promise of multimedia learning: Using the same instructional design methods across different media. *Learning and Instruction, 13*, 125–139.

Mayer, R. E. (Ed.). (2005). *The Cambridge handbook of multimedia learning*. New York: Cambridge University Press.

Mayer, R. E. (2008). Applying the science of learning: Evidence-based principles for the design of multimedia instruction. *The American Psychologist, 63*, 760–769.

Mayer, R. E. (2009). *Multimedia learning* (2nd ed.). New York: Cambridge University Press.

Mayer, R. E. (2011). *Applying the science of learning*. Upper Saddle River, NJ: Pearson.

Mayer, R. E. (2013). Multimedia learning. In J. M. Spector, M. D. Merrill, J. Elen & M. J. Bishop (Eds.), *Handbook of research on educational communications and technology* (4th ed.). New York: Springer.

Mayer, R. E., Bove, W., Bryman, A., Mars, R., & Taangco, L. (1996). When less is more: Meaningful learning from visual and verbal summaries of science textbook lessons. *Journal of Educational Psychology, 88*, 64–73.

Mayer, R. E., Heiser, J., & Lonn, S. (2001). Cognitive constraints on multimedia learning: When presenting more material results in less understanding. *Journal of Educational Psychology, 93*(1), 187–198.

Mayer, R. E., & Moreno, R. (2010). Techniques that reduce extraneous cognitive load and manage intrinsic cognitive load during multimedia learning. In J. L. Plass, R. Moreno, & R. Brünken (Eds.), *Cognitive load theory* (pp. 131–152). New York: Cambridge University Press.

Molenda, M., & Boling, E. (2007). Creating. In A. Januszewski & M. Molenda (Eds.), *Educational technology: A definition with commentary* (pp. 81–139). New York: Routledge.

Moreno, R., & Mayer, R. E. (2000). A coherence effect in multimedia learning: The case for minimizing irrelevant sounds in the design of multimedia instructional messages. *Journal of Educational Psychology, 92*, 117–125.

Morris, C. W. (1946). *Signs, language, and behavior*. New York: Prentice-Hall.

Morrison, G. R., Ross, A. M., Kalman, H., & Kemp, J. E. (2011). *Designing effective instruction* (6th ed.). Hoboken, NJ: Wiley.

National Council for Accreditation of Teacher Education (NCATE) (2000). Educational computing and technology leadership standards. Retrieved from http://www.ncate.org/

National Council for Accreditation of Teacher Education (NCATE) (2005). Educational computing and technology leadership standards. Retrieved from http://www.ncate.org/

Neisser, U. (1976). *Cognition and reality: Principles and implications of cognitive psychology.* San Francisco: Freeman.

Newcomb, T. M. (1953). An approach to the study of communicative acts. *Psychological Review, 60,* 393–404.

Ogden, C., & Richards, I. (1956). *The meaning of meaning: A study of the influence of language upon thought and of the science of symbolism* (8th ed.). New York: Harcourt, Brace.

Osgood, C. E. (1967). *The measurement of meaning.* Urbana, IL: University of Illinois.

Paas, F., Renkl, A., & Sweller, J. (2003). Cognitive load theory and instructional design: Recent developments. *Educational Psychologist, 38*(1), 1–4.

Pask, G. (1975). *The cybernetics of human learning and performance: A guide to theory and research.* London: Hutchinson Educational.

Peirce, C. S. (1931). *Collected papers.* Cambridge, MA: Harvard University Press.

Pekrun, R. (2011). Emotions as drivers of learning and cognitive development. In R. A. Calvo & S. K. D'Mello (Eds.), *New perspectives on affect and learning technologies* (pp. 23–40). New York: Springer.

Pettersson, R. (2002). *Information design: An introduction.* Amsterdam: John Benjamins.

Pettersson, R. (2007). Visual literacy in message design. *Journal of Visual Literacy, 27*(1), 61–90.

Phye, G. D., & Andre, T. (1986). *Cognitive classroom learning.* Orlando: Academic.

Potts, T. C. (1977). The place of structure in communication. In G. Vesey (Ed.), *Communication and understanding* (pp. 97–115). Atlantic Highlands, NJ: Humanities Press.

Reigeluth, C. M. (1983). Instructional design: What is it and why is it? In C. M. Reigeluth (Ed.), *Instructional design theories and models: An overview of their current status* (pp. 3–16). Hillsdale, NJ: Erlbaum.

Saussure, F. (1913/1986). *Course in general linguistics.* Peru, IL: Open Court.

Schramm, W. (1955). Information theory and mass communication. In B. Berelson & M. Janowitz (Eds.), *Reader in public opinion and communication* (2nd ed., pp. 712–732). New York: The Free Press.

Seels, B., & Richey, R. C. (1994). *Instructional technology: The definition and domains of the field.* Bloomington, IN: Association for Educational Communications and Technology.

Shannon, C. E., & Weaver, W. (1949). *The mathematical theory of communication.* Urbana, IL: The University of Illinois.

Shiffrin, R. M. (1988). Attention. In R. C. Atkinson, R. J. Herrnstein, G. Lindzey, & R. D. Luce (Eds.), *Stevens' handbook of experimental psychology: Vol. 2. Learning and cognition* (pp. 739–811). New York: Wiley.

Subramony, D. P. (2004). Instructional technologists' inattention to issues of cultural diversity among learners. *Educational Technology, 44*(4), 19–24.

Sweller, J. (2005). Implications of cognitive load theory for multimedia learning. In R. E. Mayer (Ed.), *Cambridge handbook of multimedia learning* (pp. 19–30). New York: Cambridge University Press.

Westley, B., & MacLean, M. (1957). A conceptual model for communication research. *Journalism Quarterly, 34,* 31–38.

Wilson, B. G. (2005a). Broadening our foundation for instructional design: Four pillars of practice. *Educational Technology, 45*(2), 10–15.

Wilson, B. G. (2005b). Foundations for instructional design: Reclaiming the conversation. In J. M. Spector, C. Ohrazda, A. Van Schaak, & D. Wiley (Eds.), *Innovations in instructional design: Essays in honor of M. David Merrill* (pp. 237–252). Mahwah, NJ: Lawrence Erlbaum.

Winn, W. D. (1993). Instructional design and situated learning: Paradox or partnership? *Educational Technology, 33*(3), 16–21.

Wittrock, M. C. (1990). Generative processes of comprehension. *Educational Psychologist, 24*(4), 345–376.

Wittrock, M. C. (2010). Learning as a generative process. *Educational Psychologist, 45*(1), 40–45.

Yerkes, R. M., & Dodson, J. D. (1908). The relation of strength of stimulation to rapidity of habit-formation. *Journal of Comparative Neurology and Psychology, 18,* 459–482.

Development of Design Judgment in Instructional Design: Perspectives from Instructors, Students, and Instructional Designers

Nilufer Korkmaz and Elizabeth Boling

Keywords Design judgment • Design character • Education of designers • Design competencies • Design pedagogy • Modeling • Reflection • Projects • Feedback • Justification • Vicarious learning • Qualitative exploratory study

Introduction

Scholars in the field of instructional design (ID) have noted that the activities ID professionals engage in exhibit the typical characteristics of all design fields (Boling & Smith, 2008; Goel, 1995; Murphy, 1992). ID problems are wicked problems because they have no definitive formulation and no right or wrong solution; they are unique; and there is no stopping rule telling the designer when they are solved (Becker, 2007), just like the problems in other design fields (Rowe, 1991). As early as 1992 Murphy analyzed the nature of ID problems, comparing them to the characteristics of design problems described by the architecture design scholar Lawson (1997) and concluded that instructional designers are "truly involved in design activities" (Murphy, 1992, p.281). More recently, Boling and Smith (2008) follow a similar line of reasoning, agreeing with Murphy that ID is a design field close in nature to architecture, design engineering, graphic design, and other fields of design. These authors and others posit that the education of instructional designers can benefit from study of the practices of other design fields (Bichelmeyer, Boling, & Gibbons, 2006; Boling & Smith, 2008; Cennamo et al., 2011; Murphy, 1992; Rowland, Fixl, & Yung, 1992; Tripp, 1994). Following a brief review of literature on design process models, design character, and design judgment, we will describe

N. Korkmaz (✉) • E. Boling
Indiana University, Bloomington, IN 47405, USA
e-mail: nkorkmaz@indiana.edu

B. Hokanson and A. Gibbons (eds.), *Design in Educational Technology*,
Educational Communications and Technology: Issues and Innovations 1,
DOI 10.1007/978-3-319-00927-8_10, © Springer International Publishing Switzerland 2014

the results of a study that examines how instructional design educators view and value development of design judgment and what they report in regard to how they help develop good design judgment skills in their students.

Design Process Models as the Central Focus in ID

ID models are so dominant in instructional technology that they appear to be a more significant part of our field than they appear to be in many other design fields (Wedman & Tessmer, 1993). These models have existed in the literature of the field since early 1960s (e.g., Gagne, 1962; Glaser, 1965; see those reviewed by Andrews & Goodson, 1991, and more recently Gustafson & Branch, 1997) and are a significant part of teaching and training in ID programs (Boling, 2004; Wedman & Tessmer, 1993).

However, these models have been criticized in several ways (Gibbons, Boling & Smith, in press; Gordon & Zemke, 2000; Smith, 2008; Zemke & Rossett, 2002), and studies on the actual practice of instructional designers revealed that those in practice deviate from the prescriptions of ID models (Rowland, 1992; Wedman & Tessmer, 1993). Practitioners in the field frequently skip one or more activities proposed by models (Wedman & Tessmer, 1993), and they do not systematically follow any of these models (Rowland, 1992). Schwier and his colleagues argue that "much of the extensive work describing theoretical models of ID (ID) has not been drawn from the practice of the instructional designer and, consequently, ID theory is not grounded in practice" (Schwier, Campbell & Kenny, 2004, p.2). In their review of research studies on the practice of instructional designers, Kenny and his colleagues conclude that we should focus on and study not "solely the technical aspects of how instructional designers perform the rudimentary functions of ID" (Kenny, Zhang, Schwier, & Campbell, 2005, p.23), but other dimensions of designing, such as the moral roles and responsibilities of designers. Such observations lead scholars to posit that to become good designers, novices need to develop experience designing the design process (Boling, 2004; Boling & Smith, 2008; Rowland, 1992; Rowland et al., 1992; Tracey & Boling, in press) and to have a better understanding of what design means (Nelson & Stolterman, 2003; Smith, 2008)—rather than being taught procedures—or even problem-solving heuristics.

Design Character as a Dimension Beyond Design Process

Many researchers and educators in the field have indicated that skill proficiency and knowledge in the field alone do not make students entering a field of design ready to deal with the complexities of real-world practice (Holt, 1997; Nelson, 1994; Nelson & Stolterman, 2003; Rowland, 1992; Rowland et al., 1992). With this understanding, for the last 2 decades, scholars have begun to discuss the importance of developing a *design character* (Cross, 2007; Nelson & Stolterman, 2003; Sless, 2007) in addition to acquiring field-specific skills and knowledge. Design character may be understood as the personal attributes of the individual designer (e.g., judgment, empathy, ethical perspectives, tolerance for ambiguity) associated with competent design practice (see Bichelmeyer et al., 2006; Boling, 2008; Cross, 2007; Miller & Hokanson, 2009; Rowland, 1992, 1996; Schwier, Campbell, & Kenny, 2006; Smith, 2008) and susceptible to improvement through learning (Nelson & Stolterman, 2003).

Design Judgment as an Element of Design Character

One of the personal attributes of the individual designer is judgment. According to Michael Oakeshott, as described by Fuller (1989), knowledge is composed of two parts: knowing what (information in the form of facts/rules) and knowing how (judgment). Information does not "endow us with an ability to do, or to make, or to understand and explain anything" (Fuller, 1989, p. 54). That is, information itself does not tell us how it can be used. Therefore, in Oakseshott's view, for an ability to develop, attainment of information should be followed by a judgment in order to be useful. Judgment "enables us to interpret it [information], to decide upon its relevance, to recognize what rule to apply, and to discover what action permitted by the rule should, in the circumstances, be performed" (Fuller, 1989, p. 54).

In their exploration of design as a tradition with unique ways of knowing and of building knowledge, Nelson and Stolterman (2003) differentiate design judgment from other sorts of judgment (intellectual, practical, ethical, professional, and so on) and state that "the ability to make design judgments is what distinguishes a designer as a designer" (p. 23). They define design judgment as "a form of decision-making... dependent on the accumulation of experienced consequences of choices made in complex situations" (p. 181) and "reliant on our capabilities as humans ... the character of the designer" (p. 30). They emphasize that judgment is not the same as rational decision making or colloquially understood know-how. It is a skill integrated with the designer's character. It is "the ability to gain insight onto situations that are complex, indeterminate, indefinable, and paradoxical" (Nelson & Stolterman, 2003, p.189).

Design situations are always complex and ill-defined, and design is viewed as an application of judgment (Kenny, Zhang, Schwier, & Campbell, 2005; Nelson, 1994; Nelson & Stolterman, 2003; Rowland, 1992; Rowland & Wilson, 1994). So being able to make good judgments is a crucial competency that instructional designers must possess to be able to design successful designs in addition to field-specific knowledge and skills (Holt, 1997; Nelson & Stolterman, 2003; Rowland, 1992; Rowland & Wilson, 1994; Smith, 2008). However, judgment cannot be "taught in the way in which information may be learned, recollected, or forgotten"

Table 1 Summary of number of participants by role and institutional affiliation

	Name of university	Instructors	Students	Designers
1.	University A	2	4 residential	6
2.	University B	2	2 residential	3
3.	University C	2	0	0
4.	University D	1	1 residential	0
5.	University E	1	3 online	0
6.	University F	1	1 residential	0
7.	University G	1	1 residential	1
8.	University H	1	1 residential	0
9.	University I	2	3 residential	0
10.	University J	1	0	0
11.	University K	0	0	1
	Total	*14*	*16*	*11*

(Fuller, 1989, p. 59). In other words, it cannot be reduced to principles, or rules of thumb, and explained in order to be acquired.

Purpose of This Study

This study focuses on design judgment as part of design character. Even though judgment is stated to be a very essential skill, it is reported to be included rarely in formal education (Nelson & Stolterman, 2003). In addition, although a few scholars have written about design judgment and its significance in design (Holt, 1997; Nelson & Stolterman, 2003), there is not a known empirical study about the extent to which ID educators value the development of good design judgment and how such development is addressed in the education of ID students. With this perspective, the study probes how ID educators view and value the development of design judgment, as reflected in interviews with educators, their students, and alumni, and what educators report regarding how they help develop good design judgment skills in their students.

Methods

This was an exploratory, qualitative study in which the primary data source was semi-structured interviews, augmented by mission statements, program descriptions, and course offerings as presented in program websites. Through purposeful sampling (Creswell, 1998), 11 large, well-known ID programs in the USA with good reputations in the field were chosen. These programs offer a master's degree in ID and prepare students for careers in ID in a variety of professional positions in diverse contexts, rather than focusing solely on technology integration.

Semi-structured interviews were conducted with instructors teaching introductory ID courses in these programs, current master's students in these programs, and instructional designers who had graduated recently from these programs. Table 1 summarizes institutional affiliations and roles of the participants. The participants were:

1. Fourteen faculty members from ten different programs. Each faculty member had 3 or more years of experience teaching ID. As of the time when the interviews were conducted, one was a fulltime lecturer with a Ph.D., three were assistant professors, five were associate professors, and five were full professors.
2. Sixteen then-current ID master's students from eight different programs. All students completed or would have completed 15 credit hours of coursework by the end of the semester in which the study was conducted. Two of them did not have any work experience before starting the program, while the rest of the participants had 3 or more years of professional work experiences in a variety of fields.
3. Eleven recent graduates of four different masters programs. All except one graduated from their ID program in 2005 or later. Six of the designers worked in corporate settings, four worked in higher education, and one worked for a public library.

The semi-structured interviews started with questions regarding the teaching experiences of instructors, their understanding of design and how to teach design, and their perceptions about essential skills for instructional designers and how to teach those skills. Questions about their understanding of design judgment and its relative importance followed (e.g., How do you define design judgment? How do you believe that designers develop design judgment? How important is design judgment compared to other skills that you have previously mentioned?). Thematic analysis, informed by the content of additional documents describing courses and programs and comparisons between the groups interviewed, was carried out across the 41 total interviews.

Findings

Understanding of Design Judgment in ID Among Instructors of ID

One of the major findings of this study is that design judgment is not a term commonly used among ID educators. When instructors were asked whether they were familiar with the concept of design judgment, six out of fourteen instructors stated they were familiar and provided a definition of design judgment in their own words; the rest were unsure about what was meant by design judgment. In the instances where the interviewee was not sure, the researcher made an explanation similar to the following:

> As you know, in professional practice designers need to use some kind of judgment to decide which actions to take and when to take them. For instance, when they are faced with

the choice of two instructional tactics that may be equally valid in a given context, they have to decide which one to use. Or, they may encounter some ethical dilemmas and they may have to use their own judgment to take further steps in design process.

After such an explanation, all the instructors indicated that they understood what design judgment meant. In this case, even though they did not provide their own definition of judgment, their understanding of design judgment was revealed through their answers to questions about how they teach design and the relative importance of design judgment compared to traditional ID skills and knowledge.

Twelve of the fourteen instructors indicated that strong foundational knowledge (i.e., knowledge of learning theories, instructional theories, and ID models) is the prerequisite for being able to make good judgments. For instance, Dr. Henry, an assistant professor with 3 years of experience teaching ID said:

> Of course, knowing about ID models in addition to learning theories is necessary. So having-like—a big toolbox of strategies that you can pull from. You have different learning theories, different ID models, and so forth, and different knowledge of different technologies that you can, sort of, incorporate into your training when appropriate.

In addition, subject matter knowledge is also mentioned as necessary to be able to design effectively because design judgments are informed by subject matter knowledge. For example, Dr. Daniel, a professor with 28 years of ID teaching experience, indicated that quality of design judgments is highly related to the designer's level of subject matter expertise. He explained that the ID field is "situated," but that believing you could design instruction without subject matter expertise is "anti-situated." He believed that it is "presumptuous and arrogant to think you could walk into a subject matter and tell them how to teach something where, because of your wonderful instructional models … and it is anti-situated." He expressed that instruction could be designed without subject matter expertise if you "have a good access to the subject matter expert and really trustworthy relationship in a team," but he added "a lot of us are without virtually any."

The most prominent view among instructors was that design judgment is the ability to see what is useful, that is, to make best choices among all the things that enter into design processes and products. For instance, according to Dr. Kelly, an associate professor with 8 years of ID teaching experience, a designer who could make good judgments was expected to be able to understand the context and be confident about how he/she would proceed; as she said:

> The ability to look at a situation and constraints, group of learners, context, a set of context, or goals and objectives and all of the situational characteristics and all of the demands of the design task. And to look at that not to feel overwhelmed but to say "Here are the steps I need to take procedurally; here are the things that I need to understand systemically. And here are the things that constrain me but they are not barriers. They are just challenges." I think for me design judgment is all of those things wrapped together.

Another prominent view was that design judgment is the ability to evaluate the effectiveness of the decisions that were made during design process. Even though some emphasized the effectiveness of forms the designer created, many indicated that design judgment is goodness of fit, which means how well what is created meets expectations based on the specifics of context. However, when the interviewees mentioned goodness of fit or expectations, they explained that they meant not only the expectations of the client, learners, or others in the design team but also expectations of the designer himself/herself. As Dr. Scott, a lecturer who had been teaching ID for 3 years, articulated, "...once time and energy invested in an idea or design, of course, in result, it has to be judged to answer: Are they satisfactory to the designer? Are they going to be satisfactory to the designer? To the client? Or any other stakeholders?"

Participants mentioned that quality of design judgment is revealed over time through the consequences of decisions and that design judgment happens all the time throughout the design process and even after the process ends. For instance, Dr. Jane, an associate professor with 10 years of ID teaching experience, said design judgments are made,

> ...when you are evaluating, when you are looking back at the decisions you made and critiquing them. So knowing what kinds of questions to ask in analysis, knowing how to interpret that analysis information you gather to be able to make the decisions...You are using your judgment at every stage and in every level.

Understanding of Design Judgment in ID Among Practitioners of ID

Similarly, Lisa, a designer who had been working in a corporate setting for 4 years, stated that the design process is iterative and any time we go through an iterative process we have to bring our judgment into play. Then she pointed out that the designer begins to make judgments when she understands the problem, even if the client is unsure of what the problem is exactly. As she expressed it, "Being able to move in the face of ambiguity" requires making a lot of judgments on the part of the designer.

Moreover, participants expressed that there are not already existing alternatives/choices in design situations; instead, the conditions of the context determine the available alternatives. They explained that the designer has to come up with alternatives and make the best choice from among those. As explained by Mary, a designer in a pharmaceutical company, the designer needs to make judgments to decide what actions to take; as she said:

> ...you cannot say under circumstance A, be flexible; under circumstance B, be firm. What you can do is say these are several factors that you have to take into consideration. And then depending on the response of the client, how do you then deal with it? Or depending on the responsible team members how do you deal with it?

Relative Importance of Design Judgment in ID. All the instructors and designers indicated that design judgment is a critical competency for successful instructional designers. They believed, furthermore, that design instructors can help novice designers develop better design judgment. The instructors asserted that they had been addressing the development of design judgment in their teaching in various ways, like creating an open environment for their students to exercise judgment.

The instructor interviews revealed that some instructors purposefully address design judgment, and a majority believed that all the activities they had been doing naturally do address the development of good judgment.

Addressing Development of Design Judgment

The findings suggest that development of design judgment is being addressed in ID education in five major ways: (1) projects, (2) feedback on projects, (3) justification and reflection activities, (4) vicarious learning, and (5) modeling by experienced individuals.

Projects

The most common view among the study participants was that the most effective way of learning to make better judgments in design is to engage in project-based activities. Instructors stated that people develop the ability to make informed decisions through experiences. They believe that one does not develop a good design overnight; it is only through the accumulation of many experiences that one can make good judgments and create a good design.

Authentic projects, real projects with real clients, or made-up projects are believed to provide experiences that help develop design judgment. Novice designers can exercise judgment when they are required to make choices during the design process by actually working on creating an ID product. Instructors and designers both stressed that real projects play an especially important role in developing design judgment because real projects require students to deal with the complexity of actual design situations and to satisfy client needs. Dr. Angela, an assistant professor with 8-year experience teaching ID, explained that since ID is an applied field, simple classroom activities do not provide sufficient experiences for students to learn how to make better judgments when they enter into the field. Therefore, she argued that students needed to work on real projects. As she said:

> [when you are doing a real project] you make choices and see how they work, how they play out, and you figure out, if it has turned out to be a bad decision, how you are going to fix it. So I think real world experience is what fills that ability to make good judgments, which I think, by the way, pretty much with any applied field.

According to participants, when working on real projects, students need to be able to evaluate the effectiveness of their judgments and be able to justify them when the client asks. Five out of the fourteen instructors participating in the study stated that they required students to work on a real project with a real client. In these participants' view, when students are engaged in real projects, they start to make decisions and take risks which are essential in design learning. However, three instructors mentioned that they found it challenging to have their students get started with making decisions themselves when they engage in projects. One instructor, Dr. Anna, a professor with 15 years of ID teaching experience, explained that her students did not want to make mistakes and she tried to help them understand that "ID is an iterative process and you can't sit and bear great thoughts. You have to think and do. And you are getting feedback several times and you are adjusting what you are doing based on the feedback you are getting."

Another common view among participants was that by doing real projects students get the opportunity to see consequences of their design judgments, since designers learn from consequences of their designs. They stated that when those designs are used by real people, the designer can see what works and what does not work so that next time she/he can make better design judgments. For instance, Bill, who had been practicing ID at a community college for 8 years, indicated that it was very important for novice designers to gain more experience in real business situations to "actually understand the implications of decisions that they are suggesting." He believed that since the graduate school environment is not realistic enough, students usually forget about the fact that their design decisions have a business impact.

All the designers interviewed stated that they began to develop design judgment when they were working on real projects during their education. The most commonly stated reason was that when they worked on real projects, they had to communicate with real clients and find ways of satisfying their needs and desires. Abby, a designer in a corporate setting for 3 years, stated, "In the ideal world the learners are more important, but the reality of the situation is—just keeping the project owner happy is important at that time." She added, "Without working with a real client you can only make up or guess what is important at that point." Casey, a designer at a university for over 2 years, shared Abby's view and stated that "Seeing what a real life client would argue with has been really nice to know."

All the designers mentioned the significance of having students begin to work on real or authentic projects as early as possible during their education, in order to improve their judgment making skills, hence their design skills. Nine out of the eleven designers interviewed stated that instructors should take more responsibility to make sure their students gain experience with real ID situations, or at least very authentic experiences. However, practicing designers and current students complained that their instructors did not always try to help their students to get the best out of these projects. For instance, Lisa believed that the instructors in her instructional program were very experienced and had "a wealth of knowledge that they were not entirely using." She mentioned especially two instructors who had worked in the corporate world more than 10 years as designers. She thought that they both knew very well what it was like to work with the constraints of a client, but in their courses they did not require their students to work with real clients. She suggested that they could have created a realistic case with their wealth of experience and students could have had an experience closer to working with a real client.

Feedback

Instructor and peer feedback were pointed out by respondents as effective methods to develop and improve judgment. All participants indicated that detailed feedback is critical, regardless of the nature of ID projects, and that meaningful, constructive, and honest feedback must accompany practice in order to get the most out of project experiences. They argued that when design students complete a product, they should receive meaningful feedback in order to see the effects of their judgments, specifically whether their judgments fulfilled the requirements of the project. For instance, Brian, a student, stated that gaining experience in working with real clients had been the best way for him to hone his judgments because feedback from clients had been insightful. However, a couple of designers further pointed out that when it was not possible to work with real clients and get their feedback in graduate school, "honest" feedback should be received from other knowledgeable people around. It was expected that instructors or peers would make comments about whether their ID product was working or not working, or how it could further be improved. Colson, a designer with 5-year ID experience in higher education and corporate training, emphasized the significance of practice and feedback as he stated:

> I don't just learn something by doing. I learn by doing and then getting feedback about it. Without the feedback it doesn't matter. I don't know if I've done a great job or a horrible job unless I get honest feedback from somebody that knows what they are doing. Feedback from somebody that doesn't know what they are doing—they are just making it up; is not going to help to me to be effective. Feedback that is just trying to be nice is not going to help me to be effective. What I need is honest feedback from somebody that really knows the area, whatever it is that happen to be.

Two instructors believed that design is an iterative process and students need to receive feedback before making too much progress on a design. These instructors required students to submit drafts/work in progress to receive feedback from them. In this case, the instructors did not give a letter grade on the draft but provided formative feedback to students so that, as Dr. Daniel said, "Incrementally, they are seeing what we are looking for and make sure they don't get too far off with what we are looking for." They stated that students cannot develop design judgment if they do not get feedback on whether their judgments are good or bad.

All of the instructors claimed that they provided good quality feedback to their students in oral and/or written forms. In contrast to what these instructors said about the amount and quality of feedback they provide, eight of the sixteen students indicated that the feedback they received from their instructors was not detailed. Six students stated that the feedback they received was mostly a grade/score on their assignment and "good job." These students mentioned that having a good grade was important to them, but that they would like to know if their design was good, why it was good, and, if it needed improvement, how it could be improved. For instance, Rebecca shared that she received mostly high grades on her assignments and she was also frustrated with the instructor feedback she received; as she said:

> It is usually all positive. It is never very constructive. It doesn't tell me… It says good job, you thought about this, you thought about that. But it never quite probes further "What

would you do if this resource was not available to you? What would you do if your client did something else?" I think that would be very helpful. Or "What would you do if all the sudden this happened to your project and you are given this budget constraint?" That doesn't really happen in the projects. It is always you have unlimited resources. You have unlimited time. It made it easy. It also made it easy to give feedback because there were really no probing questions.

In addition to instructor feedback, all instructors reported using peer feedback in a variety of forms and at several levels. Some instructors required students to give critique to a certain number of peers in a formal way and document their feedback. On the other hand, some instructors encouraged them to give feedback to each other but did not require any documentation. Several instructors did both.

The instructors believed that students learned both when receiving feedback on their work from their peers and also when critiquing others' work. In fact, five of the instructors indicated that the main purpose of peer critique activities in their courses is to help students gain critiquing skills. Dr. Angela pointed out that critique is a big part of her class. In her class, students do critiques in class informally and also give comprehensive written feedback to each other on their ID products. When she assigns students to critique each other's work, she shared that she reminds her students that the whole critique activity should be useful both to the author of the design work and also to the person who provides feedback. She explained:

> It is the idea that designers engage in dialogue and they learn from each other. And then I tell them my best ideas come from other designers, in other words, when you look at another designer's work you will learn things about design just by looking at and evaluating that work.

Dr. Jane stated that putting their work in front of others to be critiqued, and critiquing others, was one of the most effective ways of requiring students to exercise judgment. She explained that students need to defend their judgments and decisions in peer critique and that they have to make adjustments accordingly based on the feedback they get. She stated that when they receive feedback on one aspect of their design work, they sit and think about their judgments. Like Dr. Jane, Dr. Angela also believed that it was critical for students to learn how to evaluate the effectiveness of a design. She explained that those who teach ID "give up, or find it challenging to teach design judgment, as they tend to rely on their own personal judgments as to decide whether something is good or bad rather than trying to teach students how to evaluate whether it is good or bad." To nurture her students' ability to evaluate the work of others, she explained that in one fourth of her visual design class, she has her students do peer critiques. She said:

> ...because as they critique each other's design and articulate what works or what doesn't work they are sharpening their design judgment skills. It is one thing to design that something you like yourself. It is another thing to be able to design for others and take their wants and needs into account. So that ability to critique is critical in developing design judgment.

A common view was that instructor's modeling and scaffolding how to give peer feedback is important to improve students' ability to critique. Several instructors mentioned that they did not provide students any guidelines on giving feedback except telling them to be "courteous" and polite and to give useful feedback more than "nice job." However, five instructors reported that because a majority of students do not have prior experience with peer critique, it is necessary to model and scaffold how to give critiques. They stated that when students are unsure about what to look for to make comments about others' designs, it is not appropriate to expect them to develop judgment to evaluate effectiveness of forms created by other students. They believed that it was essential to scaffold and model giving critique to each other in order to improve students' ability to critique.

Four instructors mentioned that students get better at critique over time. For instance, Dr. Kelly believed that peer feedback is a powerful way of developing design judgment, and she stressed that peer feedback is "one of things that they feel the least confident about when they begin and the most gratified with when they are finished." She had her students do a peer feedback activity every time they bring a component of their design to class so that they can gain ideas from each other. Dr. Kelly pointed out that even though students felt that they did not have any expertise to give critique in their first course, by the second semester they gained so much confidence that they really were able to critique each other's work. She added, "They were able to sit back and say 'I can make judgments about design and I can see when things are done well or not so well, effectively or not so effectively.' That grows powerful."

Reflection and Justification Activities

Reflection and justification activities were commonly cited as effective ways of helping students develop design judgment skills. Eleven of the fourteen instructors mentioned that students should be able to defend their design decisions to others and evaluate the quality of their own judgments. Therefore, they stated that they have their students justify their design decisions in different ways and also have them reflect about how well their designs meet expectations of the design situation. For instance, Dr. Joseph, a professor who had taught ID for 17 years, stated, "It is very important in terms of being able to reflect upon it and to be open to understand why it's working or why it's not working." He further explained that it was essential for students to understand that they would have to justify their decisions all the time in real life practice because what they design would likely be somewhat different than what the client expected.

Reflection and justification activities take place in many forms in ID courses. Three instructors reported that they require their students to complete a form and function matrix in which they explain how a form they plan to create would meet a certain function in a matrix worksheet or as a narrative. On the other hand, six instructors asked their students to write their design rationales in their project reports or keep a design journal throughout the class in which they reflect on and evaluate their design decisions. Instructors expressed that, whatever justification it takes, it is important to make students aware they will have to justify their decisions to other designers and/or other stakeholders in real life practice. Students and designers shared that being forced to reflect on and justify their design decisions helps them improve their judgment.

Bill, a designer in higher education, mentioned that they had to write about their design rationales—why they chose the particular things they chose to do—in one of the ID courses he had taken. He said, "That activity I think was quite beneficial because the ability to rationally think through and to be able to answer the questions like 'Why did you choose this over this? What are the limitations for choosing this? Does that work given the current business environment? Why not?' helped me improve my design skills."

Many of the students also mentioned that writing design rationales that explained their design decisions helped them to reflect on their design decisions. For instance, Emily said:

> I think [the] design justification document that went along with our projects was really help-ful because knowing that you have to turn in that design justification project really made you think about your judgments and your decisions while you were doing the project because you knew that you have to justify in this design document. You couldn't just make things up and then go back and justify it later. I think being accountable for those decisions, proving your judgment, that was a really helpful part.

Another student, Amber, indicated that when her instructor or peers questioned the way they (students) designed, having to justify design decisions prepared them for real life practice because she thinks that clients would be very likely to ask for justification for their decisions in their projects. She pointed out that when they had to present their proposal for a training or instruction, it gave them the "ability to think on their own feet" as people could ask about anything; as she further emphasized, "You need to be prepared for everything and you got to have that ability to really back yourself up... You got to start off knowing how you are going to justify it."

Vicarious Experiences

All of the instructors believed that instructors need to develop in students the ability to look around the world as a designer and see something that is useful for their own designs. Instructors reported that they try to expose students to examples from pro-fessional designers, previous students' projects, peers' projects, examples from web, and examples from the instructor's own designs. Instructors and designers stated that students are able to develop design judgments by looking at and analyz-ing those examples, as they develop a sense of noticing good and bad aspects of those examples.

Those instructors who were familiar with other design fields compared the ID field with architecture or graphic design as did Dr. Susan, a professor with 18-year ID teaching experience. She stated:

> While [an] average graphic design student has seen and thought about hundreds of thousands of examples of his or her professional art by the time they graduate from their undergraduate or graduate program, ID students are exposed to a very limited number of examples.

There were instructors who reported exposing their students to as many examples as possible because they believed in the power of seeing and analyzing examples in improving design skills. For example, Dr. Kelly indicated that she brings lots of examples to class because she believes that "access to many examples and full range of possible options increase our ability to make judgment among the many options in a reasonable way." Similarly, Dr. Henry also stated that he showed multiple examples of good and bad ID because he thought it helped develop students' design judgment.

However, several instructors complained that the field did not provide constant access to multiple ID examples even though examples were believed to be effective tools of teaching design. For instance, Dr. Daniel stated that although he believed that seeing examples was an effective way to learn, he admitted that he was not showing examples much in his class because it was not easy for him to find and get access to examples.

All of the students interviewed mentioned that looking at examples of finished ID products was helpful for them to develop as designers and improve their judgment. Ben said, "If you had a collection of 10 or 20 varieties of different instructional materials and hear or read about how they were created, that would be really useful for ID students." Ben explained that especially if a student did not have any experience in the field, examples would be beneficial to communicate the language or style of the field. He further added that vicarious learning from examples would be effective as he said, "When you are not actually developing and when you are not actually working in a real setting, the way you get some of that experience [is] from looking at examples that are already developed." Valerie echoed Ben as she said, "I think one of the best ways to develop judgment skills might be to analyze the final products that are already there."

While students and designers appreciated their instructors sharing their own design experiences and found them helpful, especially since they were able to talk about the context and their design judgments, they did not believe using case studies from ID case study books was effective in helping them make better judgments. They stated that those case studies miss a lot of important information and do not represent the complexity of real-world design situations.

Four students stated a desire to see examples of professional designs and hear about the design processes behind those designs, in addition to seeing examples from their instructors' own experience and projects created by previous students or their classmates. For instance Rebecca said:

> That [examples from professional designers] would be really cool and helpful if we were given the ability to talk about it to analyze it. If I can understand the thought process behind it will be helpful for development of design judgment. If, for example, I was given an instruction from an alumnus or something and it was an activity in class where we had to reverse engineer it then that would be a very useful activity. It would be even more useful probably that they taught also how that designer talked to that designer, what made you do this, what was the reasoning behind that. That is I think how you really develop design judgment: looking at the example, breaking it down, talking to an expert about that.

Modeling

All the designers and the students indicated that modeling by others who had more design experience helped them learn and develop better judgment. All the instructors claimed that they were good models or they were trying to be good models for their students because, in their view, judgment is nurtured under guidance of an expert instructor. They believed that students can observe how the instructor with more ID experience approaches a problem, what types of things they consider during design process, and how to take considered actions in design. It was evident that each instructor thought they modeled good ID practice in a different way and at different levels. However, some instructors seemed to put an exceptional effort into being good models for their students as they felt responsible for the development of their students and to provide a good quality education to them.

Each student reported a different experience with their instructors' modeling. However, in general students reported that the instructors who had ID experience in the workplace, outside the classroom, or who were currently working as consultants were perceived to be more effective models since they shared their experiences with students more often. On the other hand, instructors who did not practice ID in a work setting or who did not have their doctoral degree in ID/educational technology were not perceived as good models. As Hannah said, "The professors of ID are not necessarily practicing instructional designers. So it is very hard to mentor someone in a field that you don't practice in. Professors who have previous experiences bring those experiences to the table though." Similarly, Ben stated that he took a majority of his ID courses from two assistant professors who did not have ID background themselves and were not good models for him. He was frustrated with these instructors as the instructors themselves admitted several times verbally that, "I am learning this as you are too," and to him that meant they did not have an approach to ID themselves. He further said: "That is pretty frustrating when I am paying a lot of money to come and learn how to do these things. [...] He [the instructor] didn't really have a good basis for how to design and how to talk about some of those things."

Five instructors believed that students could benefit from each other's expertise in developing their judgment skills. Therefore, these instructors reported that they facilitated sharing among students in different ways to encourage collaboration. Even though each instructor encouraged students to learn from each other in different ways, three instructors clearly expressed their belief in the necessity of apprenticeship or mentorship relationship among students in their classes and in their program in general. For instance, when talking about the development of students as designers, one of the points Dr. Angela stressed was that there was always value to having students interact with people who were more experienced. She believed that inexperienced students learned from students who came to the program with more knowledge and experience, so she tried to encourage such interaction among students. She deliberately looked for opportunities to expose her students to more models, mentioning that once a former Ph.D. student co-taught one of her ID classes with her. She believed that it was a wonderful experience for her students, saying: "They had two designers who had more experience than them and they could get two different perspectives and two different people modeling." Another instructor, Dr. Jane, indicated that she tried to use students who have a lot of prior industry experience as mentors to other students who had less experience.

Eight students shared that they have found peer feedback helpful in improving their judgment. For instance, Daisy mentioned that she learned a lot through listening to and observing another student in her team who was an instructional designer with corporate ID experience. She stated that her peer's views helped her improve her designs as her peer was able to tell about how designing happens in real life and added:

> Exposure to so many people that some of them are teachers, some are instructional designers, you do pick up design judgment from them because you see what they do from projects they work on, you see the mistakes that are made, from there you learn.

However, not all students seem to have a positive attitude toward learning from peers. Finally, seven instructors stated that interacting with professional designers and observing them while they design help students have an understanding of real-world ID practice and develop students' judgment skills. Students were looking forward to learning from practicing designers. The students in programs where professional designers were invited as guest speakers thought that it was wonderful to interact with practicing designers. In addition to "brown bags," panels or seminars in which one or more professional designers/alumni came and talked about projects they worked on helped students looking for more interactions with ID professionals. They want to hear more about thought processes of designers. For instance, Laila, a student, believed that having some exposure to information about what experts do and how they design would be very helpful "to identify where the better judgments would make, where the better design is in." She reflected on a guest talk by a professional instructional designer with more than 10 years of experience:

> … that is very valuable. Because not only do we learn about his experience of a designer, but we are learning something that he has learned and we can apply to what we are doing and we have a very good takeaway in that because the full spectrum of his experience and we actually do have an application to transfer in at the end. I would like to an expert to come in and speak to us. Even the instructors who practice for ages, I would like to see the projects they have done. We need the exposure to real world designers.

Discussion

Understanding of Design Judgment

This study suggests that design judgment is seen as an important faculty for designers. Although it is not explicitly used or addressed much in the literature, it is being addressed in instructional design programs in a variety of ways as discussed. However, efforts to develop judgment may be much more effective if we openly discuss this important concept in our teaching. If we could address and reflect on judgment making skills intentionally with our students, our students would be much more aware that foundational skills and knowledge will not suffice in the workplace and, hence, put more effort toward improving their judgment skills so that they would become better designers.

However, it is worth noting that the participants in this study did not mention design judgment as a skill that is inseparable from the designer, or discuss it in a way to suggest that they saw it as such. This implies a question regarding how design judgment can be taught as part of a design program if, in fact, we attempt to teach it as a rational process. If it is true that design judgment is unique to each individual, that is, constructed based on each individual's unique experiences, it may be especially challenging to address design judgment in the field of instructional design. This is because instructional design aims to standardize instruction and to consistently produce efficient and effective learning (Bichelmeyer, 2004; Morrison, Ross, & Kemp, 2001)—suggesting, if not stating outright, that every student in a well-designed course should learn the same things to the same standard of performance; this is, in fact, hardly considered worth questioning. A traditional instructional design approach may work well for skills and knowledge that can be deconstructed and taught to learners in the same way across contexts. However, that systematic approach may be limiting when teaching complex performances (such as design judgment) to learners with different backgrounds and capacities. We may not be able to ensure that all learners gain design judgment skills in exactly the same way and at exactly the same level, even if they are exposed to the same experiences, and this will require some basic rethinking of how our designers are taught.

Addressing Design Judgment

Project-Based Learning. The findings from this study suggest that students are expected to exercise design judgment through completing instructional design projects. Scholars of instructional design emphasize the necessity of engaging students in authentic experiences that allow them to integrate the skills and knowledge they learn in their courses in the complexity of real-world instructional design situations (Rossett, 1981; Wedman & Tessmer, 1993; Winn, 1995). Students in this study reported that it is not possible to see the consequences of their design judgments in hypothetical projects, especially when there is limited feedback from the instructor with no client or real learner involved. The importance of authentic learning experiences for students under the guidance of experts has been emphasized by many ID scholars (Ertmer & Cennamo, 1995; Quinn, 1994, 1995; Rowland, 2004; Tripp, 1994).

Practicing designers and students believed that their instructors had not expended enough effort to help students find real and authentic projects. Instructors can create real project opportunities through collaborations at department, school, and university levels, as well as with community agencies as also suggested in the literature. Requiring students complete real ID projects has been discussed in the literature. It is suggested that through cooperation with community agencies, students can be assigned real design projects and present their completed designs formally to clients (Cennamo & Holmes, 2001; Ertmer & Cennamo, 1995; Kapp & Phillips, 2003;

Quinn, 1994; Rossett, 1981). This may be the method of promoting development of design judgment most frequently employed in the field presently.

Feedback. All participants of this study indicated that design judgment could be developed through meaningful feedback on projects. Formative feedback on work in progress is perceived to be important in helping students evaluate their judgments and make better judgments. That is consistent with the literature as Benson (2003) suggests that feedback that is meaningful, of high quality, and timely helps students become actively engaged in the content and environment of learning. Ertmer and Cennamo (1995) found that expert feedback is instrumental in engaging students in reflective thinking and moving them forward along the continuum of design exper-tise. The findings in this study suggest that students expect to have individualized, detailed feedback with probing questions that lead them to think more deeply and evaluate their decisions. However, even though students from a few of the programs acknowledged that they received immediate guidance and individualized feedback from their instructors during their projects, a majority of students and designers complained about lack of quality feedback from their instructors. There is clearly a gap between what instructors report and what students experience in their courses. Students would like to hear particularly about what they could have improved in their designs from an expert's view so that they can improve their judgment making skills. Instructors are expected to spend more time with students and observe closely how students are doing in their projects with intermittent feedback and also ask probing questions to make students aware of their judgments and have them think more deeply about what can be improved in their designs. In this regard, the chal-lenges may come in finding instructors who have the experience themselves to offer such feedback rooted in their own experiences and in restructuring courses which include real, or realistic, projects, but are still structured around content (process, principles, theories, and so on).

Peer Critique. Another important finding in this study is that instructors felt that students develop design judgment through giving and receiving peer feedback. When they give feedback, they are able to evaluate the effectiveness of forms cre-ated by their peers and make suggestions for improvements. When they receive feedback, they are to evaluate their own judgments because they need to explain why they created the design the way they did. Even though peer critique is a signa-ture pedagogy in other design fields (Parnell, Sara, Doidge, & Parsons, 2007; Shulman, 2005), this is not the case in instructional design education. Moreover, it seems that there is not a unified approach to peer critique in ID. Students are not always trained or, in most cases, even given models for how to give and receive peer critique. Participants indicated that this eventually affects the value and benefit stu-dents receive from the critique experience. Since the success of peer feedback depends greatly on how the process is designed and managed (Topping, 1998), peer critique should be carefully organized, delivered, and coached. Otherwise, peer feedback does not help much to improve students' capacity to judge. If students were trained how to give critique, through instructor modeling, and then able to practice, in the long run they would eventually gain confidence; they could make better evaluative judgments about their own and others' designs and give better feedback to their peers. Again, if instructors have not been trained in critique themselves, they may not be effective models. They may assume they are giving more valuable feedback than they actually are, carry forward negative practices from other domains in which critique is practiced (Anthony, 1991), or even assume that critique is something it is not.

Reflection and Justification Activities. The findings from this study reveal that instructors help their students develop design judgment through reflection and justification activities and that students believe these activities help them to think more deeply about their judgments and make sure they have a justification behind their decisions. This also helps them be aware that they are responsible for their decisions and they need to be able to justify those to others (e.g., clients, colleagues) when asked and also to assess the potential consequences of their actions as Rowland (1993) expressed. Engaging in reflective conversation with oneself and others in different ways helps designers make sense of their learning experiences and expand their understanding (Rowland, 1992).

Moreover, guidance of the instructor in reflective activities is emphasized in this study and in the literature. Ge and Hardre (2010) found that with continuous scaffolding of reflection through asking "why" questions about particular strategies they used in an activity helped students think more intentionally and strategically. In addition, Schön (1983) states that mastering the process of reflection-in-action is an important aspect of becoming a designer and discussed that providing students an environment that promotes reflection under the guidance of an expert instructor/ practitioner is necessary. Julian (2001) found that instructors who coach students through their projects and help them reflect on their options and evaluate their decisions are appreciated. However, it appears that data in this study suggest that not all instructors are good models of expert instructional designers in the eyes of ID students and recent graduates.

In addition, the discussion from these participants of justification for decisions sounds distinctly traditional; specifically, it sounds as though the justifications are expected to have been rational and systematic. Lawson and Dorst (2009) explain the valid process of discovering rationale ex post facto, explainable in light of the notion of "parti," or an unconscious, but nevertheless disciplined, notion which gives rise to a design and is examined after it is expressed to discover its rationale (Nelson & Stolterman, 2003). If justification is understood only in terms of which articulated principles have been followed, design judgment will not be fostered but suppressed. It will be relegated to the status of choice—choosing which principle is appropriate, rather than perceiving which factors in a situation are to be foregrounded, for example.

Vicarious Learning. In his discussion of developing design judgment in novice instructional designers, one of the suggestions Tripp (1994) makes is to provide students with opportunities to study the product and process masterpieces of the field. He states that exposure to masterpieces can provide instructional design students with opportunities to closely observe good practices of instructional design and also familiarize themselves with thought processes of an experienced designer. One problem cited by instructors is access to exemplary and non-exemplary works of ID. There are not readily available resources of complete ID products with detailed descriptions (Boling, 2010). In addition to examples, the findings suggest that observing thought processes of expert designers would be a powerful way of developing design judgment because when they see examples, they do not have any idea about how the designer started the design and why they ended up with that design, what kind of decisions were made and why they were made. So seeing examples can help to some degree, but observing expert designers can help to a greater degree as Quinn (1995) also suggested.

Modeling. Tripp (1994) and Quinn (1995) argue that novice designers can be better prepared for professional practice through an apprenticeship model. In their "cognitive apprenticeship" model, Collins, Brown, and Newman (1989) include modeling (demonstration) of expert skills to develop expertise in design. Consistent with the literature, the findings of this study suggest that participants believe novice designers can better develop design judgment if it is modeled for them by their instructors, students with more experience, and practicing instructional designers.

This study reveals that not all instructors have real-world instructional design experience, defined as creating ID products for external clients. Students in this study feel that their instructors who do not have such experience do not always model good ID practice. This finding is consistent with the finding of Rowland and Divasto's (2001) study on powerful learning experiences of adult learners. These researchers found that personal interaction with an expert teacher who has a high level of expertise in the domain and who also participates actively in the learning process as a role model is believed to be a powerful learning experience. However, in this study, even though instructors believed they model good instructional design practice to their students, a large number of students believed that their instructors are not good role models and do not model what they preach in their courses. We speculate this finding may be further confused by a disconnect between the novice ID's understanding of design practice and the messages given to them by instructors who understand something about real-world practice but do not have credibility based on real-world experience. Put simply, an instructor with years of professional experience can argue with the textbook and be believed, whereas an instructor without such experience will be doubted even if he is offering realistic feedback.

In addition, expert modeling has been suggested by several scholars to better prepare student designers for real-world instructional design (Cennamo & Holmes, 2001; Rowland, 2004; Rowland et al., 1992). Findings from this study reveal that modeling by practicing designers can help develop design judgment in novice designers because they learn more about real-world experiences and challenges, and practicing designers can bring to the classroom another viewpoint in addition to what students learn from their instructors. Several programs in this study involve practicing designers in their programs to a limited degree. They invite professional designers as guest speakers and have them talk about their job and how they tackle problems in their job. Students do find this very helpful because they can directly communicate with professionals and ask questions to get a better picture of real life practice. This finding confirms Rowland (1991) and Silber's (2007) claims that novice instructional designers need to understand more about what practicing instructional designers do, rather than just memorizing procedures in an instructional design model.

Observing and shadowing expert designers is also desired by students because they believe this will help them see how expert designers design. Gilbert and Gilbert (1988) argued that observation-based training is the most effective method to learn from experts. Even though there are privacy issues with companies, shadowing could be achieved through internships in which student interns are supervised by experienced designers. Internships provide real-world experience for students in real settings where they can observe how professional designers design (Rowland, 2004). While internships are perceived to be "eye-opening" by participants of this study because they provide students opportunity to deal with real-world design situations and observe professional designers while they are designing, internship is required in only three of the programs included in this study.

Suggestions for Future Studies

Case studies of individual programs, especially those which have a distinct curriculum, such as a studio curriculum or internship-based curriculum, need to be studied in depth to investigate how development of this judgment is addressed in these programs. Studying expert instructional designers in their workplace while they are designing, using observations and interviews, can help us better understand uses of design judgment in instructional design practice. While a number of studies have been conducted in the field looking directly at instructional design, the approach has been to ask to what extent those designers are following prescribed processes or how they are using the models developed by academics. We need studies that start from the premise that design activity in the field is legitimate in its own right and seek to discover how it is being accomplished. Finally, studies that compare the ways design judgment is addressed in instructional design and other design fields need to be conducted.

This study was exploratory, involving a small subset of the instructors, students, and designers working in the field. We consider it to be provocative, however, demonstrating as it does that a positive, albeit imprecise, understanding of design judgment does exist in the field and is perceived as important. We propose that design judgment needs to be viewed as more important still and that more clarity in this area could lead to marked improvements in the preparation of our students for ID practice.

References

Andrews, D. H., & Goodson, L. A. (1991). A comparative analysis of models of instructional design. In G. J. Anglin (Ed.), *Instructional technology, past, present, and future* (pp. 133–155). Eaglewood, CO: Libraries Unlimited. Reprinted from the Journal of Instructional Development, 3(4), 2–16.

Anthony, K. H. (1991). *Design juries on trial: The renaissance of the design studio.* New York, USA: Van Nostrand Reinhold.

Becker, K. (2007). Wicked ID: Conceptual framework for considering instructional design as a wicked problem. *Canadian Journal of Learning and Technology, 33*(1), 85–108.

Benson, A. D. (2003). Assessing participant learning in online environments. *New Directions for Adult and Continuing Education,* 100, 69–78.

Bichelmeyer, B. (2004). Instructional theory and Instructional design theory: What's the difference and why should we care? *IDT Record.* Retrieved January 5, 2009, from http://www.indiana.edu/~idt/articles/documents/ID_theory.Bichelmeyer.html

Bichelmeyer, B., Boling, E., & Gibbons, A. (2006). Instructional design and technology models: Their impact on research, practice and teaching in IDT. In M. Orey, J. McLendon, & R. Branch (Eds.), *Educational media and technology yearbook 2006.* Westport, CT: Libraries Unlimited.

Boling, E. (2004). Teaching a design model vs. developing instructional designers. *IDT Record.* Retrieved January 10, 2009 from http://www.indiana.edu/~idt/shortpapers/documents/IDTf_Boling.pdf

Boling, E. (2008). *The designer as human instrument.* Presented as part of a panel organized by Dr. Jonassen, Alternative perspectives on design. Annual Meeting of the Association for Educational Communications and Technology, Orlando, FL.

Boling, E. (2010). The need for design cases: Disseminating design knowledge. *International Journal of Designs for Learning, 1*(1), 1–8. Retrieved from http://scholarworks.iu.edu/journals/index.php/ijdl/index

Boling, E., & Smith, K. M. (2008). Artifacts as tools in design. In D. Merrill & M. Specter (Eds.), *Handbook of research in educational communications and technology* (3rd ed.). New York, NY: Taylor & Francis.

Cennamo, K., Brandt, C., Scott, B., Douglas, S., McGrath, M., Reimer, Y., et al. (2011). Managing the complexity of design problems through studio-based learning. *Interdisciplinary Journal of Problem-based Learning, 5*(2), 11–36.

Cennamo, K. S., & Holmes, G. (2001). Developing awareness of client relations through immersion in practice. *Educational Technology, 41*(6), 44–49.

Collins, A., Brown, J. S., & Newman, S. E. (1989). Cognitive apprenticeship: Teaching the crafts of reading, writing, and mathematics. In L. B. Resnick (Ed.) *Knowing, learning, and instruction: Essays in honor of Robert Glaser* (pp. 453–494). Hillsdale, NJ: Lawrence Erlbaum Associates.

Creswell, J. W. (1998). *Qualitative inquiry and research design: Choosing among five traditions.* Thousand Oaks, CA: Sage.

Cross, N. (2007). *Designerly ways of knowing.* Basel, Switzerland: Birkhäuser Verlag.

Ertmer, P. A., & Cennamo, K. S. (1995). Teaching instructional design: An apprenticeship model. *Performance Improvement Quarterly, 8*(4), 43–58.

Fuller, T. (1989). *The voice of liberal learning.* New Haven: Yale University Press.

Gagne, R. M. (1962). The acquisition of knowledge. *Psychological Review, 69,* 355–365.

Ge, X., & Hardre, P. L. (2010). Self-processes and learning environment as influences in the development of expertise in instructional design. *Learning Environments Research, 13*(1), 23–41.

Gibbons, A., Boling, E., & Smith, K. (in press). Design models. In M. Spector, D. Merrill, M. J. Bishop, & J. Elen (Eds.), *Handbook for research in educational communications and technology* (4th ed.). New York, NY: Springer.

Gilbert, T. F., & Gilbert, M. B. (1988). The art of winning. *Training, 25*(8), 33–39.

Glaser, B. G. (1965). The constant comparative method of qualitative analysis. *Social Problems, 12*(4), 436–445.

Goel, V. (1995). *Sketches of thought.* Cambridge, MA: MIT Press.

Gordon, J., & Zemke, R. (2000). The attack on ISD. *Training, 37*(4), 43–53.

Gustafson, K. L., & Branch, R. M. (1997). *Survey of instructional development models* (3rd ed.). Syracuse, NY: ERIC.

Holt, J. E. (1997). The designer's judgement. *Design Studies, 18*(1), 113–123.

Julian, M. F. (2001). *Learning in action: The professional preparation of instructional designers.* University of Virginia, VA: Unpublished dissertation thesis.

Kapp, K. M., & Phillips, T. L. (2003). Teaching the business of instructional technology: A collaborative corporate/academic partnership. *TechTrends, 47*(1), 46–51.

Kenny, R. F., Zhang, Z., Schwier, R. A., & Campbell, K. (2005). A review of what instructional designers do: Questions answered and questions not asked. *Canadian Journal of Learning and Technology, 31*(1), 9–16.

Lawson, B. (1997). *How designers think: The design process demystified* (3rd ed.). Boston, MA: Architectural Press.

Lawson, B., & Dorst, K. (2009). *Design expertise.* New York, NY: Taylor & Francis.

Miller, C., & Hokanson, B. (2009). The artist and the architect: Creativity and innovation through role-based design. *Educational Technology, 44*(4), 27.

Morrison, G. R., Ross, S. M., & Kemp, J. E. (2001). *Designing effective instruction* (3rd ed.). New York: Wiley.

Murphy, D. (1992). Is instructional design truly a design activity? *Education and Training Technology International, 29*(4), 279–282.

Nelson, H. G. (1994). The necessity of being "un-disciplined" and "out of control": Design action and systems thinking. *Performance Improvement Quarterly, 7*(3), 22–29.

Nelson, H. G., & Stolterman, E. (2003). *The design way: Intentional change in an unpredictable world: Foundations and fundamentals of design competence.* Englewood Cliffs, NJ: Educational Technology.

Parnell, R., Sara, R., Doidge, C., & Parsons, M. (2007). *The crit: An architecture student's handbook* (2nd ed.). England: Architectural Press.

Quinn, J. (1994). Connecting education and practice in an instructional design graduate program. *Educational Technology Research and Development, 42*(3), 71–82.

Quinn, J. (1995). The education of instructional designers: Reflections on the Tripp paper. *Performance Improvement Quarterly, 8*(3), 111–117.

Rossett, A. (1981). Instructional technology as link between university and community. *NSPI Journal, 20*(1), 26–28.

Rowe, P. G. (1991). *Procedural aspects of design thinking* (Design thinking, pp. 39–113). Cambridge, MA: MIT Press.

Rowland, G. (1991). *Problem-solving in ID.* Unpublished doctoral dissertation, Indiana University, Bloomington, IN.

Rowland, G. (1992). What do instructional designers actually do? An initial investigation of expert practice. *Performance Improvement Quarterly, 5*(2), 65–86.

Rowland, G. (1993). Designing and ID. *Educational Technology Research and Development, 41*(1), 79–91.

Rowland, G. (1996). "Lighting the fire" of design conversation. *Educational Technology, 36*(1), 42–45.

Rowland, G. (2004). Shall we dance? A design epistemology for organizational learning and performance. *Educational Technology Research and Development, 52*(1), 33–48.

Rowland, G., & DiVasto, T. (2001). Instructional design and powerful learning. *Performance Improvement Quarterly, 14*(2), 7–36.

Rowland, G., Fixl, A., & Yung, K. (1992). Educating the reflective designer. *Educational Technology, 32*(12), 36–44.

Rowland, G., & Wilson, G. (1994). Liminal states in designing. *Performance Improvement Quarterly, 7*(3), 30–45.

Schön, D. A. (1983). *The reflective practitioner: How professionals think in action.* USA: Basic Books.

Schwier, R. A., Campbell, K., & Kenny, R. (2004). Instructional designers' observations about identity, communities of practice, and change agency. *Australian Journal of Educational Technology, 20*(4), 69–100.

Schwier, R. A., Campbell, K., & Kenny, R. (2006). Instructional designers' perceptions of their interpersonal, professional, institutional, and societal agency: Tales of change and community. In M. J. Keppell (Ed.), *Instructional design: Case studies in communities of practice* (pp. 1–18). Hershey, PA: Idea Group.

Shulman, L. S. (2005). Signature pedagogies in the professions. *Daedalus, 134*(3), 52–59.

Silber, K. H. (2007). A principle-based model of instructional design: A new way of thinking about and teaching ID. *Educational Technology, 47*(5), 34–37.

Sless, D. (2007). Designing philosophy. *Visible Language, 41*(2), 101–126.

Smith, K. M. (2008). *Meanings of "design" in instructional technology: A conceptual analysis based on the field's foundational literature*. Indiana University, Bloomington, Indiana: Unpublished doctoral dissertation.

Topping, K. (1998). Peer assessment between students in colleges and universities. *Review of Educational Research, 68*(3), 249–276.

Tracey, M., & Boling, E. (in press). Preparing instructional designers. In M. Spector, D. Merrill, M.J. Bishop, & J. Elen (Eds.), *Handbook for research in educational communications and technology* (4th ed.). New York, NY: Springer.

Tripp, S. D. (1994). How should instructional designers be educated? *Performance Improvement Quarterly, 7*(3), 116–126.

Wedman, J., & Tessmer, M. (1993). Instructional designers' decisions and priorities: A survey of design practice. *Performance Improvement Quarterly, 6*(2), 43–57.

Winn, W. (1995). Instructional design and situated learning: Paradox or partnership? In B. Seels (Ed.), *Instructional design fundamentals: A reconsideration* (pp. 159–169). Englewood Cliffs, NJ: Educational Technology.

Zemke, R., & Rossett, A. (2002). A hard look at ISD. *Training, 39*(2), 26–28.

Ethics and Design: Rethinking Professional Ethics as Part of the Design Domain

Stephanie Moore

Keywords Ethics • Professional standards • Code of conduct • Social responsibility • Design ethics • Design domain • Instructional design

Introduction: A Way, Way Back Background

In the classical piece *Phaedrus* by Plato (1990), one of the central debates is over writing and its introduction into the Academy. As the Greeks traveled more, they imported ideas from other cultures, and papyrus from Egypt was among those. As with any new idea, there was much discussion and consternation over the introduction of this new *techne*: How would it change the relationship between the teacher and learner, how would it change the nature of instruction, how does it affect memory, and is this desirable or even ethical? Plato's position, as voiced through his teacher Socrates in the piece, viewed writing as a destructive presence in the Academy. Borrowing another idea from the Egyptians, Socrates relates the myth of Theuth and Thamus to explain this opposition. In the myth, Theuth—the embodiment of all inventors who has invented math and other ideas—runs with excitement over his latest invention to his god, Thamus, to tell him about the "invention of all inventions—writing." After listening to Theuth for a while, Thamus replies,

> You, who are the father of letters, have been led by your affections to ascribe to them a power the opposite of that which they really possess. For this invention will produce forgetfulness in the minds of those who learn to use it, because they will not practice their memory.... You have invented an elixir not of memory, but of reminding; and you offer your pupils the appearance of wisdom, not true wisdom, for they will read many things without instruction and will therefore seem to know many things, when they are for the most part ignorant and hard to get along with, since they are not wise, but only appear wise. (p. 140)

S. Moore (✉)
University of Virginia, Charlottesville, VA, USA
e-mail: stephanie.moore@virginia.edu

B. Hokanson and A. Gibbons (eds.), *Design in Educational Technology*,
Educational Communications and Technology: Issues and Innovations 1,
DOI 10.1007/978-3-319-00927-8_11, © Springer International Publishing Switzerland 2014

What seemed like an invention with so much promise in fact held many pitfalls in the eyes of Thamus and in the eyes of the ancient Greek academy. As Socrates' argument progresses, he calls upon the cultural meaning of locusts that buzz when someone or something is inspired, describing the scene of a teacher and his students beneath the plane tree with locusts humming around them. The traditional teaching was sacred and inspired. This new techne was not. Socrates worries that words written on the papyrus can be "bandied about": Their original speaker is not there to defend them against attacks or misinterpretations. Written words could not protect themselves and were therefore too prone to misunderstanding, leading to false wisdom and, even worse, arrogant students who thought they understood because they had read something when in fact they were "ignorant" … and, in a fun interpretation that many teachers may be able to relate to, "hard to get along with" because of that ignorance.

But in the piece it is also clear that this debate over technology is not solely a deep, abiding concern over the introduction of technology itself, but rather a proxy for sharp political divides that were reaching a fever pitch at the time *Phaedrus* was written. There had been growing debate between the sophists, who had long been the principle architects of the Academy and its methods, and the growing body of philosophers who had a very different sense of the purpose of the Academy. Sophists had traditionally emphasized the art of speaking well, for the way a leader led the masses was through ability to persuade. A good leader could persuade the masses to support or oppose a matter, thus this art of persuasion was a critical skill. The philosophers advanced a different purpose—a leader was someone who sought the truth and used the art of persuasion in service of the truth. While it was still important for students at the Academy to learn how to speak well, it was most important that they learn how to discern the truth and construct a message that had logos (logic), ethos (ethics), and eros (passion). These two major camps within the Academy were increasingly in conflict with each other, even beginning to fight over prized students. And that is how the story of *Phaedrus* begins: Phaedrus is one of the prized students, a student of Socrates, and he has just returned from listening to a speech by one of the sophistic teachers. Phaedrus has in his pocket a scroll with the speech of that teacher written out. He is so excited by this speech and by this written word in his pocket that as soon as he sees Socrates, he tells Socrates all about it. Naturally, Socrates then sets about poking holes in the argument—this is his prized student, after all, clearly swept up in the sophistic arguments and their use of this new techne. So he starts his argument first by attacking the medium of instruction—the written word, which seems so helpless there on the page and unable to defend itself against Socrates' assault—and by the end of *Phaedrus*, the sophistic tradition and its mechanisms like writing along with it are merely pieces on the intellectual floor of the Academy.

What is most interesting for our purposes here is that Phaedrus has a subtitle. The full title of the piece is *Phaedrus; Or, the Ethical, or Beautiful*. The entire piece is a discussion on ethics and beauty. Today, much of the treatment of ethics around educational technology tends to emphasize codes of conduct and standards of practice.

While those are important aspects of the dialogue on ethics in the profession, in this piece I want to explore ethics from a different angle, one which I think finds its roots in these classical pieces. For Socrates, there was an immediate, pressing ethical issue with the introduction of writing. Politics aside, he asked some very astute questions of the technology ... and found it lacking (even if his analysis was erroneous). He was concerned with how it would impact the nature of knowledge and knowing itself—wondering whether it would facilitate memory or be just a way of reminding, questioning if a student who had only read some words on a page could be said to truly know or understand, asking what happens if a misunderstanding arose and the teacher was not present to catch or correct that. And he was concerned deeply about how it would impact the most sacred space of the relationship between students and instructors. Many of these questions and concerns still get raised today by instructors considering the introduction of any given technology into the learning environment. It is a sacred space, a cherished relationship between teacher and student, and fraught with lingering questions about the impact of technology on memory, knowledge, and relationships. Socrates ultimately concluded that, because of these troubling questions, writing had no place in the Academy.

But we know the history of writing doesn't end where Socrates and Plato left it. Writing did not remain intellectual litter on the floor of academic history but instead has become one of the most valued and regarded forms of expression around the world—artistic, academic, and more. In describing the educational benefits—and detriments—of writing, Quintillian (1990) gives voice to perhaps one of the earliest instructional design treatments that exists, if we could call it such. In his *Institutes of Oratory*, Quintillian lays out an entire curriculum for the Academy, almost 400 years after Plato. In it, he devotes an entire book (Book X) to the place of writing in the learning process. Perhaps what Quintillian has also provided is an excellent roadmap for the discussion of any educational technology. Instead of accepting or rejecting writing in toto, he goes to great lengths explaining when writing is valuable, when it is not, why in each case, and the best instructional uses of it (as well as when to cease using it). He explains that writing is excellent for helping students learn to craft ever better articulations of their arguments. It gives them almost unlimited opportunities to continually practice how they will say things along with the ability to stop, reflect, and revise. Through much practice, almost like a laboratory, students can continually craft and re-craft messages, increasing their efficacy and efficiency over time until they are able to craft finely tuned messages extemporaneously. However, the revision process is never ending: One can always find something to change or improve or tweak, and the leader who does not emerge from writing to actually speak is no leader at all. The student must be able to recognize the point at which writing should stop and speaking and leading should begin. Writing could encourage too much internal process and not enough external engagement, at which point it becomes more of a hindrance to learning and growth rather than a supporting technology.

Indeed, Quintillian displays some notable analysis of the usefulness and limitations of writing along with suggested uses based on this analysis, all before the days of cognitive science. And he, too, is concerned not just with the learning result (Did something stick in the learner's mind, or did the learner display strong writing ability?) but also with the impact of this technology on the student's ability to eventually lead. He was profoundly concerned with what this educational approach led to in terms of the type of leaders the academy developed and graduated into the world. Societal impact was his guidepost for his instructional system design; and, as with Socrates, this suggests a way of thinking and talking about the ethical considerations of instructional design and technology that is different from the current codes-and-standards approach.

From these works by Plato and Quintillian, we can begin to see parts of the broad outline for a different sort of discussion: How does research on learning with technology inform ethics? (Not just how do ethics inform the conduct of such research.) How do we consider the systemic impacts of the introduction of technologies into human systems like education? How do we plan and design the integration of technology into instructional systems with societal impact as a guidepost? How do we communicate research to the broader public in a way that can guide decision making and implementation—much the way Quintillian exemplified? And even how do we develop reflective practitioners?

Zooming Forward

The current status of dialogue on ethics of educational technology in the literature of the field is rather sparse. This is a typical trend, though, for technology-oriented disciplines, but not for reasons one might assume, like technology as a "fairly recent phenomenon," which is not historically accurate. Rather, technology was long considered either not worthy of philosophical consideration (Scharff & Dusek, 2003) or viewed as the derivative of science under a positivist paradigm and, therefore, assumed the objective high ground as a product of science. After all, how could something derived from the scientific process have moral characteristics or negative consequences? And this trend was persistent across nearly all disciplines for a long time as well. Davis (1999) provides accounts of ethics across the university, tracking the emergence of ethics in disciplines outside philosophy as serious societal issues arose. For example, as technological developments increased in medicine, there was growing discussion over how these technologies changed practices and some of the tough decisions or trade-offs doctors felt increasingly faced with in practice. Purchasing a new machine for treatment of patient with serious illnesses who represented a small part of the population could mean not building another clinic that provided basic services to a larger number of people. As doctors were presented with numerous dilemmas, ethics started appearing in the curriculum and then the literature. In engineering, bribery scandals that included the White House and large-scale disasters such as passenger airplane failures prompted the field to start teaching ethics as part of its curriculum, and resulting research emerged as well. Other fields such as business, military, nursing, and law all began to confront complex challenges and respond by developing strands of discourse, research, and curriculum focused on ethics of the field.

Curiously absent from Davis' account is any mention of education fields. There are likely several reasons for this, but based on Davis' rationale of public scandals or backlash preceding a discipline's attention to ethics, the field of education had not yet faced its national scandal and did not have a corresponding depth of curricular or literature treatment. For educational technology specifically, even though codes of ethics had existed for several decades, the most expansive treatment did not appear until 1994 in a special issue of *Educational Technology* guest edited by Yeaman, Koetting, and Nichols. That edition presented a discussion beyond codes of ethics that explored the application of postmodern theory to the field; however, it has not managed as of yet to find broader integration into practice, research, or broad curricular integration.

In a review of research on ethics in the field of educational technology, Moore and Ellsworth (2013) report that to date the presence remains very slim. In the major research journal of the field, *Educational Technology Research and Development*, only 1.5 % of articles, a total of 39 out of 2,501 articles, since 1950 have some mention of ethics. Out of those 39, only four treated ethics as the primary topic; the remaining 35 mentioned ethics in passing, often in conclusions as further consideration. This was consistent across the major research journals. For applied, juried journals, the rate of inclusion was a bit higher. For example, in *TechTrends*, 4.8 % of articles, a total of 111 out of 2,307 articles, since 1980 had some mention of ethics. For this analysis, ethics was defined very broadly to include articles that mentioned the term as well as articles on topics considered part of the construct, such as accessibility, copyright, intellectual property, and cultural considerations. In addition, Moore (2005, 2009) found that curricular integration as of 2005 was equally as sparse. In a review of curricula in the USA and Canada, only one in five educational technology programs offered any course that explicitly considered ethics; very few had an entire course on the topic. Less than 10 % of programs included ethics as part of the objectives or outcomes for program graduates, and less than 6 % of programs included ethical practice of technology as part of its overall mission or vision, even when ethics was as broadly defined as possible.

Given this, it seems clear that ideas related to ethics have not diffused throughout educational technology's research, design models, or curricula. Additionally, Moore and Ellsworth (2013) suggest that most of the existing literature is more rightly classified as focusing on legal issues, not ethical considerations. Much of the work on codes of ethics or standards have this same sort of legalistic tendency, with their emphases on understanding the law and compliance with legal statutes. What literature does deviate from this presents a compelling case for the social responsibility of the discipline but so far has not translated into design models or yielded a broader body of research and publications.

That is the focus here—to begin building that bridge from philosophical consideration into application and research. To do so, I am proposing that the key relationship to focus on in the discipline is the relationship between ethics and design. As the core function of all professional activity, whether it be what professional practitioners do or what researchers seek to inform, design represents the essence of the discipline.[1] It has the ability to speak to the practitioner and researcher personas alike in our field. Design also represents the very space in which a translation process occurs, where research findings are translated into design features or constraints, where a designer's ideas and reflections and considerations start to manifest a solution or new creation. If we take the view of design as a nexus of activity for professionals in the field, then it makes most sense to ask whether we can position ethics at that nexus.

Why Design

In order to understand the relationship of design with ethics and social responsibility, we have to first explore what design is. While practitioners engage in this activity on a daily basis and researchers may study processes or theories that inform design, we may not often stop to remind ourselves what it means to design, much less realize how central this skill set is to addressing major life and global challenges.

In studies of student approaches to scientific experimentation, researchers have identified two classes of problem solvers. Klahr and Dunbar (1988) labeled these two groups theorists and experimenters. Schauble, Klopfer, and Raghavan (1991) labeled these differently: One was focused on engineering goals, while the other was focused on scientific goals. The second group—theorists, or scientific problem solvers—developed hypotheses and designed a series of tests to determine whether their model was accurate in explaining or predicting results. The first group—experimenters or engineering problem solvers—manipulated the various inputs until they achieved a desired outcome. In short, when it came to understanding and solving problems, there were two major categories of approach: inquiry and design. Although the literature talks about these as dichotomous constructs, these function more like a yin to the yang in real life, with inquiry informing design and design suggesting new areas of inquiry. And yet we can also clearly identify them as very different and distinct processes and even ways of viewing and approaching the world. The theorist develops a model for explanation and tests that model, whereas the designer starts with an end goal in mind and views the rest of the inputs as malleable to that goal.

Most of such literature comes from science education and how to teach students the scientific method. A possible unfortunate side effect of this is that much of this research exhibits a subtle bias towards the pure scientific (inquiry) process to solving problems, often viewing the engineering (design) process as less sophisticated. For

---

[1] This is akin to viewing engineering design as the central function engineers engage in, or architectural design for architects, etc. This is not intended to be dismissive of the role of research, but it is an argument that design is the convergence point for all the actors and activities in the field of instructional design/educational technology in much the same manner as it is in other design- and technology-oriented fields.

example, in their study on scientific problem solving in a simulation on infectious diseases, Feldon and Gilmore (2006) categorized learners into either the scientific or engineering approach based on two measures: accuracy and robustness (of their mental models). Participants who increased in both accuracy and robustness were categorized as those following a successful scientific model of inquiry. Participants whose accuracy increased but the robustness of their mental model did not were classified as following a successful engineering model (they do not even label this a design model). In the other studies cited earlier, they described scientific approaches as rigorous testing but described engineering approaches as manipulating variables to achieve specific results: the former a state of serious investigation, the latter a state of play. The very description of design-oriented problem solving as "manipulation" of variables or "play" in itself suggests a negative disposition towards such an activity, as well as a mischaracterization of the design process denying it status as a possible separate but equal approach to problem solving.

Design, a defining process for professional engineering and many other disciplines, is a goal-oriented activity. The characterization of design-focused approaches to problem solving as less sophisticated, however unintentional, suggests a less-than-accurate understanding of the design process and how that can vary in sophistication and emphasis. As a design-oriented discipline, most engineers would likely object to the characterization of their professional practice as merely the manipulation of variables to achieve an outcome. Furthermore, they do develop a mental model of the problem under study, but it is likely to be a very different sort of mental model than a theory-based model or representation of the problem that was under study.

Nigel Cross, in his book *Design Thinking* (2011), provides a more expansive conception of what design is. He states that "designing is not a search for the optimum solution to the given problem, but that is it an exploratory process" (p. 8). Unlike scientific reasoning, which looks for many cases to substantiate a rule, the process of design looks for a case or set of cases that give a satisfactory result. It is a form of reasoning that attempts to satisfy a range of considerations—including functional, aesthetic, social aspects—with a solution or solution set that yields desirable results (often a range of desirable results, not just a single result). Design is concerned with real-world context, results, and consequences.

Banathy (1996), perhaps more widely associated with systems theory than design, offers up a wide range of definitions of design that represent an array of perspectives from various design fields such as architecture, organizational design, industrial design, and social systems design. These definitions vary so widely that similarities are general at best, but all emphasize some sort of orientation or process for finding a solution, often in search of improving the future or some part of the designer's universe. For example, Rittel and Webber (1973) explains that the motivation is consequential action, not understanding or explanation. Simon's definition (1969) asserts that design is concerned with how things ought to be, and the designer "devises a course of action aimed at changing existing situations into preferred ones" (Banathy, 1996, p. 12). Many of the definitions reiterate these same themes. Although not included in Banathy's text, these themes are very similar to existing literature in the field that we have not often looked at through this lens. For example, Kaufman's (2000) mega planning model for strategic organizational planning is at its core a systems planning, design, and evaluation model that begins and ends with outcomes and has a heavy consequentialist emphasis. Kaufman's work emphasizes how to make the future world a better place for tomorrow's children, and in answering that question derive solutions and operational plans that can accomplish systemic changes in a more systematic manner.

This host of definitions of design begins to lay out the clearest logical relationship yet between design and ethics. Design and ethics both operate in a space concerned about consequences, solutions, and whether the world around us or the future will be a better place for the decisions made or the solutions implemented. Often, ethics are defined as a process for determining a morally correct course, which tends to suggest there is a most optimal solution or only one correct course that is the most moral. However, authors from various design-oriented disciplines are starting to explore how we can rethink ethics through design. In short, the application of design to ethics suggests that rather than identifying the elusive single morally correct course of action, another possible way to view ethics that emphasizes action rather than judgment is ethics as a process of devising possible solutions to social problems based on a complex set of considerations and the possible or desired results. The process is far more participatory and extended over a longer period of time than we may tend to think of for design; the considerations now include societal impact (e.g., safety), justice, and cultural or contextual factors as well as aesthetics, technical, or other constraints; and the desired results are a set of results rather than a singular objective that in the case of learning technologies would include learning outcomes but also considers other systemic or large-scale results, all the way from impact on the brain in individuals to increased access to education to shifts in an entire educational landscape that impact the larger social system it serves.

All this suggests (at least) two types of relationships between ethics and design: One is the use of design for social problems, termed *design for good* or *ethics as design* or other similar phrases in other design fields; the second is the integration of ethics into the design process for design problems that are not social problems on their face. As an example of the latter, an educational technologist may be working on a project where the purpose is to assemble asynchronous learning modules and make those available via a website. Any of the design models in the field would focus on the learning strategies, etc., but none to date would lead the designer to consider accessibility of the materials for users with disabilities or question whether the content going into the modules perpetuates stereotypes and promotes discrimination.[2] These two relationships will be explored in the remainder of this chapter as the relationship between and ethics and design are drawn from a range of authors outside and inside the field.

---

[2] One response to accessibility would be that laws would require this, such as Section 508, but accessibility is raised here because of the topics that do arise in the small body of literature on ethics in the field, accessibility is one of the most common themes. For more discussion on a distinction between a legal treatments and design treatments of topics related to ethics, see Moore and Ellsworth (2013).

Design for Good

In 2010, the Smithsonian Cooper-Hewitt, National Design Museum in New York hosted an exhibit entitled "Why Design Now?" The exhibit featured designs of all kinds—products, architecture, message, clothing, landscapes, and so forth—that address some of the major societal challenges around the world today. The themes focused on energy, mobility, community, materials, prosperity, health, communication, and simplicity. Ideas and products in the exhibition ranged from very low-cost eyeglasses that the user can adjust, AdSpecs, which addresses the needs of an estimated half billion people living in poverty around the world, to a neonatal incubator using car parts that makes incubators easy and quick to repair or fashion out of scrap in remote or impoverished parts of the world, to social housing designs that rely on a grid of renewable energy sources and offer low-income residents high quality environments and ability to individualize their spaces in a way that adds aesthetic appeal as well, and many more examples of "design for good."

The examples and exhibits were selected based on how they represented the role that design plays in making the world a better place. In each case, the designer or developer or entrepreneur had identified a *social* gap that was then methodically addressed through the design or development of new and improved products or materials or even new design processes altogether. These weren't idealized visions of the future, but practical solutions to a range of problems intended to improve the quality of life for a few, for a town, or for half a billion.

What was also reflected in this exhibit is the growing role that design-oriented professions are playing in defining what heretofore have been abstract muddy concepts—like social responsibility, ethics, and "good"—in more concrete or practical terms. Rather than defining "good" as solely a value or an ideal state, these projects all defined "good" as an end goal and a realizable result. They represent an articulation of a good that can be done, a value that can be added, if only we set an intentional gaze upon it, rather than a hopeful or wistful gaze. In short, they reflect a dynamic shift that is taking place at the intersection of design and ethics. When ethics meet the design process, we can wake up a tired and exhausted (and exhausting) concept that we all know to be important but don't really know how to tackle beyond trying to be a good person, turn it around to see it from a new angle, and even engage the creativity and innovativeness that designers thrive on. Rather than ethics being something externally imposed on us, lurking around a corner for some professional body to jump on our next infraction of some rule intended to "regulate" us into good behavior, they become the very things that we *do*, that we *produce*.

Ethics and Design Domain?

In recent years, Reeves has been emphasizing the importance of the little understood but highly relevant conative domain. Distinct from the cognitive and affective domains, the conative domain was long ago identified, but has not received attention

Table 1 Comparison of cognitive, affective, and conative domains (adapted from Kolbe, 1990, emphasis mine)

Cognitive	Affective	Conative
To know	To feel	To act
Thinking	Feeling	Willing
Thought	Emotion	Volition
Epistemology	Esthetics	*Ethics*
Knowing	Caring	Doing

or development like the others—to great detriment to learners, according to Reeves (2006). Conation is the act of striving and has to do with intention, will, and drive or desire. Kolbe (1990) provides a good summary comparison of domains (Table 1):

In this context, specific attention is drawn to "ethics" as part of the conative domain—in the same category as doing, acting, and volition. These are the very same definitions and descriptors often used to define design. Separate from performance, design is a goal-oriented activity that seeks not just to understand, but to produce and act upon a problem. This would imply that the very act of design itself is a manifestation of ethics, and conversely that the most accurate way to discuss ethics is not as contemplation, or knowing, but as a goal-oriented activity that requires us to engage sophisticated design processes.

This emphasis on design as a framework for thinking about ethics (or rethinking ethics) is an emerging theme across some bodies of literature that will be covered here as representative ideas: Barbour's *Ethics in an Age of Technology*; Whitbeck's (1996) "ethics as design;" Pinch and Bijker's (1984) "social construction of technology" model; and finally ending back within our own literature with Kaufman's (2000) Mega planning and evaluation model. These bodies of work tend to converge on the same story: Design (and planning) play a crucial role in addressing what we might classify as "ethics." Specifically, it defines the space of "applied ethics" which authors in other disciplines, such as health, have developed into a typology that includes professional ethics and social responsibility (Porter, 2006). What literature does exist in our field focuses primarily on these two areas—professional ethics and social responsibility—and these have been the primary guiding constructs for development and revision of professional codes of ethics. However, our body of literature has not connected design to these two areas yet; Barbour (1993), Whitbeck, Pinch and Bijker, and Kaufman suggest the connection points.

Barbour: Technology as Design in Context

In order to explain a design disposition towards technology, Barbour (1993) first debunks two pervasive and fallacious ways of thinking about technology, both fundamentally deterministic. One common view of technology is that it is beneficial and any innovation is necessarily an improvement of society, akin to "innovation bias" explored by Rogers (2003). This view derives from positivist and technocratic strands throughout history and helps to explain popular mental models of technology. New innovations are sold and marketed all the time on the promise they will revolutionize a "bad" system. As Nye (2007) states, this is the language of salesmen and politicians. MOOCs will change higher education as we know it. iPads will change education and learning. We can trace back through every single educational technology and find volumes of such language used to sell these technologies to policy makers and education administrators. The second common view is the pessimistic version of the first—technology detracts from human and social relationships and processes and we are wise to be wary. Rather than improving a given context, technology will have adverse effects. For example, internet access in schools may be great for research, but it introduces substantial security threats into the school environment and turns social interactions between students into interactions between a student and a computer screen.

What both perspectives share is a deterministic view—a linear process wherein technology is developed in isolation then implemented in social systems where human actors must react, often in an accept/reject manner. Such determinism even begins to show up in some pockets of educational authors. For example, Cuban (1986, 2003) and Healy (1990, 1999) both ardently question the value of technology in education, arguing that technology either has had no visible effect and is a waste of resources or that technology will have a negative effect on learners' cognitive functioning. As tempting as these lines of thought are, they are both inconsistent with the research on technology in social systems, including research on technology in educational systems, because they both neglect the influence of design in failures and successes. Barbour's third view of technology, which he advocates for instead of the previous two, proposes a design view rather than a deterministic view of technology.

Barbour (1993) advocates a "contextualist" view of technology, holding that "technology is neither inherently good nor inherently evil but is an ambiguous instrument of power whose consequences depend on its social context" (p. 15). His is an interactive model in which different members of the social system, including the designer, work together to create the best possible solution. He states:

> … historical analysis suggests that most technology are already molded by particular interests and institutional goals. Technologies are social constructions, and they are seldom neutral because particular purposes are already built into their design. Alternative purposes would lead to alternative designs. Yet most designs still allow some choice as to how they are deployed. (1993, p. 15)

The impact of any given technology is a function of design—both front-end definitions and inputs, such as interests and goals, as well as ongoing revision processes. This view—that it is the design that matters and that no given technology possesses an inherent ability to change things for the better or worse—is internally consistent with both the media comparison studies history of our field and with analyses of technologies from other fields of historical and cross-cultural comparisons. The most comprehensive of the latter type of analyses is Carlson's seven-volume collection of *Technology in World History* (2005) that examines all kinds of technologies across world history and world cultures. Carlson started with the question of how technology has impacted history, but as he gathered evidence over historical periods and across cultures, he had to modify his own question to instead focus on how different societies use technology differently to achieve their priorities. In essence, societies and cultures make different decisions about the design and adoption or even adaptation of technologies. Design is a far better explanation of technological phenomena than determinism.

Some may argue that Barbour's quote blurs design with implementation or deployment. However, Cross (2011) would remind us that design is an iterative process, and when the concept of iteration is mapped onto the social nature of the process as described in Carlson (2005) and Pinch and Bijker (1984, explained in more detail below), we can begin to see how all innovations go through a revisive process that is not limited just to pre-deployment but in fact technologies are modified over a more extended time as feedback from end users, failure analyses, market responses, etc., all influence the constant shaping and reshaping of technologies (especially in democratic societies[3]). Thus, design is not a time-limited activity nor is it limited in who participates to just the designer or innovator or even a narrow set of users. Design is a participatory activity that unfolds over time guided by purpose and intent, often with competing or even oppositional definitions of purpose or intent.

Pinch and Bijker: Social Construction of Technology

The temporal and participatory aspects of design, especially when we are talking at the scale of systems, are probably best captured in Pinch and Bijker's theory of social construction of technology (SCOT). In 1984, Pinch and Bijker first advanced the argument that "technology" was not something we could represent with a linear development process but instead looks more like an interactive web or network that shifts and changes over time. A traditional view of the innovation process was linear with six stages: basic research, applied research, technological development, product development, production, and usage. This sort of linear perspective is still predominant today in many developers' minds and operates as a fundamental mental model of how innovations are developed and diffused; it is the mental model bedfellow of the deterministic perspective described by Barbour. In analyzing the history of the development of the bicycle—a seemingly simple technology—Pinch and Bijker explain that the design we have today did not derive from a linear process nor was it predetermined; instead, it evolved over time as various "relevant social groups" influenced the design and variations of design over time. Some of the design variants "die" as they prove to be less useful or advantageous (Rogers' characteristics of innovations explain this phenomenon with more

---

[3] For additional treatment, Carlson (2005) does discuss at length the relationship between technology and all forms of sociopolitical systems and provides and descriptive model for these relationships.

specificity, 2003). Other design variants emerge to serve different social groups with varied interests. For example, Pinch and Bijker explain how women cyclists influenced the adaptation of the early bicycle designs to yield a design better suited to female cyclists.

Today the bicycle is still probably one of the best examples of a design for which there are multiple thriving variations of the idea all suited to differing uses and users—racing, road bikes, mountain bikes, hybrids, cruisers, men's, women's, children, family, recumbent, and so on. This one example helps narrate the temporal and participatory aspects of technological design. The designs that exist today were not the first designs and did not even stem from a small-loop design or brainstorming process before the first bicycle ever hit the street. Instead, these design modifications and variations appeared over a great length of time and continue to do so today as different user groups reshape the technological artifact and as other discoveries are made such as improved materials or safety standards.

The bicycle is also a great example of how no technology operates in isolation but instead is part of a larger socio-technical system or infrastructure. Adoption of cycling is not as simple as purchasing a bike. The nature of the supporting system or infrastructure around a cyclist can greatly impact his or her ability to make use of the artifact—and the values of a given society define how extensive that infrastructure is. For example, in Colorado cycling and healthy lifestyles are highly valued and even strongly encouraged by employers and government. This support shows up in investments in infrastructures such as bike lanes throughout most of the major cities and bike paths between cities that allow more extended commuting or recreational use of bikes. Safety standards both for the bicycles and for all traffic on the road establish a culture of "sharing the road." In Virginia, however, there is less investment in such infrastructure and therefore far less use of bikes for transportation or commuting. In contrast, most European cities are even more advanced than Colorado in their infrastructure for integration. In addition to bike lanes and streets designed to accommodate bicycle traffic, there are ramps for bikes beside nearly every staircase so users can push their bikes upstairs in their office buildings or roll it down the stairs to the train, where there is even a designated space on the train to rest the bicycle between stops. In Denmark, they have even built a "superhighway" for bikes designed for commuting to work and plan to add 26 additional routes to connect Copenhagen to suburbs and beyond. So in addition to design variations of the artifact itself, there are next-order design variations in the systems that support or hinder adoption of the technology.

When it comes to educational technologies, these variations in user groups, their interests, and their value systems are actually quite widely understood and represented in a great deal of research in the field. Research on change and technology integration into schools continually emphasizes stakeholder involvement (stakeholders = relevant social groups). Context and culture make a difference as well in terms of what technologies are a best match, and differences in infrastructure greatly impact whether a school or system can make best use of a technology. Where we may be lacking is in the more participatory role that educators play in the design and development of technologies before introduction and throughout a more extended revision cycle that most technologies naturally go through.[4] In fact, exploration of Pinch and Bijker's (1984) SCOT to the specific context of educational-technical systems could offer some critical insights as we shift from thinking of technology as something we do in or to schools to thinking of the whole system as an integrated socio-technical system. For example, application of SCOT in education highlights that one-size-fits-all-policy for technology in education neglects contextual factors that influence effectiveness; educator participation in the technological system is necessary and desirable at every point in time including conception as well as ongoing revision and redesign; technology integration is possibly a fallacious construct because it assumes that educators and schools are merely in a receptive or reactive position, and technology construction is a more accurate, fair, and ethical approach to technology in education.

Barbour (1993), Pinch and Bijker (1984), and others help us to understand the contextual and systemic aspects of technological design that inform what Strijbos (1998) calls "system ethics" that are necessary as we recognize the interconnectedness of designs, decisions, and their impacts. In addition, we can also drill downward into the design process itself and explore how and where ethics integrate with design.

Whitbeck: Ethics as Design

In other design-oriented disciplines, such as engineering, there is increasing recognition that the act of design is also one of developing solutions to meet societal challenges. For example, in a Hastings Center report Whitbeck (1996) writes about "ethics as design," explaining that ethics are embedded in the design process itself. She offers what is probably the best clarification for how we might rethink ethics, suggesting that solving moral problems "is not simply a matter of choosing the 'best' of several possible responses. It is also a matter of *devising* possible responses" (p. 1, emphasis added). She explains that moral problems are practical challenges and bear many striking similarities to another class of practical problems—the design problem. Developing a response to an ethical problem requires one to take multiple considerations into account—and often there is some tension or conflict between these demands. Traditionally, a philosophical approach to ethics would conclude that these are irresolvable conflicts, so a person must "opt" for a solution.

---

[4] There appears to be far less patience with the temporal aspects of technological reshaping in educational contexts, at least on the part of policy makers and innovators. One might argue that much of what looks like "resistance" in schools is actually the range of relevant social groups acting upon the technologies to reshape them, which appears to "slow down" the adoption process and is more accurately described as a redesign process rather than resistance/adoption. This has also likely led to less participatory design models in educational technology because the core relevant social groups are viewed as "resisters" rather than codesigners. Further exploration, which I hope to encourage in others through this chapter, of the implications of SCOT for educational technology could yield some more effective models and relationships for the educational-technical system.

However, design processes tend to approach these competing demands as varying needs or constraints that can often be at least partially satisfied through a more considered design. Whitbeck notes, for substantive design problems, that "there is rarely, if ever, a uniquely correct solution or response" but emphasizes that this is an entirely different claim than saying there are no right or wrong answers. Whereas the latter is an extreme expression of relativism in ethics, the former is a practical approach to ethics offered by design. While there may be no one correct solution or response, it *is* possible to devise—or design—a response or solution that effectively balances the competing requirements.

An example in instructional technology can help illustrate application of similar ideas to design and development in our field. One of the topics typically classified as "ethics" in the literature is accessibility. Accessibility relates to the ability of users with disabilities to have equal access to a physical or virtual environment. Because these are often discussed as requirements for compliance with the Americans with Disabilities Act (ADA) and Section 508 regulations, the tendency is to discuss what designers must do in order to be compliant. A compliance orientation often suggests there is one morally correct course of action, thus a lot of the resulting recommendations are a generation of rules. So, for a website, a designer must have alt tags, D links, cascading style sheets, and closed captioning (and the closed captioning must be in a specific font and size). Some of these recommendations have stemmed from studies on what format works best (such as font and size for closed captioning), but the resulting discourse tragically misses all the possibilities that are afforded by a more design-oriented approach to the topic.

A framework for design with promise in this area is Universal Design for Learning (Rose & Meyer, 2002), developed by the Center for Applied Special Technology (CAST) at Harvard. While universal design has caught on in many teacher preparation programs, it has received very little attention in educational technology. This is rather curious because Rose and Meyer (2002) envision that technology plays a particularly crucial role in accomplishing universal design principles in learning environments. They argue that the use of technology in a learning environment will lead to a more flexible and individualized environment. However, any given technology can maintain rigid structures or barriers just as well as it can remove barriers or change structures. Its ability to do so, however, rests with the design decisions that are made by all those participating in the system, from designers to administrators to those responsible for its integration and use. Educational technology literature *is* replete with analyses of why the simple "adoption" model of technology is a failed model. But while Rose and Meyer's model of Universal Design—and specifically the role of technology in accomplishing that—can be improved, conversely educational technology can be improved by integrating more universal design principles into the design process and by studying this area more to determine evidence-based practices.

In short, accessibility and flexibility of learning technologies cannot be assumed; rather, they result from intentional design considerations and features that seek to understand multiple users, operates from a pluralistic definition of learners, and seeks out solutions to make a design functional for as many users as possible.

Much like Whitbeck's (1996) examples in engineering, the practical functionality of accessible design also yields desirable societal results in the educational sphere—primarily reduction of barriers and increased access to learning for groups of learners who are traditionally underserved.

Design and Planning for Socially Desirable Results

Within our own field we have some excellent foundations already—but we are only likely to see them as such when we reframe ethics through the design lens. In the area of needs assessment, planning and evaluation, Kaufman's (2000) model for organizational performance presents a robust framework for planning and evaluating multiple levels of impact which includes societal impact. In Kaufman's (2000) model, societal impact is both the basis for planning or design (a process that starts there then plans or designs "downward" into organizational outcomes, performance outcomes, inputs, and processes) and the longitudinal measure of an organization's success (as results at each level align back from the inside out). He presents an operational definition of societal outcomes as well as a framework that assesses and employs societal needs as the basis for design, implementation, and evaluation—in short, one that not merely hopes, but *plans* for ethical outcomes. This same sort of purposeful design shows up in other design disciplines as well. For example, McDonough, award-winning architect and designer in sustainability, explains in a discussion on his book, *Cradle to Cradle Design*, "… it's no longer acceptable for us to say this isn't part of our plan… because it's part of our *de facto* plan. It's the thing that's happening because we have no other plan. Then we realize as a culture that we have become strategically tragic" (2006). By not defining these ends, we deliver a future and a world to our children that are unintentionally tragic, and potentially irreversible. Here again in Kaufman and McDonough we find the same concept of design as the earlier definitions reviewed by Banathy—a focus on what should be and on improving the future through intentional action.

While this might seem to be large—and daunting—in focus, there are many areas in which professionals in the field are working on projects with direct societal impact. At the simplest level, any distance learning initiative is not just about learning outcomes but is about a positive impact on society by providing access to education for those who could not previously access it. International settings offer some of the clearest examples. In reviewing education in fragile states (states that are in conflict or crisis), the Inter-Agency Network for Education in Emergencies (INEE), in a study commissioned by the World Bank, explained that education is not an assumed positive influence but instead can mitigate *or contribute to* fragility, depending on how it is implemented. INEE's analyses show both the complexity and the criticality of determining impact; their analysis of four states revealed a continuum of education's impact on a society ranging from actively reinforcing or perpetuating fragility, through inadvertently favoring it, to mitigating against it. In Afghanistan, schools are often a target for insurgents because they are used as polling places and because of the push to allow girls to receive an education, as evidenced by the recent shooting of Malala Yousafzai in neighboring Pakistan. INEE observed that building physical schools can inadvertently *increase* fragility by consuming resources *and* inviting attacks on the community's children and best-educated adults. In this case, radio-based distance education was employed, enabling safer schooling and measurably reducing fragility (INEE, 2011). In addition to accomplishing learning outcomes, this use and design of an educational technology also accomplished societal outcomes such as stability and safety as well as access to education for underserved populations and strengthening those populations to counter discrimination in the long run.

In other situations that INEE observed, learning materials perpetuated social divides. For example, in Bosnia and Herzegovina, biased curricula, textbooks and teacher training had been designed to maintain ethnic and language divisions. These biases reproduced patterns of inequality that ultimately determined outcomes and employment opportunities for students on an ethnically differentiated basis, maintaining or even increasing fragility in that society. In the face of these results, the country's educational leadership is currently working to reduce these negative societal results through increased national governance and intentional deigns of curricula, texts, and training that promote social cohesion (INEE, 2011).

Such examples reveal a layer of design considerations we may not normally confront: How do our designs work with—or *against*—other parts of the educational system to affect learning? How could our choices increase or decrease participants' safety? To exactly what are we providing access—and is that contributing to desirable outcomes, or maintaining *undesirable* ones like social inequalities? These questions challenge us to clarify the actual needs and objectives we pursue and highlight that *learning* outcomes are not the only results of instructional designs, but rather a subset of the ethical considerations that should inform the design process.

So What Do We Do With This: Three Touchpoints

The broad goal of this chapter has been to suggest that we can rethink ethics, and in return rethink design as well, because of how these two constructs interact. In doing so, the intent was not to suggest that every possible relationship or model has emerged but rather if the conversation gets triggered and others begin to reflect on the ideas suggested herein, that we can more collectively generate a body of insights around this topic. But I want to close by focusing on three "touchpoints" that I think are practical and tangible places to start for applied ethics as they relate to design in the field.

1. *Reflective practitioners*: First, through the participation in the design symposium, it was very clear from other members that the idea of the "reflective practitioner" resonated strongly with this topic (or vice versa). In another chapter in this collection, Tracey writes about the reflective practitioner and how we develop such an individual. Although my own work does not tend to focus on the

individual designer, there is a great deal of attention in this area and it adds vital dimensionality. In this sense, Tracey and others emphasize that we start both with *design* and the *designer*. Many participants discussed how our field has tended to dehumanize the designer, but ethics reminds us to treat the designer as a person who will bring certain values and beliefs to the design. The designer, whether as an individual or a group, lies at the core of the design process. Developing more reflective practitioners strengthens that core, as depicted in Gordon's chapter in this same collection. Self-reflective practitioners go beyond compliance with codes or standards to ask themselves questions such as whether there are certain audiences they would not design for, what is one's epistemology and how does that intersect with what is being asked, what is the context for the design, what is one's agency, how (for example in the case of considering accessibility) are "learners" being defined." These reflective questions don't require "right" answers but rather can be used to prompt students and give them (and us) tools for developing habits of design mind one might call "ethical."

2. *Research-informed design*: One of the more subtle themes in this chapter has been the relationship between research and design. Typically when "research" and "ethics" are put in the same equation, "institutional review board" comes after the equal sign. While this is one way to think of the relationship between these two, the introduction of design into the equation suggests a different interaction that yields research-informed design. While there are all manner of people using "instructional designer" as a title on a business card, the professional instructional designer is one who uses understanding of how people learn and how designs facilitate learning in his or her work. Research defines professional practice and guides it, and design in the absence of such research can produce an array of ill effects from false evidence of a technology being ineffective to bad policies around technologies in educational systems that end up hurting multiple stakeholders and wasting resources. Ongoing research continues to inform how we do this well, with "well" including not just learning outcomes but positive desirable impacts on learner populations, on educational systems, and on the social systems the education seeks to serve. The body of research is larger around learning outcomes, but additional research on access, educational systems and other types of societal impact can greatly inform practice. Beabout (2013) offers an excellent example of this type of work, writing on social justice aspects of redesigning the education system in a post-Katrina New Orleans. In addition to providing an example approach, he explores the more complicated relationship research has with design, especially when designing at a social systems level. He writes:

The core ethical dilemma of this [work] ... is the tension between adopting 'what works' architectures or using an overly structural lens when looking at educational change. Particularly in public schools ... communities (I argue) have a right to have a say in the development and maintenance of systems that impact their lives. Bureaucracies fudge on this participation in the name of 'excellence' or in the name of expediency, but with pretty singularly bad results. (personal communication, 2012)

His work reiterates much of what this chapter has been about—planning and design at a systems level, participatory design processes, recognition of cultural and contextual influences on designs, and use of design to accomplish a societal good—specifically in an educational setting. Emerging models for research such as design-based research, which Nelson explores in this volume as well, may offer more naturalistic and integrative ways of studying instructional and educational design as a communal and participatory process that unfolds over time rather than a singular event that occurs, after which we measure outcomes. Far more research and exploration can be done along these lines in any setting.

3. *Ethics as design*: Finally, ethics can be integrated directly into design processes even at a very fundamental level. Earlier I suggested a definition of ethics that was a design-oriented definition. That definition suggested several characteristics of ethics in design: participatory process that identifies and involves stakeholders, or relevant social groups, all throughout; consideration of societal impact, social justice, and cultural and contextual factors as positive design constraints; definition of desired results that includes systemic or societal impacts as well as learning outcomes. One's task may be to design a website, but "learners" can be more broadly defined so the website doesn't inadvertently exclude a population from the educational process. One's task may be to lead an online learning initiative, but involvement of stakeholders from the very beginning can greatly inform the design to shape it into something the users will actually want to use and be invested in.

These are things any designer could start doing today.

References

Banathy, B. (1996). *Designing social systems in a changing world*. New York: Plenum Press.

Barbour, I. (1993). *Ethics in an age of technology: The Gifford Lectures* (Vol. 2). San Francisco: HarperCollins.

Beabout, B. R. (2013). Community leadership: Seeking social justice while recreating public schools in post-Katrina New Orleans. In I. Bogotch & C. Shields (Eds.), *International handbook of social (in) justice and educational leadership*. Dordrecht, Netherlands: Springer.

Carlson, B. (2005). *Technology in world history* (Vol. 1–7). New York: Oxford University Press.

Cross, N. (2011). *Design thinking: Understanding how designers think and work*. New York: Berg.

Cuban, L. (1986). *Teachers and machines: The classroom use of technology since 1920*. New York: Teachers College Press.

Cuban, L. (2003). *Oversold and underused: Computers in the classroom, 1980–2000*. Cambridge, MA: Harvard University Press.

Davis, M. (1999). *Ethics and the university*. London: Routledge.

Feldon, D. F., & Gilmore, J. (2006). Patterns in children's online behavior and scientific problem-solving: A large-N microgenetic study. In G. Clarebout & J. Elen (Eds.), *Avoiding simplicity, confronting complexity: Advances in studying and designing (computer-based) powerful learning environments* (pp. 117–125). Rotterdam, The Netherlands: Sense.

Healy, J. (1990). *Endangered minds: Why our children don't think*. New York: Simon & Schuster.

Healy, J. (1999). *Failure to connect: How computers affect our children's minds—and what we can do about it*. New York: Simon & Schuster.

INEE Working Group on Education and Fragility. (2011). *Understanding education's role in fragility: Synthesis of four situational analyses of education and fragility: Afghanistan, Bosnia and Herzegovina, Cambodia, and Liberia*. Paris, France: International Institute for Educational Planning (IIEP).

Kaufman, R. (2000). *Mega planning: Practical tools for organizational success*. Thousand Oaks, CA: Sage.

Klahr, D., & Dunbar, K. (1988). Dual search space during scientific reasoning. *Cognitive Science, 12*, 1–48.

Kolbe, K. (1990). *The conative connection: Acting on instinct*. Reading, MA: Addison-Wesley.

McDonough, W. (2006). Cradle to cradle design. *iTunesU—Stanford series*. December 3, 2006. Retrieved January 15, 2008.

Moore, S. L. (2005). *The social impact of a profession: An analysis of factors influencing ethics and the teaching of social responsibility in educational technology programs*. Doctor of Philosophy dissertation, University of Northern Colorado.

Moore, S. L. (2009). Social responsibility of a profession: An analysis of faculty perception of social responsibility factors and integration into graduate programs of educational technology. *Performance Improvement Quarterly, 22*(2), 79–96.

Moore, S. L., & Ellsworth, J. (2013). Ethics and standards in educational technology. In M. Spector (Ed.), *Handbook of research on educational communications and technology*. Bloomington, IN: Association of Educational Communications and Technology.

Nye, D. (2007). *Technology matters: Questions to live with*. Cambridge: MIT Press.

Pinch, T. J., & Bijker, W. E. (1984). The social construction of facts and artefacts: Or, how the sociology of science and the sociology of technology might benefit each other. *Social Studies of Science, 14*, 399–441.

Plato. (1990). Phaedrus; Or the ethical, or beautiful. In P. Bizzell & B. Herzberg (Eds.), *The rhetorical tradition: Readings from classical times to the present* (pp. 113–143). Boston: Bedford Books.

Porter, R. (2006). *The health ethics typology: Six domains to improve care*. Hampton, GA: Socratic Publishing.

Quintillian. (1990). Institutes of oratory. In P. Bizzell & B. Herzberg (Eds.), *The rhetorical tradition: Readings from classical times to the present* (pp. 297–363). Boston: Bedford Books.

Reeves, T. (2006). How do you know they are learning?: The importance of alignment in higher education. *International Journal of Learning Technology, 2*(4), 294–309.

Rittel, H., & Webber, M. (1973). Dilemmas in a general theory of planning. *Policy Sciences, 4*: 155–169. In N. Cross (Ed.) (1984). *Developments in design methodology* (pp. 135–144). Chichester: Wiley.

Rogers, E. (2003). *Diffusion of innovations* (5th ed.). New York: Free Press.

Rose, D., & Meyer, A. (2002). *Teaching every student in the digital age: Universal design for learning*. Alexandria, VA: Association for Supervision and Curriculum Development.

Scharff, R., & Dusek, V. (Eds.). (2003). *Philosophy of technology: The technological condition, an anthology*. Malden, MA: Blackwell.

Schauble, L., Klopfer, L., & Raghavan, K. (1991). Students' transition from an engineering model to a science model of experimentation. *Journal of Research in Science Teaching, 18*(9), 859–882.

Simon, H. (1969). *The science of the artificial*. Cambridge: MIT Press.

Strijbos, S. (1998). Ethics and the systemic character of modern technology. *Techne: Journal for the Society for Philosophy and Technology, 3*(4), 1–15.

Whitbeck, C. (1996). Ethics as design: Doing justice to moral problems. *The Hastings Center Report, 26*(3), 9–16.

Yeaman, A., Koetting, R., & Nichols, R. (1994). Critical theory, cultural analysis, and the ethics of educational technology as social responsibility. *Educational Technology, 34*(2), 5–13.

EDISYS: A Tool for Enhancing Design Inquiry

Gordon Rowland

Keywords Design inquiry • Inquiry system • Design inquiry system • Educational innovation • Design-based research • Over-the-edge thinking • Trustworthiness • Design way • Learning • Designing • Disciplined inquiry • Inquiry • System • Systems design • Powerful learning experience • Second-order cybernetics • Reflection in design • Designing the design • Design case • Expert behavior • First principles • Interdependence • Emergence • Dimensionality • Requisite variety • Complexity • Half-known world

The Context of Educational Innovation

At the 2012 AECT Research Symposium for which chapters in this volume were drafted, I began my presentation with a poll regarding current circumstances in education. I asked participants to raise their hands if they felt the following statements were true: (1) There has been adequate innovation in education to meet current and future challenges. No hands were raised. (2) Educational innovation is guided sufficiently by research. No hands were raised. (3) Design has great potential for contributing to educational innovation. All hands were raised.

G. Rowland, Ph.D. (✉)
Roy H. Park School of Communications, Ithaca College,
Ithaca, NY 14850, USA
e-mail: rowland@ithaca.edu

B. Hokanson and A. Gibbons (eds.), *Design in Educational Technology*,
Educational Communications and Technology: Issues and Innovations 1,
DOI 10.1007/978-3-319-00927-8_12, © Springer International Publishing Switzerland 2014

Perhaps the poll results were a consequence of self-selection in the audience, but there is growing recognition that design has something special to offer education that research alone does not. Steps to more fully embrace design are being taken in a number of different directions, including the following:

- New approaches to inquiry are being developed. For example, design-based research involves conducting research through collaborative design (Anderson & Shattuck, 2012). These types of approaches better contextualize research by moving inquiry into actual settings, although they continue to privilege research and the researcher over design and educators and maintain a belief in universal, generalizable laws (e.g., see Willis, 2011b).
- A body of precedent material and, in particular, the methods and media for sharing design cases have begun to be developed (Howard, 2014). Gaver (2012) recently described the associated concept of "annotated portfolios."
- There are calls for focusing on designing for learning experience as opposed to instruction, that is, the transactions between individual learners and the learning environment rather than just how subject matter is delivered (e.g., Parrish, 2009), and for more powerful outcomes (e.g., Wilson, Switzer, Parrish, & the IDEAL Research Lab, 2007).
- There is increasing interest in approaches and design principles that go beyond the purely rational, for example, creative processes (Clinton & Hokanson, 2012) and aesthetic principles (Parrish, 2009). A concept that a colleague and I have been developing in this area is "over-the-edge thinking," which recognizes that innovations more often come from finding or creating relationships between things just across previously defined boundaries than from simply "thinking out of the box."
- There are interesting new views of design, especially Krippendorff's *Semantic Turn* (2006), and a call for a richer instructional design (ID) language (e.g., Gibbons & Brewer, 2005).
- Standards and criteria for judging quality, for example, trustworthiness criteria drawn from naturalistic inquiry, have been suggested (Smith, 2010).
- Many of these directions have been brought together under the umbrella of a "design way" (Nelson & Stolterman, 2012).

Other directions could be taken as well. For example, careful attention could be given to rewards and incentives in academia, which are currently heavily biased toward traditional research, and more sophisticated tools and techniques could be developed to assist/enhance design processes. This chapter focuses on the latter.

Key Concepts: Learning, Design, Inquiry, and System

Before describing the tool that I have developed, I should make clear how I am defining some key concepts.

Typically, *learning* is defined as the development of knowledge, skills, and attitudes, or a semipermanent change of behavior. For the purposes of this chapter, I define learning broadly, encompassing any such definitions, and including:

(a) Learning that occurs within the intended context, that is, by learners in the setting/situation for which a design was created, as well as the co-learning by learners and instructors
(b) Learning by the designer, that is, knowledge and knowing that is gained and may transfer to subsequent designs
(c) Learning by others outside the context, for example, transfer by designers who learn from precedent materials such as design cases

Learning defined so broadly thus relates directly to the symposium's themes of design thinking, design process, and design studio and includes educational innovation. While this broad definition might include informal and incidental learning, the concern in this chapter is learning environments that are intentionally designed.

Designing involves creating something new that serves a practical purpose. As with learning, I would add a few clarifications:

(a) We, the symposium participants and authors of chapters in this book, seek to go beyond "idealized representations of design in educational technology [that] tend to characterize design as being oriented on process, conducted as systematic work, represented by models, based on theory, grounded in data, characterized by subdivision and specialization, and focused on problem-solving" (Smith & Boling, 2009, p. 3). We see these idealized representations as limiting, particularly in terms of the development of designers' personal style and voice—those things that make a designer great, not just competent.
(b) Consequently, rather than a simple definition of design that would include, in the context of education, the routine act of preparing to teach, I/we are referring to something more specific—the skillful designing done as a professional occupation, based on training, experience, knowledge of precedent, processes, theories and principles, and so on. Design in this sense involves sophisticated discipline and judgment (Boling & Smith, 2009) and is a distinct form of inquiry—a decision-oriented disciplined inquiry (Banathy, 1996).
(c) Design conducted as a disciplined inquiry involves activities that would be readily recognized as a form of research and is influenced by the depth and quality of those activities.
(d) And as Krippendorff states, "Designers are motivated not by a quest for knowledge for its own sake but by: challenges, troublesome conditions, problems, or conflicts that have escaped (re)solution; opportunities to change something for the better—not recognized by others—to contribute to their own or other communities' lives ..." (2006, p. 28). In doing this search for knowledge, designers can draw upon scientific principles and processes, yet not be acting as scientists. Rather, design is a tradition on par with science (and art) (Cross, 1982; Nelson & Stolterman, 2012). In other words, design, as an inquiry specifically dedicated to meeting these challenges and to taking advantage of opportunities, is as essential as scientific research and may have greater impact on learning.

Inquiry is "an activity which produces knowledge" (Churchman, 1971, p. 8), so it includes various forms of reasoning (e.g., inductive, deductive, and abductive) and a wide range of approaches (e.g., quantitative/rationalistic, qualitative/naturalistic, pragmatic, and critical). Different types of inquiry (e.g., basic research, applied research, and evaluation) have different purposes, use different methods, and result in different forms of knowledge. Since design processes create knowledge, and design products can be thought to embody knowledge, design can be considered a type of inquiry.

A *system* is an integrated whole composed of elements/parts and relationships. The whole has special properties that emerge from the relationships among parts, and when parts are especially well aligned, the resulting synergy can dramatically increase the system's potential. Consequently, we can facilitate the achievement of a system's purposes by examining and intentionally attempting to align parts and strengthen relationships, which is an application of *systems thinking*.

Systems thinking can be very useful in designing. In fact, it is essential for designs to be sustainable (Nelson & Stolterman, 2012). There are some aspects of systems thinking, though, that are not obvious. To appreciate these, try the following activity. You will need a single piece of blank paper.

1. Consider a learning experience in a formal setting to be a whole. Identify the parts of that whole (e.g., learners, goals/objectives, setting, instructional strategies). Write the names of the parts in a circle or oval around the outside of your paper.
2. Identify two learning experiences that you have had, or in which you have been involved, in a formal context such as a class or training program. Identify one that was especially good and another that was especially poor.
3. Now consider what made the one experience good and the other poor. If it was the quality of an element(s), circle that element. If it was the quality of a relationship between elements, draw a line between those elements.

What do you see? If your experience is anything like that of the symposium participants, then you will notice that both the parts and the relations were important (and *which* of these are important varies significantly between instances). This means we are concerned with learning *systems* — with relationships, not just parts or elements — and this representation of the design artifact or *product* also implies that we need to think systemically in the *process* of creating such systems, hence *systems design*.

Had you participated in the symposium, you would have seen, also, that every individual's representation was different. (Try the activity with colleagues to see this.) What this implies is that *we* define the parts, the relationships, and the system as a whole, and we do so through language. In other words, we create and/or select the constructs that we use in thinking about and describing parts and patterns. And while we may choose to collaborate with others and to agree on the constructs we use for a specific project or for work in general, we define the system. It is artificial. There are certainly interdependencies that exist without our presence, observation, or intervention, but the *system* is what we call the system. (If you do not believe this, try identifying the boundary of any system in a way that no one else who identified the boundary would disagree. Try our "solar system," for example. Where does it end? Similarly, ask individuals from two different stakeholder groups to represent the system in which they hold stakes).

There is an important relationship here. Krippendorff (2006) argues that we respond to the individual and cultural meanings of things rather than to their physical properties. This is true not only in the use of the objects/artifacts that we design. It is true of designing itself. We define what we call parts of systems, give them names, and ascribe meanings to them. We fashion them into patterns, which have meanings for us, also. This requires much reflective skepticism on our part. For example, how we relate to a design may be entirely different from how a user or another stakeholder does. (Empathy is important and insufficient in user design.) It requires that we develop considerable design judgment, choosing constructs and defining them in ways that experience tells us has beneficial consequences, carefully monitoring and adjusting those definitions, and consciously questioning whether definitions are shared by other stakeholders throughout the design process.

Another important nuance is that while systems design is important, this does not require that systems be fully specified in advance or fully controlled. In fact, in our most powerful/transformative learning experiences, the elements appear to combine in special ways that are unpredictable and unique to the situation (e.g., Reuning-Hummel, 2011; Rivera & Rowland, 2008; Wilson et al., 2007). We may find greater potential in overconceptualized and underspecified (Weick, 2004) dynamic learning systems that are intelligently and creatively guided than in highly specified instruction.

There are insights to gain from applying other systems concepts, also, if we go beyond the typical nod to systems science as an historical root of our field. For example, references to general systems theory or the "systems approach" offer some information on how approaches in our field developed, but they barely take us beyond 1960s systems science, in the same way Bishop (2014) points out how the field of communication has developed far beyond the communication models that are typically cited in ID texts. To suggest one possibility, if we looked at inquiry systems in terms of second-order cybernetics (or double-loop learning), we would see not only the interaction of the designer and situation, but the designer stepping back to gain a perspective of how she or he and the situation have influenced each other in organizing that interaction, which is a part of reflection in design (Tracey & Baaki, 2014). This could help us do more than improve an existing design process. It could lead us to more powerful alternative processes, what Banathy (1996) called "designing the design."

Concepts Combined: Design Inquiry, Inquiry Systems, and Design Inquiry Systems

As can be seen with "systems design," the terms that were defined above can be combined in a variety of ways. In several specific cases, this is quite useful: design inquiry, inquiry systems, and design inquiry systems. Following the systems principle of emergence, these combined concepts create something with special properties not possessed by either alone.

Design inquiry can be defined as a disciplined search for knowledge that will take the form of something new that has practical value. That search is more than everyday design or problem solving and more than just creating an artifact. It is an integration of research and design, with all the discipline and rigor associated with both: for example, formal processes, explicit purposes and criteria, acknowledgement of assumptions and beliefs, careful documentation, and public sharing of results. The outcome of design inquiry is not just the design artifact or product. It is a thorough description of the process, in particular the decisions that were made and the rationale for choices. This is called the design case (see Howard, 2014), and it opens the inquiry to criticism and to learning, as broadly defined earlier. As I have argued elsewhere (Rowland, 2008, 2007), the whole created by integrating research and design has greater capacity for educational innovation than design and/or research conducted separately.

The formal, disciplined nature of design inquiry might represent one end of a continuum of design, with everyday, unskilled design or problem solving at the other end. The phrase design inquiry thus makes the reference to a particular form or approach to design explicit. Similarly, the phrase inquiry system highlights particular properties of this inquiry.

An *inquiry system* is a whole dedicated to the search for knowledge, and, presumably, the potential knowledge from that whole is greater through the synergy of parts. The parts or elements of an inquiry system are the key constructs that one uses in representing processes and products. For example, in the case of research, these constructs might include research questions, methods, findings, criteria, and assumptions. Or in the case of typical approaches in the instructional design (ID) context, constructs might include need, task, context, learner, environment, approach, strategies, tactics, and media.

The relationships of an inquiry system might mean the sequence of consideration in a method (e.g., in an ID process model: $A \rightarrow B \rightarrow C$) or the structure of a prescription (e.g., Conditions + Outcomes $\rightarrow$ Methods), although these examples may be deceptively simple in terms of expert behavior. We find that experts view learning systems and their design in much more sophisticated ways (e.g., Perez, Johnson, & Emery, 1995). For example, their thinking is more bidirectional ($A \rightarrow B$, $A \leftarrow B$), multidimensional (AB, ABC, ABCD), and complex (AB, ABC, ABCD as integrated wholes). (To consider examples, substitute the ID constructs above, such as need and task, for the letters in parentheses).

Finding evidence for these points regarding expert views, Anne Marie Adams and I conducted a study (Rowland & Adams, 1999) in which we found relationships among constructs that were more nuanced than those suggested in ID texts and that were largely invisible in typical ID models (see Fig. 1; my apologies for the small font size necessary to show these relationships simultaneously). In fact, we asked experts to do only pair-wise comparisons of constructs, as opposed to more multidimensional comparisons, and they stated that this underestimated the complexity of their design thinking. Also, while we did not study process directly, we came to a sense of "emphasis-shifted and mutual-shaped defining of system components." This is consistent with the findings of those who have studied design behavior in other fields (e.g., Cross, 2011; Lawson, 2006). It is also understandable given the

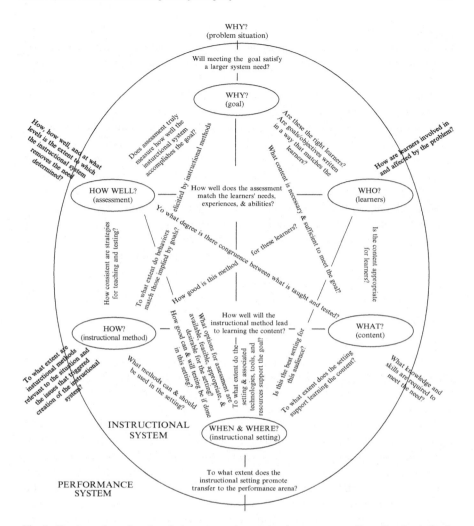

Fig. 1 Key issues/questions in relations among instructional systems parts. From Rowland, G., & Adams, A. M. (1999). Systems thinking in instructional design. In J. van den Akker, R. M. Branch, K. Gustafson, N. Nieveen, & T. Plomp (Eds.), *Design approaches and tools in education and training* (pp. 29–44). Boston: Kluwer Academic Publishers

cognitive limitations that Christakis (1996) points out: If three things (A, B, C) form a system, then thinking about this system actually involves seven concerns (A, B, C, AB, AC, BC, ABC). We reach Miller's (1956) magic number seven plus or minus two with only three parts, and this assumes unidirectionality (i.e., A → B or A ← B, not A → B and A ← B)!

Combining the three concepts — design, inquiry, and system — thus creates something that is especially complex — a design inquiry system. A *design inquiry system* can be defined as (1) a system for doing design inquiry, that is, a whole whose purpose is to help designers do research-AND-design, and to strengthen their ability to create new things that have practical utility, including learning experiences, or (2) an inquiry system for design, that is, a whole for advancing knowledge of design, including the development of precedent material. Both are relevant to the symposium and this volume, and both could be beneficial. My main focus for the remainder of this chapter is the former—the likelihood of greater learning being increased by thinking in terms of design inquiry *systems* and by strengthening these systems. Strengthening these systems means working toward stronger parts and, particularly, stronger relationships, since what makes something a system is in the relationships not the parts. The basic argument, therefore, is that aligning and building on interdependence among the constructs of the design inquiry will enhance potential learning. (And recall that learning is broadly defined here to include knowledge advancement from the inquiry by the designer and by others who vicariously come to know about the design process and product.) Given the inquiry system's complexity, this is a challenge. What I have attempted to create is a tool that will help.

The Tool

Some tools exist that might help us improve designs and design processes. For example, we have checklists for the quality of products such as e-learning courseware (e.g., NHS Shared Learning, 2009), and we have lists of competencies of instructional designers (e.g., Richey et al., 2001). Unfortunately, though, these tools, and our literature in general, tend to focus highly on parts or skills associated with parts. We have many books and book chapters on steps in processes, and, typically, relationships are ignored or portrayed in a simplistic fashion. For example, a text may call for matching an instructional strategy to a learning style, without any sense of how that match may be influenced by other factors in the situation, and a competency may refer to reflecting on the situation before finalizing decisions, without a sense of what would constitute quality of that reflection. I am aware of few existing tools in our field that are intended to enhance design by focusing on relationships and by embracing contemporary systems concepts and principles. Perhaps the closest are Kaufman's (2009) notion of levels of planning and Rummler and Brache's (1990) management of the white space in the organizational chart, though neither is focused on design. As a start, I have been developing a tool called EDISYS, which stands for Enhanced Design Inquiry System.

Before getting into details, it is important to consider what EDISYS is and what it is not.

EDISYS is:

- A system for enhancing design inquiry
- A set of coherent heuristic questions and statements intended to help the designer strengthen the inquiry and the design
- An attempt to more fully embrace systems concepts

- A prompt for reflection, consistent with Tracey and Baaki's thoughts on reflection in action (2014)
- A tool to help us compose coherent cases that can be shared, argued, criticized, improved, and used to educate and to build the knowledge base through precedent material that has greater transferability

EDISYS is not:

- A process model or tool to guide designing, although it might assist design processes by focusing attention on relationships
- A set of specific criteria (e.g., those that establish trustworthiness, drawn from naturalistic and action research; Smith, 2010), a view of design (e.g., ISD process, systems approach, organizational, design language, operational principle, team process, architectural, or functional-modular view; Gibbons, 2014), or a particular perspective of design (e.g., principle based, problem solving, language and layers, aesthetics, agency and design character, performance improvement; Boling & Smith, 2012)

In some ways that I am aware of, and in other ways that I am not, EDISYS is a result of the context for which it was developed. I teach a course titled Critical Issues in Organizations, which is a capstone in our Communication Management and Design undergraduate major. Students in the major are interested in a wide range of communication areas such as public relations, event management, employee communication, and web design. Few have specific interest in instructional design, but some discover it in their courses and pursue related jobs or graduate study.

Faculty members who taught the course before me selected a particular issue, and the class conducted research on that issue for the term. I redesigned the course for student teams to explore multiple issues in which they had special interest and to not only do research—understand *what is*—but to design—seek to resolve the issue by composing *what might be*. (I use "resolve" here to mean to solve or to find an answer to, but in the design sense of seeking so powerful an answer that it does not merely counter the immediate forces or factors; it makes the underlying causes and conflicts disappear or become irrelevant.)

In my first attempts, I found that students had difficulty integrating research and design. They had taken courses in research methods and media design, but they had little experience in bringing the two together, at least with respect to an issue at the level of significance proposed: changing workplace demographics, emerging technologies, new organizational structures, globalization, and so on. They were intimidated by the scope and by the expectation that they could resolve something with which professionals—even professions—were struggling. And their reports often showed from a lack of coherence among questions, findings, ideas, and proposals that they had not well aligned their research and design activities.

EDISYS is a tool that I have been developing to help them. It is a work in progress, but it has resulted in much improvement in their results, as evident in their papers and presentations, many of which have now been presented and published, and in greater learning, as broadly defined earlier in this chapter. To give a flavor of their work, here are some issues that teams explored in spring 2012: fear in

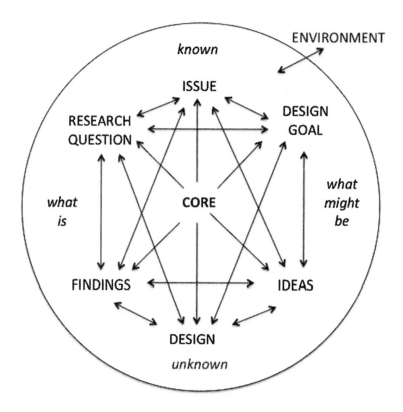

Fig. 2 EDISYS

twenty-first century organizations; management of social media; generations in the workplace, cyberloafing and productivity; fear in decision-making in organizational crises; knowledge management during turnovers; and aligning organizational values across cultures.

Overall Structure

As can be seen in Fig. 2, the major constructs of EDISYS are arranged in a symbolic journey from known to unknown (top to bottom) through two spaces (left and right): *what is* (research) and *what might be* (design). Again, EDISYS is not a process model, so a specific order to construct definition should not be inferred. Rather the tool can be applied throughout the design journey, particularly toward the conclusion, and the constructs can be seen as placeholders that are iteratively filled.

Elements

Each of the parts or elements is defined by a stated response to a set of questions. At the top is the issue driving the inquiry and defining what is known about the past and present.

Issue. What is the problematic situation or matter in dispute that you are addressing? What is known and unknown about this situation? Who are the stakeholders, what are their needs and views, when and where does the situation occur, and why is the issue important to address?

To the left is the analytic process of researching *what is*, the unknown past and present. The research question is key.

Research plan: (*question(s), methods, and sources*). On what has your research focused? In order to inquire into the key unknown(s) regarding the issue, what research question(s) have you posed? What methods have you used? What sources?

Findings and implications. What have you learned from your research? What does that imply with respect to the issue and its possible resolution?

To the right is the synthetic process of designing *what might or should be*, the unknown future. Here design goals are key, and recall that they are constructed, not given. The designer goes beyond givens, and the goals (and the design brief overall) coevolve with all other elements.

Design brief: (*goal(s), requirements, constraints, and criteria*). What are you seeking to create in order to resolve the issue? What needs and desires are you seeking to satisfy? Under what constraints? Against what criteria is the quality of the design to be judged?

Alternative ideas and arguments. What possible alternatives have you found, generated, and considered? What are the strengths and limitations of each alternative?

At the bottom is the selected design.

Design. Through what form of intervention (strategy, actions, tools, etc.) do you propose to resolve the issue?

Surrounding the elements is the systemic environment.

Environment. In what social context(s) does the issue exist?

And in the center is the core.

Core. What beliefs, assumptions, values, ethical and theoretical commitments, ideas, and metaphors underlie the inquiry?

Strengthening the Elements

One step in strengthening the system is to criticize and improve each of the elements. To do this, the elements are succinctly stated such that ratings can be given by peers, for example, by adding a Likert scale (strongly agree, agree, disagree, strongly disagree) to the statements below. The ratings, along with comments/explanations, are given as feedback to the designer(s).

Issue. The issue is clearly framed; that is, boundaries are clarified, particular aspects or things are selected for attention, and coherence is developed to guide further moves.

Research question. The question directly and in an unbiased manner focuses research on a key unknown(s).

Findings. The findings clearly express something important and relevant that was unknown prior to research.

Design goal. The goal clearly expresses the requirements of something of value that could be created through design.

Alternative ideas. The ideas represent a wide range of possibilities.

Design. The design is clearly described as a strategy, action, tool, or other form of intervention.

Strengthening Relationships

Similarly, the relationships among elements, and between elements and the systemic environment, can be criticized and strengthened. The more obvious relationships among adjacent pairs of constructs (e.g., research question and findings) can be considered first order, while relationships among nonadjacent pairs of constructs (e.g., findings and issue) can be considered second order. Where our literature addresses relationships, they tend to be first order only.

Environment ←→ *issue.* The issue is important in the systemic environment.

Issue ←→ *research question.* The research question(s) focused attention on the key unknown(s) regarding the issue.

Research question ←→ *findings.* The methods measured what was intended and lead to valid/trustworthy answers to the question.

Findings ←→ *issue.* The findings offer new insights into the issue.

Findings ←→ *design goal.* (a) The findings assisted in the identification of requirements for the design. (b) Requirements of the design are explicitly linked to research findings.

Design goal ←→ *issue.* Achieving the goal would resolve the issue.

Design goal ←→ *ideas.* The goal inspired a sufficient range of ideas.

Findings ←→ *ideas*. Ideas are related to findings in such a way that their strengths and limitations are obvious.

Ideas ←→ *design*. The selected alternative has the greatest potential.

Design ←→ *design goal*. The design satisfies the design goal.

Design ←→ *findings*. Implementing the design would alter findings in the future.

Design ←→ *issue*. The design will resolve the issue.

Design ←→ *environment*. The design will have a positive impact in the systemic environment.

Core

The core underlies the whole structure and consists of one's beliefs, assumptions, and commitments. Aspects of the core that might be articulated include the following:

Worldview. What do you believe to be the nature of reality (ontological beliefs)? How do you assume humans come to know anything (epistemological assumptions)? To what types of actions, for example, inquiry methods, do these beliefs and assumptions lead (methodological choices)?

Values and ethical commitments. With respect to work in this area (e.g., in organizational communication and learning), what should be given priority and why?

Theoretical commitment(s). What theoretical lens(es) or way(s) of seeing have you adopted for this inquiry?

First principles. What first principles of learning, instruction, performance, systems, and/or design do you seek to apply in this inquiry?

Core ideas and metaphors. What core ideas or metaphors underlie your design and inquiry?

Articulating a coherent worldview might be assisted by comparison to traditions of inquiry, for example, rationalistic, naturalistic, critical, or pragmatic.

Examples of core values might be Kaufman's (2009) mega level service to society or a commitment to simultaneously embracing (as opposed to trading off) individual freedom, social justice, and ecological harmony (Banathy & Rowland, 2002).

A theoretical commitment might be to specific theories within Willis' (2011a, 2011b) suggested "families" of ID scholarship and practice—behaviorist, cognitive and learning/instructional science, constructivist, and critical. Rather than a simple reference to eclecticism, this would include an articulation of theories that contributed to design judgments, examining the results of one's "critical flexibility" (Yanchar & Gabbitas, 2011).

First principles are basic and override instrumental goals. For example, Cross (2011) describes that the highly accomplished racecar designer Gordon Murray adopts the first principle "win the race," while others tend to become distracted by technical requirements and specifications. Examples in relevant domains for EDISYS include Merrill's (2002) first principles of instruction (demonstration, application, activation, integration, and task centered), Gibbons' (2009) operational principles, and Clark's (2009) active ingredients.

Core ideas and metaphors might include one's view of the human mind (e.g., as a pump, information processor, design artifact, autopoietic or homeopoietic system), view or perspective of ID mentioned earlier (Gibbons, 2014; Boling & Smith, 2012), or perhaps one's commitment to a primary systems level (which is different than the level in a systems hierarchy; Banathy, 1991).

Strengthening the Core and the Overall System

In the same way as elements and their relationships, statements about the core can be criticized and improved, perhaps by peer rating and comments.

Core. Beliefs, assumptions, and commitments are clearly articulated.

Core ←—→ *elements*. The elements and the system as a whole are coherent with core beliefs, assumptions, and values. (An example of this would be a consideration of methodology—a rationale for one's choice of methods that connects to epistemological assumptions.)

Reflecting on the Value of EDISYS

The EDISYS described above is clearly context bound. It was developed to assist a specific type of design inquiry conducted by undergraduate students in the field of communications. It would need to be adapted, or new types of EDISYS developed, for ID. However, even though it is a work in progress, it has provided much assistance to date. Salient to the symposium and this volume, I believe it offers evidence of the value of incorporating design and systems principles into a tool for enhancing inquiry, and perhaps even more importantly, the value of a deeper embrace of systems thinking in ID. Some of the systems principles incorporated into EDISYS include:

- *Interdependence*—relationships among all elements, going beyond steps in a systematic process model
- *Emergence and holism*—coherence and alignment of elements and their contribution to a greater whole
- *Dimensionality*—a focus on pairs of constructs, with others in the background of a common space; this could go beyond two dimensions in the future
- *Requisite variety*—for example, the sufficiency of the range of alternative ideas, as opposed to simply the number of ideas (see Boling & Smith, 2014)
- *Complexity*—a start to incorporating an understanding of nonlinearity and unpredictability, for example, by seeking to help recognize and manage complex interactions rather than impose a linear process

- *Second-order cybernetics*—for example, recognizing that all of the EDISYS constructs, including the "known" issue, are artificial

A fitting definition of design that the link to second-order cybernetics implies is *a journey through the known and unknown in order to create a half-known world* (see Parrish, 2014). Weick's (2004) point that we should seek to overconceptualize and underspecify designs, as opposed to the reverse, applies here well.

EDISYS is also consistent with current literature on design. For example, Cross (2011, p. 75) identifies "Three key strategic aspects of design thinking … (1) taking a broad 'systems approach' to the problem rather than accepting narrow problem criteria; (2) 'framing' the problem in a distinctive and sometimes rather personal way; and (3) designing from 'first principles.'" Nelson and Stolterman (2012) concur that systems thinking is an important part of design thinking, and Akin (1994) emphasizes that problem framing or problem setting is as important to design as problem solving.

The second aspect of problem framing relates, also, to Boling and Smith's (2014) point that we need to keep in mind the presence of the designer and what she or he brings to the design. EDISYS constructs are defined by the designers in the specific situation, and from the initial activity in this chapter, recall that those described here are just the constructs I have suggested for a single context of my own work.

Similar tools for other contexts await development, and a pattern for doing so could follow this particular EDISYS' lead: identify primary constructs/parts; create key questions that lead to construct definitions; create statements that incorporate quality criteria to be used for gaining feedback; identify relationships that are most salient; create statements that incorporate quality criteria to gain feedback on the relationships; and test and refine the system for the specific context. For ID, development of an EDISYS might begin by considering the analytic side to be what Archer (1995) refers to as options research, and findings could be succinct statements describing needs, tasks, learners/performers, and learning and performance environments. These statements would form a subsystem, with quality criteria for parts and relationships.

An essential part of the tool would be the core, and my experience is that constructing the questions and statements that help the user define the core is a challenge. For my course, I created an activity that helped students identify their worldview as rationalistic, naturalistic, critical, or pragmatic, then helped them compare their worldview to how they had defined the system parts and relationships. The results were useful.

Summary

Design has great potential as a source of educational innovation, particularly when it is engaged in as a formal, disciplined inquiry. That disciplined inquiry, or "design inquiry" to distinguish it from everyday design, involves a deep integration of research and design. This integration can be fostered through examining and strengthening relationships between key constructs, for example, between research questions and design goals and between research findings and design ideas. This also represents a deeper application of systems thinking than typical ID and can even be referred to as a design inquiry system, hence the name EDISYS. EDISYS is a tool that I have developed and tested with critical issues in organizations, that is, for seeking potential resolutions of such issues, and it could be adapted for ID.

References

Akin, O. (1994). Creativity in design. *Performance Improvement Quarterly, 7*(3), 9–21.

Anderson, T., & Shattuck, J. (2012). Design-based research: A decade of progress in educational research. *Educational Researcher, 41*(1), 16–25.

Archer, B. (1995, January). The nature of research. *CoDesign: Interdisciplinary Journal of Design, 2*, 6–13.

Banathy, B. H. (1991). *Systems design of education: A journey to create the future.* Englewood Cliffs, NJ: Educational Technology.

Banathy, B. H. (1996). *Designing social systems in a changing world.* New York: Plenum Press.

Banathy, B. H., & Rowland, G. (2002). *Guiding our evolution: If we don't do it, who will?* Self-published 2014: http://www.guidingourevolution.com

Bishop, M. J. (2014). Reconceptualizing instructional message design: Toward the development of a new guiding framework. In B. Hokanson (Ed.), *Design in educational technology.* Heidelberg: Springer.

Boling, E., & Smith, K. M. (2012). The changing nature of design. In R. A. Reiser & J. V. Dempsey (Eds.), *Trends and issues in instructional design and technology* (3rd ed., pp. 358–366). Boston: Pearson Education.

Boling, E., & Smith, K. M. (2014). Critical issues in studio pedagogy: Beyond the mystique and down to business. In B. Hokanson (Ed.), *Design in educational technology.* Heidelberg: Springer.

Christakis, A. N. (1996). A people science: The CogniScope TM system approach. *Systems, 1*(1), 16–19.

Churchman, C. W. (1971). *The design of inquiring systems.* New York: Basic Books.

Clark, R. E. (2009). Translating research into new instructional technologies for higher education: The active ingredient process. *The Journal of Computing in Higher Education, 21*(1), 4–18.

Clinton, G., & Hokanson, B. (2012). Creativity in the training and practice of instructional designers: The Designer/Creativity Loops model. *Educational Technology Research and Development, 60*, 111–130.

Cross, N. (1982). Designerly ways of knowing. *Design Studies, 3*(4), 221–227.

Cross, N. (2011). *Design thinking.* Oxford, UK: Berg.

Gaver, W. (2012). *What should we expect from research through design.* Proceedings from CHI 2012, May 5–12, Austin, TX. Retrieved from http://dl.acm.org/citation.cfm?id=2208538&dl=ACM&coll=DL&CFID=108653450&CFTOKEN=72893826

Gibbons, A. S. (2009). The value of the operational principle in instructional design. *Educational Technology, 49*(1), 3–8.

Gibbons, A. S. (2014). Eight views of instructional design and what they should mean to instructional designers. In B. Hokanson (Ed.), *Design in educational technology.* Heidelberg: Springer.

Gibbons, A. S., & Brewer, E. K. (2005). Elementary principles of design languages and design notation systems. In J. M. Spector, C. Ohrazda, A. Van Schaak, & D. Wiley (Eds.), *Innovations in instructional design: Essays in honor of M. David Merrill.* Mahwah, NJ: Lawrence Erlbaum.

Howard, C. D. (2014). Instructional design cases: Documenting precedent in instructional design. In B. Hokanson (Ed.), *Design in educational technology.* Heidelberg: Springer.

Kaufman, R. (2009). Mega thinking and planning: An introduction to defining and delivering individual and organizational success. *Performance Improvement Quarterly, 22*(2), 5–15.

Krippendorffff, K. (2006). *The semantic turn.* Boca Raton, FL: CRC Press.

Lawson, B. (2006). *How designers think*. Oxford, UK: Architectural Press/Elsevier.

Merrill, M. D. (2002). First principles of instruction. *Educational Technology Research and Development, 50*(3), 43–59.

Miller, G. A. (1956). The magical number seven, plus or minus two: Some limits on our capacity for processing information. *Psychological Review, 63*(2), 81–97.

Nelson, H. G., & Stolterman, E. (2012). *The design way: Intentional change in an unpredictable world* (2nd ed.). Cambridge, MA: MIT Press.

NHS Shared Learning. (2009). *Quality assurance checklists for learning objects and online courses*. Retrieved from http://www.knowledge.scot.nhs.uk/media/4088630/quality_assurance_checklists.pdf

Parrish, P. E. (2009). Aesthetic principles for instructional design. *Educational Technology Research and Development, 57*, 511–528.

Parrish, P. E. (2014). Designing for the half-known world: Lessons for instructional designers from the craft of narrative fiction. In B. Hokanson (Ed.), *Design in educational technology*. Heidelberg: Springer.

Perez, R. S., Johnson, J. F., & Emery, C. D. (1995). Instructional design expertise: A cognitive model of design. *Instructional Science, 23*(5–6), 321–349.

Reuning-Hummel, C. (2011). *Preludio: Powerful learning experiences of teenaged musicians through three vantage points*. Unpublished master's thesis. Ithaca College, Ithaca, NY.

Richey, R., Fields, D., Foxon, M. (with Roberts, R. C., Spannaus, T., & Spector, J. M.). (2001). *Instructional design competencies: The standards* (3rd ed.). Syracuse, NY: Eric Clearinghouse on Information and Technology.

Rivera, B., & Rowland, G. (2008, March). Powerful e-learning: A preliminary study of learner experiences. *Journal of Online Learning and Teaching, 4*(1), 14–23.

Rowland, G. (2007). Educational inquiry in transition: Research and design. *Educational Technology, 47*(2), 14–23.

Rowland, G. (2008, November–December). Design and research: Partners for educational innovation. *Educational Technology*, 3–9.

Rowland, G., & Adams, A. M. (1999). Systems thinking in instructional design. In J. van den Akker, R. M. Branch, K. Gustafson, N. Nieveen, & T. Plomp (Eds.), *Design approaches and tools in education and training* (pp. 29–44). Boston: Kluwer Academic.

Rummler, G. A., & Brache, A. P. (1990). *Improving performance: How to manage the white space on the organization chart*. San Francisco: Jossey-Bass. Ch. 2.: Viewing organizations as systems.

Smith, K. M. (2010). Producing the rigorous design case. *International Journal of Designs for Learning, 1*(1). Retrieved from http://scholarworks.iu.edu/journals/index.php/ijdl/issue/view/67

Smith, K. M., & Boling, E. (2009, July-August). What do we make of design? Design as a concept in educational technology. *Educational Technology*, 3–17.

Tracey, M. W., & Baaki, J. (2014). Design, designers, and reflection-in-action. In B. Hokanson (Ed.), *Design thinking, design process, and the design studio*. Heidelberg: Springer.

Weick, K. (2004). Rethinking organizational design. In R. J. Boland & F. Collopy (Eds.), *Managing as designing* (pp. 36–53). Stanford, CA: Stanford University Press.

Willis, J. (2011a). The cultures of contemporary instructional design scholarship, part one: Developments based on behavioral and cognitive science foundations. *Educational Technology, 51*(3), 3–20.

Willis, J. (2011b). The cultures of contemporary instructional design scholarship, part two: Developments based on constructivist and critical theory foundations. *Educational Technology, 51*(3), 3–17.

Wilson, B. G., Switzer, S. H., Parrish, P., & the IDEAL Research Lab. (2007). Transformative learning experiences: How do we get students deeply engaged for lasting change? In M. Simonson (Ed.), *Proceedings of selected research and development presentations*. Washington, DC: Association for Educational Communications and Technology.

Yanchar, S. C., & Gabbitas, B. W. (2011). Between eclecticism and orthodoxy in instructional design. *Educational Technology Research and Development, 59*, 383–398.

Improving Instructional Design Processes Through Leadership-Thinking and Modeling

Marcia L. Ashbaugh and Anthony A. Piña

Keywords Instructional design • Instructional design leadership • Leadership-thinking • Leadership model • Quality courses • Design process • Design practice

It is the aim of this chapter to focus attention on the leadership competencies and thinking considered critical for improving the instructional design (ID) processes that create academic courses. The course designer role has long been regarded as one that supports the academic goals of an institution (Smith & Ragan, 1999), but has not often been associated with that of a leader (Kenny, Zhang, Schwier, & Campbell, 2005). However, a recent phenomenological study (Ashbaugh, 2011) of expert instructional designers in practice found that leadership competencies and thinking in any role are critical to the design process. In other words, there is a perceived need to enhance ID students' skillsets with leadership characteristics with which to better negotiate what has become a fluid and complex framework of modern education (Shaw, 2012; Sims & Koszalka, 2008). To further develop the notion of leadership in terms of the ID process, definitions, descriptions, and discussions from the business, organizational, and educational leadership literature were extracted and synthesized with the Ashbaugh (2011) study's findings. The results were encapsulated into a leadership model contextualized for ID—one that encourages thinking about the ID practice and its processes from a fresh perspective. Following a discussion of the literature analysis and study findings, the model is

M.L. Ashbaugh, Ph.D.
University of the People/MLA Instructional Designers, 442 Gardner Street,
Castle Rock, CO 80104, USA
e-mail: marcia.ashbaugh@gmail.com

A.A. Piña, Ed.D. (✉)
Sullivan University, 2100 Gardiner Lane #220, Louisville, KY 40205, USA
e-mail: apina@sullivan.edu

B. Hokanson and A. Gibbons (eds.), *Design in Educational Technology*,   223
Educational Communications and Technology: Issues and Innovations 1,
DOI 10.1007/978-3-319-00927-8_13, © Springer International Publishing Switzerland 2014

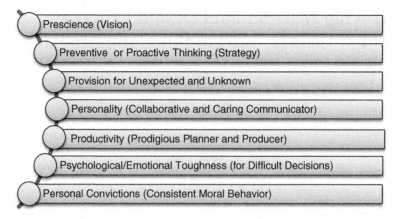

Fig. 1 A summary of the 7Ps of leadership for ID model with brief descriptions of each characteristic: prescience, preventive or proactive thinking, personality, productivity, psychological/emotional toughness, personal convictions

presented later in the chapter. Meanwhile, previews the model—the 7Ps of leadership for ID—which includes practicing with *prescience* (vision), engaging in *preventive* or proactive thinking (strategy), making *provision* for the unexpected and unknown, communicating with a collaborative and caring *personality*, leading a project with *productivity*, possessing *psychological* and emotional toughness for making difficult decisions, and consistently acting on *personal* convictions, including ethical and moral purposes Fig. 1.

Context and Purpose of the Study

Given the extent of various conceptualizations of leadership, there is no one description that adequately characterizes an educator facing the challenges of the current social environment of ambiguity, complexity, and chaos. The multifarious issues of modern society perplex the efforts and test the skills of most leaders from any discipline to effect change where it is needed (Durdu, Yalabik, & Cagiltay, 2009). One dominant theme in the literature describes leadership as transformational (Tichy & Ulrich, 1984/2008) in that it instigates and guides change. From this perspective, leadership may be considered more of a broad approach, a mindset, although activated for the purpose of conducting business in a given domain for particular situations and environments (Gelo, Braakmann, & Benetka, 2008). When comparing the notion of transformation and the situations instructional designers find themselves working in (Gelo et al., 2008), a discrepancy proved troublesome: although a course designer is responsible for envisioning and strategizing for the educational materials that transform students (through changes in personal knowledge, understanding, skills, and consequently to the institutions and society students engage with), the notion of leader is rarely ascribed to the ID situation or personality. Regarded as more of a technologist, it is generally assumed that an instructional designer understands the importance of providing excellent courses to students; indeed, the implications are significant for long-term harm if the job is not done well (Hall, 2010; Smith & Ragan, 1999). Quality courses engage students, while interest and motivation to learn wane in poorly designed learning events (Nimon, 2007).

Although being more than technologists or academic support, most course designers are guided by an innate sense of responsibility for shaping lives that tends to motivate them through and beyond modern design challenges with a magnitude not often experienced by the previous generation of instructional designers. This was partly because, in the past, leadership was often bracketed as a role or position of authority and regarded as not necessary for those considered to be 'support staff.' Spector (2009) traced the history of the field and those called upon to reconceptualize the standards and models for practice in light of a paradigm shift in learning deliveries in the early twentieth century. As a result of his reflections, Spector envisioned design professionals who would advance education and serve as leaders—particularly in web-based learning. At the same time, the potential for acquiring and applying new competencies such as leadership skills represents a major shift in approach for many practitioners who, in a study by Campbell, Schwier, and Kenny (2009), acknowledged their influence on the institution and society, although they felt a lack of power in making significant changes. It is our hope that the work we are presenting will inspire instructional designers to recast themselves in a leadership role.

Inspiration for modern instructional designers to adopt a leadership mentality comes from Zenger and Folkman (2009) who enunciated the journey, the goals, and the noble burden of leadership,

> The highest expression of leadership involves change. Caretaker managers can keep things going on a steady path, but leaders are demanded if the organization is to pursue a new path or rise to a significantly higher level of performance. (p. 14)

We recognize that reconceptualizing the ID role and process will require a change in thinking and an elevation in certain competencies. In their large-scale study of leaders, Zenger and Folkman (2009) observed, "We have not given much attention to the competencies that will be required in the future. Thus, much of the leadership analysis and development has been 'looking in the rearview mirror' and not looking out over the horizon" (p. 5). Fullan and Scott (2009) sounded a similar charge stating, "There is often little attention paid to the capabilities and experience necessary to lead change in higher education" (p. 39). At the same time, Kowch (2009) expressed concern for a lack of awareness of the leadership competencies required for developing quality education for modern learning needs. Moreover, a vision put forth by Reeves, Herrington, and Oliver (2004) for educational technologists to map a new direction, as well as a potential for leading new initiatives for education expressed by Spector (2009), will be diminished if a reconceptualization of designers as leaders is not forthcoming.

Responding to these and earlier calls for enhancing design practice competencies in a rapidly changing ethos of education (Beaudoin, 2007; Dooley et al., 2007;

Kowch, 2009; Naidu, 2007; Reeves et al., 2004; Sims & Koszalka, 2008), Ashbaugh (2011) identified certain competencies and characteristics of leaders in design practice deemed critical to the efficacy of course design outcomes. The study results informed the leadership model displayed in Fig. 1 which is explicated later in the chapter. Consequently, this discussion represents an extension of the previous work of the first author, whose study is referenced frequently in this chapter as an underpinning source.

In order to focus on what we consider an important and current, albeit complex, issue, the following discussion is oriented toward leadership-thinking for design processes as a viable framework for reexamining ID thinking, approaches, and processes. Chapter goals include (a) a call for attention to the critical need for leadership from its practitioners, (b) a reconceptualization of the scope of the ID role and process to embrace a leadership-driven approach, and (c) introduction of a leadership for ID model for enhancing designer-thinking. To conclude the chapter, a suggestion is made for increasing integration of leadership training into ID academic and training programs, and research is suggested for exploring the critical issues facing the ID field in a continuously changing world of technology, including the notion of interpolating leadership into its daily practices.

Definitions of Leadership

Definitions from Cross-Disciplinary Literature

A review of the cross-disciplinary literature informed the ideas and assumptions presented in this chapter with numerous definitions of leadership. What most scholars thought of leadership coalesced around key attributes, behaviors, and skills (Dooley et al., 2007; Drucker, 1981; Fullan & Scott, 2009; Kowch, 2009). Zenger and Folkman (2009) organized leadership under a model of five expressions — character, leading organizational change, focus on results, personal capability, and interpersonal skills. From this basic understanding, leadership was observed in persons that direct and influence both tasks and people (Howard & Wellins, 2008) and was represented in both positional and nonpositional roles (Gressick & Derry, 2010). Additionally, some regarded leadership as transformational (Bass & Riggio, 2006; Tichy & Ulrich, 1984/2008) in that it instigates and guides change from a holistic approach through collaboration and teamwork with all stakeholders. To this point in the review and analysis, the various metaphors of leadership resonated with the course designer's role, processes, and practices, particularly when situated within the dynamics of design and development teams and stakeholder relationships.

Other perspectives on leadership included Katz (1955) who developed an early leadership model of three skill categories — *technical*, *human*, and *conceptual* — which serves as a useful construct for paralleling leadership to the work of ID. For example, focusing on the *technical* aspects, or duties, involved in educational changes, Kotter (1996) formulated a developmental process for organizational leadership; he later distinguished leadership functions from the more managerial tasks of controlling and problem-solving (Kotter, 2008). From the *human* orientation, Kouzes and Posner (2007) summarized leadership into five practices—model the way, inspire a shared vision, challenge the process, enable others to act, and encourage the heart. With a similar personal application, Senge (2006) elaborated on the disciplines, habits, and traits of leaders. More to the topic of this discussion, Spitzer and Evans (1997) *conceptualized* strategic thinking as a key to leadership. Similarly, the elements of technology, the human impact, and conceptualizing for effective learning are each represented in the daily challenges of ID practice and resonate with the three categories of leadership organized by Katz (1955).

What was most obvious from the literature review, however, was that leadership embodies copious philosophies, characteristics, attributes, positions, roles, attitudes, and essentials which are applied to a multitude of professions (Zenger & Folkman, 2009). In other words, leadership, as a concept, transcends organizations, institutions, and traditions. Indeed, Paulsen, Maldonado, Callan, and Ayoko (2009) posited that a quality of leadership is one that envisions and predicts new ideas and inventions for advancing knowledge in multiple disciplines, which would include education and its course designers.

Contextualized for ID, Beaudoin (2007) defined leadership as "a set of attitudes and behaviors that create conditions for innovative change, enable individuals and organizations to share a vision and move in the appropriate direction, and contribute to the management and operationalization of ideas" (p. 519). Earlier, Schuller (1986) declared that the educational leader will "bring about significant change" (p. 3). Change is a fluid phenomenon and the one who develops "a vision of the future along with the strategies for producing the changes needed to achieve that vision" (Gallos, 2008, p. 7) will be prepared for the educational fluctuations and challenges ahead. In this regard, leadership is a fitting description as instructional designers are continually analyzing current and future trends for strategizing student needs into cohesive learning events that will adapt to future changes, all the while working to satisfy shifting institutional and faculty goals and ideals.

Definitions from an ID Study

Leadership was defined for ID in a recent study (Ashbaugh, 2011) of expert instructional designers who revealed how design process thoughts and decisions, informed by a leadership mindset, impact the quality of online learning designs. Participants' expert statuses were established from an average of 16 years of design experience with active involvement in higher education. In their daily practices, the group—consisting of two staff instructional designers, one senior online faculty, two higher education department heads, and one dean of online studies—acknowledged and activated ID standards such as those proposed by the International Board of

Table 1 Design decisions made by IDs as leaders for exemplary design processes

Instructional strategies for the design	Learning components in design
Theory-based	Clear objectives
Values-based	Relevant assessments with clear measurements
Invite learner engagement	Authentic tasks
Afford learner-control	Activities for personal knowledge construction
Ensure learner satisfaction	Interaction
Guarantee alignment of objectives, assessments, & activities with the instructional strategy	Afford problem-solving
	Afford higher-level thinking

Standards for Training, Performance and Instruction (IBSTPI, 2000). This was not a surprise as those aligned with the ID occupation are usually expected to be trained in, and to excel at, applying best practices for design (Wilson, 2005), especially for innovative technologies and deliveries. However, certain decisions and actions were identified by participants as leadership competencies that are critical to the ID process, including research and selection of instructional strategy approaches and learning components listed in Table 1. The participants were conveying that course designers will lead as they envision and strategize not merely for best practices but for exemplary practices and design selections.

Additionally, instructional designers demonstrate leadership competency when they are called upon to (a) communicate effectively in visual, oral, and written form (Larson & Lockee, 2009; Wakefield, Warren, & Mills, 2012), (b) apply current theory to solve practical problems (Dooley et al., 2007), (c) identify and resolve ethical and legal implications of educational/training product development in the workplace (IBSTPI, 2000), (d) lead design teams and mentor junior designers, and (e) pass on ID knowledge to faculty and subject matter experts (SMEs) (Kenny et al., 2005). From these definitions, it is clear that the comprehensive nature of creating and producing academic designs will inevitably move an instructional designer into a leadership role at some point, regardless of position or job description.

Leadership-Thinking for the ID Process

Comparison of Design-Thinking and Leadership-Thinking

In spite of the emerging inevitability of leadership's place in the ID purview, there are those in the field that have pushed back on the notion of ascribing leadership to instructional designers in any capacity, including one participant of the Ashbaugh (2011) study. The participant was a senior member of the group and perceived an ID in a supportive role with minimal personal power in the process of designing courses and training. One reason for questions surrounding the role of leadership in ID is that the standards and requirements of design and leadership are closely aligned and may not easily be parsed. As we have shown in the previous section, commonalities include innovation, strategy, problem-solving, and people skills. However, while reflecting on how leadership is different and how its qualities represent additions to the typical ID skillset, a characterization developed from the majority of Ashbaugh's (2011) study group responses that depicted leadership as a *mindset*—a way of thinking that transcends tasks, roles, and positions of power.

Subsequently, we observed the similarities in thinking processes ascribed to leadership and how design professionals in other industries think. The basic elements of ideation, collaboration with a team, and forging an ill-structured process into a logical learning design resonate with the underlying theories of numerous design-based fields—industrial, structural, mechanical, electrical, and various arts. Over a decade ago Smith and Ragan (1999) articulated common threads in each of these and compared certain approaches with ID:

> Many fields use the term *design* [emphasis in original] as part of their title.... The term **design** [emphasis in original] implies a systematic or intensive planning and ideation process prior to the development of something or the execution of some plan in order to solve a problem. Fundamentally, design is a type of problem solving and has much in common with problem solving in other [design] professions (p. 4).

Although elements of Smith and Ragan's earlier observations have since evolved, such as Jonassen's (2011) recent work on problem-solving, the description resonates with contemporary thought that most design projects involve a series of decisions and specific ways of thinking about the design goal during the various stages of the process, such as acquisition of relevant knowledge, how to proceed, and team leadership (Taura & Nagai, 2010). Earlier, Schön (1984) described a way of designer-thinking and emphasized the value of reflection on the process for advancing innovation. From such reflective thoughts, designers generate concepts, build heuristics, and devise systems in order to determine the best approach for a workable solution (Gero, 2010) to a design problem. In comparison to a designer's way of thinking, leaders gather knowledge, reflect on best procedures, and rely on indigenous systems and teamwork for holistic solutions in a given environment (Lawson, 2006; Pisapia, 2009; Senge, 2006). Beyond reliance on systems and checklists, leaders make decisions from an inner source of wisdom and courage (Jaworski, 2012). Similarly to designers in any industry, the burden for instructional designers is to ensure quality and to provide solutions (for learning), which often demands an unusual capacity for designing with leadership-thinking.

Leadership-Thinking Inspires a Better Product

A finished product in any industry represents a series of thoughts and decisions. Likewise, the decisions and outcomes of leadership are characterized, in one way, by one's thinking. Kepner and Tregoe (1997) stressed the need for leaders to engage in systematic analysis through rational *thinking*; while Spitzer and Evans (1997) promoted strategic and critical *thinking* for leaders. Kotter (1996, 2008) updated his earlier leadership model by distinguishing project management skills from leadership *thinking* and actions, or decisions. During the creation and implementation of courses, Dooley et al. (2007) concluded that critical decisions underpin high quality, effective, and relevant designs. From more recent observations, it was found that leadership interpolates strategic and visionary decisions into the workplace (Campbell et al., 2009; Gelo et al., 2008), including into the ID process. When taken together, an inference is made from the literature that leadership-thinking aligns with and predicts the value of its outcomes. A link between leadership-thinking, the design process, and quality outcomes was evident in the personal artifacts submitted in the Ashbaugh (2011) study by the participants, who identified leadership characteristics that were applied to academic course design samples. In brief, the designs were underpinned by envisioning for current and future learner needs, environment-relevant and theory-based decisions, exemplary instructional strategies, and thoughtful, engaging activities. Together, the decisions made during the ID process culminated in quality-rated educational products—the ratings were determined by using a modified version of the Quality Matters Rubric™ (Maryland Online, 2010).

In comparison to leadership as a predictor of quality products, industry has shown that leadership impacts both products and their quality. For example, when Lee Iacocca assumed leadership of Chrysler in 1978, through strategic changes in the design processes, the products improved. Iacocca, author of *Where Have all the Leaders Gone?* (2007), assumed oversight of the near-bankrupt Chrysler Corporation and changed the direction and fortunes of the giant auto manufacturer when he introduced the Mustang, compact cars, and the minivan. Second, Steve Jobs returned to Apple in 1997 and through visionary leadership and extraordinary design-thinking, the products improved and evolved rapidly (Isaacson, 2011). The extent of the innovative products' impact on the world is evident in the tools provided with unharnessed learning potential, including the iPhone and the iPad. Demonstrating a trait of leadership recorded by Kouzes and Posner (2007), Jobs not only possessed a personal vision but inspired others in future-oriented thinking for the digital future.

Models of extraordinary leadership are stimulating; however, an issue of significant concern arose from evidence that leadership is not being passed on to subordinates by a majority of leaders (Howard & Wellins, 2008). The lack of trained leadership found by Howard and Wellins (2008) in a wide-scale study has the potential to impact quality and successful outcomes. From United States history, a tragic incident provided a haunting example for product outcomes *without* a leadership element in the design process. The underlying causes of the 1986 Challenger space shuttle disaster were eventually determined to be design flaws and a lack of leadership demonstrated in a nonmanagerial position (Boisjoly, Curtis, & Mellican, 2004). In the case, one engineer appeared to lack personal leadership skills when he was powerless to achieve an additional scenario-based test of the spaceship's component in question—the infamous O-ring. It was known that certain low temperatures could affect the functionality of the O-ring, but those conditions were not considered by the management to be likely for the typical balmy Florida weather. However, the temperature forecast for launch day was well below previous test conditions.

Although he attempted to alert the project managers, nevertheless, the engineer gave in to administrative pressure, failed to assert his expert opinion at a crucial moment in the project, and allowed a launch to proceed with a predicted potential to fail—the result was a total loss.

Admittedly, this example is extreme and appears far removed from the ID process; however, the parallel to ID lies in the seriousness of a role in educating learners who may go on to actually be that engineer, or operate in another capacity that may be responsible for life and death situations (Smith & Ragan, 1999). Leadership is something that is passed on, taught, and mentored. Ultimately, leading in the design effort intimates the power of influence an instructional designer has through the course design that will in turn influence the learner for positive or negative outcomes.

Leadership-Thinking Strategizes for the Unforeseen and Innovation

Being proactive in nature, the practice of leadership extends beyond positional responsibilities and enables the leader to make informed choices for effective outcomes, purposes to press for change where change is needed, and formulates alternatives for unforeseen barriers (Sonnenfeld & Ward, 2007). Sonnenfeld and Ward (2007) found that leaders plan strategically for the unexpected; while Scott, Coates, and Anderson (2008)) reported that leaders collaborate for best possible solutions to not only current but unforeseen problems and challenges. Scott et al. (2008) regarded this characteristic as a capacity to see the *big picture* and to "read and respond to a continuously and rapidly changing external environment" (p. 11). Likewise, strategizing for innovation includes the ability to see beyond the immediate toward a larger purpose with future potential. Leadership-thinking predicts future scenarios as well as potential failures, provides multiple perspectives, and tests for unusual conditions in much the same way as design theory prescribes (Collins, 1993), and is synonymous with visionary thinking (Power, 2012). In other words, leaders peer long and hard in order to spot the roadblocks (Sonnenfeld & Ward, 2007). As a result, they make decisions that will steer the project and colleagues around and away from such obstacles (Moore & Kearsley, 2005).

In this way, leaders do not get caught up with changing fads of technology (Rothwell & Kazanas, 2008), but examine the evidence for viability of a new affordance in specific situations. For example, learning designers will need to consider the potential pitfalls of the social media learning strategies offered by Web 2.0 technologies when inculcated into the academic course structure—security, privacy, resistance by students, instructor unease with the technology, adverse physical effects (Ashbaugh, 2013)—and make the necessary corrections before implementation. However, Ashbaugh (2011) found that predicting the consequences of a new pedagogical technology is, at best, problematic. A dimension of ID beyond best practices and what usually works is urgently needed to project for, meet, and overcome unforeseen barriers of modern learning—we need a leadership mindset.

A Reconceptualization of ID Roles

ID Leadership as a Personal Role

Development of academic course designs may be dispersed over various roles—faculty, academic departmental staff, contractors, and administrators—and serve multiple environments, such as the traditional classroom, online course room, hybrid class, or a mobile delivery. Added to this, the functions of a course designer, project manager, or a team leader may be distributed or all of these roles may be assumed by one individual (Williams van Rooij, 2011). From this understanding, there is a need to acknowledge that the characteristics of leadership are as operational on a personal level as when fulfilling an executive role (Gressick & Derry, 2010). For example, designers often find themselves in the position of being, as Siemens (2008) suggested, an "educator to educators" (p.18), as when the designer instructs a SME on current technologies or alternative, web-based resources. Rather than assume a positional leadership role to the SME, the designer may instead *lead* her to a new understanding for making effective selections or changes.

In the past, instructional designers have been viewed as course developers and support staff (Kenny et al., 2005) capable of putting together various units of specific content for the introduction of concepts and facts to students. Subsequently, it was up to the student to read, memorize, and rehearse the knowledge presented and, hopefully, pass a fact-based test, perhaps write a cogent essay, or produce a subject-relevant project. Arguably, the traditional format described does not require leadership to design in the familiar process; it takes technical competency. The process may require project management, but even in that role often very little demand is expected of the designer for envisioning and strategizing for new technologies (Williams van Rooij, 2011). This scenario has led to a pervasive view of a task oriented, 'worker-bee,' academic support role begging for respect (Rossett & Papaila, 2005). A perception of a lesser impact on the design's significance exists in spite of the routine higher-level thinking required of the course designer, such as:

- Intricately interweaving new technologies and emerging learning theories with diverse instructional environments
- Adapting to diverse cultural and societal influences
- Interpreting and applying a rapidly growing global knowledge base to design affordances for the learning outcomes required by twenty-first century clients and learners

In this way, the designer is called upon to be more than a technician, technologist, or project manager; rather, the job more accurately represents a design engineer or an architect, a highly trained professional with extraordinary responsibility for the personal decisions—including those of leadership magnitude—that culminate in an effective learning structure.

Returning to the Challenger shuttle disaster example, Boisjoly et al. (2004) described a scenario in which leadership was acceptable only in a top-down, militaristic form. Decisions made at high levels were not to be questioned, in spite of the knowledge and, as in the engineer's case, the prescience and personal convictions of those in lesser roles. The prevailing environment did not recognize workers as being capable of having the 'bigger picture,' and as a result, workers were limited in their value and in their ability to contribute to leadership-level decisions. In this case, leaders at NASA were wrestling with decisions weighted down by political and organizational ramifications that would drown out the warnings of a sole engineer. Although the engineer reported to those in charge that the conditions were ripe for a flaw in design to affect the successful completion of the mission, the deceptively larger issues retained priority. In the end, personal leadership—the proactive characteristic that acts to prevent failure in spite of resistance or personal consequences—was not only lacking but unavailable to the engineer who was relegated to a position of powerlessness. In protest of the modern day limitations of power placed on the professional ID, the Ashbaugh (2011) study included an underlying assumption that improvement of educational products is possible, in part, through leadership-thinking and behavior in the design process from all participants.

ID Leadership as a Positional Role

Leading people requires a different skillset than leading design tasks. Participants of the Ashbaugh (2011) study expressed that, whether leading a team or an individual design project, some characteristics span the roles—the ability to strategize in the now with an eye on the future. For example, to help distinguish the role of project manager from that of a leader, Williams van Rooij's (2011) study of ID competencies concluded, "project management is a distinct and evolving discipline, with its own methodology, body of knowledge, and professional standards and practices" (p. 140) and infiltrates all manner of projects in any industry, including educational design. The researcher listed the project management function as (a) coordinating all aspects of a project with the client, (b) establishing project objectives, (c) assigning design team members' duties, (d) scheduling team meetings, (e) scheduling and tracking progress of each phase of the project while ensuring deadlines are met, (f) implementing and follow-up, (g) resolving design and team issues, and (h) making quality control decisions (Williams van Rooij, 2011). The competencies were then compared to the ID function list which revealed skills common to both project management and ID (e.g., quality control). Further, the project manager functions were compared to a general leadership competencies list with distinct characteristics found in the leader category: (a) communicate effectively in visual, oral, and written form; (b) apply current theory to solve practical problems; and (c) identify and resolve ethical and legal implications of educational/training product development in the workplace. While functions of all three roles or positions— manager, designer, and leader—overlapped in various ways, the leader category suggested a more prescient and proactive approach.

ID Leadership as an Interpersonal Role

Implicit, but often overlooked in the literature and training of instructional designers, is the fact that ID is a process that is dependent upon successful interaction with
people. The competencies for ID established by IBSTPI (2000) and its creators
include the following:

- Communicate effectively in visual, oral, and written form
- Identify and resolve ethical and legal implications of design in the workplace
- Promote collaboration, partnerships, and relationships among the participants in
  a design project (Richey, Fields, & Foxon, 2001).

Commenting on the role and importance of *effective communication*, Spannaus
and Spector (2001) stated, "The foundational research supporting this competency
was perhaps most consistent, and insistent, in affirming that this particular competency was indeed essential for all instructional designers" (p. 59). The authors
(Spannaus & Spector, 2001) then explained that this communication goes beyond
the instructional designer merely providing clear messages to others and suggested
a leadership role for designers:

> Instructional design is not a solitary activity and designers must work effectively in group
> settings, often in a position of leadership. Typically, instructional designers organize meet-
> ings with clients, sponsors, other project groups, and instructional design team members to
> discuss and explain various aspects of an instructional design project. Those with whom
> instructional designers typically interact often come from different disciplines, have differ-
> ent backgrounds, and represent different roles within a project or organization.
> Understanding group dynamics and being aware of group expectations is essential for
> effective teamwork. (p. 59)

With regard to *ethical and legal issues*, the IBSTPI (2000) standards and competencies vary between instructors and course designers. Instructors are expected to
comply with established ethical and legal standards and avoid breaches of ethics
(Klein, Spector, Grabowski, & Teja, 2004), while the designers have an additional
responsibility to *resolve* ethical and legal implications of design in the workplace
(Richey et al., 2001). Lin (2007) found that research on "how professional technologists deal with ethical issues in their work activities is still underspecified in the
literature" (p. 433). In his study of ethical concerns and strategies used by instructional design and training professionals, Lin found that setting up team environments to facilitate collaboration and discussion of ethical issues was the most
commonly used coping strategy used by these professionals, which may be viewed
as a leadership activity.

Spannaus and Spector (2001) defined the IBSTPI (2000) instructional design
competency of *promoting collaboration, partnerships, and relationships* in terms of
components, into various components, each indicating a leadership role for instructional designers. These included "build and promote effective relationships that
may impact a design project" and "promote and manage the interaction of team
members" (p.84). Although the training of designers has historically endowed them
with knowledge skills in learning and instructional theory, instructional design,

development, and evaluation, it typically does not focus on competencies in relationship building, group dynamics, conflict management and dispute resolution, interpersonal communications, or other leadership skills. This can result in instructional designers being ill-prepared to assume leadership roles and professional advancement and may limit the influence of both individual designers and the field of ID as a whole (Ashbaugh & Piña, 2012).

Given the leadership-thinking skills demanded of the designer in various functions, roles, and capacities within a specific domain, a dedicated and context-relevant leadership component should be considered critical and foundational to the instructional designer's training and skillset. Therefore, a model of leadership specific to ID is presented below as a tool for improving the ID process through leadership-thinking.

The 7Ps of Leadership for ID Model

This chapter has introduced and discussed the notion of how a robust leadership model might impact the quality of instructional course designs, the design process, and the design field as a profession, which is unveiled here as the 7Ps of Leadership for ID model. The model is a synthesis of the literature and concepts presented in this chapter; it contains seven characteristics for leadership from which to guide an effective practice of modern educational design—prescience, proactive or preventive thinking, provision, personality, productivity, psychological toughness, and personal convictions.

Prescience

Leaders conceptualize the world through a prescient mindset; they discern the future and formulate a vision for what needs to be done (Scott et al., 2008). Subsequently, leaders are stewards of a vision, live the vision through decisions, promote and convey the vision, and encourage others to share in the vision as well as enliven others to their vital role in the vision (Kouzes & Posner, 2007; Sackney & Mergel, 2007). They look for patterns and trends to predict future possibilities and look for connections between the past and the future. Leaders possess an innate sense of what is the right thing to do, a reservoir of wisdom that guides decisions for the moment based on what is perceived for the future (Jaworski, 2012). In other words, leaders test and plan in the present while keeping the *big picture* (Scott et al., 2008) in view, and do not allow themselves to be bogged down or distracted by minutiae.

Application for ID. Design leaders will communicate with and encourage either a design team or designer/instructors to contrive new approaches for satisfying learners' needs and goals. They will never be satisfied with the answer, 'Because that is the way we have always done it.' They will specify methods and techniques which are framed by a vision of future global changes with unanticipated societal and work duty skill demands (Durdu et al., 2009; Reimers, 2009). An ID leader will take full advantage of opportunities to interact with and learn from other visionary professionals by becoming active in professional associations, attending conferences and professional meetings, and reading scholarly and trade publications (Ashbaugh, 2011). ID visionary leaders will participate in and inspire field-relevant research and dissemination on the future challenges and potential for education, particularly as technology advances and changes the landscape of academia (Reigeluth et al., 2008). For example, how will social media support, enhance, or perhaps dominate online education? What are researchers predicting? Will online education grow as expected? What will the new standards be for distributed pedagogies? How can we as ID leaders set the standards? Instructional designers as leaders consider these questions of the future while working on the designs of today.

Preventive (Proactive) Thinking

Leaders reflect on strategies to prevent problems rather than waiting for them to happen; moreover, they engage others in the process, collaborating for best possible solutions (Campbell et al., 2009) to not only current but also to unforeseen problems and challenges (Scott et al., 2008). They know where to go for answers—knowledge sources from which to create the answers. In other words, they make the right connections through diverse technologies (Siemens, 2004) by drawing from a network of colleagues for collective and innovative thinking (Piña, Sadowski, Scheidenhelm, & Heydenburg, 2008). Leaders learn and rely on best practices; they test and prove solutions to difficult problems. They research current and future trends.

Application for ID. It may be conceptualized that preventive thinking is a way of planning for the future and avoiding the pitfalls that have caused degradation of education in the past (Reeves et al., 2004). ID leaders will, without exception, infuse theory- and evidence-based strategies into the design structure (Dooley et al., 2007). The proactive leader will make (a) strategic decisions for the organization in preparation for rapid growth in learning technologies, (b) strategic decisions for the design team to research best options for providing strict alignment of measurable objectives to assessments, content, and activities (Sims, 2011), and (c) strategic decisions for the design structure to afford engagement with context-relevant learning, flexibility for personalized learning, and rapid adaptivity to personal and societal fluidity. An example is creating a new interface design to accommodate Web 2.0 technologies (Ashbaugh, 2013), more learner disabilities, or emergent delivery modes (Dede & Bjerede, 2010). Will social media help or hinder learning for a given topic? What is the latest research on connections between cognitive processes and tactile information? Who has done the most research in the area of mobile devices as pedagogical agents and what have they found? An ID leader works now to solve the problems of the future.

Provision (for the Unexpected) Thinking

In the event of failure, leaders have backup plans and resources in reserve, alternatives and options as a way of providing for the unexpected. From a mindset of provisional thinking and planning, the impact of failure is diminished. Moreover, leaders know how to endure and to not give up after an unforeseen failure (Scott et al., 2008; Sonnenfeld & Ward, 2007); they bounce back and stand the test of time. Leaders seek advice from others in and outside of the team and are ready to offer best scenario solutions.

Application for ID. In terms of designing for education, leaders will provide for unexpected design failures. An ID leader will strategize for potential context-related roadblocks for learners as well as for the design team. Leaders of design teams will rally colleagues in times of intense institutional and societal challenges. Examples include (a) providing alternate realistic and reliable means of completing and forwarding assignments when students experience technology interruptions, (b) ensuring that multiple recovery plans are in place in the event of institutional upheavals from technology failures, (c) completing projects on time in lieu of heavy scheduling demands or budget shortages, and (d) drafting and teaching a plan to a team for handling ethical complaints. Leaders may ask questions such as the following: What is in the institutional pipeline for support of mobile deliveries and social media integration? Is it time to demand system-wide upgrades? Will operating with one less team member require unpaid overtime? Was adequate protection provided during interactive video meetings that may have prevented harm to students? Are the online course organizers warning students of the risks of media use by referring them to studies on cognitive overload through media learning?

Personality

Leaders convey personality through a high degree of professionalism; they possess a sense of presence through confidence and strength; and they act maturely in all manners and ways (Kirkpatrick & Locke, 1991; Kouzes & Posner, 2007). Leaders articulate and mediate with diplomacy and never waffle or sidestep the tough questions, and they communicate with inherent and exceptional interpersonal skills (Larson & Lockee, 2009) demanded in the modern workplace (Wakefield et al., 2012). Additionally, leaders are sincere, show compassion, demonstrate self-control, and are humble yet self-aware (Ashbaugh, 2011).

Application for ID. Instructional designers will exhibit confidence and professionalism by offering academic and relevant arguments for their design, strategic, and team decisions. Leaders will listen carefully to impassioned arguments by the team or clients and will articulate decisions from a practical, firm position, yet will take care to be considerate of others. One example of this characteristic is a disagreement on how much an SME will be allowed to modify a completed design. The situation requires leadership to find a balance between instructor flexibility and maintaining the integrity of the design. Moreover, a designer will lead by reconciling design perspectives and decisions with all the stakeholders. Whenever possible, the effective ID leader will seek "win–win" solutions to lessen adversarial feelings among members of the design team (Covey, 2004). In this way they will lead projects and teams with a sense of purpose (Fullan, 2001; Sergiovanni, 2003).

Productivity

Leaders show up on time, every time. Leaders encourage others to finish the task with excellence in spite of obstacles (Moore & Kearsley, 2005). Leaders work as hard as what they expect from others; and, they get the job done with expertise and extraordinary skill. Leaders are producers, a quality found to be preferred over being a visionary (Chen, Wu, Yang, & Tsou, 2008). Leaders can be counted on to meet schedule and budget constraints and are not afraid to go beyond the minimum expectations. Leaders rally the team to better practices; they strive for and apply innovative, creative, and effective measures (Ashbaugh, 2011).

Application for ID. Moving the process along toward completion, the ID leader will encourage the team to think and act efficaciously with openness to new ideas and theories that enhance learning designs. A successful leader is constantly reflecting and asking, "Is this way the best, most efficient and effective way, or is there a better way to do this?" If in a team leadership position, he or she will allocate the most appropriate resources and personnel to ensure production of efficacious and high quality learning events. For example, if a web design is required, and the design leader is the most skilled member of the team in that area, he or she will perform the task even though a different task may be more interesting or desirable. Likewise, if another team member has more expertise or ability in an area of interest to the leader, he or she will assign the more skilled member to the task. For another example, halfway through a design project funding is pulled, yet administration demands a completed course anyway. The ID finds a way to gracefully accept new budget restrictions and complete the project without burning out her colleagues in the process.

Psychological (Emotional) Toughness

Leaders think rationally, make good choices, and avoid knee-jerk reactions (Kepner & Tregoe, 1997; Scott et al., 2008; Sergiovanni, 2003). They will do the right thing, even when it is uncomfortable to do so. Leaders operate on the offensive, not from the defensive, with openness to other ideas, opinions, and criticisms

(Maxwell, 2007). Leaders apply logic tempered with practicality and common sense; they weigh the evidence to distinguish truth from fiction; and they rely on fairness, not dogma. Moreover, leaders exhibit patience with and respect for clients and co-workers and are highly self-disciplined (Ashbaugh, 2011).

Application for ID. Instructional designers acting from the personal leadership attribute of psychological toughness communicate capability through personal self-regulation and discipline. They exhibit strength and pragmatism in being patient with the design process and team members. They will behave with respect toward other stakeholders when sorting out conflicting ideas on theories of learning needs in order to adopt the best, most relevant practices for targeted learners and environments. For example, a disagreement in affordance selection for a hybrid accounting course will have various perspectives with legitimate arguments. The leader will encourage civil discussion, yet make the tough decision if consensus is not reached.

Personal Convictions

Good leaders are considered to be honest (Wolumbwa, Avolio, Gardner, Wernsing, & Peterson, 2008); they don't cheat personally or in business and they never lie. In other words, they possess integrity in all areas of their lives (Covey, 1992). Leaders align their actions with their beliefs (Argyris & Schön, 1992) and live by conscience not rules (Sergiovanni, 2003). Leaders act with moral purpose (Campbell et al., 2009) and they will consider the higher good of a matter at the risk of bending an inflexible rule. Leaders are trustworthy, faithful, and consistent in their beliefs. Leaders offer truthful support for decisions, including those that cause errors and delays; and take care to act on personal moral principles when confronted with a conflicting mandate (Ashbaugh, 2011). Consequently, leaders will work to bring change where needed in an ethical manner.

Application for ID. An ID leader will demonstrate a willingness to confront old paradigms and regimes to do what is believed to be efficacious for the learner. For an educational leader positioned for change, Fullan (2001) argued for an overarching moral purpose that Campbell et al. (2009) found to be present in instructional designers to guide decisions. As a matter of lifestyle, a design leader will exemplify high moral conduct, mindful of his or her responsibility to a vulnerable population of learners (Covey, 1992). For example, while honoring the budget, copyright laws will be followed meticulously at any cost while providing best possible course materials. Furthermore, ethical considerations will be afforded in each academic design, giving preference only to the success of the learning process and not personal or political gain. An instructional designer acting with a leadership mindset will set the tone for fellow team members in consistent kind, caring, and unselfish behavior, remembering that 'we're all in this together'.

Going Forward

Training for ID Leadership

Pressure is increasing for more rigor in academic courses (Arum & Roksa, 2011) which is afforded by the instructional designers of those courses. However, the complexity of new technologies requires a new way of thinking and training in leading the field in new ways as articulated by Kowch (2009),

> New leaders need new ways to address these issues beyond the instructional leadership literature, which was found lacking due to a classical focus on the supervision of instructors/teachers more than with the leading of the instructional process (design and development, as we know it). (p. 45)

Academic instruction is given on critical thinking, process thinking, risk management thinking, ethical thinking—all of which require higher-level cognitive adaptations, so why not add leadership-thinking to the repertoire of analytical skills curricula?

Since higher education may be viewed as a means of elevating cognitive and analytical skills, it is hoped that institutions offering programs of educational technology training will take notice of the need emphasized in this chapter for budding instructional designers to interpret their roles more broadly as leaders and will consider providing more leadership-thinking opportunities. The challenge before us, then, is how to provide for leadership-thinking in current ID programs. The concept is relatively unheard of. Williams van Rooij (2011) found that less than 23 % of such programs offer any project management courses, which called into question the number of related leadership courses available. Another startling discovery was made from a survey of 21 highly regarded graduate programs in instructional technology, that only one-third offered a leadership-related course and, of those, less than half specified actual leadership (not management) instruction (see Table 2). The net results showed a mere 15 % of ID programs that train in leadership as a comprehensive topic. Without appropriate training, the potential is limited for designers to become leaders, which could be problematic for a profession that is ultimately responsible for the advancement of effective course designs (Moore & Kearsley, 2005).

Implications for ID Research

Ultimately, our goal is to provide a validated leadership model specified for ID and the design process. A suggestion for accomplishing this is to rely on design and development research (Richey & Klein, 2007), which provides a rigorous method for infusing research and theory into the development of models. In the Ashbaugh (2011) study, existing theory was applied to practice and resulted in confirmation that instructional designers tend to perceive themselves as leaders. At the same

Table 2 Institutions with degree programs in instructional technology and leadership courses

Institution	Degree	Leadership course offered?	Type
Arizona State University	Master's in Educational Technology	No	
	PhD in Educational Technology		
Boise State University	Master's in Instructional and Performance Technology	Yes	Change Mgmt
Brigham Young University	Master of Instructional Psychology and Technology	No	
	PhD of Instructional Psychology and Technology		
Capella University	PhD, Education: Instructional Design for Online Learning	Yes	Leadership
Florida State University	Master of Science in Instructional Systems	No	
Indiana University	Master's in Instructional Systems Technology	No	
Jones International University	Master of Education: e-Learning Technology & Design	No	
Kaplan University	Master of Science in Education in Instructional Technology	No	
Nova Southeastern University	Master's in Instructional Technology & Distance Education	Yes	Leadership
Old Dominion University	PhD in Instructional Design & Technology	No	
Penn State World Campus	Master of Education in Instructional Systems-Educational Technology	No	
San Diego State University	Master of Educational Technology	No	
Syracuse University	Master of Science, Instructional Design, Development, & Evaluation	Yes	Curriculum, instructional, change
	Master of Instructional Technology		
	PhD, Instructional Design, Development, & Evaluation		
University of Arizona South	Master of Science in Educational Technology	No	
University of Memphis	Master of Science in Instructional Design & Technology	Yes	Curriculum
University of Northern Iowa	Master's of Instructional Technology	No	
University of West Georgia	Ed.S in Media, Emphasis in Instructional Technology	Yes	Administration
University of Wisconsin-Stout	Instructional Design Online Graduate Certificate	No	
Utah State University	Master of Science in Instructional Technology	No	
	PhD, Instructional Technology & Learning Sciences		
Walden University	Master's in Instructional Design and Technology	Yes	Organizational
Western Illinois University	Master's in Instructional Design and Technology	No	
	Quantitative Data Summary	7 of 21 include leadership courses	3 of 7 courses specify leadership
	Ratios/Percentages	1/3 institutions	15 % of all programs

time, new theory was created from a new understanding of what it means to be a leader in the ID field. The method exemplified one of the definitions of design and development research (Richey & Klein, 2007), which offers an approach that provides an effective avenue for exploring a novel leadership model.

In addition, a critical issue to be taken from this study is the foundation that course designers are laying for the future and how they are approaching their duty for doing the job with integrity by embracing the role of leadership. One way practitioners can lead is by participating in ongoing research to allow examination of personal decisions and habits that drive ID process decisions. Self-evaluation may lead to a more complete awareness of their vital role in the world of education. Articulating a similar concern, Kenny et al. (2005) foresaw that ID practice was in need of personalized and contextualized research,

> In order to truly understand what instructional designers do and how to help them develop more effective practice, we not only need to further study their actual practice, but also to help them more fully understand the roles they play as leaders in the enterprise of learning. (Discussion, Beyond process: Looking under the Rock section, par. 4)

Therefore, future research should continue to query practitioners, including the less experienced, for conceptions of what leadership is and for how its characteristics may be adopted for producing exemplary academic pedagogies, and, further, toward building a knowledge base of leadership competencies in use and how they inform the design process. Instructional designers in all roles and capacities, including those in community colleges and technical schools, public and private universities, international and online schools, designer/instructors, consultants, and staff course developers, may lend unique perspectives on this important profession. In this way, improvement is expected in the alignment of competencies and quality of practice, guided and driven by ID leadership.

Conclusion

What destroyed the Challenger space shuttle? Some would say it was a lack of leadership on the part of the engineer who was the victim of a system that led "individuals to defer to the anonymity of the process and not focus clearly enough on their individual responsibilities in the decision chain" (N.R.C. Report, in Boisjoly et al., 2004, p. 133). In addition, science would prove that the now infamous O-ring worked in most scenarios, but under rare conditions would prove to be fatally flawed. From this tragedy, it was confirmed that the utility of design must be proven in its most complete perspective for a successful outcome, including for educative purposes. Sharing responsibility for the fatal decision to continue the flight were those in positions of leadership who would not entertain the warnings of the design engineer and the engineer who did not press harder for an audience. Likewise for ID, knowledge building is a shared responsibility which includes multiple course design stakeholders. We need to build leadership-thinking into a more perfect design process for hedging against potential error-prone decisions by learners.

One implication from this study is that leadership, when activated in the design process, acts as a predictor of quality products, specifically, of academic courses. Hence, leadership training in the educational technology programs will effectively influence the overall quality of the compendium of learning events. In order to avert the same failures in education as those the world has witnessed in government, space exploration, finance, and business, great opportunity affords itself to impress leadership competencies on future designers for creating high quality and effective academic training courses.

In summary, leadership exhibits a mindset that will guide the design process and underpin innovative course creations through a more skilled instructional design function. It is important that the field of instructional design pays attention to the critical leadership skills needed to drive the changing ethos of education. It is with sincere hope that interested readers will add expertise and insight to what has been presented, will continue the conversation, and will promote research for developing a leadership model for elevating the instructional designer's role and process—the 7Ps of Leadership for ID.

References

Argyris, C., & Schön, D. (1992). *Theory in practice: Increasing professional effectiveness.* San Francisco: Jossey-Bass.

Arum, R., & Roksa, J. (2011). *Academically adrift: Limited learning on college campuses.* Chicago: University of Chicago Press.

Ashbaugh, M. L. (2011). *Online pedagogical quality questioned: Probing instructional designers' perceptions of leadership competencies critical to practice.* Retrieved from http://gradworks. umi.com/34/60/3460621.html

Ashbaugh, M. L. (2013). I-Design 2.0 strategies for Web 2.0 adoption: Appropriate use of emerging technologies in online courses. In P. Blessinger & C. Wenkel (Eds.), *Increasing student engagement and retention in e-learning environments: Web 2.0 and blended learning technologies* (Vol. 7, pp. 17–56). Bingley, UK: Emerald Publishing Group. DOI: http://dx.doi. org/10.1108/S2044-9968(2013)000006G004.

Ashbaugh, M. L, & Piña, A. A. (2012, July). *Design-thinking for engineering quality instructional design processes through leadership competencies and modeling.* Presented at the 2012 Annual Research Symposium of the Association for Educational Communications & Technology, Louisville, KY.

Bass, B. M., & Riggio, R. E. (2006). *Transformational leadership* (2nd ed.). Mahwah, NJ: Lawrence Erlbaum Associates.

Beaudoin, M. F. (2007). Distance education leadership: An appraisal of research and practice. In M. G. Moore (Ed.), *Handbook of distance education* (2nd ed., pp. 391–402). Mahwah, NJ: Erlbaum.

Boisjoly, R. P., Curtis, E. F., & Mellican, E. (2004). Roger Boisjoly and the challenger disaster: The ethical dimensions. In T. E. Beauchamp & N. E. Bowie (Eds.), *Ethical theory and business* (7th ed., pp. 123–135). Upper Saddle River, NJ: Pearson Prentice Hall.

Campbell, K., Schwier, R., & Kenny, R. (2009). The critical, relational practice of instructional design in higher education: An emerging model of change agency. *Educational Technology Research and Development, 57*(5), 645–663. doi:10.1007/s11423-007-9061-6.

Chen, C. J., Wu, J., Yang, S. C., & Tsou, H-Y. (2008). Importance of diversified leadership roles in improving team effectiveness in a virtual collaboration learning environment. *Educational*

Technology & Society, 11(1), 304–321. Retrieved from http://www.ifets.info/journals, http://www.educause.edu/eq

Collins, J. A. (1993). *Failure of materials in mechanical design: Analysis, prediction, prevention* (2nd ed.). New York: Wiley.

Covey, S. R. (1992). *Principle-centered leadership: Strategies for personal and professional effectiveness.* New York: Simon & Schuster.

Covey, S. R. (2004). *The seven habits of highly effective people* (15 anniversaryth ed.). New York: Free Press.

Dede, C., & Bjerede, M. (2010). *Mobile wireless devices that empower engagement, learning, and assessment.* Presented at the ISTE Annual Conference & Exposition, June 27–30, 2010, Denver, CO.

Dooley, K., Lindner, J., Telg, R., Irani, T., Moore, L., & Lundy, L. (2007). Roadmap to measuring distance education instructional design competency. *Quarterly Review of Distance Education, 8*(2), 151–159. Retrieved from http://www.infoagepub.com/index.php?id=89&i=4

Drucker, P. (1981). *Why management consultants?* Retrieved from http://anoovaconsulting.biz/drucker.pdf

Durdu, P., Yalabik, N., & Cagiltay, K. (2009). A distributed online curriculum and courseware development model. *Educational Technology & Society, 12*(1), 230–248. Retrieved from http://www.ifets.info

Fullan, M. (2001). *Leading in a culture of change.* San Francisco: Jossey-Bass.

Fullan, M., & Scott, G. (2009). *Turnaround leadership for higher education.* San Francisco: Jossey-Bass.

Gallos, J. V. (2008). *Business leadership: A Jossey-Bass reader* (2nd ed.). San Francisco: Jossey-Bass.

Gelo, O., Braakmann, D., & Benetka, G. (2008). Quantitative and qualitative research: Beyond the debate. *Integrative Psychological & Behavioral Science, 42*(3), 266–290. doi:10.1007/s12124-008-9078-3.

Gero, J. S. (2010). *Design computing and cognition'10.* New York: Springer.

Gressick, J., & Derry, S. J. (2010). Distributed leadership in online groups. *International Journal of Computer-Supported Collaborative Learning, 5*(2), 211–236. doi:10.1007/s11412-010-9086-4.

Hall, B. (2010). Nonmaleficence and the preparation of classroom teachers in instructional design. *Journal of Elementary and Secondary Education, 1*(11), 1–16. Retrieved from http://www.theelearninginstitute.org/journal_pdf/JESE%20-%20Nonmaleficence%20and%20the%20Preparation%20of%20Classroom%20Teachers%20in%20Instructional%20Design.pdf

Howard, A., & Wellins, R. S. (2008). Global leadership forecast 2008|2009: Overcoming the shortfalls in developing leaders. Retrieved from http://www.ddiworld.com/pdf/globalleadershipforecast2008-2009_globalreport_ddi.pdf

Iacocca, L. (2007). *Where have all the leaders gone?* New York: Scribners.

International Board of Standards for Training, Performance and Instruction (IBSTPI). (2000). *Instructional design competencies report.* International Board of Standards for Training, Performance and Instruction. Retrieved from http://www.ibstpi.org/downloads/InstructionalDesignCompetencies.pdf

Isaacson, W. (2011). *Steve Jobs.* New York: Simon & Schuster.

Jaworski, J. (2012). *Source: The inner path of knowledge creation.* San Francisco: Berrett-Koehler.

Jonassen, D. H. (2011). *Learning to solve problems: A handbook for designing problem solving learning environments.* New York: Routledge.

Katz, R. (1955). Skills of an effective administrator. *Harvard Business Review, 33*(1), 33–42.

Kenny, R. F., Zhang, Z., Schwier, R. A., & Campbell, K. (2005). A review of what instructional designers do: Questions answered and questions not asked. *Canadian Journal of Learning and Technology, 31*(1). Retrieved from http://www.cjlt.ca/index.php/cjlt/article/view/147/140

Kepner, C. H., & Tregoe, B. B. (1997). *The new rational manager: An updated edition for a new world.* Princeton, NJ: Princeton Research Press.

Kirkpatrick, S. A., & Locke, E. A. (1991). Leadership: Do traits matter? *Academy of Management Executive, 5*(2), 48–60. Retrieved from http://journals.aomonline.org/amp

Klein, J. D., Spector, J. M., Grabowski, B., & de la Teja, I. (2004). *Instructor competencies: Standards for face-to-face, online and blended settings.* Greenwich, CT: Information Age Publishing.

Kotter, J. P. (1996). *Leading change.* Boston: Harvard Business School Press.

Kotter, J. P. (2008). What leaders really do. In J. V. Gallos (Ed.), *Business leadership: A Jossey-Bass reader* (2nd ed., pp. 5–15). San Francisco: Jossey-Bass.

Kouzes, J. M., & Posner, B. Z. (2007). *The leadership challenge* (4th ed.). San Francisco: Wiley.

Kowch, E. (2009). New capabilities for cyber charter school leadership: An emerging imperative for integrating educational technology and educational leadership knowledge. *TechTrends, 53*(4), 41–48.

Larson, M. B., & Lockee, B. B. (2009). Preparing instructional designers for different career environments: A case study. *Educational Technology Research and Development, 57,* 1–24. doi:10.1007/s11423-006-9031-4.

Lawson, B. (2006). *How designers think: The design process demystified* (4th ed.). Burlington, MA: Architectural Press.

Lin, H. (2007). The ethics of instructional technology: Issues and coping strategies experienced by professional technologists in design and training situations in higher education. *Educational Technology Research and Development, 55,* 411–437. doi:10.1007/s11423-006-9029-y.

Maryland Online. (2010). *Quality Matters rubric standards 2008–2010 edition with assigned point values (QM™ 2010).* Retrieved from http://qminstitute.org/home/Public%20Library/About%20QM/RubricStandards2008-2010.pdf

Maxwell, J. C. (2007). *The irrefutable of laws of leadership: Follow them and people will follow you* (Rev., 10 anniversaryth ed.). Nashville, TN: Thomas Nelson.

Moore, M., & Kearsley, G. (2005). *Distance education: A systems view* (2nd ed.). Belmont, CA: Thomson Wadsworth.

Naidu, S. (2007). Instructional designs for optimal learning. In M. G. Moore (Ed.), *Handbook of distance education* (2nd ed., pp. 247–258). Mahwah, NJ: Erlbaum.

Nimon, S. (2007). Generation Y and higher education: The other Y2K. *Journal of Institutional Research, 13*(1), 24–41. Retrieved from http://www.aair.org.au/2006Papers/Nimon.pdf

Paulsen, N., Maldonado, D., Callan, V. J., & Ayoko, O. (2009). Charismatic leadership, change and innovation in an R&D organization. *Journal of Organizational Change Management, 22*(5), 511–523. doi:10.1108/09534810910983479.

Piña, A. A., Sadowski, K. P., Scheidenhelm, C. L., & Heydenburg, P. R. (2008). SLATE: A community of practice for supporting learning and technology in education. *International Journal of Instructional Technology and Distance Learning, 5*(7).

Pisapia, J. (2009). *The strategic leader: New tactics for a globalizing world.* Charlotte, NC: Information Age.

Power, D. (2012). *Why innovation needs design thinkers.* Harvard Division of Continuing Education. Retrieved from http://www.dce.harvard.edu/professional/blog/why-innovation-needs-design-thinking-5-29-12.jsp;jsessionid=HPOHOGNECCCL

Reeves, T. C., Herrington, J., & Oliver, R. (2004). A development research agenda for online collaborative learning. *Educational Technology Research and Development, 52*(4), 53–65.

Reigeluth, C. M., Watson, W. R., Watson, S. L., Dutta, P., Zengguan, C., & Powell, N. (2008). Roles for technology in the information-age paradigm of education: Learning management systems. *Educational Technology, 48*(6), 32–40. Retrieved from http://cardinalscholar.bsu.edu/bitstream/123456789/194511/1/LMS.pdf

Reimers, F. M. (2009). Leading for global competency. *Educational Leadership: Teaching for the 21st Century, 67*(1). Retrieved from http://www.ascd.org/publications/educational_leadership/sept09/vol67/num01/Leading_for_Global_Competency.aspx

Richey, R. C., Fields, D. C., Foxon, M. (with Roberts, R. C., Spannaus, T., & Spector, J. M.). (2001). *Instructional design competencies: The standards* (3rd ed.). Syracuse, NY: Eric Clearinghouse on Information and Technology.

Richey, R. C., & Klein, J. D. (2007). *Design and development research*. Mahwah, NJ: Erlbaum.

Rossett, A., & Papaila, D. (2005). Instructional design is not peanuts. In J. M. Spector, C. Ohrazda, A. van Schaack, & D. A. Wiley (Eds.), *Innovations in instructional technology: Essays in honor of David Merrill* (pp. 91–110). Mahwah, NJ: Erlbaum.

Rothwell, W. J., & Kazanas, H. C. (2008). *Mastering the instructional design process: A systematic approach*. San Francisco: Pfeiffer.

Sackney, L., & Mergel, B. (2007). Contemporary learning theories, instructional design and leadership. In J. M. Burger, C. Webber, & P. Klinck (Eds.), *Intelligent Leadership* (Vol. 11, pp. 67–98). Dordrecht, Netherlands: Springer. doi: 10.1007/978-1-4020-6022-9_5

Schön, D. A. (1984). *The reflective practitioner: How professionals think in action*. USA: Basic Books.

Schuller, C. F. (1986). Some historical perspectives on the instructional technology field. *Journal of Instructional Development, 8*(3), 3–6. Retrieved from http://www.aect.org/Publications/JID_Collection/H3_V8_N3/3_Schuller.PDF

Scott, G., Coates, H., & Anderson, M. (2008). *Learning leaders in times of change: Academic leadership capabilities for Australian higher education*. [Report]. University of Western Sydney and Australian Council for Educational Research.

Senge, P. (2006). *The fifth discipline: The art & practice of the learning organization*. New York: Doubleday.

Sergiovanni, T. (2003). A cognitive approach to leadership. In B. Davies & J. West-Burham (Eds.), *Handbook of educational leadership and management* (pp. 12–16). New York: Pearson/Longman.

Shaw, K. (2012). Leadership through instructional design in higher education. *Online Journal of Distance Learning Administration, 12* (3). Retrieved from http://www.westga.edu/~distance/ojdla/fall153/shaw153.html

Siemens, G. (2004). *Connectivism: A learning theory for the digital age*. Retrieved from http://www.elearnspace.org/Articles/connectivism.htm

Siemens, G. (2008). *Learning and knowing in networks: Changing roles for educators and designers*. Presentation at ITFORUM for Discussion, January 27, 2008. Retrieved from http://www.ingedewaard.net/papers/connectivism/2008_siemens_Learning_Knowing_in_Networks_changingRolesForEducatorsAndDesigners.pdf

Sims, R. (2011). Reappraising design practice. In D. Holt, S. Segrave, & J. Cybulski (Eds.), *Professional education using e-simulations: Benefits of blended learning design*. Hershey, PA: IGI Global.

Sims, R. C., & Koszalka, T. A. (2008). Competencies for the new-age instructional designer. In J. M. Spector, M. D. Merrill, J. van Merriënboer, & M. P. Driscoll (Eds.), *Handbook of research on educational communications and technology* (3rd ed.). New York: Earlbaum.

Smith, P. L., & Ragan, T. J. (1999). *Instructional design* (2nd ed.). New York: Wiley.

Sonnenfeld, J., & Ward, A. (2007). *Firing back: How great leaders rebound after career disasters*. Boston: Harvard Business Press.

Spannaus, T., & Spector, J. M. (2001). The ID competencies: Discussion and analysis. In R. C. Richey, D. C. Fields, & M. Foxon (Eds.), *Instructional design competencies: The standards* (3rd ed.). Syracuse, NY: Eric Clearinghouse on Information and Technology.

Spector, J. M. (2009). Reflections: Reconsidering the notion of *distance* in distance education. *Distance Education, 30*(1), 157–161. doi:10.1080/01587910902846004.

Spitzer, Q., & Evans, R. (1997). *Heads, you win!: How the best companies think—and how you can use their examples to develop critical thinking within your own organization*. New York: Simon & Schuster.

Taura, T., & Nagai, Y. (2010). *Design creativity*. New York: Springer.

Tichy, N. M., & Ulrich, D. O. (1984/2008). The leadership challenge—a call for the transformational leader. In J. Steven Ott, S. J. Parkes, & R. B. Simpson (Eds.), *Classical readings of organizational behavior*. Belmont, CA: Thomson-Wadsworth.

Wakefield, J., Warren, S., & Mills, L. (2012). Traits, skills, & competencies aligned with workplace demands: What today's instructional designers need to master. In P. Resta (Ed.),

Proceedings of Society for Information Technology & Teacher Education International Conference 2012 (pp. 3126–3132). Chesapeake, VA: AACE. Retrieved from http://www.editlib.org/p/40070

Williams van Rooij, S. (2011). Instructional design and project management: Complementary or divergent? *Educational Technology Research & Development, 59*, 139–158. doi:10.1007/s11423-010-9176-z.

Wilson, B. G. (2005). Foundations for instructional design: Reclaiming the conversation. In J. M. Spector, C. Ohrazda, A. Van Schaack, & D. A. Wiley (Eds.), *Innovations in instructional technology: Essays in honor of M. David Merrill* (pp. 237–252). Mahwah, NJ: Erlbaum.

Wolumbwa, F. O., Avolio, B. J., Gardner, W. L., Wernsing, T. S., & Peterson, S. J. (2008). Authentic leadership: Development and validation of a theory-based measure. *Journal of Management, 34*(1), 89–126. doi:10.1177/0149206370308913.

Zenger, J. H., & Folkman, J. (2009). *The extraordinary leader: Turning good managers into great leaders*. New York: McGraw-Hill.

Higher Education Leaders as Designers

Paul F. Zenke

Keywords Leadership • Higher education • Higher education leadership • College leadership • University leadership • Change leadership • Design • Design thinking • Design education • Designers • Colleges of design • Leaders as designers

Higher Education Leaders as Designers

American higher education faces unprecedented financial, institutional, and political challenges (Duderstadt, 1999). "Declining federal funding, record reductions in state funding, erosion of endowments, soaring tuition costs reaching unaffordable limits, intensifying, internal as well as global competition, increasing compliance and reporting requirements, as well as the loss of political and public confidence in the value of university-based research" threaten the health and accessibility of higher education (The Research Universities Futures Consortium, 2012, p. 10). Institutions are under increasing pressure from politicians, citizens, and students to address these challenges through creative new approaches; however, scholars have noted higher education is largely "impervious to outside forces" (Johnson, Hanna, & Olcott, 2003, p. 11) and plagued by inertia (Duderstadt, 2000; Hanna, 2000; Trowler, 2008). American college and universities' steadfast allegiance to their missions, traditions, and culture is undoubtedly a large part of their success, but for higher education leaders responsible for helping to shape the future of their organizations, these cultural preferences for slow and measured change often lead to conflicts with campus stakeholders (Kezar, 2001).

P.F. Zenke (✉)
The University of Wisconsin-Madison, Madison, WI, USA
e-mail: pfzenke@gmail.com

B. Hokanson and A. Gibbons (eds.), *Design in Educational Technology,*
Educational Communications and Technology: Issues and Innovations 1,
DOI 10.1007/978-3-319-00927-8_14, © Springer International Publishing Switzerland 2014

Nonetheless, college and universities as institutions are not exclusively responsible for their perceived opaqueness and inertia. Higher education leaders themselves rise through the administrative ranks largely because of their demonstrated enculturation in these tradition-laden institutions, and university boards recruit and continue to support the preservation of that culture by favoring candidates with risk-averse analytical thinking skills (Plinske & Packard, 2010). These leadership approaches "espouse predictability and control," but during this time of unprecedented financial, institutional, and political turmoil, analytical thinking alone "provides less and less direction and guidance for reliable action" (Woodward & Funk, 2010, p. 297), suggesting that higher education must attract and develop new kinds of leaders (Skinner & Miller, 2012). College and university leaders need new approaches that will empower them to view constraints as opportunities, guide them towards considering issues systemically, and encourage them to create and test many possible solutions to increasingly complicated problems (Dunne & Martin, 2006). Scholars and practitioners concerned with how institutions and their leaders will respond to these emerging challenges have taken a renewed interest in design thinking and leadership practice. In an effort to address the challenges facing higher education leaders, this chapter will explore the affordances of design thinking and will further the concept of higher education leaders as designers.

Design Thinking

University of Minnesota College of Design, Dean Thomas Fisher describes this tremendous period of social and economic transformation as a "world of flows" (2006, p. 2). In this world, Fisher suggests capital, talent, and ideas flow freely without regard for political, geographic, or disciplinary boundaries. For Fisher "a world of flows... favors those who have learned to see similar patterns among disparate things and underlying relationships among apparently unrelated functions. It favors, in other words, the designer" (pp. 11–12). Borja de Mozota posits "designers have always been agents of change in society" (2010, p. 186) because their future-oriented dispositions and willingness to frame and address pressing issues in a holistic way force us to ask fundamental questions and create new solutions that move our society beyond the fracture-critical systems that defined the twentieth century (Fisher & Larsen, 2010). Simon (1969) describes designers as "concerned with what ought to be—how they ought to be in order to attain goals, and to function" (p. 5). Krippendorff (2006) asserts designers are driven by "challenges, opportunities to change something for the better, [and] possibilities to introduce variations into the world that others may not dare to consider" (pp. 28–29). Recently, there has been a resurgence of scholarly interest in how designers address problems because some believe that the "skills of designers that will most help decision makers face their current challenges" (Borja de Mozota, 2010, p. 185). This section will argue that the way designers frame and address problems through design thinking is well-suited to help higher educational leaders

. . . develop the capacity for change; remove the constraints that prevent institutions from responding to the needs of the rapidly changing societies; remove unnecessary process and administrative structures to question existing premises and arrangements and to challenge, excite, and embolden all members of the campus community. (Duderstadt, 1999, p. 1)

Fisher describes design thinking as a "rigorous process by which we come up with things that do not exist" (Fisher & Larsen, 2010, p. 1). It is future oriented, primarily concerned with "the conception and realization of new things" and focused on "planning, inventing, making, and doing" (Cross, 1982, p. 221). Design thinking is an inherently "human-centered" process "that draws from the designer's toolkit to integrate the needs of people, the possibilities of technology, and the requirements" for success (IDEO, 2012, p. 1). However, design thinking is not a new idea. For decades scholars like Simon (1969), Rittel and Webber (1972), Cross (1982, 2011), Schon (1987), Margolin (1984), Norman (1988), Lawson (2004, 2005), and Visser (2006) have conceptualized design thinking "as problem solving, as part of the industrial process, as social engineering, as a question, as a research activity, as a discourse rather than a thing, as a label, [and] as an art form" (Borja de Mozota, 2010, p. 185). Design thinking has recently reentered the scholarly conversation as an approach for helping organizations succeed in the "world of flows" because design thinking helps "loosen up restrictive identities in an increasingly complex and ambiguous world in which a purely rational approach is no longer tenable" (Rylander, 2009, p. 15).

Designers employ "abductive logic," which Fisher and Larsen (2010) describe as "a method of logical inference that considers a set of seemingly unrelated facts— and then connects them" (p. 1). First codified by Aristotle and later rediscovered by the late nineteenth century philosopher Charles Sanders Peirce, abductive logic differs from deductive logic "of what must be," and inductive logic "of what is operative" by searching for "what could possibly be true" (Martin, 2009, pp. 62–63). Abductive logic "sits squarely between the past-data-driven world of analytical thinking and the knowing-without-reasoning world of intuitive thinking" (Martin, 2009, p. 26). Designers rely on abductive logic and design thinking to build and test solutions to "wicked problems."

"Wicked problems" are "ill defined and characterized by incomplete, contradictory, and changing requirements and complex interdependencies" (Rylander, 2009, p. 10). Rittel and Webber (1972) developed ten distinguishing properties of wicked problems, including they have "no definitive formulation" are "essentially unique," "can be considered to be a symptom of another problem," and have solutions that "are not true-or-false, but good-or-bad" (pp. 162–166). Dunne and Martin (2006) posit that whereas leaders and organizations typically avoid engaging with wicked problems because of their inherent ambiguity, "designers embrace these problems as a challenge" (p. 522). Addressing higher education's wicked problems, like decreasing state and federal aid and preparing students to contribute in the "world of flows," requires design thinking.

Design thinking is often described in terms of "designerly ways of knowing" (Cross, 1982) or as a "design attitude" (Boland, Collopy, Lyytinen, & Yoo, 2008). Contrary to the common cultural understanding of designers' work, these ways of knowing are not the sole domain of formally trained designers (Cross, 1982). Design thinking is learned and can be developed by adopting the "stance, tools, and experiences" of designers (Martin, 2009, p. 30). Cross (1982) canonically described the five aspects of "designerly ways of knowing" as: tackling ill-defined problems, being solution-focused, thinking constructively, translating abstract requirements into concrete objects, and being able to read and write in object languages. Similarly Boland et al. (2008) studied architect Frank Gehry and from their observations concluded a "design attitude" is an "ongoing expectation that each project is a new opportunity to create something remarkable, and to do it in a way that has never been done before" (p. 13). Furthermore, a "design attitude" understands the constraints of a project "anticipates that these conditions could be other than they are, and they strive to change them for the better" (p. 13). For higher education leaders to meaningfully address the wicked problems facing their institutions, they would benefit from adopting "designerly ways of knowing" and a "design attitude."

The implementation of design thinking is not driven by a rigid set of steps but rather is best conceptualized as "a system of overlapping spaces", including, "inspiration, ideation, and implementation". (IDEO, 2012). IDEO describes the inspiration space as the "problem or opportunity," the ideation space as "the process of generating, developing, and testing ideas" and the implementation space as "the path that leads from the project stage into people's lives" (2012). However, this is only one of many possible ways to understand design thinking in practice, but is useful for our discussion because it reflects many of the common features discussed in the literature (Beckman & Barry, 2007; Gloppen, 2009; Joziasse, 2011; Martin, 2009; Melles, Howard, & Thompson-Whiteside, 2012; Rylander, 2009). Design thinking has incredible potential for reinvigorating higher education. The next section will discuss the application of design thinking within higher education leadership.

Leaders as Designers

Donald Schön posited "architecture offers clues to the reform and revitalization of higher education" (1986, p. 96). Although at the time he was advocating for the broader application of design thinking in undergraduate education, Schön's comment is also applicable for higher education leaders today. Bell (2010) echoes Schön's thoughts, "What can design thinking offer to higher education? In a word, change. It's a roadmap for future-proofing one of society's most valued resources" (p. 1). Schön and Bell describe design thinking as a powerful lens for viewing the challenges facing higher education; however, change in higher education comes slowly, and rarely, if ever, is the result of one group or person (Bolman & Gallos, 2011). Kezar's (2001) research suggests that for higher education change initiatives to be successful, they need to be contextualized within higher education. Therefore, this section describes how change in higher education is possible by highlighting two examples of how design thinking can spur change and collaboration in two contexts: conceptually redesigning an administrative unit inspired by the design studio and redesigning higher education leadership. These examples demonstrate the potential of design thinking in higher education and work to further the concept of higher education leaders as designers.

The design studio has been called the "heart and head of architectural education" (Dutton, 1987). Although design programs have distinctive pedagogies and often champion different architectural schools of thought, there are "certain central, more or less constant features" of all design studios (Schon, 1986, p. 6). Four of these constant features germane to our conversation include "learning-by-doing, problem setting, public prototyping, and open critique" (Brown, 2006; Dutton, 1987; Rylander, 2009; Schon, 1986). Students in the design studio learn by doing instead of through studying and analysis (Lawson, 2006, cited in Rylander, 2009). The design studio encourages moving "from problem solving to problem setting," suggesting properly framing a problem is equally important as the design process (Schon, 1986). As students work through their designs, this process is public, and prototypes and their iterations are on display for other students to see (Brown, 2006). This demonstrates how students are working through the problem-setting process, often using drawings and sketches to "think with their hands" (Collopy, 2004). Once students have completed a solution, they share their work and receive critiques from their fellow students. This helps students learn from each other and practice explaining and receiving feedback on their "design choices and constraints that led to the final result" (Brown, 2006, p. 16). Also, because the critique process is public, even students who are not receiving critiques benefit from what Lave and Wenger (1991) describe as "legitimate peripheral participation" (p. 4) by exposing them to "the sensibilities, beliefs, and idiosyncrasies of the particular community of practice" (Brown, 2006, p. 20). The design studio is well-suited as an organizational platform for revitalizing higher education leadership.

Architect and higher education scholar Shannon Chance recently proposed using the design studio format within higher education leadership because "it can help overcome many of the limitations inherent to bureaucratic structures that rely on vertical hierarchy and that inadvertently suppress creativity and pluralistic thinking" (2009, p. 112). The challenges facing higher education require a new organizational framework for prototyping, testing, and receiving feedback on solutions to our most pressing issues, and Chance suggests the design studio "provides an ideal and well-established model for promoting inventive, proactive, and increasingly productive responses to unfolding events and opportunities that confront academia" (2009, p. 116). Within the design studio's structure, design thinking can flourish so that higher education's wicked problems can be addressed in a holistic, collaborative way. Although Chance introduces the design studio concept to address the specific needs of institutional advancement units, for the purpose of this paper, I will discuss the opportunities for more broadly applying Chance's work to other units within colleges and universities.

Using institutional advancement as an example, Chance posits that the first step for creating a new higher education leadership design studio, or atelier, would be to rethink institutional divisions, dissolving as many offices as possible to avoid compartmentalization. The Institutional Advancement Atelier "will be housed in a single building to catalyze collaboration and creativity" within an office that is as open as possible to "promote staff interaction, [and] ingenuity" (2009, p. 116). The atelier would be organized into three large teams—"Development Programs," "Integrated Marketing," and "Student and Alumni Relations"—each run by an Associate Vice President. What would have traditionally been many offices, often spread across campus, will be reformed as several design studios organized by topics and areas of common interest, such as the "Alumni Relations Studio" and the "Development Studio." Design studios require space that encourages "radical collaboration" (Hasso Plattner Institute of Design at Stanford, 2010) and that facilitates "chance encounters" to promote the creation of new ideas. The collaborative, less fragmented studio approach to higher education units is essential for "pooling talent and resources and for promoting nonlinear, creative, and collaborative thinking" (Chance, 2009, p. 123). Iarrobino's research (2006) on the successful formation of institutional advancement units supports the design studio model and lays our criteria for its translation to other units across campus including providing "(a) a collectively constructed vision; (b) increased availability of supervisors and colleagues; (c) effective communication (with feedback, praise and constructive critique); (d) well- formulated and widely understood strategies for business and hiring; (e) competency-based performance criteria and reward systems; (f) improved flexibility (in scheduling, comp-time, and opportunities to work from home); and (g) access to professional development, promotion and new learning experiences" (cited in Chance, 2009, p. 115). Utilizing Iarrobino's criteria, and building on the previous section on design thinking, the design studio emerges as a natural fit and organizational model for supporting higher education leaders as designers.

Beyond breaking down traditional divisions and fostering collaboration, emerging higher education leadership research supports the atelier model. Antiquated leadership approaches focused on "heroic leaders," and "static, highly structured, and value-neutral leadership frameworks" has given way to contemporary scholarship on "dynamic, globalized, and processed-oriented perspectives of leadership that emphasize cross-cultural understanding, collaboration, and social responsibility for others" (Kezar, Carducci, & Contreras-McGavin, 2006, p. 2). The atelier model personifies Kezer et al.'s vision for the next generation of leadership. Birnbaum (2012) research suggests higher education leadership is impacted by the organization's structure, and conversely, the organization is impacted by leadership practice which underscores the importance of adopting a structure like the atelier model to support change throughout the organization. The atelier model for higher education leadership forces units on campus to co-create and form collaborative teams that become accustomed to building from, and critiquing, each other's work. Ann Pendleton-Jullian, Director of the Knowlton School of Architecture at Ohio State University, has also proposed an organizational model inspired by design education which is well-suited for supporting higher education leaders as designers.

Pendleton-Jullian (2009) argues that higher education should adopt "design labs where the organizational structure is light, emergent, networked, and elastic" and are "different from design studios in that they are driven by inquiry rather than organized around pedagogy" (p. 27). These design labs would be more useful than research centers because of the relative ease with which the labs could "plan, build, and reconfigure as projects shift and move in other direction" (p. 27). Similar to Chance (2009), Pendleton-Jullian suggests grouping people around their research interests and talents. However, unlike Chance, Pendleton-Jullian recommends these micro-labs should be highly distributed, possibly across institutions and even continents. Pendleton-Jullian's micro-lab model also represents a unique, design-centered approach to higher education leadership. Drawing on the metaphor of a four-person cycling team, Pendleton-Jullian suggests that these nonhierarchical micro-labs should draw on collective leadership that rotates depending on the "terrain." Cycling teams rely on each other to take turns in the lead while the other team members "draft at the rear, to rest, recuperate, and regenerate" (p. 28). Unlike traditional higher education units, the leadership of the micro-labs would be a collective effort relying on "hyperdisciplinary" collaboration between "faculty, research assistants, industry researchers and consultants, artists, film makers, business, and anyone valuable from anywhere with the necessary talent for the situation at hand" (p. 39). Chance's design studio model and Pendleton-Jullian's micro-lab model addresses the general leadership opportunities within design-based structures, but John Maeda, president of the Rhode Island School of Design (RISD), has made significant contributions to this line of inquiry by translating his experiences as a world famous designer to higher education leadership.

When John Maeda became president of RISD in June, 2008, he approached his new leadership role from the unique prospective of an award-winning artist and designer. Along with his RISD colleague Becky Bermont, Maeda has openly chronicled his leadership journey on social media platforms and university websites. However, Maeda's attempts at digital leadership did not translate well to RISD's culture, and in March, 2011, the faculty passed a vote of "no confidence" by a margin of 142-32 (Tischler, 2011). "I was the high-risk candidate," he acknowledged, "but I'm not worried about getting fired. I could get another job. If you have no fear, no one has power over you" (Tischler, 2011).

Around the same time, his book coauthored with Bermont, *Redesigning Leadership,* was released, and since then Maeda has continued to iterate on the idea of "Creative as Leader" (Maeda & Bermont, 2011a). Maeda remains one of higher education's most interesting presidents and has undoubtedly forwarded the concept of higher education leaders as designers better than anyone else. Irrespective of Maeda's standing at RISD, his work refining the idea of higher education leaders as designers is important to the future of higher education leadership literature.

Meada and Bermont have since codified six principles of creative leadership: build from foundations, craft the team, sense actively, take leaps, fail productively, and grow from critique (Maeda & Bermont, 2011b). Building from foundations is a familiar idea in design education. Maeda describes how RISD students learn to draw by sketching buildings and then improve their skills by breaking buildings down to simple shapes. Like design students, leaders need to "start with core foundations and basic principles" (Maeda & Bermont, 2011b). In *Redefining Leadership*, Maeda adds "a creative leader is someone who leads with dirty hands, much the way an artist's hands are often literally dirty with paint" (2011a, pp. 9–10). However, it has been a struggle for Maeda to translate getting his hands dirty transitioning from an artistic to a leadership context. Maeda describes how Bermont helped him realize that running RISD's day-to-day operations is how he gets his hands dirty, or "meta-dirty," as he likes to call it (Maeda & Bermont, 2011a).

Maeda's second principle of creative leadership is crafting the team. Like any creative project, materials matter, and in a leadership context Maeda describes people as the most important material. Similar to Collin's (2001) axiom "first who, then what," Maeda stresses the importance of crafting your team wisely and then engaging collaboratively with the best materials available to do great work. When Maeda does creative work, he often works alone, and so he actively reminds himself while at RISD not to operate as a "lone wolf creative" (Maeda & Bermont, 2011b).

Third, Maeda suggests creative leaders must sense actively. As the world continues to change rapidly, leaders need to be responsive and sense actively to changes in their environment. Maeda described how, just as kites help make the wind visible, leaders need to be responsive to changes and help communicate those changes to their institutions in tangible ways. Sensing actively requires what Maeda describes as "5-bars of signal" or the clearest possible way of receiving information about changes in the environment (Maeda & Bermont, 2011b). Leaders are only as successful as their ability to collect and analyze high-quality institutional data.

Fourth, creative leaders take leaps. Maeda relates in *Redesigning Leadership* that "artists... attempt to make giant leaps to a solution, seeming to ignore all constraints. By making those leaps, they sometimes miss the solution completely. But they are not afraid to miss the target" (2011a, pp. 22–23). Creative leaders learn to trust their intuition and develop skills in abductive thinking. Maeda suggests "in the end, it's about learning to hear your own voice as a leader" (Maeda & Bermont, 2011a, p. 21).

The fifth principle of creative leaders is failing productively. Leaders are not accustomed to viewing failure positively. However, designers and other creatives understand failure as an opportunity to improvise and adapt. One way for leaders to utilize failure is by using setbacks as an opportunity to connect new people to collaborate on a problem. Maeda describes that designers always learn something that they can apply to their next project, and leaders would equally benefit from failing productively.

And sixth, creative leaders grow from critique. Traditionally leaders are averse to asking for feedback, especially in public. However, Maeda relishes critique often starting meetings with colleagues by asking, "How am I doing?" Designers benefit from critique and solicit honest feedback to improve their work. Maeda discusses how the higher people rise in organizations the harder it is to receive feedback on their work from colleagues because people often fear retribution. Also after receiving a critique, "part of the challenge inherent in welcoming feedback is dealing with the inevitable expectation that you will act on all of the input given to you" (Maeda & Bermont, 2011a, p. 21). Creative leaders can help create an open and reflective culture by inviting critique and growing from it (Maeda & Bermont, 2011b).

Shannon Chance's design studio model, Ann Pendleton-Jullian's micro-lab model, and President John Maeda's emerging theory of "creative as leader" are important examples for understanding higher education leaders as designers. The current challenges to higher education (The Research Universities Futures Consortium, 2012, p. 10), the failings of traditional higher education leadership theories within this changing context (Kezar et al., 2006), and the well-suited affordances of design thinking to meet these challenges forward the concept of higher education leaders as designers.

Summary and Implications

Professor David Gosling, in the forward of Donald Schon's classic text *The Design Studio* (1986) writes "to suggest that other professions taught in institutions of higher learning have much to learn from architectural [design] education is a radical, if not unique, point of view." About three decades ago it seemed impossible that design and design thinking would occupy its current home as one of the most discussed topics in organizational design, education, and innovation studies. Entire new fields and discourses are emerging from the scholarship first codified in the 1960s. However, as Buchanan (2008) contends "enthusiasm alone, however, will not be enough to sustain interest in design, particularly when the concept of design as a discipline of thinking and making is still widely misunderstood" (p. 3). He concludes, "there will have to be tangible benefits, and the benefits will have to be understood as a clear outcome of design thinking" (p. 3). This chapter took Buchanan's advice to heart and attempted to lay the groundwork for future research on design thinking within higher education leadership.

Higher education faces a challenging and uncertain future (Skinner & Miller, 2012). Revitalizing our institutions "will require organization, innovation, direction, and the ability to imagine new possibilities" (Gloppen, 2009, p. 37). However, as Kezar et al. (2006) notes "the importance of the leadership process in producing learning so that people can be more successful in creating change, providing organizational direction, and supporting organizational effectiveness is not emphasized in the higher education literature" (p. 12). It's clear that now is the moment for higher education leadership to reinvent itself. Arizona State University President Michael Crow recently launched the New American University project by posing the question to the ASU community: "Do we replicate what exists or do we design what we need?" Irrespective of ASU's implementation of the New American University project, higher education needs more of design thinking-inspired questions. There is reason for hope that design thinking has a future in higher education leadership. The University of Kentucky recently created the Laboratory on Design Thinking in Education (dLab), an issue-based laboratory within the Kentucky P-20 Innovation Lab dedicated to "applying design thinking to create new solutions to challenges in education and the community" (dLab Website, 2012). UK's dLab serves as a model for training the next generation of educational leaders as designers. This chapter has argued that design thinking represents a meaningful way forward and a new frame for higher educational leadership within "the world of flows."

References

Beckman, S. L., & Barry, M. (2007). Innovation as a learning process: Embedding design thinking. *California Management Review, 50*(1), 25.

Bell, S. (2010). "Design thinking" and higher education. Inside Higher Ed. Retreived 2012 from http://www.insidehighered.com/views/2010/03/02/bell

Birnbaum, R. (2012). *The cybernetics of academic organization and leadership*. San Francisco: Jossey-Bass.

Boland, R. J., Jr., Collopy, F., Lyytinen, K., & Yoo, Y. (2008). Managing as designing: Lessons for organization leaders from the design practice of Frank O. Gehry. *Design Issues, 24*(1), 10–25.

Bolman, L. G., & Gallos, J. V. (2011). *Reframing academic leadership* (p. 288). San Francisco: Jossey-Bass.

Borja de Mozota, B. (2010). Design management as core competency: From "Design you can see" to "Design you can't see. *Journal of Design Strategies, 4*(1), 91–98.

Brown, J. S. (2006). New learning environments for the 21st century: Exploring the edge. *Change: The Magazine of Higher Learning, 38*(5), 18–24.

Buchanan, R. (2008). Introduction: Design and organizational change. *Design Issues, 24*(1), 2–9.

Chance, S. (2009). Proposal for using a studio format to enhance institutional advancement. *International Journal of Educational Advancement, 8*(3–4), 111–125.

Collins, J. (2001). *Good to great: Why some companies make the leap… and others don't*. New York, NY: HarperBusiness.

Collopy, F. (2004). On balancing the analytical and the intuitive in designing. In R. J. Boland & F. Callopy (Eds.), *Managing as designing* (pp. 164–168). Stanford, CA: Stanford University Press.

Cross, N. (1982). Designerly ways of knowing. *Design Studies, 3*(4), 221–227.

Cross, N. (2011). *Design thinking: Understanding how designers think and work* (pp. 1–3). New York: Berg Publishers.

dLab Laboratory on Design Thinking in Education at the University of Kentucky. (2012). University of Kentucky. Retrieved from http://dlab.uky.edu/

Duderstadt, J. J. (1999). Can colleges and universities survive in the information age? In R. N. Katz (Ed.), *Dancing with the devil: Information technology and the new competition in higher education* (pp. 1–25). San Francisco: Jossey-Bass.

Duderstadt, J. (2000). *A university for the 21st century*. Ann Arbor, MI: University of Michigan Press.

Duderstadt, J. J., Atkins, D. E., & Houweling, D. V. (2002). *Higher education in the digital age*. New York: American Council on Education.

Dunne, D., & Martin, R. (2006). Design thinking and how it will change management education: An interview and discussion. *The Academy of Management Learning and Education, 5*(4), 512–523.

Dutton, T. A. (1987). Design and studio pedagogy. *Journal of Architectural Education, 41*(1), 16–25.

Ekman, R. (2010). The imminent crisis in college leadership. *The Chronicle of Higher Education, 57*, A88.

Fisher, T. (2006). *In the scheme of things: Alternative thinking on the practice of architecture*. Minneapolis: University of Minnesota Press.

Fisher, T., & Larsen, T. (2010, June). Design thinking: A solution to fracture-critical systems. *DMI News & Views*.

Gloppen, J. (2009). Perspectives on design leadership and design thinking and how they relate to European service industries. *Design Management Journal, 4*(1), 33–47.

Hanna, D. E. (2000). *Higher education in an era of digital competition: Choices and challenges*. Madison, WI: Atwood Publishing.

Hasso Plattner Institute of Design at Stanford. (2012). Bootcamp bootleg. Retrieved 2012 from http://dschool.stanford.edu/wp-content/uploads/2011/03/METHODCARDS2010v6.pdf

Iarrobino, J. D. (2006). Turnover in the advancement profession. *International Journal of Educational Advancement, 6*(2), 141–169.

IDEO. (2012). *IDEO website*. Retrieved 2012 from http://www.ideo.com/about/

Johnson, M. J., Hanna, D. E., & Olcott, D. (Eds.). (2003). *Bridging the gap: Leadership, technology, and organizational change for university deans and chairpersons* (p. 173). Madison, WI: Atwood Publishing.

Joziasse, F. (2011). The soul of design leadership. *Design Management Review., 22*, 34–42.

Kezar, A. J. (2001). Understanding and facilitating organizational change in the 21st century (No. 28). In *Recent research and conceptualizations* (4th ed., p. 162). Jossey-Bass Incorporated Pub.

Kezar, A. J., Carducci, R., & Contreras-McGavin, M. (2006). The revolution in leadership. In *Rethinking the "L" word in higher education* (Vol. 31, pp. 1–14). ASHE Higher Education Report.

Krippendorff, K. (2006). *The semantic turn*. Boca Raton, FL: CRC Press.

Lave, J., & Wenger, E. (1991). *Situated learning: Legitimate peripheral participation*. Cambridge: Cambridge University Press.

Lawson, B. (2004). *What designers know*. London: Taylor & Francis Ltd.

Lawson, B. (2005). *How designers think: The design process demystified*. London: Routledge.

Maeda, J., & Bermont, R. J. (2011a). *Redesigning leadership*. Cambridge, MA: The MIT Press.

Maeda, J., & Bermont, R. J. (2011b). *Creative mornings*. New York, NY. Retrieved from http://vimeo.com/29166945

Margolin, V. (Eds.). (1984). *Design Issues, 1*(1).

Martin, R. L. (2009). *The design of business: Why design thinking is the next competitive advantage*. Cambridge, MA: Harvard Business School Press.

Melles, G., Howard, Z., & Thompson-Whiteside, S. (2012). Teaching design thinking: Expanding horizons in design education. *Procedia—Social and Behavioral Sciences, 31*, 162–166. doi:10.1016/j.sbspro.2011.12.035.

Norman, D. A. (1988). *The design of everyday things*. New York: Broadway Business.

Pendleton-Jullian, A. (2009). *Design education and innovation ecotones*. Columbus, OH: The Ohio State University.

Plinske, K., & Packard, W. J. (2010). Trustees' perceptions of the desired qualifications for the next generation of community college presidents. *Community College Review, 37*(4), 291–312.

Research Universities Futures Consortium. (2012). *The current health and future well-being of the American research university* (pp. 1–66). New York: Elsevier.

Rittel, H. W. J., & Webber, M. M. (1972). Dilemmas in a general theory of planning. *Policy Sciences, 4*(2), 155–169.

Rylander, A. (2009). Design thinking as knowledge work: Epistemological foundations and practical implications. *Design Management Journal, 4*(1), 7–17.

Schon, D. (1986). *The design studio: An exploration of its traditions and potentials*. Portland, OR: Intl Specialized Book Service Inc.

Schon, D. (1987). *Educating the reflective practitioner*. San Francisco: Jossey-Bass.

Simon, H. A. (1969). *The sciences of the artificial*. Cambridge, MA: MIT Press.

Skinner, R. A., & Miller, E. R. (2012). Colleges must seek new kinds of leaders. *The Chronicle of Higher Education*.

Tischler, L. (2011, May). RISD old guard clashes with its tweeting President John Maeda. *Fast Company*. Retrieved from http://www.fastcompany.com/1747593/risd-old-guard-clashes-its-tweeting-president-john-maeda

Trowler, P. (2008). *Cultures and change in higher education*. London: Palgrave Macmillan.

Visser, W. (2006). *The cognitive artifacts of designing*. London: CRC Press.

Woodward, J. B., & Funk, C. (2010). Developing the artist-leader. *Leadership, 6*(3), 295–309.

Designing for the Half-Known World: Lessons for Instructional Designers from the Craft of Narrative Fiction

Patrick Parrish

Keywords Design process • Narrative design • Learning experience • Learner analysis • Fiction writing • Practice theory • Esthetic experience • Esthetics • Empathy • Design imagination • Design creativity • Design stories • Story paradigms

The Practice of Instructional Design

It is not all that unusual, I suspect, for those in a practice to have debates about the fundamental nature of that practice, and I suspect the sides of the debate show parallel differences across disciplines. They may relate to a natural and culturally reinforced human spectrum of predispositions that run between desire for control and uncertainty avoidance at one end, to desire for unrestraint and uncertainty acceptance at the other. Indeed, researchers have been finding this spectrum a prominent feature explaining everything from political viewpoints to learning and teaching preferences (Hatemia et al., 2009; Nisbett, 2003; Parrish & Linder-Vanbershot, 2010; ProCon.org, 2012). It is natural to expect that a divide in thinking about the essential nature of instructional design might occur along this same spectrum.

The long-standing agreement to apply the term "design" to the processes of creating instruction does not bring consensus, because the concept of design is rather fluid and used in both technical and creative professions. "The conception and realization of new things" is the functional (and poetic) definition of design that was offered in the 2012 AECT Summer Research Symposium, from which this work arose. But while the creation of new things will always involve a venture into limited control and some degree of uncertainty, some practitioners will embrace that

P. Parrish (✉)
WMO, Geneva, Switzerland
e-mail: pparrish@wmo.int

B. Hokanson and A. Gibbons (eds.), *Design in Educational Technology*,
Educational Communications and Technology: Issues and Innovations 1,
DOI 10.1007/978-3-319-00927-8_15, © Springer International Publishing Switzerland 2014

uncertainty and some will work diligently to reduce it with models and methods and prescriptions that resemble those from engineering disciplines. There is a long, but frequently not well-structured debate among instructional designers regarding these two tendencies. The distinction is often manifested along the lines of constructivist versus instructivist approaches to solutions and between artistic versus engineering design processes.

But there is another way to conceive of instructional design that is more embracing of the diversity that exists. Adopting a practice-based orientation (Wilson, 2013) suggests a method of approaching the complex design tasks of instructional design by embracing the social realm it inhabits, a realm composed both of traditions and the evolving influences from an interconnected web of varied contemporary social activities. Practice-based instructional design places grounded tasks above theories and methods. To meet the needs of grounded tasks, it calls upon the inclinations and gathered experiences of the individual practitioner as well as the society of practitioners, alongside theories and principles about the processes of learning and performance. Practice theory (in the sense of *professional* practice, not the repetition required for learning) suggests taking an open-minded stance in regard to theory and orientation for the sake of developing a coherent (perhaps elegant) and customized solution to the problem at hand. It implies a degree of control, but also embraces the unknown, or the half-known, as a stimulant to fresh approaches and effective solutions. Wilson (2013) offers that:

> [Design] coherence can be achieved in configuring an elegant response to a learning need, a problem of practice, or curriculum goal. Design elements may borrow eclectically from different theories, in pastiche or bricolage form, similar to how a bird fashions a nest based on available sticks and twigs and wires. The coherence and elegance of design does not reflect theoretical purity or consistency of origins, but rather in how elements hang together and support a coherent experience for learners. Practice-oriented designers face the same complexity in the situation, but they are more open to the paths and solutions afforded by the situation, not dictated by theory or ideology.

One can notice the central place of the learning experience reflected in this passage. Learning experience is a broader goal than learning outcomes as traditionally conceived. Learning experiences contain the cognitive qualities that receive the bulk of the discussion in the literature of instructional design theories and models (but not *all* the discussion—see Reigeluth, 1999, 2009), but they also have emotional, social, cultural, political, and esthetic qualities (Parrish, 2009). All these come into play in determining the immediate qualities and enduring outcomes of a learning experience.

> Experience is the inward way of looking at activity—similar to how the inward-looking construct of culture is different from the outward looking construct of society. Experience as a construct is useful because of its relevance [its long history of being connected] to education—and because of its mystery and undefined, subjective nature. A vocabulary that includes "experience" opens the door for esthetic considerations such as ritual, myth, dramatic pacing of learning experience, and so forth—which are increasingly important in today's mediated worlds. (Wilson, 2013)

Practice-based instructional designers are concerned with experience over theory and process, because they are concerned with the full range of impacts of what they do. When experience is the focus of concern for designers, new outcomes and processes need to be called upon to aid in understanding and impacting this broader realm. A practice-based orientation, without dispensing with the strong traditions of cognition-oriented instructional design, will include a wider variety of influences drawn not only from the "fringes" of our own discipline but also from those disciplines concerned with broader experience, including the other design fields, as well as the arts. Central to these are dispositions and tools for understanding the end experience of a designed product or activity, or strategies for the development of designer empathy and tools for stimulating empathy during design. The arts, particularly the narrative arts, offer fruitful resources.

The Narrative Nature of Learning Experience

All experiences, including learning experiences, by definition have beginnings, middles, and ends. This is not as simplistic as it sounds. Beginnings involve the presentation of conflict (a problem, question, ethical dilemma, confrontation of values, etc.) that demands resolution, or at least exploration. Middles include that exploration, the uncovering of related and probably deeper conflicts, and the slow march toward resolution (denouement). Endings bring the emotional intensity of the impending resolution, and finally a time of reflection that connects everything that has come before into logical and organic unity. The process of learning, powerful learning at least, clearly demonstrates these parts.

Kenneth Burke offers a more intricate grammar of the narrative pattern. He sees as fundamental to any narrative the presence of an Agent, an Action, a Goal, a Setting, and a Means (Burke, 1969). Dewey, in his work on developing a theory of inquiry, also outlined the principles of narrative, which he later realized and developed into his theories of general and esthetic experience (Dewey, 2000/1938). The pattern of experience he outlined, as applied to learning, unfolds like this:

- A felt need, tension, or puzzlement that impels a learner to resolve an indeterminate situation.
- A sustained anticipation of outcomes that helps to maintain the initial engagement.
- Intent action, participation, or observation on the part of the learner, including a concern for the immediate task (not merely a focus on goals or instruction as a means to an end).
- Consideration of how these tasks and observations contribute to the anticipated end.
- A consummation that unifies the experience (not merely terminates it) and makes it significant, through reflection and/or integrative activity.

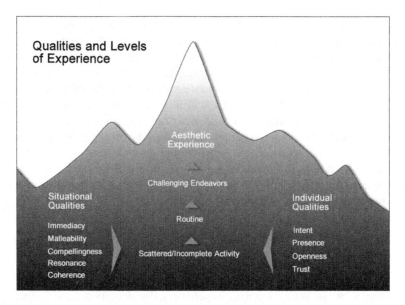

Fig. 1 Contributors to the quality of an experience. The individual qualities are those least in control of instructional designers

The elemental nature of these expressions of the components of a narrative reveals the powerful role narrative plays in our framing of experiences and in our forming of experiences as well.

Experiences are not equal in their power to generate change in our lives nor to stimulate learning. Parrish, Wilson and Dunlap (2011) outline a framework describing the qualities of an experience that lead to its ability to generate higher levels of engagement in experience. The framework assumes (like Burke's narrative grammar) a transaction view of experience, with people and their worlds mutually interacting and cocreating a future (Dewey, 1925/2000). Unlike the colloquial meaning of experience as just "happening" to someone, experience in the transaction sense is an active process, immediately felt, but unfolding over time, located in a historical, geographical, and cultural setting, and then reconstructed over time as well in reflection.

In this context, the framework describes situational and individual qualities that contribute to the level or potential impact of an experience, from scattered activity to coherent esthetic experience Fig. 1.

Traditionally, the realm of instructional design has been to affect the situational qualities of learning experiences, particularly at cognitive levels, and instructional design began as a set of principles for affecting the "conditions of learning" (Gagné & Briggs, 1979). The range of individual qualities required of good teachers also has its body of literature, and even the required individual qualities of instructional designers (as agents) are sometimes discussed (Schwier, Cambell, & Kenny, 2004). However, instructional designer qualities are typically described in terms of their competencies for impacting the situational qualities of learning experiences, not their personal/individual qualities. But the individual qualities of learners, and how these will contribute to an experience, are always only half-known and not something that can be directly impacted. We can go through the process of learner analysis, but that is often a relatively superficial process, yielding only general characteristics. To understand learners in a way that helps design experiences, one needs empathy.

Developing Empathy

Empathy describes our ability to use our imaginations to vicariously experience the experience of others. It has been argued that empathy is more than a virtue, but that it brings evolutionary advantages that create group cohesion and support survival—being able to anticipate the response to our actions within a group, to negotiate, to bond, to anticipate the moves of our enemies, and even to hunt prey (de Waal, 2009). It is likely the single most important quality that a designer or artist can possess, the ability to anticipate the response of people to design options. Even though we have product testing, formative evaluation, or reviewers, even these are unlikely to be effective without the empathy to anticipate, receive, interpret, and respond to their results. It is better to begin with empathy and to exercise it throughout the design process.

Empathy is the ability to see the narrative inherent in a situation and to understand how another perceives the situation participating in that narrative. And because narratives unfold over time, shifting in the transactions of experience, empathy never gives us a fully known world of another. Empathy provides a compass only.

The same way novice fiction writers are often told to exercise empathy by outlining everything they can about the characters' histories before beginning to write (called "creating a backstory"); instructional designers are told to learn everything they can about their learners. One piece of guidance for writers proposes that the story shows only the tip of the iceberg about what the author actually knows about his characters, but that without understand the entire iceberg, a story with psychological depth could never be written. Learner analysis is typically much less ambitious, primarily because the consideration of those things that comprise the important aspects of a learning experience is limited. It often includes questions about learners' prior knowledge, attitudes toward content, academic motivation, education and ability level, learning preferences, and attitudes toward the organization and group. While these questions do touch upon some of the individual qualities that have a fundamental effect on the quality of a learning experience, they go only so far, and they can potentially do harm by creating the illusion that a person IS their set of analysis characteristics, and that they cannot be persuaded to change.

Not all writing instructors propose comprehensive backstory as a necessary or even healthy process to ensure a compelling narrative. For example, novelist Robert Boswell, in his collection of essays on the craft of writing, *The Half-known World* (2008), suggests that too much preparation of backstory "cuts a character off at the knees" and prevents both revelation to readers of depth of character and allowance for the author to learn more about her characters as she works. In Boswell's perspective, limiting the backstory or being willing to change or expand it in the process of writing preserves some of the mystery that is truer to life, allowing a character to grow in non-stereotyped ways. For the reader, this means a richer, less predictable plot progression and greater depiction of life's complexity. Granted, such fictional worlds are more suited to literary works than much of popular fiction, which rely more heavily on genre standards and stereotypes to create an easy reading experience. For the writer, limiting the backstory allows greater flexing of imagination and empathy. It of course places more emphasis on the imagination as the source of good literary decisions, and assumes that the creative mind has greater resources for generating good fiction than the analytical one. Perhaps the same can be said for much of instructional design.

In Parrish (2006), it was suggested that instructional designers might use design stories to stimulate their creative powers and generate higher degrees of empathy to anticipate the range of learner engagement in a learning experience. Design stories are short first-person narratives written by designers from the imagined point-of-view of a user. They explore either an episode of use of a key design feature or a complete, coherent experience with the designed product. They take into account the expected qualities of instructional settings and of learners, including their motivations, ambitions, desires, and potential frustrations in learning, not just narrowly defined learner characteristics.

The act of creating design stories can help designers imagine learning experiences in a degree of detail not possible through traditional analysis processes and not possible in the often-constrained conditions of formative evaluation either. Writing design stories, which stimulates a thought process that exhibits a blend of analysis and synthesis, also makes the compositional nature of design more explicit, avoiding an artificial division of analysis and synthesis in design deliberations (Lawson, 1997; Nelson & Stolterman, 2003). Imagined stories of user experience likely arise in the minds of all designers when they are considering possible impacts of designs or design features, but written design stories can help make learning experiences more tangible and detailed, allowing designers to catch qualities of potential user experience that might be missed in analysis or in those brief, imagined episodes of experience. In addition, written stories also have the advantage of becoming a document for creating shared vision within the design team, reminding subject matter experts about the less tangible instructional goals, and communicating the rationale and value of a design to clients.

Several of the suggested tactics for writing good design stories are borrowed from guidelines commonly used by fiction writers to open up the author to the potential of a story. For example:

- Inhabit the learner in the story as you imagine his or her responses during the learning experience.
- Improvise and allow yourself to be surprised with the outcome.
- Write rapidly, almost automatically, to avoid rationalization.
- Give the action immediacy. Use present tense and include learner reflections only as a response to tangible elements of the design.
- Explore as many aspects of the learner's experience as possible, including setting, motivations, desires, ambitions, and frustrations. Consider how values (of the designer, client, and learner) and political factors come into play.

In the final section of this chapter, several more elaborated tactics are offered that can help those with no experience in creative writing tackle these more difficult design story writing tasks. These exercises are primarily for use in the analysis stage of a project, but they could also be useful even if a designer is moving into the design stage and wants to check their assumptions.

Techniques for Designing for Half-Known Learning Experiences

Some novice and even experienced designers may resist trying out these techniques due to the new uncertainty and complexity they introduce into instructional design processes. They are offered to complement the standard learner analysis processes and in the hope that they might stimulate more creative design considerations. The techniques might be used in design courses to help novice designers consider the deeper impacts of the designs they create, or to help experienced designers find refreshing viewpoints on their work.

(a) *Alternative questions for learner analysis*

For each of the following questions, try to imagine several responses for different types of learners. Then consider how you might adjust your design to accommodate, mitigate, or enhance what you discover in your responses.

- What will make learners say "Wow! I wish I had known that before"?
- What are your learners most likely to forget, misunderstand, undervalue, resist, and fail to connect to?
- What will incite their curiosity and make them want to come back to the next class?
- What will learners most likely skip or skim over, put off until the end, or feel is unnecessary?
- Why do your learners think they may fail to learn?
- What will learners want to share with their family or friends at dinner?
- What kind of learner might feel out of place or disenfranchised?
- In what learning experience did your learners previously struggle that may intimidate them now?
- What part of the learning experience will keep your learners awake at night?
- What part of the instructional design will learners see as reflecting your own personality or personal biases as a teacher or ID?
- What part of your design DOES reflect your own biases or past experiences? How and why have you used similar designs in the past?
- What related interests might be triggered in learners?
- What might learners want to explore more deeply than can be covered in this learning experience?

(*b*) *What is the theme of the instruction? (Theme should be evident throughout, returned to directly, infused in the content, or obvious in each learning activity)*

An instructional theme can be manifested as a generative goal (the learner has to solve a problem, complete a project, perform a series of experiments, etc.). Narrative themes are not just ideas, but action-ideas (Egri, 1942), ideas played out in a plot. Learning themes are also actions, just like learning is an action and not just an outcome. Subject matter alone is an insufficient basis for instruction. However, subject matter couched in an action-idea creates the potential for esthetic experience by turning it into tangible activity.

- Summarize the "plot" and "theme" of your course in the way a novel is enticingly summarized on a book jacket, or the way a film idea is pitched to a Hollywood producer.

(*c*) *What is your motive for teaching the class/developing the product? What motive do you want/expect of your students?*

Answer the following questions for yourself first, and then imagine how your students feel about the course and about your attitudes toward teaching of the course.

- What excites you about the course topics? Why did you study in this field? What do you like to teach about it? What do you dread about teaching it?

(*d*) *How can you use location to ground instruction in a context to enhance theme and "conflict"?*

Stories are not set just anywhere convenient for the author, they need to stimulate the plot or reflect character.

- How does your location (country, state, cultural or geographical region, school) offer opportunities to embody your course and make it more tangible?

(*e*) *How can you introduce new mysteries, challenges, and problems with each new concept, theory, and piece of information you provide?*

How can you keep students engaged, curious, and compelled to complete their learning experience? "Dramatic questions" are those questions that arise in the mind of a reader of fiction about the tensions that need to be resolved in a plot. For example, Will the protagonist be reconciled with his wife/father/child? What clue will allow the thief to be discovered? How will the hero escape in time to save the heroine? Dramatic questions might be strategically planned, or naturally arising from the narrative.

- Can you provide something to decode—a thread that must be discovered, and not just be told?

- What dramatic questions will your learners experience as they proceed through the learning experience? What content or activities, at what points, will generate dramatic questions? For example, "How is this content related to the theme of the course? What will I likely learn next? What am I missing or not understanding sufficiently?" How can you help ensure dramatic questions occur to students?

(f) *How could you design your course to fit each of the two most basic, paradigmatic story patterns?*

When and why would you choose one over the other? How would the same learning event play out differently by shifting from one paradigm to another? What is the instructional equivalent of a stranger and journey? (Consider content, concepts, personal challenges, skills, discipline, culture.)

- A stranger comes to town.
- Someone goes on a journey.

Or, choose a more fine-grained paradigm and choose from those below if they seem more compelling to you:

- Overcoming the monster.
- The quest.
- Journey with a return.
- Comedy (misunderstanding and resolution).
- Tragedy (tragic flaws in less-than-expert practitioners).
- Rebirth.
- Rags to riches.

(g) *Play with time*

Writers, novelists especially, have a critical decision to make in how they treat time. Choices about what events are depicted or merely referenced, when they occur within the story, and in what order events appear provide shape to a story. Authors can slow down time, skip forward, leap backward, switch back and forth between time periods, leave meaningful gaps, and use time to create tension, focus, and variety. They can tell an entire life, or they can focus on a single event that reflects an entire life. Time can be linear, discontinuous, or even circular.

- In what ways can you shape the time experienced by your students by changing the content and activity sequences? What might this add to the learning experience?
- What parts will you accelerate and slow down?
- Is the learning experience linear? Is it cyclical in any way? How could you add a circular quality?
- How can you accentuate this so that students notice and it becomes a driving quality of the learning experience?

References

Boswell, R. (2008). *The half-known world*. Saint Paul, MN: Graywolf.

Burke, K. (1969). *A grammar of motives*. Berkeley: University of California Press.

de Waal, F. (2009). The age of empathy: Nature's lessons for a kinder society. New York: Harmony Books.

Dewey, J. (1925/2000). Experience and philosophic method. In J. J. Stuhr (Ed.), *Pragmatism and classical American philosophy* (2nd ed., pp. 460–471). New York: Oxford University Press.

Dewey, J. (2000/1938). The pattern of inquiry. In J. J. Stuhr (Ed.), *Pragmatism and classical American philosophy* (2nd ed., pp. 482–491). New York: Oxford University Press.

Egri, L. (1942). *The art of dramatic writing: Its basis in the creative interpretation of human motives*. New York: Touchstone.

Gagné, R. M., & Briggs, L. J. (1979). *Principles of instructional design* (2nd ed.). New York: Holt, Rinehart, and Winston.

Hatemia, P. K., Funka, C. L., Medlanda, S. E., Maesa, H. M., Silberga, J. L., Martina, N. G., et al. (2009). Genetic and environmental transmission of political attitudes over a life time. *Journal of Politics, 71*(3), 1141–1156.

Lawson, B. (1997). *How designers think: The design process demystified* (3rd ed.). Amsterdam: Architectural Press.

Nelson, H. G., & Stolterman, E. (2003). *The design way*. Englewood Cliffs, NJ: Educational Technology.

Nisbett, R. E. (2003). *The geography of thought: How Asians and westerners think differently… and why*. New York: Free Press.

Parrish, P. E. (2006). Design as storytelling. *TechTrends, 50*(4), 72–82.

Parrish, P. E. (2009). Aesthetic principles for instructional design. *Educational Technology Research & Development, 57*(5), 511–528.

Parrish, P. E., & Linder-Vanbershot, J. A. (2010). Cultural dimensions of learning: Addressing the challenges of multicultural instruction. *International Review of Research in Open and Distance Learning, 11*(2), 1–19.

Parrish, P. E., Wilson, B. G., & Dunlap, J. C. (2011). Learning experience as transaction: A framework for instructional design. *Educational Technology, 51*(2), 15–22.

ProCon.org. (2012). Differences in conservative and liberal brains: 16 peer-reviewed studies show liberals and conservatives physiologically different. *ProCon.org* http://2012election.procon.org/view.resource.php?resourceID=004818. Retrieved 11/12/12.

Reigeluth, C. M. (Ed.). (1999). *Instructional-design theories and models: A new paradigm of instructional theory*. Mahwah, NJ: Lawrence Erlbaum Associates.

Schwier, R. A., Campbell, K., & Kenny, R. (2004). Instructional designer's observations about identity, communities of practice and change agency. *Australasian Journal of Educational Technology, 20*(4), 69–100.

Wilson, B. G. (2013). A practice-centered approach to instructional design. In M. M. Spector, B. B. Lockee, S. E. Smaldino, & M. Herring (Eds.), *Learning, problem solving, and mind tools: Essays in honor of David H. Jonassen*. New York: Routledge.

Index

B. Hokanson and A. Gibbons (eds.), *Design in Educational Technology*,
Educational Communications and Technology: Issues and Innovations 1,
DOI 10.1007/978-3-319-00927-8, © Springer International Publishing Switzerland 2014

CPSIA information can be obtained
at www.ICGtesting.com
Printed in the USA
LVOW04*1822050516

486886LV00010B/66/P